Student Assessment and Learning Guide

for use with

Understanding Business

Sixth Edition

William G. Nickels
University of Maryland

James M. McHugh
St. Louis Community College at Forest Park

Susan M. McHugh
Applied Learning Systems

Prepared by
Barbara Barrett
St. Louis Community College -Meramec

 **McGraw-Hill
Irwin**

Boston   Burr Ridge, IL   Dubuque, IA   Madison, WI   New York   San Francisco   St. Louis
Bangkok   Bogotá   Caracas   Kuala Lumpur   Lisbon   London   Madrid   Mexico City
Milan   Montreal   New Delhi   Santiago   Seoul   Singapore   Sydney   Taipei   Toronto

McGraw-Hill Higher Education

A Division of The McGraw·Hill Companies

Student Assessment and Learning Guide for use with
UNDERSTANDING BUSINESS
William G. Nickels, James M. McHugh and Susan M. McHugh

2 3 4 5 6 7 8 9 0 QPD/QPD 0 9 8 7 6 5 4 3 2 1

ISBN 0-07-245584-5

www.mhhe.com

This study guide is designed to give you, the Introduction to Business student, every advantage in mastering the concepts presented in the fifth edition of *Understanding Business,* sixth edition, by Bill Nickels, Jim McHugh and Susan McHugh.

Using this study guide will give you an edge; you will go beyond just memorizing terms, to developing and using the critical thinking and creative problem solving skills that are so important in today's dynamic business environment.

Using The Study Guide

There are many different ways to learn, so I can only make suggestions about how to use this guide more effectively. You may find a different way, which suits you better.

First, this study guide is not designed to replace reading the text! In fact, reading the text is an integral part of using this study guide. You can use the guide to help point out places where you need more work, or need to review. The guide is very detailed, and requires you not only to remember facts, but also to apply concepts in a way that will help you to develop a better understanding of today's business environment.

You will find that there is a lot of writing in completing these exercises. Writing the answers to the questions, rather than just choosing a number or matching a term with a letter, will help to reinforce the material. You will also be better prepared to answer essay or short answer questions when you have studied by writing out answers in your own words.

Finally, to make effective use of this study guide, I suggest that you:

- Read the text before each class period, and outline important concepts. You will probably have a syllabus that outlines the reading assignments for each class.
- Attend class and take good, detailed notes. Ask questions in class; get involved!
- Do the exercises in the study guide *after* you have completed the first two steps. . I would suggest that you do the exercises in stages, and not try to do the whole chapter at one sitting. For example, if there are 6 learning goals, do the exercises pertaining to the first three learning goals on one day, and then complete the remaining exercises the next day. Or, do the factual based exercises one day, the critical thinking exercises the next, and so on.
- Do *all* the exercises in the guide, not just the ones that take less time!
- Review your answers, and mark the questions you had problems answering. Then, reread the section of the text that deals with those areas.
- Before a test, review your class notes, the text and the study guide material.
- Remember, your instructor may add material in class that is not in the text, and the study guide won't cover that material. That takes us back to the first suggestions: read the book before class, attend every class, take notes, and get involved!

Design Of This Study Guide

Each chapter in this guide contains the following sections to help you be successful in this Introduction to Business course.

- **_Learning goals:_** Each learning goal is listed in the order in which it appears in the text. This is to help you focus on what is important throughout the chapter. The appropriate learning goal for each exercise is also noted in the side margin as you go through the chapter.

- **_Learning the Language:_** This section identifies the key terms and definitions from the chapter. This is a matching section, in which you read the definition then choose the appropriate term. Many of the definitions will be direct quotes from the chapter, or a slight variation.

- **_Assessment Check:_** These exercises help you to learn the facts of the material from the text. You will be writing answers to factually based questions from the chapter, organized by learning goals. This section is designed to develop your knowledge of the text material. I suggest you keep the book nearby while doing these exercises, but do as much as you can without opening the book. This will help you to determine the areas where you need to review.

- **_Critical Thinking Exercises:_** Business people need a variety of skills. Among the most important skills you can bring to a job is the ability to think for yourself, analyze problems, develop solutions based upon your analysis, and present the solutions in written form. There are many opportunities to hone these skills with this text. In this section of the study guide, the questions will require you to think and apply the material from the chapter to come up with a solution to the situation presented. These application questions are designed to provide you with the opportunity to enhance your decision-making skills and understanding of the material. In some cases, there are no definitive answers, only suggested answers.

- **_Practice Test:_** In all likelihood, you will be required to take some objective exams. The practice test is divided into two sections, multiple choice, and true false. Keep in mind this is only a sample of the types of questions you could see on an exam, and these are not the actual questions you will see on a classroom test! The practice exam will give you the chance to find out what areas of the chapters you need to take some extra time with before your classroom exam.

- **_You Can Find It On The Net:_** Business research is an integral part of being a successful businessperson. These Internet exercises provide an opportunity to practice your research skills on the Internet. The web addresses listed are only an entry to the information available; there is so much to explore on the Internet! Use your imagination to see where you can "travel"! The web sites were valid at the time of this writing. Please understand that the Internet changes daily, and not all the web sites may be available when you are completing the exercise.

- **_Answers:_** The answers to all the Retention Check, Critical Thinking Exercises and Practice Tests are at the end of each chapter.

There is no substitute for just plain hard work. To be successful in tomorrow's work world, you will need to work hard today to develop the skills employers are looking for. The text, _Understanding Business,_ and this study guide are designed to help you to be successful by starting you on the road to developing those skills. The rest is up to you. Good Luck!

Acknowledgements

Many thanks are due, and I will be brief. First, thanks to Bill Nickels, Susan McHugh and Jim McHugh, and to McGraw-Hill/Irwin for allowing me to continue my involvement with this wonderful text. Sarah Reed, thanks for your patience. To Ryan and Chad, thank you for your support, understanding, and computer consultation! And to all my colleagues at the Meramec campus of St. Louis Community College, thanks for your support and encouragement.

Barbara Barrett

CONTENTS

CHAPTER 1
MEETING THE CHALLENGES OF TODAY'S DYNAMIC BUSINESS ENVIRONMENT

LEARNING GOALS

After you have read and studied this chapter, you should be able to:

1. Describe how businesses and nonprofit organizations add to a country's standard of living and quality of life.

2. Explain the importance of entrepreneurship to the wealth of an economy and show the relationship of profit to risk assumption.

3. Examine how the economic environment and taxes affect businesses.

4. Illustrate how the technological environment has affected businesses.

5. Identify various ways that businesses can meet and beat competition.

6. Demonstrate how the social environment has changed and what the reaction of the business community has been.

7. Analyze what businesses must do to meet the global challenge.

8. Review how trends from the past are being repeated in the present and what that will mean for the service sector.

LEARNING THE LANGUAGE

Listed below are important terms found in the chapter. Choose the correct term for each definition and write it in the space provided.

Business	Factors of production	Revenue
Database	Goods	Return on Investment
Diversity, multiculturalism	Loss	Risk
Dot-com company	Nonprofit Organizations	Services
Demography	Productivity	Stakeholders
E-commerce	Profit	Standard of living
Empowerment	Quality of life	Telecommuting
Entrepreneur		

1.	The resources businesses use to create wealth are called _____.

2.	_____ is the total output of goods and services in a given period of time divided by work hours.

3.	Buying and selling products and services over the Internet is known as _____.

4.	_____ refers to the general well-being of a society.

5.	An _____ is the person who risks time and money to start and managing a business.

6.	Products which are intangible, such as heath care and education are known as _____.

7.	A _____ is any activity which seeks profit by providing goods and services to others.

8.	When a business's costs and expenses are more than its revenues a _____ has occurred.

9.	Entrepreneurs take a _____ when they take a chance that they will lose time and money on a business that may not prove to be profitable.

10.	A society's _____ is the amount of goods and services people can buy with the money they have.

11.	A _____ is an organization whose goals do not include making a personal profit for its owners.

12.	An electronic storage file where information is kept is known a(n) _____.

13.	When we study _____, we are looking at a statistical study of the human population to learn its size, density and characteristics.

14.	Known as _____, this means giving frontline workers the responsibility and freedom to respond quickly to customer requests.

15.	Houses, food, clothing and TV sets are tangible products known as _____.

16. _____ is the money a business earns above and beyond what it spends for salaries, expenses and other costs.

17. A organization's _____ are the people who stand to gain or lose by its policies and activities.

18. Workers who stay home and keep in touch with the company through telecommunications are said to _____.

19. The process of optimizing the contribution of people from different cultures is known as _____ or _____.

20. The total amount of money a business earns in a given period by selling goods and services is called _____.

21. A businessperson's _____ is the return he and other owners get on the money they invest in the firm.

22. An Internet company whose Web address ends with.com is a _____.

ASSESSMENT EXERCISES

Learning Goal 1   **What is a business?**

1. Contrast "standard of living" with "quality of life"

2. Describe how entrepreneurs and the businesses they create benefit the communities in which they are located.

3.   How do non-profit organizations benefit our society?

Learning Goal 2   **Entrepreneurship versus working for others**

4.   What are two ways to succeed in business, according to the text?

5.   What are the statistics regarding minorities and entrepreneurship?

6.   What is the difference between revenue and profit?

7.   When does a company experience a loss?

8.   What is the relationship between risk and profit?

9.   What are the 5 factors of production?

   a._____   d._____

   b._____   e._____

   c._____

10.   Which two factors of production are noted in the text as the key ingredients to making countries rich?

   a._____   b._____

11.   What three factors contribute to keeping poor countries poor?

   a._____   b._____   c._____

Learning Goal 3   **The Business Environment**

12.   What are the 5 key environmental factors that are key to business growth and job creation?

   a._____

   b._____

   c._____

   d._____

   e._____

13.   Why is a healthy business environment important?

The Economic Environment

14.   How does the tax rate have an impact on entrepreneurship?

15.   According to the text, what are four actions governments must take to foster entrepreneurial growth?

a. _____

b. _____

c. _____

d. _____

Learning Goal 4   **The Technological environment**

16.   What are three characteristics of the Internet that are affecting business and user access to business information?

a. _____

b. _____

c. _____

17. What factors of e-commerce attract businesses?

a. _____

b. _____

c. _____

d. _____

e. _____

f. _____

18. What are the two major types of e-commerce transactions? Which is larger?

19. How would you describe a "click and mortar" business?

20. How has e-commerce affected marketing intermediaries, such as car dealers and bookstores?

21. How have databases helped businesses become more responsive to their customers?

22.   What is the role of a CIO or a CKO in a company?

Learning Goal 5   **The Competitive Environment**

23.   What are the three basic things U.S. companies have found they must offer in order to stay competitive in today's world markets?

a._____   b._____   c._____

24.   Companies compete by:

a. _____

b. _____

c. _____

d. _____

e. _____

25.   What does it mean for a company to "compete with speed?

26.   Who are a company's stakeholders?

27.   How will the jobs and roles of managers, supervisors and employees change in the era of empowerment and self-managed teams?

Learning Goal 6   **The Social Environment**

28.   What are the ways is which the social environment is changing?

a. _____

b. _____

c. _____

d. _____

29.   How will the demographics of the population of the U.S. change in the next 50 years?

30.   In what ways can a multiculturally diverse population benefit U.S. businesses?

31.   The desire for a more comfortable lifestyle combined with an interest in careers outside the home have created a surge in the number of two income families. There has also been an increase in the number of single parent families in the United States. These families have different needs than workers of the past. How have companies responded to those needs?

Learning Goal 7   **The Global Environment**

32.   What is considered to be the number one global environmental change?

33.   How have U.S. firms responded to the increase in global competition?

34.   What are two ways in which changes in the global market will affect you?

a. _____

b. _____

Learning Goal 8   **The Evolution of American Business**

35.   Describe how the agricultural industry changed in the 20th century.

36.   What are the changes expected in the service industry in the future?

CRITICAL THINKING EXERCISES

Learning Goal 1

1. Monika lives in Germany, works for the Mercedes plant in her hometown and makes the equivalent of $55/hour American. Her cousin Joe lives in the United States and works for the Chrysler plant in his hometown. When Monika visits Joe she is amazed at how big his house is compared to where she lives, his stereo equipment and how well he seems to live. "Boy" says Monika, "I sure can't live like this at home. Why not?"

Learning Goals 1, 2

2. Revelle Industries is a small company located in an area of the country where unemployment has been very high for the last 5 years. In 1990, Revelle was struggling. There were only 20 employees, and profits were low. With new management things began to turn around, and now Revelle employees almost 75 people. This year they sold 120,000 units of their only product line, a component part used in the manufacture of automobiles. The price of their product is $20/unit. The costs of salaries, expenses and other items was $2,050,000. Sales forecasts look good for the next several years, as Revelle has customers world wide and will be expanding their product line in the next 18 months.

    a. What are Revelle's revenues?

    b. What are Revelle's profits?

    c. How has the company generated wealth and created a higher standard of living?

Learning Goal 3

3. "If you were to analyze rich countries versus poor countries to see what caused the differences, you would have to look at the factors of production..."

    Russia and other areas of Eastern Europe experienced dramatic changes during the 1990's, with changes in both government and economic policies. The newly formed countries have struggled for the last decade with questions about how to be successful in the 21st century. What will be the key to developing the economies of these countries?

Learning Goal 4

4. Schnucks is a large grocery retailer located in the St. Louis, Missouri area. The company is expanding, and continually improving the technology in their stores. How can a database help Schnucks better serve its customers? How do you think a grocery store such as Schnucks will compete in the area of e-commerce?

Learning Goal 5

5. Consider your college or university:

   a. Who are its competitors?

   b. How does the school "please" its customers?

   c. How does the school "compete with speed?"

   d. Who are the school's stakeholders? Does it meet the needs of the stakeholders? Why or why not?

   e. How do you think it meets the needs of its employees?

   f. How do the answers to these questions affect the school's competitive situation?

   g. Do you see a concern for the environment?

Learning Goal 4, 5, 6, 7

6. Take a look at a company with which you are familiar, for example where you or one of your family are currently employed.

   a. How important is technology to the business? Does the company participate in e-commerce? Does it have a Web site?

   b. What kinds of programs has the company implemented to meet the needs of two career families and other employees?

   c. Does the company appear to be competing in the manner described by your text, by speed, meeting the needs of its employees, the community and the environment?

   d. Does the company do business internationally? Does the company have a diverse workforce?

Learning Goal 6

7.   How do the changes and programs companies have implemented to meet the needs of two career families help these companies to be more competitive?

Learning Goal 7

8.   How can increased global competition benefit the United States and U.S. workers?

Learning Goal 8

9.   How do the changes in the agricultural industry in the early 1900's parallel the changes we have seen in the industrial sector recently?

PRACTICE TEST

Multiple Choice: Circle the best answer.

1. Taxes would not be used to support which of the following activities?

   a. Build a new school
   b. Support people in need
   c. Keep a clean environment
   d. Help run a privately owned day care center

2. A clean environment, safety, free time and health care are elements which contribute to our:

   a. standard of living.
   b. quality of life.
   c. economic environment.
   d. factors of production.

3. Which of the following would be considered a non-profit organization?

   a. Microsoft
   b. UPS
   c. The Red Cross
   d. Chrysler

4. Businesses owned by _____ grew at a rate faster than all other businesses in the early 1990s.

   a. Asians
   b. Hispanics
   c. American Indians
   d. Pacific Islanders

5. A loss occurs when a company:

   a. has revenues greater than expenses.
   b. hires too many new workers.
   c. has expenses greater than revenues.
   d. has taken a risk.

6. In general, the _____ the risk, the _____ the profit.

    a. higher/higher.
    b. lower/higher.
    c. higher/lower.
    d. faster/quicker.

7. Which of the following is (are) not considered a factor of production?

    a. Information
    b. Capital
    c. Labor
    d. Taxes

8. According to the text, the two factors of production that contribute most to making countries rich are:

    a. land and labor.
    b. capital and land.
    c. entrepreneurship and use of knowledge.
    d. use of knowledge and taxes.

9. All of the following would create an environment that would foster entrepreneurial growth except:

    a. raising taxes and increasing regulations.
    b. passing laws which allow businesses to write enforceable contracts.
    c. establishing a currency that is tradable in world markets.
    d. developing governmental policies eliminating corruption.

10. Which of the following statements is false, regarding Internet selling?

    a. Transaction costs are higher.
    b. Companies can build customer orders.
    c. The Internet allows for larger catalogs.
    d. Customers frequently order a larger amount than they would ordinarily.

11.   The greatest proportion of Internet sales is:

     a.   Consumers selling to other consumers.
     b.   Businesses selling to other businesses.
     c.   Consumers trying to sell to small businesses.
     d.   Businesses selling to consumers.

12.   Internet marketing has risen rapidly, and

     a.   many dot-com companies have proven to be less successful than people had hoped.
     b.   the old brick and mortar companies are losing out and are not participating in Internet marketing.
     c.   there has been little effect on the roles of intermediaries, such as wholesalers and retailers.
     d.   B2C e-commerce will exceed B2B commerce.

13.   In today's environment, business have found they must do all but which of the following in order to remain competitive?
     a.   Meet the needs of all stakeholders of the business.
     b.   Meet the needs of employees by supervising them more closely.
     c.   Delight customers by exceeding their expectations.
     d.   Be aware of potential damage and hazards to the environment.

14.   Which of the following is true regarding the changes to the population of the United States?
     a.   The population will be come less diverse in the next 50 years, and then the trend will reverse.
     b.   There will be fewer older Americans as the birth rate declines.
     c.   The number of two income and single parent families will increase.
     d.   Projections are that the actual population of the U.S. will begin to decline.

15.   The trend toward two-income families has lead to:

     a.   businesses paying lower wages and hiring fewer workers.
     b.   policies allowing only one family member to work for the same company.
     c.   programs such as flexible work schedules, child care and cafeteria benefits.
     d.   fewer opportunities in the area of human resource management.

16. The process of maximizing the business contributions of a diverse workforce is known as:

    a. multiculturalism.
    b. ethnocentrism.
    c. globalism.
    d. nationalism.

17. The number one global environmental change is considered to be:

    a. the increase in the number of large companies.
    b. the loss of jobs in the U.S. as a result of competition from Japan.
    c. the increase of U.S. worker productivity.
    d. the growth of international competition and free trade.

18. As businesses increasingly serve global markets, it is likely that:

    a. fewer jobs will be created in the United States.
    b. students who expect to prosper will have to compete in a changing environment, and continually update their skills.
    c. U.S. firms and their workers will become less productive.
    d. cooperation among firms will become less likely.

19. Since the mid-1980s, the _____ has generated most of the increases in employment in the United States.

    a. manufacturing sector
    b. agricultural sector
    c. service sector
    d. goods producing

20. Cars and machine tools are a part of the _____ .

    a. goods producing sector
    b. services sector
    c. agricultural sector
    d. intangible services sector

True-False

1. _____ Mariko, who lives in Tokyo, makes the equivalent of approximately $35,000 per year, while Donada, living in the United States makes only $25,000. From this you can assume Mariko has a higher standard of living than Donada.

2. _____ Business skills are useful and necessary in non-profit institutions.

3. _____ Opportunities for minority entrepreneurs have grown rapidly.

4. _____ An entrepreneur is an individual who has worked for a nonprofit organization for their entire career.

5. _____ As a potential business owner, you should invest your money in a company with a lot of risk, in order to earn a lot of money quickly.

6. _____ Profit refers to the difference between risk and revenue.

7. _____ High taxes and increased government regulations can actually drive entrepreneurs out of a particular country, state or city.

8. _____ Few technological changes have had a greater impact on business than the Internet and various forms of information technology such as computers and modems.

9. _____ While Internet usage has grown in the past, usage is expected to level off and decline in the next few years.

10. _____ In today's marketplace, competing with speed has become less important as companies focus on the quality of the product over speed of delivery.

11. _____ The new role of supervisors will become to support employees by providing training to do their jobs well, including handling customer complaints effectively.

12. _____ The Bureau of the Census predicts that the U.S. population will remain essentially the same throughout the next century, in terms of diversity.

13. _____ A more diverse, multicultural population will give U.S. workers an advantage when working and competing in a global marketplace.

14. _____ Cooperation among international firms could lead to the downfall of many economies as people are laid off due to increased competition.

15. _____ When workers in the industrial sector were laid off, many of them went back to work in the agricultural sector.

YOU CAN FIND IT ON THE NET

This is an additional exercise for your own exploration and information. The answers for this section aren't provided.

The purpose of this exercise is to gather data regarding trend in occupations and in the population and the social environment and to analyze how these changes affect Americans and American businesses. To answer these questions, begin with the Census Bureau homepage on the Internet at www.census.gov

1. Select the population Clock from the Census bureau's homepage. Record the time and population of the United States. Try to find the population of the world. What proportion of the world's population is represented by the United States?

2. What is the fastest growing occupation? What could contribute to the increase in this profession? (The Bureau of Labor Statistics is a good place to search for occupational growth stats.)

3. What is the population of your home state? What percentages of the population of your home state are from minority groups?

4. What are the average salaries for individuals with high school degrees, college degrees, master's degrees and professional degrees? What is the trend, and what does that indicate about incomes in the United States for the future?

5. Return to the Census Bureau's homepage. What is the population of the country now? If you come back to the homepage for three consecutive days, you will see how quickly the population is growing. How can businesses use this information?

ANSWERS

LEARNING THE LANGUAGE

1. Factors of production	9. Risk	17. Stakeholders
2. Productivity	10. Standard of living	18 Telecommute
3. e-commerce	11. Non profit organization	19. Diversity/Multiculturalism
4. Quality of life	12. Database	20. Revenue
5. Entrepreneur	13. Demography	21. Return on Investment
6. Services	14. Empowerment	22. dot-com company
7. Business	15. Goods	
8. Loss	16. Profit	

ASSESSMENT EXERCISES

What is a business?

1.   Standard of living refers to the amount of goods and services people can buy with the money they have to spend. Quality of life refers to our general well being, such things as freedom, a clean environment, schools, access to health care, safety, free time, and other things that lead to a sense of satisfaction

2.   Entrepreneurs provide employment not just for themselves but for other people in the communities in which they locate. Employees pay taxes that the federal government and local communities use to build hospitals, schools, playgrounds, and other facilities. Taxes are used to keep the environment clean and to support people in need. Businesses pay taxes that benefit the communities. The businesses these entrepreneurs start are part of an economic system that contributes to the standard of living and quality of life both in the local community and in the country as a whole.

3.   Non-profit organizations help make our country more responsive to the needs of citizens.

Entrepreneurship versus working for others

4.   According to the text, the two main ways to succeed in business are to rise up through the ranks of a business, and to start your own business.

5.   Minority groups have benefited tremendously from opportunities in entrepreneurship. The number of minority owned businesses grew rapidly in the early 1990s, with Hispanic owned businesses experiencing the greatest growth. The number of businesses owned by women has also increased dramatically in the last 20 years.

6. Revenue is money generated by selling goods or providing services, while profit is the money left over after a business has paid its expenses.

7. A company will have a loss when expenses of doing business are greater that the revenues generated.

8. In general, the companies that take the most risk can make the most profit.

9. The five factors of production are:
   a. land and other natural resources
   b. labor
   c. capital, such as money, machine tools, and buildings
   d. entrepreneurship
   e. knowledge

10. The key ingredients to making countries rich are considered to be
    a. entrepreneurship
    b. information

11. The factors which contribute to keeping poor countries poor are
    a. lack of entrepreneurship
    b. absence of knowledge workers
    c. lack of freedom

The Business Environment

12. The five key environmental factors critical to the success of business are:
    a. the economic environment
    b. the technological environment
    c. the competitive environment
    d. the social environment
    e. the global business environment

13. A healthy business environment helps businesses to grow and prosper. Job growth and wealth make it possible to have a high standard of living and a high quality of life. The wrong environmental conditions lead to job loss, business failures and a low standard of living and quality of life.

The Economic Environment

14. Entrepreneurs are looking for a high return on investment. When the government takes away much of what their business earn through high taxes, entrepreneurs may no longer take the risk of starting a business, because their return isn't high enough to warrant the risk.

15. To foster entrepreneurial growth a government can
   a. Reduce the risk of being an entrepreneur by passing laws which allow for enforceable contracts.
   b. Take economic steps to ensure that the country's currency is tradable on world markets.
   c. Create policies eliminating corruption in business and government. This allows for freer competition and helps businesses to flourish.
   d. Keep taxes and government regulations to a minimum. High federal, state and local taxes are disincentives for entrepreneurs, who are looking for a high return on their investments of time and money.

The Technological Environment

16. a. The Internet allows business to communicate with a worldwide audience.
   b. Users can access information whenever it is convenient for them, day or night.
   c. Business can operate without borders because there are no geographical limits.

17. a. Low transaction costs, which reduces cost of customer service. With no sales tax, things can be less expensive than in the stores.
   b. Larger purchases per transaction. Customers tend to buy more than they might in a traditional store.
   c. Integration of business processes. The Internet offers a company the ability to make a great deal of information available to customers.
   d. Flexibility. Companies can build custom orders, as well as compare prices between many vendors
   e. Large catalogs.
   f. Improved customer interaction. Companies can send e-mail and confirm orders instantaneously.

18. The two major types of e-commerce transactions are B2C business to consumer and B2B, business to business. B2B is by far the largest.

19. A click and mortar business is a traditional retailer, or store, that has expanded onto the Internet.

20. There are an increasing number of companies that make and sell their product direct to the consumer. The need then for companies that ship and store goods has changed, and we could eventually see the elimination of certain kinds of retailers or other marketing intermediaries.

21. A database can be used to store a great deal of information about a company's customers. This information could be provided, for example, by a bar code on a product package. The information from the bar code, combined with a customer's name and address on a mailing list can give a retailer enough information to enable it to send you catalogs and other direct advertising that offer the kind of products you want.

22. The CIO or CKO is responsible for managing the vast amount of information available to managers and workers.

The Competitive Environment

23 For U.S. companies to stay competitive in today's global market, they must offer
   a. quality products
   b. great service
   c. competitive prices

24. Companies compete by:
   a. pleasing the customer
   b. competing with speed
   c. meeting community needs
   d. restructuring and meeting the needs of employees
   e. demonstrating concern for the natural environment

25.   Customers want fast delivery of their products. Businesses must respond to that customer need, or they risk losing business.

26.   A company's stakeholders are all the people who stand to gain or lose by the policies and activities of an organization, including customers, employees, stockholders, suppliers, dealers, bankers, people in the local community, environmentalists, and elected government leaders.

27.   Supervisor's jobs will become to train and support front line people with training and the technology to do their jobs, including handling customer complaints. With self-managed teams and cross-functional teams, managers may be eliminated. Companies that have implemented self-managed teams expect a lot more from lower-level workers and can do without various levels of management. Such workers need more education. Increasingly managers jobs will be to train, support, coach and motivate lower level employees.

The Social Environment

28.   The social environment is changing through:
   a.   increased diversity
   b.   an increase in the number of older Americans
   c.   more two income families
   d.   more single parent families

   These trends are affecting how we live, and are expected to provide many opportunities for businesses in the next century.

29.   The population of the U.S. will increase significantly, with the demographic makeup very different from today. It is estimated that the Hispanic population will increase significantly, as well as the Asian and African American populations.

30.   A multicultural population gives U.S. citizens the opportunity to live and work with people from many different cultures and backgrounds. That should give us an advantage when it comes to working with people in global markets. Further, a diverse population provides businesses with ideas and concepts that will enhance and enrich the business community and culture.

31.   A number of programs have been implemented to help two income families. Pregnancy benefits, parental leave programs, flexible work schedules and eldercare programs are some examples. Many companies either offer day care on site or offer some type of child-care benefits. Others offer cafeteria style benefits packages, enabling families to choose from a "menu" of benefits. Many companies have increased the number of part-time workers they employ, while others allow workers to stay home and work, by telecommuting. Single parents have benefited from family leave programs and flextime.

The Global Environment

32. The number one global environmental change is the growth of international competition and the increase of free trade among nations.

33. In order to become world-class competitors, U.S. manufacturers have been analyzing the best practices from around the world, and many have implemented the most advanced quality methods. U.S. firms are changing the way they operate by going beyond competition, and have learned to cooperate with international firms. That cooperation has the potential to create rapidly growing world markets.

34. a. It will be important to be prepared for a rapidly changing environment, by studying technology, telecommunications and foreign languages.
     b. Continuous learning will be required.

The Evolution of American Business

35. The agricultural industry led the way for economic development in the U.S. in the early part of this century. That industry became so efficient through the use of technology that the number of farmers dropped dramatically. Small farms were replaced by much larger farms, but agriculture is still a major industry in the U.S.

   Many of the farmers that lost jobs in agriculture went to work in factories. Like agriculture, the manufacturing industry used technology to become more productive. This meant fewer jobs in manufacturing, but by increasing productivity new jobs have been created, and many of those displaced manufacturing workers have found employment in the service sector.

36. Almost all of our economy's employment increases have been in service industries, and although growth in the service industries has slowed, it remains the largest area of growth. There are now more high paying jobs in the services sector than in the goods producing sector, in such areas as health-care, accounting, finance, telecommunications and other areas. Projections are that some areas will grow rapidly, such as telecommunications, and others will have much slower growth.

CRITICAL THINKING EXERCISES

1. Monika is surprised at the standard of living Joe seems to have attained compared to hers, while working at a similar job. While Monika makes more per hour (equivalent U.S. dollars) than Joe, the cost of food, housing and other services is probably much higher for her. Therefore she can't buy as much with her money as Joe can—it simply costs too much. A similar situation exists in the United States when you compare one region to another. Compare average housing prices for example in San Francisco, California to those in St. Louis, Missouri or your own city. When you compare per capita income for those areas, you will also find a difference.

2.   a. $2,400,000 in revenue

       b. Profit is $350,000 after taking expenses of $2,050,000.

       c. Companies like Revelle generate wealth and create a higher standard of living in many ways. Workers pay taxes that federal and local governments use to build hospitals, schools, roads and playgrounds. Tax money is also used to keep the environment clean. Businesses also pay taxes to the federal government and the local community.

           Standards of living go up because people can buy goods and services with the money they earn from being employed. When businesses start, grow and prosper, and generate wealth, our quality of life improves as the taxes the workers and the business pay provide for good schools, good health care, and a clean environment.

3.   In the analysis of the factors of production, the most important factor is not capital, natural resources or labor. Countries in Eastern Europe have land and labor, but are still poor. Capital is available, thus countries have money for machinery and tools. The key to developing an economy appears to be entrepreneurship and the effective use of information. In many of these countries businesses have been owned by the government, and there has been little incentive to work hard or create profit.

        A government interested in developing its economy must encourage business and entrepreneurship and provide the information necessary to help people to move ahead.

        Many of these countries do not have laws which enable companies to write enforceable contracts, necessary to do business. This makes the risk of starting a business much higher. Further, these countries are still attempting to stabilize the value of the their currency. The governments are corrupt in many cases, making it impossible to get permits without expensive bribes. Lastly, taxes in many developing countries are high, minimizing a businesses' return on investment.

4.   The new retailing technology allows a retailer to determine what kind of products customers purchase, in what amount, in what size and at what price. That information, plus information such as the name, address and family information about a customer will go into a databank. With that information Schnucks can send direct mail pieces to customers offering exactly what they want. It will allow Schnucks to carry inventory specifically for a customer base in different areas around the city. For example, if there is an area with a large Italian population, the Schnucks store in that area will carry more of the type of products those customers might buy. If there is a large Jewish population in another area of the city, the store serving that area may carry fewer of the Italian products, and more for the dietary needs of the Jewish customer, and so on. These stores will also be able to replace the items quickly through contact with the suppliers, who also have the bar code information. If Schnucks is interested in developing direct mail pieces or other types of services, this technology will help decision makers to know exactly what to feature, and mailing lists will be readily available.

5. a. Competitors for some schools will be the other colleges and universities in the local community. For others it may be other schools in the region or the nation.

    b. A college or university may please its customer (students) by offering classes at convenient times (many schools offer weekend college programs for example), in convenient locations (off site locations), encouraging faculty to be accessible to students through designated office hours or mentoring programs, offering a variety of programs, offering Internet or other technology based courses, and of course having winning sports teams!

    c. A college or university can compete with speed by making registration easy and fast by providing for registration by phone or online. College affiliated bookstores can allow students to order books ahead of time, bundle all of a student's books together, and also reduce waiting in line.

    d. The stakeholders are students, parents of students, employees, taxpayers, the community in which the school is located and alumni for example. How schools meet the needs of its stakeholders may be through a variety of course offerings, tuition and rate of tuition increases, level of community involvement by the school's administrators, responsiveness to student organizations, cooperation with alumni groups, and so on.

    e. Students may have difficulty answering how the school meets the needs of employees. You may find out if there is a structure for faculty and staff to communicate openly with their manager, for example, or how employees view the administration and the school's policies.

    f. By being responsive to students, parents, employees and the community, and working together, any organization can create a better "product". A college or university is more than just the courses it offers. For example, the quality of student life on campus can directly affect enrollment.

    g. There may be courses on your campus in Environmental Management, Recycling Management and so on. There may be paper or can recycling programs, or student sponsored clubs or activities relating to the environment.

6. Answers to this question will vary. Most companies make use of computers for everything from inventory management to payroll. Students will find that companies are using technology in hundreds of different ways. Most large companies will have a Web site, and some small companies will also. Many companies today are offering benefits such as time off to work as a volunteer, day care centers and more. Most will also find that the company is involved in some way in the international market, even if it is just selling or buying a few products imported from overseas. Many of these companies will have a diverse workforce, and employ a variety of international workers at all levels.

7.   By developing programs such as those mentioned, companies better meet employee needs. This can make a company more competitive by fostering a positive environment with satisfied workers who may then be more productive. Further, these programs can be used to attract the kinds of skilled workers companies will need in the future to remain competitive.

8.   If U.S. firms want to be competitive in today's global environment, they must continue to focus on quality issues in the same way that countries like China, India, South Korea and Mexico have done. These countries are often able to produce high quality goods at low prices. U.S. manufacturers have taken ideas from around the world, and implemented the most advanced quality methods to make U.S. workers among the most productive in the world. Further, U.S. firms have begun to realize that in order to be competitive, they must cooperate with other international firms to continue to serve the growing global markets with the highest quality products and services at the lowest possible prices. This has provided U.S. workers with jobs by expanding our global marketplace.

9.   As the agricultural industry became more productive through advances in technology, fewer people were needed to produce the same or greater volume of goods. So, agricultural workers had to find jobs elsewhere, in other industries, and learn new skills. Many of these people went to work in manufacturing, helping to make the United States a world manufacturing power in the first half of this century.

       The same trend has occurred today in the industrial, or manufacturing sector. As factories have been able to improve productivity through technology, fewer workers are needed to produce the same or greater volume of high quality products. Factory workers today have found new employment in the service industries, which have generated almost all of the employment growth increases since the mid-1980s.

PRACTICE TEST

MULTIPLE CHOICE   **TRUE/FALSE**

1.	d		11.	b		1.	F		9.	F
2.	b		12.	a		2.	T		10.	F
3.	c		13.	b		3.	T		11.	T
4.	b		14.	c		4.	F		12.	F
5.	c		15.	c		5.	F		13.	T
6.	a		16.	a		6.	F		14.	F
7.	d		17.	d		7.	T		15.	F
8.	c		18.	b		8.	T			
9.	a		19.	c						
10.	a		20.	a						

LEARNING GOALS

After you have read and studied this chapter you should be able to:

1.   Compare and contrast the economics of despair with the economics of growth.

2.   Explain the nature of capitalism and how free markets work.

3.   Discuss the major differences between socialism and communism.

4.   Explain the trend toward free market economies.

5.   Use key terms (e.g. GDP, CPI, PPI, productivity, inflation, recession, monetary policy, fiscal policy and national debt) to explain the U.S. economic condition.

LEARNING THE LANGUAGE

Listed below are important terms found in this chapter. Choose the correct term for each definition below and write it in the space provided.

Capitalism	Gross domestic product (GOP)	Oligopoly
Command economies	Inflation	Perfect competition
Communism	Invisible hand	Producer price index (PPI)
Consumer price index (CPI)	Macroeconomics	Recession
Demand	Market price	Resource development
Deflation	Microeconomics	Socialism
Depression	Mixed economies	Supply
Disinflation	Monetary policy	Unemployment rate
Economics	Monopolistic competition	
Fiscal policy	Monopoly	
Free market economies	National debt	

1.   The quantity of products that manufacturers or owners are willing to sell at different prices at a specific time is known as _____.

2.   The part of economic study that looks at the behavior of people and organizations in particular markets is called_____.

3.   The country is in a _____when GDP has declined for two consecutive quarters.

4.   The economic system known as _____ is one in which all or most of the factors of production and distribution are privately owned and operated for profit.

5.   _____ is the quantity of products that people are willing to buy at different prices at a specific time.

6.   We define the _____ as the number of civilians at least 16 years old who are unemployed and have tried to find a job within the prior four weeks.

7.   Buyers and sellers negotiating prices for goods and services are working within _____, in which decisions about what to produce and in what quantities are decided by the market.

8.   The _____ consists of monthly statistics that measure changes in the prices of about 400 goods and services that consumers buy.

9.   The results of a series of government deficits when the government spends more money than it collects on taxes, over time, is called the _____.

10. A course in _____ will teach us how society chooses to employ resources to produce various goods and services and to distribute them for consumption among various competing groups and individuals.

11. Government economists keep a close watch on _____, which is the general rise in the price level of goods and services over time.

12. One key economic indicator is _____, the total value of goods and services produced in a country in a given year.

13. Some countries operate under a _____in which the government largely decides what goods and services will be produced, who will get them, and how the economy will grow.

14. In developing _____ the government is managing the amount of money placed into the economy and managing interest rates.

15. _____ is a condition where price increases are slowing.

16. A severe recession is known as a(n)_____.

17. _____ is an economic system based on the premise that most basic businesses should be owned by the government so that profits can be evenly distributed among the people.

18. When the government makes an effort to keep the economy stable, it may use _____, by increasing or decreasing taxes and/or government spending.

19. A _____ exists where some allocation of resources is made by the market and some by the government.

20. The economy is experiencing _____ when prices are actually declining.

21. A _____ is a market in which there is only one seller.

22. The market situation known as _____ is where there are many sellers of nearly identical products and no seller is large enough to dictate the price of the product.

23. Adam Smith coined the term _____ to describe the process that turns self-directed gain into social and economic benefits for all.

24. A form of competition where the market is dominated by just a few sellers is called a(n)_____.

25. The part of economic study called _____ looks at the operation of a nation's economy as a whole.

26. The study of _____ focuses on how to increase resources and to create the conditions that will make better use of those resources.

27. The _____ is the price determined by supply and demand.

28. _____ is the market situation in which there are a large number of sellers that produce similar products, but the products are perceived by buyers as different.

29. The economic and political system called _____ is where the state makes all economic decisions and owns all the major forms of production.

30. The index that measures prices at the wholesale level is the _____.

ASSESSMENT CHECK

Learning Goal 1   **The Importance of the Study of Economics**

1. What do followers of Thomas Malthus believe? How do the views of the neo Malthuasians differ from others?

2. What did Adam Smith believe was vital to the survival of any economy?

3. How does the economy benefit if workers can keep the profits from the work they do?

4. Describe Adam Smith's theory of the "invisible hand."

5.   In a capitalist system, who/what owns the businesses and decides what to produce, how much to produce, how much to pay workers, and how much to charge for goods?

6.   What is the foundation of the U.S. economic system?

7.   What are the four basic rights of a free market (capitalist) system?

   a. _____

   b. _____

   c. _____

   d. _____

8.   In general, how do consumers in the U.S. and other free market systems send signals to producers – in other words, what tells producers what and how much to produce?

9.   What is "supply" and what happens to quantity supplied as price goes up?

10.   What is demand and what happens to demand as price goes up?

11.   What is the key factor in determining quantity supplied and quantity demanded?

12.   Label the graph

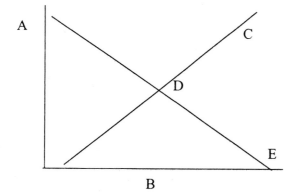

13.   What does the equilibrium point represent and how is price determined?

14.   Why could it be argued that there is no need for government planning or intervention in a free market system?

15.   Describe:

a. perfect competition

b. monopolistic competition

c. oligopoly

d. monopoly

16.   Even in the face of prosperity, how does the free market system also create inequality in a society?

Learning Goal 3   **Understanding Socialism**

17.   What is the basic premise of socialism? In a socialist system what is the government expected to provide?

18.   What is the major benefit of socialism? Why?

19.   What are the negative consequences of socialism? What results from those consequences?

Learning Goal 3   **Understanding Communism**

20.   Who is considered to be the father of communism?

21.   In a communist system, who/what makes economic decisions?

22.   What has been a problem with communism, and what has been the result?

Learning Goal 4   **The Trend Toward Mixed Economies**

23.   What are the two major economic systems "vying" for dominance in the world?

   a. _____

   b. _____

24.   What is the major principle of each of the two major economic systems?

   a. _____

   b. _____

25. Experience has shown that neither capitalism nor socialism has had optimal results in terms of the economy. What are the problems with:

a. Capitalism (a free market system)

b. Socialism/communism

c. What has been the result of those problems?

26. What is considered a "mixed economy?"

27. What kind of economic system do we have in the United States? Why is it considered to be this type of system?

Learning Goal 5 **Understanding the Economic System of the United States**

28. What are three major indicators of economic health?

a. _____

b. _____

c. _____

29. Why is the level of G.D.P. actually larger than what the figures show? What is one major influence on the growth of G.D.P.?

30.   Describe the four types of unemployment.

a. _____

b. _____

c. _____

d. _____

31.   List two measures of price changes over time.

a. _____

b. _____

32.   Why is the CPI an important figure?

33.   The income earned from producing goods and services goes to:

a. _____

b. _____

34.   Is the government running a budget surplus or deficit? What is the controversy surrounding this issue?

35. What is productivity?

36. What does an increase in productivity mean, and what is the benefit of an increase in productivity?

37. What is the difficulty in measuring productivity in the service sector?

38. Two ways to describe inflation are:

    a._____

    b._____

39. What does the CPI measure?

40. What is the difference between inflation and deflation?

41.   What is the difference between inflation and disinflation?

42.   What is a recession?

43.   What three things happen when a recession occurs?

a. _____

b. _____

c. _____

44.   What are three consequences of a recession?

a. _____

b. _____

c. _____

45.   What is the difference between a recession and a depression?

The Issue of Monetary Policy

46.   What are two areas managed by monetary policy?

a. _____

b. _____

47.   What is the Fed? What powers does the Fed have?

The Issue of Fiscal Policy

48.   What two areas are managed by fiscal policy?

a. _____

b. _____

49.   How is a budget deficit created, and what does the government do when there is a budget deficit? Does the U.S. have a surplus or a deficit?

50.   What is the difference between the federal deficit and the national debt?

51.   How high is the national debt?

52.   What are 3 issues being discussed in deciding how to handle the surplus?

        a. _____

        b. _____

        c. _____

CRITICAL THINKING EXERCISES

Learning Goal 1

1.   They're everywhere! McDonald's hamburgers can be purchased in cities and suburbs, on riverfronts, in college football stadiums and in discount stores. There are fast food restaurants at most major road intersections, and billions of dollars are spent annually to advertise everything from fast food frozen yogurt to kid's meals. Grocery stores have even gotten into the act with their own versions of fast food restaurants.

        Families with sick children can stay in Ronald McDonald houses located close to the hospital where the children are receiving treatment, and grocery stores in the Midwest and California, along with many other businesses came to the aid of flood victims in the mid and late 1990's.

        How does the story of the founding and growth of entrepreneurial ventures like McDonald's and the resulting growth in other, similar businesses illustrate Adam Smith's invisible hand theory?

Learning Goal 2

2.   There are four basic rights under the capitalist economic system;

a. Private property   c. Competition

b. Profit   d. Freedom of choice

Read the situations below and determine which of these is being demonstrated.

a. The owners of Pro Performance, Inc. make a profit for the owners for the first time in their history and decide to pay themselves a dividend. _____

b. The owners of Pro Performance, Inc. bought a piece of land for investment purposes._____

c. Proctor and Gamble spends over $2 billion a year on advertising._____

d. Tom Oswalt decided not to join the union at the shop where he is employed for the summer._____

e. Arthur Tower receives a patent for a new method he devised to make metal springs._____

f. Alfred Rockwood, after he retired, decided to move to northern Michigan and start his own fly-tying business._____

g. Sony introduces a new, upgraded version of its popular Play Station video game in order to grab a larger share of the toy market. _____

h. The Andersens, a young, dual-income couple, draw up a will, making their children the beneficiaries of their home, property and other assets. _____ _____

3. Plot a supply curve using the information below:

Unit price (dollars)	Amount supplied (units)
$125	500
100	400
75	300
50	200
25	100

Now, plot the demand curve using the information listed below.

Unit price (dollars)	Amount demanded (units)
$125	100
100	200
75	300
50	400
25	500

a. What is the equilibrium price? _____

b. How many units will be supplied and purchased at the equilibrium price?

_____

4. Indicate whether the market price of a product will most likely go up or down in the following situations:

a. There is a drought in the Midwest (bushel of wheat) _____

b. Strawberries are in season with a bumper crop. _____

c. It's the ski season (price of motel rooms)._____

d. A nutrition study indicates that red meat should be eaten only in moderation, if at all. (price of red meat) _____

e. A major corporation announces that it has to borrow money from the government in order to stay in business. (price of its stock)_____

5. There are four degrees of competition:

a. perfect competition   c. oligopoly

b. monopolistic competition   d. monopoly

Match the type of competition to the situation described below"

a. Murray Barnard takes his soybean crop to the grain elevator in Decatur Illinois. He found that because of government price supports he would make a nice profit this year.

_____

b. Because it is the only provider of electrical service in the area, AmerenUE is carefully regulated by the Missouri Public Service Commission. _____

c. Cheer cleans in all temperatures. Ivory Snow is gentle enough to launder a baby's clothes and Tide cleans the dirtiest clothes. Procter and Gamble makes these brands, as well as several others, which all appear to be different. Procter and Gamble competes with many other manufacturers and retains control over advertising, branding and packaging. _____

d. The purchasing agent for Missouri Rolling Mills says that he buys the steel the company uses to make their sign posts primarily on the basis of the best delivery date and the highest quality, rather than price, since all of his suppliers charge the same dollar amount per ton.

_____

Learning Goal 2, 3

6. Julie Marshall's first cousin, Jean-Paul, lives and works in Belgium. They have had long "discussions" via e-mail about the benefits and drawbacks of living in the U.S., a capitalist system, versus living in Belgium a socialist economic system. Both Julie and Jean-Paul defend their country's system. What do you think Julie would say about the benefits of living in the U.S. and the drawbacks of living in Belgium, and how would Jean-Paul respond?

7.   Four basic economic systems are:

a. Capitalism   c. Socialism

b. Mixed Economy   d. Communism

Read the following examples and using the table on page 53 of the text, determine which system is most likely being described:

a. _____ John works for a local television station in the country in which he lives. He is considered to be a government employee, but his brother owns his own small printing business.

b. _____ Because the market is "ruled " by supply and demand with little government involvement, Maria has a wide variety of goods and services available for purchase where she lives.

c. _____ Many of the products Maria purchases have been made or assembled outside her country. These products are available because the government of her country does not control or interfere with trade with other countries.

d. _____ Hong's uncle works for a large corporation where promotions and raises are given to those who work hard and do a good job. The only problem is, the tax rate is so high there is little incentive for anyone to work that hard. Hong is a teacher in a public school, and the government controls his wages.

e. _____ Sam is a farmer in his country, and has been paid by the government for the last 3 years not to plant and harvest his land.

f. _____ Ramon works hard at his job because where he lives and works, profits are kept by the owners of the company, and he is one of the owners. Workers are well rewarded for high productivity, and they work hard.

g. _____ Vladimir would like to change jobs, but his government restricts his ability to do so.

h. _____ Enrique has a cousin in another country who tries to supply him with blue jeans and other products which are in very short supply in his country. Enrique often has to obtain some basic things, such as some food and clothing products, illegally.

Learning Goal 5

8. Discuss the relationship between productivity and price levels. What is the relationship between productivity and Gross Domestic Product?

9. There are four types of unemployment:

a. frictional   c. cyclical

b. structural   d. seasonal

Match the situation being described to the type of unemployment

a. As sales of new homes decline, the construction industry lays off thousands of workers.
_____

b. A migrant worker, finished with his job in the potato fields in Idaho, travels to Michigan to look for a job harvesting fruit. _____

c. A middle manager is laid off. His job has been eliminated with the installation of high tech information processing equipment. _____

d. A businessman quits his job over a major disagreement with company policy. _____

10. Determine whether fiscal policy or monetary policy is being discussed:

a. Congress debates a major income tax revision. _____

b. The Federal Reserve raises interest rates to its member banks. _____

c. A candidate for major political office promises to cut spending for social programs to reduce the national debt. _____

d. Major government programs lose federal funding. _____

e. In an attempt to ease unemployment, the Fed increases the money supply. _____

f. A proposal is made to cut defense spending, but to raise taxes to fund defense spending. _____

g. American taxpayers express concern over tax loopholes for the rich._____

h. A debate centers on whether to lower the national debt through an increase in the tax rate, less spending, or both. _____

11. Political campaigns often revolve around the issue of taxes and how an increase or a decrease will affect government spending and revenues. Since government revenues come from collecting taxes, discuss how a tax *decrease* could have the effect of *raising* government revenues. (Some of this answer will come from what you learned in Chapter 1)

PRACTICE TEST

MULTIPLE CHOICE - Circle the best answer

1. Bill Ding started his own construction company to support his family. The going was slow at first but after some time, Bill got so busy he had to hire 3 workers. Bill and his workers do high quality work, and now, there is quite a demand for their services . Bill is considering hiring 2 more people. He also has an exclusive deal with a local lumber yard. Because of Bill's business, the yard has added another employee. This is an example of the_____ in action.

    a. marketing concept
    b. invisible hand
    c. benefits of communism
    d. resources development theory

2. The challenge for economists today is to:

    a. determine how rich countries can remain rich.
    b. reduce population growth so that resources will be conserved.
    c. ensure that all countries of the world become capitalist.
    d. implement policies and programs that will lead to increased prosperity for all people in all countries.

3. One of the problems with_____ is that it naturally leads to unequal distribution of wealth.

    a. communism
    b. socialism
    c. a command economy
    d. capitalism

4. Karl Marx believed that:

    a. businesses should be owned by workers and economic decisions should be made by the government.
    b. business and government should not mix, and so all businesses should be privately owned by stockholders.
    c. capitalism was not the kind of system where wealth could be created.
    d. eventually all of the countries in the world would operate under capitalist beliefs.

5. Citizens of socialist nations can rely on the government to provide all of the following except:

   a. education.
   b. health care.
   c. unemployment and retirement benefits.
   d. money to start a business.

6. What kind of a system exists when the marketplace largely determines what goods and services get produced, who gets them and how the economy grows?

   a. command economy
   b. socialist economy
   c. free market economy
   d. communist economy

7. The country of Amerensk has, for the last several years, been moving from a communist country to a more mixed economic system. All of the following could be observed in Amerensk except:

   a. an increase in the level of government involvement in trade
   b. private ownership of business
   c. an increase in the rate at which jobs are created
   d. more incentives for workers to work harder

8. Most countries in the world have a _____ economy.

   a. capitalist
   b. socialist
   c. mixed
   d. communist

9. Which of the following is not one of the four basic rights of a capitalist system?

   a. The right to have a job.
   b. The right to private property
   c. The right to compete
   d. The right to freedom of choice

10. Typically, the quantity of products that manufacturers are willing to supply will _____ when prices _____.

   a. increase/increase
   b. decrease/increase
   c. stay the same/increase
   d. increase/stay the same

11. A(n)_____shows the amount people are willing to buy at the prices at which sellers are willing to sell.

   a. supply curve
   b. demand curve
   c. marginal revenue point
   d. equilibrium point

12. One holiday season a few years ago, there was a toy called Tickle My Elbow that was all the rage. Demand for this toy was so high, that stores couldn't keep them on the shelf! There was quite a shortage of Tickle My Elbow that year. When a shortage such as this exists, what generally happens?

   a. the price goes up
   b. the price stays the same, and mothers everywhere fight for the last toy
   c. the government intervenes, and forces the manufacturer to make more of the toy
   d. when customers realize they can't get the toy, they give up, and the price goes down

13. What's going on here? As soon as Dewey Cheatum and Howe Motors increases the prices on their sport utility vehicle, then so does their only competitor, You Betcha Motors! Their prices are basically the same for similar vehicles, although their advertising says their products are really very different. What kind competition exists here?

   a. perfect competition
   b. monopoly
   c. oligopoly
   d. monopolistic competition

14. Which of the following would not be considered a key economic indicator?

   a. GDP
   b. The unemployment rate
   c. The tax rate
   d. The price indexes

15. Juan Valdez was laid off from his job at the coffee factory, because the demand for coffee has weakened. The kind of unemployment Juan is experiencing would be:

   a. frictional.
   b. seasonal.
   c. structural.
   d. cyclical.

16. Measures to increase productivity:

   a. are failing in manufacturing, as productivity is slowly decreasing.
   b. can improve quality of service providers, but not always improve worker output.
   c. are always successful in manufacturing and services industries.
   d. are becoming unimportant in today's competitive market.

17. Which of the following would not occur during a recession?

   a. high unemployment
   b. increase in business failures
   c. drop in the standard of living
   d. increase in interest rates

18. Monetary policy involves:

   a. raising and/or lowering interest rates and inflation.
   b. raising and/or lowering government spending.
   c. raising and/or lowering interest rates and the money supply.
   d. raising and /or lowering government spending and the money supply.

19. Fiscal policy is at issue when:

   a. The Federal Reserve raises interest rates to its member banks.
   b. The Federal Reserve debates combating inflation by cutting the money supply.
   c. Congress debates a proposal to cut defense spending, and raising taxes to support spending. for education
   d. Unemployment goes up as the country slides into a recession.

20. The results of all the government deficits over time is known as the:

   a. fiscal policy.
   b. gross national debt.
   c. national debt.
   d. aggregate demand for money.

True-False

1. _____ Adam Smith believed that as long as workers, or entrepreneurs, had the freedom to own property (or a business), and could see economic reward for their efforts, they would work long hours.

2. _____ One of the consequences of a socialist system is a high tax rate on those who do work, in order to pay for services for those that don't or can't work.

3. _____ The United States is a purely free market economy.

4. _____ In a free market system, price is determined through negotiation between buyers and sellers.

5. _____ When there is a surplus of products, manufacturers will tend to raise the price so that they will make a profit from those products they are able to sell.

6. _____ As capitalist systems evolved in the United States and other parts of the world, wealth became more equally distributed.

7. _____ A communist system is based upon the premise that the government owns all major forms of production and all economic decisions are made by the government.

8. _____ Socialism and communism are popular terms used to describe free market economies.

9. _____ Mixed economies exist where some allocation of resources is made by the marketplace, and some by the government.

10. _____ Monopolistic competition exists when there is only one supplier of a good or service.

11. _____ Total Gross Domestic Product in the United States in 1999 was over $6 trillion.

12. _____ Betty Bixler worked for Chrysler for 20 years before being laid off when her job was eliminated because updated technology made her job obsolete. Betty is structurally unemployed.

13. _____ The CPI is important because some government benefits, wages and salaries, rents and leases, tax brackets and interest rates are based upon this figure.

14. _____ Income from producing goods and services goes to the government in the form of taxes.

15. _____ An increase in productivity means the same worker produces more in the same amount of time.

16. _____ During a recession, we could experience an overall drop in our standard of living, high unemployment and increased business failures.

17. _____ During a period of disinflation, prices are actually going down.

18. _____ A major debate today is how to deal with the budget deficits we experienced in the early part of the 21st century.

You Can Find It On The Net

Many economic statistics can be found on government sites. Visit the Bureau of Labor Statistics at www.bls.gov

What is the most recent change in the Consumer Price Index?

Use the inflation calculator to determine the cost of tuition at your school in 10 years. What was tuition 10 years ago?

What is the most recent unemployment rate for the United States?

Go to the International Statistics link. How does the unemployment rate in the united States compare to other major countries such as Canada, Japan and parts of Europe?

ANSWERS

LEARNING THE LANGUAGE

1.	Supply	11.	Inflation	21.	Monopoly
2.	Microeconomics	12.	Gross Domestic Product	22.	Perfect competition
3.	Recession	13.	Command economy	23.	Invisible hand
4.	Capitalism	14.	Monetary policy	24.	Oligopoly
5.	Demand	15.	Disinflation	25.	Macroeconomics
6.	Unemployment rate	16.	Depression	26.	Resource development
7.	Free market economies	17.	Socialism	27.	Market price
8.	Consumer price index	18.	Fiscal policy	28.	Monopolistic competition
9.	National debt	19.	Mixed economy	29.	Communism
10.	Economics	20.	Deflation	30.	Producer Price Index

RETENTION CHECK

The Importance of the Study of Economics

1. Followers of Thomas Malthus believe that there are too many people in the world and that the solution to poverty is birth control. These views differ from others in that there are many who believe that a large population can be a valuable resource, especially if the people are educated. They believe that one of the keys to economic growth in the world is to educate people better.

2. Adam Smith believed that freedom was vital to the survival of any economy, especially the freedom to own land or property and the freedom to keep the profits from working the land or running a business. He believed people will work hard if they have the incentive to do so.

3. Smith believed that people would work harder if they knew they would be rewarded for work. As a result, the economy would prosper with plenty of food and available goods.

4. The "invisible hand" is what Smith believed was the mechanism for creating wealth. The idea is that people working for their own benefit will provide goods and services, which are needed by others. As a business grows and prospers, jobs are created and people are hired to work for the business. As a consequence, people will have food and goods available, and more people will have jobs. So, anyone who is willing and able to work will have a job and access to homes and opportunity for a better quality of life.

Understanding Free-Market Capitalism

5.   In a capitalist system, all or most of the factors of production and distribution are privately owned, (not owned by the government) and are operated for profit. So, in a capitalist system, business people decide what to product, how much to pay workers and how much to charge for goods and services.

6.   The foundation of the U.S. economic system is capitalism

7.   a. The right to private property
      b. The right to profits after taxes
      c. The right to freedom of competition
      d. The right to freedom of choice

8.   The consumers in a free market economy send signals to producers that tell them what and how much to make, by buying products and services, at the price we are charged. As long as we are willing to pay the price, the supplier will continue to make that supply available.

9.   Supply refers to the quantity of products that manufacturers or owners are willing to sell at different prices at a specific time. In general, as price goes up, the quantity supplied will go up.

10.   Demand refers to the quantity of products that people are willing to buy at different prices at a specific time. In general, as price goes up, quantity demanded will go down.

11.   The key factor in determining the quantity supplied and the quantity demanded is price.

12.   a. Price
      b. Quantity
      c. Supply curve
      d. Equilibrium point
      e. Demand curve

13.   The equilibrium point is the point on a graph where the quantity supplied is equal to the quantity demanded. This will tend to be the market price, as it represents the price at which sellers are willing to sell and buyers are willing to buy. So, price is determined by supply and demand.

14.   Proponents of a free market system argue that there is no need for government involvement or government planning because if surpluses develop, for example, then a signal is sent to sellers to

lower the price. If shortages develop, a signal is sent to sellers to increase the price. Eventually supply and demand will again be equal, if nothing interferes with the market forces.

15. a. Perfect competition exists when there are many sellers in a market and products appear to be identical. No one producer is big enough to dictate the price of a product. An example would be agricultural products.

b. Monopolistic competition exists when a large number of sellers produce products that appear similar, but are perceived as being different by the buyers. Product differentiation is the key to success in this type of competitive situation.

c. In an oligopoly, just a few sellers dominate the market, as is the case in the cereal and soft drink markets for example. The initial investment to enter an oligopoly is very high, and prices are similar. Product differentiation is usually the main factor in market success.

d. A monopoly exists where there is only one seller for a product or service. One seller controls supply, and could raise prices dramatically. For this reason laws in the United States prohibit monopolies, except for approved monopolies such as utility service.

16. The free market system has brought prosperity to the United States and many other parts of the world. However, it has brought inequality at the same time. A free market economy leads to inequality of wealth because business owners and managers will make more money and have more wealth than workers. Further, there will be people who are unable or unwilling to work or start a business. Others may not have the talent or drive to do so.

Understanding Socialism

17. The basic premise of a socialist system is that most basic businesses, such as steel mills, coal mines, and utilities, should be owned by the government so that profits can be evenly distributed. In a socialist system the government is expected to provide social services such as free education, free health care and free child care, for example.

18. The major benefit of socialism is social equality. There is a more even distribution of income because income is taken from richer people in the form of taxes, and redistributed to the poorer members of the population through various government programs.

19. Socialism takes away some of the incentive for business people. The income tax rates are very high, and people with high incomes are taxed very highly. As a consequence many of them leave socialist countries for more capitalistic countries with lower taxes. Socialist systems tend to discourage the best from working hard. In the business world, socialism also results in fewer inventions and less innovation because those who come up with the ideas usually don't receive as much reward as they would in a capitalist system.

Understanding Communism

20.   The father of communism is Karl Marx.

21.   In a communist system all economic decisions are made by the government and the government owns all the major forms of production.

22.   The problem with a communist system is that a government doesn't always know what is the right amount to produce. As a result, there can be shortages of many goods, even basics such as food. Another problem with communism is that it doesn't inspire businesspeople to work hard because the government takes most of their earnings.

        As a consequence most communist countries today are now suffering severe economic depression, and the people are suffering from the lack of goods and services readily available in most other countries.

The Trend Toward Mixed Economies

23.   The two major economic systems "vying" for dominance in the world are:
        a. Free market economies
        c. Command economies

24.   a. Free market economies exist when the marketplace largely determines what goods and services get produced, who gets them and how the economy grows. The popular term for this system is capitalism.
        b. Command economies exist when the government largely decides what goods and services to produce, who'll get them and how the economy will grow. Socialism and communism are terms used to describe this type of system.

25.   a. Many believe that a free market system is not responsive enough to the needs of the old, the disabled, the elderly and the environment.
        b. Socialism and communism have not created enough jobs or wealth to keep economies growing fast enough.
        c. The result has been a trend for "capitalist" countries, such as the United States, to move toward more socialism, and for "socialist" countries to move toward capitalism.

26.   Mixed economies exist where some allocation of resources is made by the market and some by the government.

27. The United States is a mixed economy. The degree of government involvement is our economy has been a matter of debate. The government is the largest employer in the United States, which means there are more workers in the public sector than in the entire manufacturing sector. There is also government involvement in healthcare, education business regulation and other parts of the economy.

Understanding the Economic System of the United States

28. a. the gross domestic product
    b. the unemployment rate
    c. the price index

29. The GDP is actually larger that what the figures show because they don't take illegal activities into account. A major influence on the growth of GDP is how productive the workforce is.

30. a. *Frictional unemployment* refers to those people who have quit work, and who haven't yet found a new job.
    b. *Structural unemployment* refers to unemployment caused by the restructuring of firms or by a mismatch between the skills or location of job seekers and the requirements or location of available jobs.
    c. *Cyclical unemployment* refers to unemployment caused because of a recession or similar downturn in the business cycle.
    d. *Seasonal unemployment* occurs where demand for labor varies over the year.

31. a. consumer price index
    b. producer price index

32. The CPI is an important figure because some government benefits, wages and salaries , rents and leases, tax brackets, and interest rates are based on the CPI.

33. The income earned from producing goods and services goes to
    a. the people who own the businesses in the form of dividends
    b. the government

34. The government is now taking in more money than it is paying out, resulting in a budget surplus. The controversy is determining whether that surplus should be used to pay off the national debt, increase social programs or go back to the people in the form of tax cuts.

35.   Productivity is the total output of goods and services one worker can produce in a given period of time.

36.   An increase in productivity means that a worker can produce more goods and services than before. Higher productivity means lower costs in producing goods and services and lower prices. This can help to make a firm more competitive.

37.   Productivity is an issue in the service industry because service firms are labor intensive. In manufacturing, machines can increase productivity, but in the service area, machines may add to the quality of the service provided, but not necessarily to the output per worker.

38.   Inflation can be described as:
        a. a general rise in the price level of goods and services over time
        b. too many dollars chasing too few goods

39.   The CPI measures the price of an average market basket of goods for an average family over time. Items included in the basket are food, automobiles, clothing, homes, furniture, drugs, and medical and legal fees.

40.   Inflation is a rise in prices of goods and services over time, and deflation is where prices are actually declining.

41.   Inflation is a rise in prices, and disinflation is a condition where the rise in prices is slowing, or in other words, the inflation rate is declining.

42.   A recession is two or more consecutive quarters of a decline in the GDP.

43.   When a recession occurs
        a. prices fall
        b. people purchase fewer products
        c. more businesses fail

44.   a. high unemployment
        b. increased business failures
        d. overall drop in living standards

45.   A depression is a severe recession.

The Issue of Monetary Policy

46.   a.   money supply

       b.   interest rates

47.   The Fed is the Federal Reserve System. The Fed is in charge of the money supply. It can add or subtract money from the economy as it sees fit.

The Issue of Fiscal Policy

48.   Two areas managed by fiscal policy are:

       a.   taxes

       b.   government spending

49.   A budget deficit is created when the government spends more money than it raises in taxes. When this happens the government borrows money to pay this deficit. The result over time is the national debt. Right now the government has a surplus.

50.   The Federal deficit is the difference between federal revenue and federal spending, The national debt is the sum of the federal deficits over time.

51.   The national debt was about $5.6 trillion in 2000.

52.   The debate is over how to handle the surplus. The questions are:

       a.   Should some money be given back to the people in the form of tax cuts?

       b.   Should the surplus go to paying off the national debt?

       c.   Should the surplus be used to create more social programs?

CRITICAL THINKING EXERCISES

1.   Adam Smith believed that an economy would prosper when people were allowed to produce needed goods and services and keep the profit in an attempt to improve their own standard of living. When people saw the potential gain from working hard and hiring others to help work, Smith argued that new businesses would be created, fueled by a desire for wealth. The invisible hand turned individual gain into social and economic benefits. Ray Kroc, the founder of McDonald's saw a need for fast food in the marketplace. He took an idea and developed it into a

multibillion-dollar corporation. He became the quintessential self-made millionaire, and spawned several companies along the way.

These companies have provided jobs for thousands of people, from high school kids working the counter after school to the franchisee who owns twenty restaurants, to the advertising executive in charge of the McDonald's account. The companies benefiting from McDonalds' success are providing a service U.S. consumers need and want, making a living providing goods and services and giving people jobs. McDonald's also goes beyond jobs and other tangible economic benefits, with Ronald McDonald Houses providing a social benefit beyond economic measure.

2.
   a. Profit
   b. Private property
   c. Competition
   d. Freedom of choice

   e. Private property
   f. Freedom of choice
   g. Competition
   h. Private property

3.

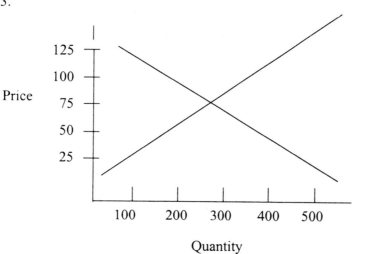

a. $75
b. 300 units

4.
   a. up
   b. down
   c. up
   d. down
   e. down

5. a. perfect competition

    b. monopoly

    c. monopolistic competition

    d. oligopoly

6. In her discussions with Jean-Paul, Julie might defend capitalism by saying that one benefit of the free-market system is that it allows open competition among companies. Businesses must provide customers with quality goods and services at fair prices with good service, or they will lose customers to other companies that do just that. She might also say that in the U.S. there is a benefit to working hard because we have the incentive of being able to keep the rewards of our work—i.e. profits.

    Julie might say further that the drawback of living in a socialist system is that the tax rate is so high that there is little incentive to work hard, be innovative and create new products because the government takes away so much of what you earn. Consequently, there are fewer Inventions and less innovation because those who come up with new ideas usually don't receive as much reward as they would in a capitalist system.

    Jean-Paul may respond that a major limitation of capitalism is the inequality of wealth distribution in a capitalist system. Business owners make more money than the workers, and some people who are old, disabled or don't have the talent to run a business can't create wealth for themselves. On the other hand, a major benefit of socialism is social equality. There is more equality because income is taken from the richer people in the form of taxes, and redistributed to the poorer members of the population through various government programs such as free education, free health care and free child care. Workers in these countries get longer vacations and tend to work fewer hours per week and have more employee benefits than workers in capitalist countries.

7. a. Socialism   e. Mixed economy

    b. Capitalism   f. Could be either capitalism or mixed economy

    c. Capitalism   g. Communism

    d. Socialism   h. Communism

8. Increases in productivity mean that the same amount of labor is able to produce a greater output. Costs are thus lower in producing goods and services, and so prices can be lower. So, efficiency in both manufacturing and the service sector can help to hold down inflation. If productivity slows, GDP growth could also slow. This would have a negative effect on the economy.

9. a. cyclical

    b. seasonal

    c. structural

    c. frictional

10. a. Fiscal policy   e. Monetary policy

    b. Monetary policy   f. Fiscal policy

    c. Fiscal policy   g. Fiscal policy

    d. Fiscal policy   h. Fiscal policy

11. Small business owners, who create many of the jobs and much of the wealth for the economy, are often severely affected by changes in the tax rates. These business owners may add jobs and hire more people when they know their tax liability will be lower as a result of a tax reduction. Consequently, while tax rates may be lower, a greater number of people will be contributing to the system, and this could have the effect of increasing government tax revenues.

PRACTICE TEST

MULTIPLE CHOICE

1.	b		11.	d
2.	d		12.	a
3.	d		13.	c
4.	a		14.	c
5.	d		15.	d
6.	c		16.	b
7.	a		17.	d
8.	c		18.	c
9.	a		19.	c
10.	a		20.	c

TRUE/FALSE

1.	T		10.	F
2.	T		11.	T
3.	F		12.	T
4.	T		13.	T
5.	F		14.	T
6.	F		15.	T
7.	T		16.	T
8.	F		17.	F
9.	T		18.	F

CHAPTER 3
COMPETING IN GLOBAL MARKETS

Learning goals

After you have read and studied this chapter, you should be able to:

1. Discuss the growing importance of the global market and the roles of comparative advantage and absolute advantage in international trade.

2. Explain the importance of importing and exporting, and understand key terms used in international business.

3. Describe the current status of the United States in global business.

4. Illustrate the strategies used in reaching global markets.

5. Evaluate the forces that affect trading in world markets.

6. Debate the advantages and disadvantages of trade protectionism.

7. Discuss the role of multinational corporations in global markets.

8. Explain how technology affects global e-commerce.

LEARNING THE LANGUAGE

Listed here are important terms found in this chapter. Choose the correct term for each definition and write it in the space provided.

Absolute advantage	Embargo	Joint venture
Balance of payments	Exchange rate	Licensing
Balance of trade	Exporting	Multinational corporation (MNC)
Common market	Foreign direct investment	Strategic alliance
Comparative advantage theory	Foreign subsidiary	Tariff
Contract manufacturing	Free trade	Trade deficit
Counter-trading	Import quota	Trade protectionism
Devaluation	Importing	World Trade Organization (WTO)
Dumping		

1. A long-term partnership between two or more companies, a _____ is established to help each company build competitive market advantages.

2. A tax known as a _____ is imposed on imported products.

3. The practice of selling products in foreign countries for less than you charge for the same products in your own country is known as _____.

4. There is a(n) _____when a country has a monopoly on the production of a specific product or is able to produce it more efficiently than all other countries.

5. The difference between money coming into a country and money leaving the country plus money-flows from other factors such as tourism, foreign aid, military expenditures and foreign investment is the _____.

6. A(n) _____is a complete ban on the import or export of certain products.

7. When there is a limit on the number of products in certain categories that can be imported, a(n) _____has been established.

8. When the value of a country's imports exceeds that of its exports, a country has a _____ .

9. The relationship of exports to imports is called the _____.

10. The _____ is the value of one currency relative to the currencies of other countries.

11. A country is involved in _____ when it is buying products from another country.

12. In a _____ a partnership has been formed in which companies often from different countries, have joined to undertake a major project.

13. A company is involved in _____when it has signed an agreement in which a producer allows a foreign company to produce its product in exchange for royalties.

14. The European Union is an example of a _____, a regional group of countries that have no internal tariffs, a common external tariff and the coordination of laws to facilitate exchange between countries.

15. A company is involved in _____ when it is selling products to another country.

16. An organization that manufactures and markets in many different countries and has multinational stock ownership and multinational management would be considered a _____.

17. A theory that asserts that a country should sell to other countries those products that it produces most efficiently is _____.

18. A company is involved in _____ when it produces private-label goods to which another company then attaches its brand name or trademark.

19. Lowering the value of a nation's currency relative to other currencies is known as _____.

20. There is _____ when the movement of goods and services among nations occurs without political or economic obstruction.

21. The use of government regulations to limit the import of goods and services is considered to be _____, which is based on the theory that domestic producers can survive and grow, producing more jobs.

22. Poorer countries will use a form of bartering among several countries which is known as _____.

23. Many countries today are involved in _____, which is the buying of permanent property and businesses in foreign nations.

24. A _____ is a company that is owned by another company in a foreign country.

25. This organization, known as the _____replaced the GATT agreement, and was assigned the duty to mediate trade disputes among nations.

ASSESSMENT CHECK

Learning Goal 1   **The Dynamic Global Market**

1.   What are some statistics that indicate the importance of international business for U.S. firms?

a. _____

b. _____

c. _____

d. _____

2.   What country is the largest exporter in the world? The largest importer?

3.   What are three reasons why countries trade with each other?

a. _____

b. _____

c. _____

4.   What are the pros and cons of free trade?

Pros	Cons
a. _____	a. _____
b. _____	b. _____
c. _____	c. _____
d. _____	

5.   Describe the basic theory of comparative advantage.

6.   What's the difference between comparative advantage and absolute advantage?

Learning Goal 2   **Getting Involved in Global Trade**

7.   Where is the greatest job potential for working in global markets?

8.   How have many individuals and entrepreneurs become involved in the global marketplace? Why has that been possible?

Measuring Global Trade

9.   What is a favorable balance of trade? An unfavorable balance of trade?

10. Why do countries prefer to have a favorable balance of trade?

11. What is the difference between the balance of trade and the balance of payments?

12. Why have some countries used the tactic of "dumping"?

Learning Goal 3 **Trading in Global Markets: The U.S. Experience**

13. How can it be said that although the U.S. is the largest exporting nation, the U.S. historically has never been focused on exporting?

14. What factors have led to American businesses going global? What is the size of the U.S. businesses involved in the global market?

15. Does the U.S. have a trade surplus or trade deficit?

16. How do economists measure a nation's economic activity? Why was the U.S. called a "debtor nation?"

Learning Goal 4   **Strategies for Reaching Global Markets**

17. List seven strategies for reaching global markets

a. _____   e. _____

b. _____   f. _____

c. _____   g. _____

d. _____

18. What are the advantages and disadvantages of licensing?

Advantages: _____

_____

Disadvantages: _____

_____

19.   What is an Export Assistance Center? What are export-trading companies?

20.   What must franchisers, such as McDonald's and KFC consider when they go global?

21.   What are the benefits of contract manufacturing?

22.   What are the characteristics of international joint ventures that make it an attractive option for
        many companies?

23.   What are the benefits and drawbacks of international joint ventures?

        Benefits   Drawbacks
        a._____   a._____

        b._____   b._____

        c._____   c._____

        d._____

24. What are the characteristics of strategic alliances?

25. How does a foreign subsidiary operate? What are the advantages? Disadvantages?

26. How can foreign direct investment be viewed? (In other words, why should we <u>not</u> worry about foreign direct investment?)

Learning Goal 5 **Forces Affecting Trading in Global Markets**

27. What are four forces affecting trading in global markets?

    a. _____

    b. _____

    c. _____

    d. _____

28. What is "ethnocentricity"? How have American business people adapted to global marketing compared to business people from other nations?

29. What are some of the sociocultural elements of which it is important to be aware in working with individuals from other cultures? How do economic forces relate to this?

30. What is "global marketing"? What is a sound philosophy to adopt with regard to global marketing?

31. What is meant by a "high value of the dollar"? What impact does a "high value of the dollar" have on U.S. businesses?

32. What is meant by a "low value of the dollar?" What impact does this have on U.S. businesses?

33. What is a floating exchange rate"?

34. How is supply and demand for currencies created?

35. How is trade conducted in many developing nations?

36. Understanding what three things is vital to a company's success in the global market?

   a. _____

   b. _____

   c. _____

37. What characteristics of the legal and regulatory forces make conducting global business so difficult?

38. What is the Foreign Corrupt Practices Act? What is the impact on American firms?

39. How can businesses increase their chances of success in foreign markets with regard to legal and regulatory forces?

40. What are the challenges, in the area of technology, that face a business entering a developing country?

Learning Goal 6   **Trade Protectionism**

41. What do advocates believe is the benefit of trade protectionism?

42. What is the idea behind the economic principle of "mercantilism"?

43. List five forms of trade protectionism

a. _____   d. _____

b. _____   e. _____

c. _____

44. What is the difference between a tariff revenue and a protective tariff?

45.   What is the difference between an import quota and an embargo?

46.   What are nontariff barriers? What are some examples of nontariff barriers?

47. What are the four trade agreements discussed in the text?

        a. _____

        b. _____

        c. _____

        d. _____

48.   What did the GATT provide for? What two areas are covered by the new GATT, passed in 1994?

49.   What organization was created by the GATT in 1995, and what is the task of that organization?

50. What critical areas are not addressed by the GATT?

51. What are two common markets?

52. What is the EU and what was it's objective?

53. What is the euro? What three things do the European nations hope to gain from the euro?

54. What countries are part of the Mercosur? What are its goals?

55. What does NAFTA stand for? What three countries are part of the NAFTA agreement?

56.   Has NAFTA been successful? What concerns about the trade agreement still persist?

Learning Goal 7   **Multinational Corporations**

57.   What are three characteristics of a multinational corporation? What distinguishes an MNC from other companies that do business overseas?

Learning Goal 8   **The Future of Global Trade: Global E-Commerce**

58.   What areas of the world is especially attractive to businesses today? Why?

59.   What are the concerns about entering the Chinese and Russia markets?

60.   What has made expansion into world markets more available?

61.   What problems still exist with technology in global trade?

CRITICAL THINKING EXERCISES

Learning Goal 1

1. How does the theory of comparative advantage relate to the development of free trade agreements around the world, such as NAFTA and the EU?

Learning Goal 2

2. Re-read the example of the ice factory in Africa, and the other examples of opportunities found in international markets. How do they illustrate the importance of entrepreneurship, capitalism and Adam Smith's "invisible hand" theory in the international market? How can you take advantage of the opportunities?

Learning Goal 3

3. The United States is the world's largest exporter, yet the text indicates that the U.S. "in general has never been very active in exporting." How can you explain these seemingly contradictory statements?

4. There are several ways to become involved in world trade:

Exporting   Franchising

Licensing   International Joint ventures

Creating subsidiaries   Foreign direct investment

Contract manufacturing

Match the term with the situations below:

a. This kind of an agreement with a Japanese food concern will give Campbell Soup a chance to increase its market share in Japan's soup market, which is very difficult to enter._____

b. In this kind of agreement, also known as outsourcing, Nike gives its name to shoes manufactured overseas and distributed here._____

c. McDonald's, Ramada Inns, and KFC have successfully used this form of operation in foreign markets, after changing their product to suit local tastes._____

d. In the late 1990's Daimler, a German automotive company, bought Chrysler, the American automotive manufacturer. _____

e. In the 1990's, Grand Metropolitan, a corporation headquartered in Great Britain, acquired a portion of Pet, Inc. of St. Louis. Grand Met, as it is known, become the parent company of Pet, Inc. _____

f. GE has a number of bilingual workers with advanced degrees in its trading department to help the corporation with this kind of international trade, selling their product to foreign markets. _____

g. Coke and Pepsi often enter foreign markets by allowing a foreign manufacturer to use its trademark and pay them (Coke and Pepsi) a royalty for that right. _____

5. How can direct foreign investment in the United States, (for example, the purchase of Pebble Beach by the Japanese) be considered a sign of strength for the American economy?

Learning Goal 5

6. Discuss the issues of the value of the dollar relative to other currencies. What impact does lowering the value of the dollar have? How would American businesses be affected if the dollar were devalued, as the Mexican peso was a few years ago?

7. The daily difficulties of doing business at home are compounded by a variety of differences between U.S. and foreign markets. Difficulties can stem from cultural and social differences, economic problems, legal and political regulations and physical and environmental forces such as technology. Keep those ideas in mind in completing the following.

    You have a successful ice cream/frozen yogurt business in the United States, and are especially interested in opening a store in the Middle East, probably Saudi Arabia. You market your product through free-standing buildings in the U.S. but are unsure of how to start up in Saudi Arabia. You have begun to seriously think about the possibility but are concerned about some of the problems you may encounter. What are the things you need to consider before going ahead with your plan?

Learning Goal 6

8.   Governments have developed a number of ways to protect their domestic industries from what they would consider the potentially negative impact of foreign trade:

Protective tariffs   Embargoes

Revenue tariffs   Non-tariff barriers

Import quotas

Match the correct type of trade protectionism to each of the following:

a.   The amount of Argentine beef brought into the United States is limited by this form of agreement._____

b.   Mexico has several of this type of tariff, designed to raise money for its government._____

c.   In early 1995, the U.S. imposed this type of "restriction" on Chinese made goods, in retaliation for the pirating of U.S. made products by Chinese manufacturers. The effect of this "restriction" was a 100% increase in the cost of Chinese made goods sold in the United States._____

d.   The U.S. has refused to allow the products of Cuba and some other countries to be sold in the U.S. under an _____ .

e.   Belgium requires margarine to be sold in cubes, cutting off those companies which manufacture margarine in tubs. _____

9.   What is the underlying principle of mercantilism?

Learning Goal 7

10.   What distinguishes an MNC from a company less involved in global business?

11. Look at the website for Ben and Jerry's ice cream (www.benjerry.com) How has today's technology enabled this company to reach a much larger marketplace? What has this company done to address the sociocultural issues involved in taking an "American" company global?

PRACTICE TEST

Multiple Choice – circle the best answer

1.   Selling products to another country is known as:

    a. importing.
    b. trade protectionism.
    c. comparative advantage.
    d. exporting.

2.   All of the following are reasons for countries to participate in foreign trade except

    a. it is just as easy to start a business overseas as it is in the U.S.
    b. no nation can produce all of the product its people want and need.
    c. even if a country were self-sufficient, other nations would seek trade with that country in order to meet the needs of its own people
    d. some nations have resources, but not technological know-how, while others have know-how, but lack resources.

3.   Producing and selling goods that we produce most effectively and efficiently, and buying goods that other countries produce most effectively and efficiently is known as:

    a. absolute advantage.
    b. free trade.
    c. international marketing.
    d. comparative advantage.

4.   When the value of exports from a country exceeds the value of imports into that country, there is a _____.

    a. trade deficit
    b. balance of payments
    c. unfavorable balance of trade
    d. favorable balance of trade

5.   The difference between money coming into a country from exports and money leaving a country due to imports, plus money flows from other factors, is known as the:

   a.   balance of trade.
   b.   dumping effect.
   c.   balance of payments.
   d.   trade deficit.

6.   The United States exports:

   a.   less volume, but a greater percentage of our products than other countries.
   b.   greater volume than other countries, and a greater percentage of our products.
   c.   about the same volume as other countries but a lower percentage of our products.
   d.   a greater volume than other countries, but a lower percentage of our products.

7.   In the 1990s Nestle acquired several U.S. firms, such as Carnation. Carnation now operates in the U.S. as a(n):

   a.   exporter.
   b.   subsidiary.
   c.   licensing agent.
   d.   franchise.

8.   Coke and Pepsi often enter foreign markets by allowing a foreign manufacturer to use their trademark and pay them (Coke or Pepsi) a royalty for that right. This is an example of

   a.   a joint venture.
   b.   exporting.
   c.   licensing.
   d.   creating a subsidiary.

9.   Nike uses this type of global strategy when it distributes products which have been manufactured by a foreign company, but which have the Nike brand name.

   a.   international joint venture
   b.   franchising
   c.   exporting
   d.   contract manufacturing

10. In franchising to foreign markets, companies such McDonald's and KFC have had to:

   a. be careful to adapt to the countries they are attempting to enter.
   b. find franchisees with money they can afford to lose if the franchise fails.
   c. be sure not to alter their products for the foreign countries, so that consumers know exactly what they are getting.
   d. find opportunities for joint ventures, as franchising doesn't seem to work in foreign markets.

11. Americans are often called ethnocentric. This means that:

   a. Americans feel their culture is superior to others.
   b. Americans welcome diversity in their workforce.
   c. U.S. firms are actively seeking international markets.
   d. U.S. businesses are pursuing a policy of multiculturalism.

12. Guillermo Martinez was concerned that his new boss, Donald Darr, an American, didn't know his job very well. Donald is continually asking Guillermo and the other workers in this plant in Mexico City, to give him their opinions before he makes a final decision. Guillermo's concern stems from _____ differences between he and Donald.

   a. economic
   b. cultural
   c. language
   d. regulatory

13. The makers of Whirlpool washers and other electrical appliance manufacturers need to be concerned about the kind and availability of electricity in the global marketplace. If there was a compatibility problem, it would be the result of a _____ difference.

   a. cultural
   b. technological
   c. economic
   d. societal

14. The law that specifically prohibits "questionable" or "dubious" payments to foreign officials in an effort to secure business contracts is called the:

   a. North American Free Trade Agreement.
   b. General Agreement on Tariffs and Trade.
   c. Securities and Exchange Act.
   d. Foreign Corrupt Practices Act.

15.   A high value of the dollar would mean

        a. your money is worth more at the stores where you shop.
        b. a dollar could be traded for more foreign currency than normal.
        c. you could trade in your money for gold.
        d. costs of foreign manufacturing would be higher.

16.   When Mexico devalued the peso, the peso became _____ valuable relative to other currencies.

        a. more
        b. less
        c. equally
        d. significantly more

17.   Using government regulations to limit the import of goods and services in order to protect domestic industries against dumping and foreign competition is called

        a. mercantilism.
        b. regulating the balance of trade.
        c. global marketing.
        d. trade protectionism.

18.   When the U.S. government imposes a tax on imported textiles, to protect the American textile industry, a(n) _____ is being levied.

        a. protective tariff
        b. import quota
        c. embargo
        d. revenue tariff

19.   Which of the following would not be considered a nontariff barrier?

        a. A requirement that all products sold in a country be packaged in a certain way
        b. A tradition of semi-permanent ties between domestic firms, which have the effect of shutting out foreign manufacturers
        c. Signing a trade agreement such as the GATT
        d. A set of quality standards that must be met by all companies wishing to do business within a country.

20. This agreement was established in 1948, and is designed to facilitate the exchange of goods, services, ideas and cultural programs.

   a. General Agreement on Tariffs and Trade (GATT)
   b. World Trade Organization (WTO)
   c. North American Free Trade Agreement (NAFTA)
   d. The European Union (EU)

21. The _____ was created by the _____ in 1995, and is assigned the task of mediating trade disputes.

   a. NAFTA/WTO
   b. GATT/ EU
   c. WTO/GATT
   d. GATT/NAFTA

22. An organization that does manufacturing and marketing in many different countries, has multinational stock ownership and multinational management is considered a

   a. common market.
   b. free trade area.
   c. global marketer.
   d. multinational corporation.

23. Which of the following is not considered to be a concern when evaluating trade with China?
   a. The one-party political system
   b. Human rights policies
   c. A shrinking market
   d. A growing trade imbalance

True-False

1. _____ It is expected that the amount of international trade will level off or decline in the next millennium.

2. _____ An example of exporting is the Meridian Group, based in the United States, selling sand from the U.S. to customers in the Middle East.

3. _____ When the country of Monrovia is buying more from the United States than it is selling to the United States, a favorable balance of trade exists for Monrovia.

4. _____ The goal of global trade is to have more money flowing into the country than flowing out of the country.

5. _____ The tactic of dumping is used to gain a foothold in a foreign market.

6. _____ Export Assistance Centers serve the role of matching buyers and sellers from different countries and providing other services to ease the process of exporting.

7. _____ One disadvantage of licensing is the cost to the company licensing its product or trademark (the licensor) to the foreign firm. (the licensee)

8. _____ An international joint venture is helpful to companies wishing to enter countries with planned economies, such as China, or in markets which for some reason are difficult to enter.

9. _____ Religion is an important element of a society's culture, and should be considered in making many business decisions.

10. _____ Economic differences between countries can affect purchasing patterns, such as quantity purchased at a given time.

11. _____ A sound global philosophy is " always assume that what works in one country will work in another."

12. _____ Trade protectionism is based upon the idea that barriers will help domestic producers grow, and create more jobs.

13. _____ Nontariff barriers can be just as detrimental to free trade as tariffs.

14. _____ In the near future, the "euro" will be the common currency in the European Union.

15. _____ Investment in China is still considered to be too risky to invest a great deal of money.

YOU CAN FIND IT ON THE NET

Find the most recent trade statistics for

a. The United States   Exports / Imports / Balance of Trade (deficit) (surplus)
b. Your state   Exports/ Imports/ Balance of Trade

What are the top ten countries with which your state trades? What is the largest category of foreign sales? How does this affect businesses and jobs in your area?

These statistics can be found on the Internet, with just a bit of looking around. A good place to start for the information regarding the U.S Trade Statistics is www.census.gov

For the state data, you may be able to start with www.ecodev.state.(state abbreviation).us, or, use a search engine, with the key words "exports" and the name of your state.

ANSWERS

LEARNING THE LANGUAGE

1.	Strategic alliance	10.	Exchange rate	18.	Contract manufacturing
2.	Tariff	11.	Importing	19.	Devaluation
3.	Dumping	12.	Joint venture	20.	Free trade
4.	Absolute advantage	13.	Licensing	21.	Trade protectionism
5.	Balance of payments	14.	Common market	22.	Countertrading
6.	Embargo	15.	Exporting	23.	Foreign direct investment
7.	Import quota	16.	Multinational corporation	24.	Foreign subsidiary
8.	Trade deficit	17.	Comparative advantage	25.	World Trade Organization (WTO)
9.	Balance of trade				

ASSESSMENT CHECK

The Dynamic Global Market

1.
   a. There are 6 billion people in the world, and most of them live outside the U.S.
   b. Americans buy billions of dollars' worth of goods from countries such as China and Japan
   c. Sales of American goods and services around the world are growing, and the U.S. is the largest exporting nation in the world.
   d. Global trade will grow more important throughout the 21st century.

2.   The United States is the world's largest exporter and importer.

3.
   a. No nation can produce all of the products its people need and want
   b. Even if a given country were self-sufficient, other nations would want to trade with that country to meet the needs of its people
   c. Trade allows nations to produce what they are capable of producing and to buy from other nations what they need.

4.   Pros
   a. Global market has over 6 billion customers
   b. Productivity grows with comparative advantage
   c. Global competition and lower-cost imports keep prices down
   d. Open trade encourages innovation
   e. Interest rates are lower due to uninterrupted flow of capital

Cons

    a.   Domestic workers in manufacturing could lose jobs

    b.   Workers face pay-cut demands from employers

    c.   Competitive pressure makes some jobs vulnerable to operations moving overseas

    d.   Domestic companies can lose comparative advantage when competitors build operations in low wage countries

5.   The theory of comparative advantage states that a country should produce and sell to other countries those products that it produces most effectively and efficiently, and should buy from other countries those products it cannot produce as effectively or efficiently.

6.   As stated in the previous answer, comparative advantage states that a country should produce and sell the products it produces most effectively and efficiently, and should buy those products other countries are better at producing and selling. A country has an absolute advantage when it has a monopoly on production of a good, or can produce it more cheaply than any other country.

Getting Involved in Global Trade

7.   The greatest job potential in global markets may be with small businesses. Today in the U.S. small businesses generate about half of the private-sector commerce, but account for only 20 percent of exports.

8.   Exporting and importing products have created a number of opportunities for individuals and entrepreneurs. Some people see a lack in the U.S. of a particularly appealing product from elsewhere. Also, just about any good or service that is used in the U.S. can be used in other countries as well, and the competition abroad is often not nearly as intense for most providers of these products as it is at home.

9.   A favorable balance of trade exists when the value of exports exceeds the value of imports. An unfavorable balance of trade occurs when the value of the country's imports exceeds that of its exports.

10.   Countries prefer to export more than they import, or have a favorable balance of trade, because the country will retain more of its money to buy other goods and services. As the example in the text illustrates, if I sell you $200 worth of goods, and only buy $100, I have an extra $100 available to buy other things.

11.   The balance of trade is a nation's relationship of exports to imports. The balance of payments is the difference between money coming into a country from exports and money leaving a country for imports, plus money flows from other factors.

12. The tactic of dumping is used to unload surplus products in foreign markets or to gain a foothold in a new market by offering products cheaper than domestic competitors.

Trading in Global Markets: The U.S. Experience

13. Even though the U.S. exports a large volume of goods globally, it exports a much lower percentage of its products than other countries do. In the past, as few as 10% of U.S. firms exported products.

14. Slow economic growth in the U.S. lured more businesses to global markets in the late 1980s and early 1990s. As we begin the 21st century, most large businesses are involved in global trade, and growing numbers of small and medium sized businesses are going global as well.

15. As of this writing, the U.S. has an overall trade deficit.

16. Economists measure a nation's economic activity by comparing the amount of money it owes to foreign creditors and the value of what foreign investors own in the country, with money foreigner owe to the country and the value of what that country owns in foreign markets. A debtor nation is a country that owes more money to other nations than they owe to it. In the 1980s it was reported that the U.S. was a debtor nation.

Strategies for Reaching Global markets

17.   a. Licensing
     b. Exporting
     c. Franchising
     d. Contract manufacturing
     e. International joint ventures
     f. Creating subsidiaries
     g. Foreign direct investment

18. Advantages of licensing are: additional revenue from a product that would not have generated domestic revenues, start-up supplies, materials and consulting services must be purchased from the licensing firm, which generates even more revenue and reduces costs of entering a foreign market; most costs are borne by the licensee.

Disadvantages with licensing include: a firm often must grant licensing rights to its product for as long as 20 years. Revenue from an especially successful product would then go to the licensee. Further, if a foreign licensee learns the technology, it could break its agreement and begin to produce the product on its own. The licensing company loses trade secrets and royalties.

19.   An Export Assistance Center (EAC) provides hands-on exporting assistance and trade finance support for small and medium sized businesses that choose to export. Export trading companies are specialists in matching buyers and sellers from different countries and providing services to ease the process of entering foreign markets.

20.   Franchisers must be careful to adapt to the customs of the countries they serve. They must consider customs, tastes, and other social factors in developing markets for their products.

21.   Through contract manufacturing a company can experiment in a new market without heavy start-up costs, which reduces risk. A firm can also use contract manufacturing temporarily to meet an unexpected increase in orders.

22.   Often, firms that participate in international joint ventures grow much faster than their counterparts that don't have such partnerships. Secondly, sometimes joint ventures are mandated by governments as a condition of doing business in their country. There are business reasons that joint ventures are developed, such as the opportunity to expand low market share in participating countries. Joint ventures often bring together unique partners, such as the example in the text, the University of Pittsburgh and the Italian government.

23.   Benefits of international joint ventures include:
   a.   Shared technology
   b.   Shared marketing and management expertise
   c.   Entry into markets where foreign companies are not allowed unless their goods are produced locally
   d.   Shared risk

   Drawbacks are:
   a.   One partner can learn the other's technology and go off on its own as a competitor.
   b.   Over time, technology may become obsolete
   c.   Partnership may become too large to be flexible.

24.   A strategic alliance is a long-term partnership between two or more companies established to help each company build competitive market advantages. These alliances can provide access to markets, capital and technical expertise, but they do not involve sharing costs, risk, management or profits.

25.   A foreign subsidiary operates much like a domestic firm, with production, distribution, promotion, pricing, and other business functions under the control of the foreign subsidiary's management. The primary advantage of a subsidiary is that the company maintains complete control over any technology or other expertise it may possess.

The major disadvantage is creating a subsidiary is that the parent company is committing a large amount of funds and technology within foreign boundaries. If relations with the host country take a downturn, the firm's assets could be taken over by the foreign government.

26.   Foreign direct investment can be viewed as a sign of strength in a nation's economy. It is time to worry when foreign investors no longer find a country attractive.

Forces Affecting Trading in Global Markets

27.   Four forces affecting trading in global markets are:

    a. Sociocultural

    b. Economic and financial

    c. Legal and regulatory

    d. Physical and environmental

28.   Ethnocentricity is the feeling that one's own culture is superior to all others. Many American businesspeople have been accused of this. Many U.S. companies fail to think globally.

29.   Some of the sociocultural elements of which it is important to be aware when working with individuals from other cultures are religious customs, cultural perspectives on time, human resources management, change, competition, natural resources and even work itself. The text gives an example of the combination of cultural and economic forces in India, where the average person consumes only three soft drinks annually, compared to 50 gallons per year per person in the U.S. The market for Pepsi and Coke would seem tremendous, until you look at this one statistic. The level of consumption relates not only to cultural differences between the U.S. and India but also to the low per capita income level of Indian consumers. Tea is less expensive than a soft drink in that country.

30.   Global marketing is selling the same product in essentially the same way everywhere in the world. A sound philosophy to adopt in global markets is to never assume that what works in one country will work in another.

31.   A high value of the dollar means that the dollar will buy, or can be traded for, more foreign currency than normal. When the dollar is high the products of foreign producers become cheaper, because it takes fewer dollars to buy them. The cost of U.S.-produced goods on the other hand, become more expensive to foreign buyers, because of the dollar's high value.

32.   A low value of the dollar means that the dollar will buy or can be traded for less foreign currency than normal. Therefore, foreign goods become more expensive in the U.S. because it takes more dollars to buy them, but American goods become cheaper to foreign buyers because it takes less foreign currency to buy American goods.

33. The floating exchange rate is a system in which currencies "float" according to the supply and demand in the market for the currency.

34. Supply and demand for currencies is created by global currency traders, who create a market for a nation's currency based upon the perceived trade and investment potential of the country.

35. In poorer, or developing nations trade is conducted through bartering, the exchange of merchandise for merchandise or service for service with no money involved. Countertrading is a complex form of bartering in which several countries may be involved, each trading goods for goods or services for services. It has been estimated that countertrading accounts for 25 percent of all international exchanges.

36. To be successful in global markets it is important to understand:
    a. economic conditions
    b. currency fluctuations
    c. countertrade opportunities

37. Some of the legal and regulatory difficulties in the global market stem from the fact that in global markets no central system of law exist, so several groups of laws and regulations may apply. Businesspeople find a myriad of laws and regulations that are often inconsistent. Important legal questions related to antitrust rules, labor relations, patents, copyrights, trade practices, taxes, product liability, child labor, prison labor and other issues are written and interpreted differently country by country.

38. The Foreign Corrupt Practices Act specifically prohibits "questionable" or "dubious" payments to foreign officials to secure business contracts. This type of legislation can create hardships for American businesses in competing with foreign competitors, because in some countries actions such as corporate bribery are acceptable, and sometimes the only way to secure a lucrative contract.

39. To be successful in global markets it is often important to contact local businesspeople and gain their cooperation and sponsorship. Local contacts can help a company penetrate the market and deal with bureaucratic barriers.

40. Technological constraints may make it difficult to build large markets in developing countries. Some developing countries have primitive transportation and storage systems that make international distribution ineffective. Technological differences also affect the nature of exportable products, such as electrical appliances. Telephone systems may also be primitive, which could inhibit effective commerce and e-commerce.

Trade Protectionism

41. Advocates of trade protectionism believe it allows domestic producers to survive and grow, producing more jobs. Countries often use protectionist measures to guard against such practices as dumping.

42. The primary idea behind mercantilism is for a nation to sell more goods to other nations than it bought from them, or in other words, to have a favorable balance of trade. This should result in a flow of money to the country that sells the most globally.

43. Forms of trade protectionism are:
    a. Protective tariffs
    b. Revenue tariffs
    c. Import quotas
    d. Embargoes
    e. Non-tariff barriers

44. A protective tariff is designed to raise the retail price of an imported good so the domestic product will be more competitive. The revenue tariff is designed to raise money for the government.

45. An import quota limits the number of products in certain categories that can be imported into a nation. An embargo is a complete ban on the import or export of certain products.

46. Nontariff barriers take a variety of forms. They are not as specific as embargoes but can be as detrimental to free trade. Japan has created relationships through keiretsu, which are close-knit groups of Japanese companies within an industry. Outsiders, such as foreign companies, cannot belong to such groups. Other countries have imposed restrictive standards that detail exactly how a product must be sold in a country.

47. a. General Agreement on Tariffs and Trade (GATT)
    b. European Union (EU)
    c. North American Free Trade Agreement (NAFTA)
    d. Mercosur

48. The GATT agreement provided a forum for negotiating mutual reductions in trade restrictions among 23 countries. The countries agreed to negotiate to create monetary and trade agreements that might facilitate the exchange of goods, services, ideas, and cultural programs.

The new GATT lowers tariffs by 38 percent worldwide and extends GATT rules to new areas such as agriculture, services and the protection of patents.

49. In 1995 the World Trade Organization (WTO) was created by the GATT. The task of the WTO is to mediate trade disputes. The WTO acts as an independent entity that oversees key cross-border trade issues and global business practices.

50. The GATT did not address critical areas such as intellectual property rights and financial services.

51. Two common markets are the EU, the European Union and the Mercosur, which is the South American Common Market.

52. The EU is a group of nations in Western Europe that united economically and formed a common market in the early 1990s. The objective was to make Europe the world's second largest economy an even stronger global competitor.

53. The euro is the currency which will be commonly used in the EU in the early part of this decade. The European nations hope that having a unified currency will bring its member nations more economic clout, more buying power and greater economic and political stability.

54. The Mercosur consists of the countries of Brazil, Argentina, Paraguay, Uruguay and associate members Chile and Bolivia. Its goals are economic in nature, and include a single currency.

55. NAFTA stands for the North American Free Trade Agreement. The three countries which are part of NAFTA are the United States, Canada and Mexico.

56. NAFTA has experienced both success and difficulties. Concerns today include issues of job loss and creation, child-labor laws and sweatshop violations, illegal immigration, environment concerns and the long-term strength of the peso.

Multinational Corporations and the Future of Global Trade

57. A multinational corporation, or MNC:
   a. does manufacturing in many different countries
   b. has multinational stock ownership
   c. has multinational management

Only firms that have manufacturing capacity or some other physical presence in different nations can truly be called multinational.

The Future of Global Trade: Global E-Commerce

58.   Asia, and specifically China are particularly attractive to U.S. businesses today. China has a population of 1.2 billion people, and a fast growing economy that appears to be shifting to a free market system. Other areas of the world that are attractive to businesses include Russia, India, Taiwan, Indonesia, Thailand, Singapore, the Philippines, Korea and Malaysia.

59.   Concerns remain about China's one-party political system, its human rights policies, the growing trade imbalance and difficulties in China's financial markets. In Russia, there are still severe political and social problems, and many firms don't expect a profit in that market until well into the 21st century.

60.   The growth of the Internet and advances in e-commerce have enabled companies worldwide to bypass normally required distribution channels to reach a large market.

61.   Problems with technology exist in global trade for a number of reasons. American Express reports that 43 percent of the small businesses polled could not find information on the Web that could help them do business globally. Many also stated that communication with companies in Asia still needed to be carried out by faxing hardcopies of documents. Some developing nations fear e-commerce will lead to the erosion of their local and national languages and culture.

CRITICAL THINKING EXERCISES

1.   The theory of comparative advantage states that a country should sell to other countries those products that it produces most effectively and efficiently and buy from other countries those product it cannot produce as effectively or efficiently. The development of free trade agreements can enable trading partners to reduce prices of traded products within those countries. They also enable these trading blocs to use comparative advantage to their benefit to realize mutually beneficial exchanges for all members. The trading blocs have an economic advantage that can make them a strong competitor in the global market, better able to take advantage of the theory of comparative advantage.

2.   It stated in chapter 2 that developing countries (particularly Eastern Europe) must allow entrepreneurship to flourish, so to speak, if their economies are to develop and become active participants in the global market. The same can be said for any part of the world. Adam Smith's idea of the "invisible hand" was simply that when an individual is allowed the incentive to work hard by being allowed to keep the profits from his business, society will benefit by getting needed goods or services. The story of the ice factory illustrates the invisible hand theory—the entrepreneur who started the factory "..is indeed wealthy.." and the country has a needed resource.

    Ways to take advantage of these ideas are by doing research, traveling, finding a need either in the United States for a product that can be imported, or overseas for a product that can be exported. The key is to be creative.

3.   While a majority of large businesses are involved in global trade, we export a much lower percentage of our products that other countries. So, by comparison, we are not as active as many other nations in the global marketplace. Further, the United States does not depend upon exporting as much as other industrialized nations, as indicated by the percentage of GDP exported by the U.S.

4.   a. International joint venture.
      b. Contract manufacturing
      c. Franchising
      d. Foreign direct investment
      e   Creating subsidiaries
      f. Exporting
      g. Licensing

5.   Many see direct foreign investment as a positive sign. They believe that the level of foreign investment has increased because the American economy has been so strong and we have been perceived worldwide as an economic leader. Property, buildings and stock have been a more attractive investment in the United States than elsewhere. The time to worry is when the level of investment begins to drop off, and other countries become more attractive.

6.   Lowering the value of the dollar means that a dollar is traded for less foreign currency than normal. Foreign goods would become more expensive because it would take more dollars to buy them. It also makes American goods cheaper to foreign buyers because it would take less foreign currency to buy them. In the long run, this could benefit U.S. firms in foreign markets. Devaluing a currency means lowering the value of a nation's currency relative to other currencies. This can cause problems with changes in labor costs, material costs and financing.

      American businesses would find their products less expensive in foreign countries, which could be beneficial for sales, but their cost of doing business in foreign countries could be negatively affected by a devaluation.

7.   One of the first things that needs to be considered is how the Saudis feel about ice cream/frozen yogurt as a product: how it's eaten, their views on dairy products (some religions have different views on dairy products and how they should be handled), where it can be marketed (do they have the same kind of grocery stores? do you open a free standing store?), even their familiarity with the product are all issues that must be addressed. There is a possibility that this may be a totally new product concept and you as a seller of the product will need to be aware of how to convince the Saudi people that this is a viable and acceptable product.

      Social and economic differences from the American market must also be considered. In the U.S. frozen yogurt and ice cream may be purchased on a trip to the grocery store, and stored at home in the refrigerator. Is that a similar life style to the Saudis? Is the type of equipment available which is needed to store the product before it is purchased? Does a typical Saudi home have the type of storage needed i.e. a freezer? American families may go to an ice cream or frozen yogurt stand as a family outing. Would that be true of a typical Saudi family? We eat ice cream or frozen yogurt as a dessert or sometimes as a snack. How would the Saudi population view the product? When might they choose to eat it?

Although Saudi Arabia as a nation may be wealthy, does the average Saudi have the money to buy a nonessential item like this?

Further questions to be answered revolve around legal and regulatory differences. The way of doing business in the Middle East is quite different from that of the U.S. Laws and regulations will vary, and practices will be different there than at home. The manner of entering business in the Middle East will be different from the U.S.

Additionally, will it be economically feasible to invest in the Middle East? How is the American dollar against the Saudi currency? That may affect the ability and willingness of the Saudi to try your product should you simply decide to export your product to the country. If you decide to attempt to produce and sell your product in Saudi Arabia, the value of the U.S. dollar will take on even more significance in light of the greater investment.

8.   a.   Import quotas
       b.   Revenue tariffs
       c.   Protective tariffs
       d.   Embargoes
       e.   Non-tariff barriers

9.   The underlying principle of mercantilism is to sell more goods to other nations than you bought from them. In other words, the goal is to have a favorable balance of trade. Mercantilism is the foundation for trade protectionism, and the various kinds of trade barriers discussed in the text.

10.   A company is only considered a multinational if it does manufacturing and marketing in more than one foreign nation. An MNC will manufacture and market in several countries, has multinational stock ownership and multinational management. The more multinational a company is, the more it will attempt to operate without being influenced by restrictions from various governments. Typically, multinationals are very large corporations.

11.   Ben and Jerry's has been able to reach their international markets conveniently through their website. A website allows them to "advertise", or promote, their product internationally because it is easily accessible to anyone with access to the Internet. It also allows Americans to see how their counterpart ice cream fans are slightly different. The website has geared its various sites to local markets by using the native language and modifying the content of the page for the "local" international market. Each page is slightly different.

PRACTICE TEST

MULTIPLE CHOICE

1.	d		13.	b
2.	a		14.	d
3.	d		15.	b
4.	d		16.	b
5.	c		17.	d
6.	d		18.	a
7.	b		19.	c
8.	c		20.	a
9.	d		21.	c
10.	a		22.	d
11.	a		23.	c
12.	b			

TRUE/FALSE

1.	F		9.	T
2.	T		10.	T
3.	F		11.	F
4.	T		12.	T
5.	T		13.	T
6.	F		14.	T
7.	T		15.	F
8.	T			

LEARNING GOALS

After you have read and studied this chapter, you should be able to:

1. Explain why legality is only the first step in behaving ethically.

2. Ask the three questions one should answer when faced with a potentially unethical action.

3. Describe management's role in setting ethical standards.

4. Distinguish between compliance-based and integrity-based ethics codes and list the six steps in setting up a corporate ethics code.

5. Define social responsibility and examine corporate responsibility to various stakeholders.

6. Analyze the role of American businesses in influencing ethical and social responsibility in global markets.

LEARNING THE LANGUAGE

Listed here are important terms found in this chapter. Choose the correct term for each definition and write it in the space provided.

Compliance-based ethics codes	Insider trading
Corporate philanthropy	Integrity-based ethics codes
Corporate policy	Social audit
Corporate responsibility	Social responsibility
Ethics	

1. Known as _____, these ethical standards emphasize preventing unlawful behavior by increasing control and by penalizing wrongdoers.

2. When a corporation performs a _____ it is conducting a systematic evaluation of an organization's progress toward implementing programs that are socially responsible and responsive.

3. _____ is the position a firm takes on social and political issues.

4. Standards of moral behavior, or _____is behavior that is accepted by society as right or wrong.

5. _____ are ethical standards that define the organization's guiding values, create an environment that supports ethically sound behavior, and stress a shared accountability among employees.

6. The dimension of social responsibility that includes charitable donations to nonprofit groups is called _____.

7. When a business shows concern for welfare of a society as a whole, it is demonstrating _____.

8. A dimension of social responsibility known as _____ includes everything from minority hiring practices to making safe products.

9. A form of investment in which insiders use private company information to further their own fortunes or that of others is called _____.

ASSESSMENT CHECK

Learning Goal 1   **Managing Business Ethically and Responsibly**

1. What is the difference between being "ethical" and being "legal?"

2. How do many Americans decide their sense of right and wrong?

3. What are some of the basic moral values found in classic literature written by Aristotle, Shakespeare, and Confucius?

4. Where does a sense of personal ethics begin?

5. How "socially minded" are Americans in general? What information does the text cite to support that claim?

6. What is an "ethical dilemma?"

Learning Goal 2
7. What are three questions to ask yourself when faced with an ethical dilemma?

   a._____

   b._____

   c._____

Learning Goal 3   **Ethics is More Than an Individual Concern**
8. Where does a sense of organizational ethics begin?

9. How do people learn standards and values?

10. What are the reasons to manage ethically?

   a. _____

   b. _____

   c. _____

   d. _____

   e. _____

   f. _____

   g. _____

   h. _____

Learning Goal 4   **Setting Corporate Ethical Standards**

11. What are two types of ethics codes?

   a. _____

   b. _____

12. What is the difference between the two types of ethical codes?

13. What are six steps to follow for a long-term improvement of America's business ethics?

   a. _____

   b. _____

   c. _____

   d. _____

   e. _____

   f. _____

14. What is the most important factor to the success of enforcing an ethics code? What makes that person effective?

Learning Goal 5   **Corporate Social Responsibility**

15. What is corporate social responsibility?

16. Describe the three dimensions of corporate social responsibility.

   a. _____

   b. _____

   c. _____

17. What are four groups that comprise the stakeholders to whom businesses are responsible?

    a. _____

    b. _____

    c. _____

    d. _____

18. What is responsibility of businesses to customers? What is the surest way of failing to please customers?

19. What could be the payoff for socially conscious behavior for a business?

20. How does socially responsible behavior affect shareholders and potential investors?

21. What responsibilities do businesses have toward employees?

22. What behaviors could result when employees feel they have been treated unfairly?

23. What are three areas of responsibility to society?

a. _____

b. _____

c. _____

24. What kinds of activities will companies undertake if they believe the business has a role in building a community beyond "giving back"?

25. What is the key for companies in determining the environmental quality activities they will undertake?

26. What is a major problem in conducting a social audit?

27.   What are some examples of socially responsible business activities?

   a. _____

   b. _____

   c. _____

   d. _____

   e. _____

28.   What is a "net social contribution?"

29.   What are four types of watch-dog" groups which monitor how well companies enforce ethical and social responsibility policies?

   a. _____

   b. _____

   c. _____

   d. _____

Learning Goal 6   **International Ethics and Social Responsibility**

30.   Are ethical problems unique to the United States? What is new about the ethical standards used to judge government leaders?

31.	What are many American businesses demanding from their international suppliers in terms of social responsibility?

32.	What are questions regarding American standards of ethics being imposed on international suppliers?

CRITICAL THINKING EXERCISES

Learning Goal 1

1.	". . . people learn their standards and values from observing what others do, not what they say." The following situation is typical of those in which businesspersons may find themselves at some time. Refer to the ethics check questions in your text and determine what you would do in the following situation.

Daryl, the general supervisor of a marketing department of a mid-sized Midwestern corporation, is an ambitious young man. He is writing a book that he hopes will make a name for himself in the business community. Because the word processing for the actual text is very time-consuming Daryl is using the secretary he shares with 2 other managers, as well as some of his market research interns to type the book while they're at work. Because they are often busy doing his book, people from the other departments are finding they can't get their work-related business done. The secretary and interns feel they have to do what Daryl says because he is their direct supervisor.

You are Daryl's peer in another department, and you also have some outside work you need to have typed. You're annoyed at Daryl's actions but would rather not inform your boss who is also Daryl's boss about what's going on because you want to maintain a friendly working relationship with Daryl. Besides, you never know how "the boss" is going to react. Sometimes you begin to think that if Daryl can get away with using company equipment, personnel, and time for his personal projects, why can't you?

2. You work for a major car manufacturer as a district manager, calling on car dealerships as a representative of the manufacturer. It is three days before the end of a sales incentive contest, and one of your dealers is close to winning a trip to Hawaii. If your dealer wins the contest for your area, you get a lot of recognition and a good chance for a promotion, which will enable you to stop traveling so much during the week. The dealer wants you to report as "sold" eight cars that he has not yet sold but will have deals on next week, several days after the end of the contest. Those eight cars will put him over the top and enable him to win the contest. Your just received a directive from the corporate headquarters on this practice of pre-reporting sales, indicating that the company would take strong action against anyone discovered taking such steps. Your boss and his superior have taken you aside and encouraged you to take whatever action is necessary to win the contest. You think you could get by with it and not get caught. An added problem is that the customer warranty starts the day the car is reported sold, so whoever purchases the car would lose several days of warranty service. What would you do?

Learning Goal 4

3. Ethics codes can be classified into two major categories:

Compliance-based   Integrity-based

Read the following examples of corporate behavior and determine which kind of ethical code the company may be using.

a. At Mary's Flowers, employees are encouraged to be active in community affairs and to be aware of their obligation to society. The company stresses honesty, provides seminars on making ethical choices and has a commitment to hire an ethnically diverse workforce.

   _____

b. At Pro-Tec, management has developed and distributed a code of ethics for employees. It defines what is acceptable behavior, and states that "behavior deemed to be unethical will not be tolerated." The policy does not define behavior that would be considered unethical, but does say that if there is a question a manager should be consulted._____

4.   "...corporate social responsibility is the concern businesses have for the welfare of society." Read the situation described below and answer the questions that follow: MUMC is a successful medium-sized firm that supplies parts for electric motors. Dan Furlong, the president, was being interviewed by the business features writer of the local newspaper. The reporter asked Dan his views on social responsibility and how MUMC reflected a socially responsive position. Dan replied that although he had never done a so-called social audit ("as the textbooks call it") he did figure that the firm was a good corporate citizen. He said, "We pay our employees a good salary, and the guys in the shop are getting paid above hourly for this area. We make a profit, and give everyone a bonus at the holidays. We take a lot or precautions in the shop, and no one has had an accident to speak of in several years. We've had a few cuts or bruises, but that's part of that kind of job. Whenever we have customer complaints I make sure someone handles them right away. We charge what I think is a fair price for our product, which I think is higher quality than most of my competitors. I pay my bills on time and don't cheat on my taxes. I guess you could say that we are a pretty socially responsible company."

   a.   In keeping with the idea of social audits and socially responsible business activities, is Mr. Furlong running the business in a socially responsible manner?

   b.   Who would you consider are Mr. Furlong's stakeholders?

   c.   What suggestions can you make to improve MUMC's position?

Learning Goal 6

5.   Who are four stakeholders to whom businesses are responsible? What does being responsible to each of these groups require?

6.   How does the increasingly global nature of U.S. business impact the issue of social responsibility and ethics?

PRACTICE TEST

Multiple Choice – Circle the best answer

1.   The difference between ethics and legality is that:

    a.   Legality reflects how people should treat each other, while ethics is more limiting.

    b.   Ethics refers to ways available to us to protect ourselves from theft, violence and fraud.

    c.   Legality is more limiting than ethics and applies to written laws

    d.   Ethics refers to a narrower range of behavior than legality.

2.   A survey revealed that

    a.   many Americans decide what's ethical behavior based upon the situation in which they find themselves.

    b.   most Americans give a considerable amount of time to their communities.

    c.   employees rarely violate safety standards or "goof off" at work. most Americans have an absolute sense of what is moral.

    d.   most Americans have an absolute sense of what is moral.

3.   Sometimes an obvious choice from an ethical standpoint has personal or professional drawbacks. An example might be when a supervisor asks you to do something unethical, and you face negative consequences if you refuse. When you are in such a situation you are faced with:

    a.   two lousy choices

    b.   an ethical dilemma

    c.   deciding the legality of your choice

    d.   a social responsibility issue

4.   Which of the following is not included as one of the questions we must ask when faced with an ethical dilemma?

    a.   Is it legal?

    b.   Is it balanced?

    c.   How will it make me feel about myself?

    d.   Is it o.k. if everyone else is doing it?

5. The most basic step in an ethics based management system is asking the question:

   a. Is it legal?
   b. Who will know?
   c. Is it balanced?
   d. Has it been done before?

6. Which of the following is not included in establishing an effective ethics program?

   a. Managers must be trained to consider ethical implications of all decisions.
   b. Outsiders such as suppliers, distributors, and customers must be told about the program.
   c. Employees must understand that they must set their own ethical standards and communicate that standard to management.
   d. An ethics office must be set up.

7. Organizational ethics begin:

   a. at the top levels of management.
   b. only with employees.
   c. with the unions.
   d. with mid level managers.

8. People learn standards from

   a. observing what others do.
   b. listening to what people say .
   c. making their own decisions.
   d. following corporate goals and standards.

9. Which of the following is not a part of an integrity-based ethics code?

   a. stresses shared accountability
   b. emphasizes penalizing of wrong-doers
   c. supports ethically sound behavior
   d. defines an organization's guiding principles

10. A _____ based ethics code stresses preventing unlawful behavior by increasing controls and penalizing wrongdoers.

   a. compliance
   b. socially
   c. integrity
   d. legally

11. Which of the following would not be considered as a dimension of the social performance of a corporation?

   a. corporate philanthropy
   b. corporate legal standards
   c. corporate policy
   d. corporate responsibility

12. Being energy conscious, ensuring that employees have a safe working environment and monitoring corporate hiring policies to prevent discrimination is part of:

   a. corporate philanthropy.
   b. corporate responsibility.
   c. corporate rules.
   d. corporate legal standards.

13. Who are the stakeholders to whom a business is responsible?

   a. employees
   b. customers
   c. investors
   d. all of the above

14. In terms of social responsibility, many people believe that:

   a. it does not make good financial sense for companies to be "up front" about potential product problems.
   b. it makes financial and moral sense to invest in companies whose goods and services benefit the community and the environment.
   c. businesses have no responsibility to create jobs.
   d. businesses have no responsibility to social causes.

15. Which of the following would not be included in a social audit?

    a. Support for higher education, the arts and nonprofit social agencies
    b. Community related activities such as fund raising.
    c. Employee-related activities
    d. Ability to compete with other major firms

16. Which of the following is not one of the watchdog groups which evaluate how well companies enforce their ethical and social responsibility policies?

    a. Socially conscious investors and consumers
    b. Environmentalists
    c. Union officials
    d. Employees

17. Government and business leaders are being held to:

    a. lower ethical standards than in the past
    b. ethical standards in the United States, but foreign leaders are not being subjected to ethical scrutiny.
    c. higher ethical standards than in the past
    d. ethical standards that cannot be met by most leaders

18. American businesses are

    a. demanding socially responsible behavior from international suppliers, particularly in the areas of environmental standards and human rights issues
    b. holding international suppliers to different standards than American companies must adhere to in the United States
    c. not concerned with the ethical or socially responsible behavior of their international suppliers
    d. are demanding that international suppliers adhere to higher standards than their American counterparts

19. All of the following contribute to the difficulty of conducting a social audit except:

    a. establishing procedures for measuring a firm's activities
    b. determining what to measure
    c. deciding whether or not positive actions should be added and then negative effects subtracted
    d. comparing charitable donations from one firm to another.

True False

1. _____ The first step in ethical behavior is following the law.

2. _____ According to the text, ethical behavior begins with observing religious leaders.

3. _____ There are usually easy solutions to ethical problems.

4. _____ With strong ethical leadership, employees feel that they are a part of a corporate mission that is socially beneficial.

5. _____ Integrity based ethics codes define an organization's guiding values, create an environment that supports ethical behavior and stresses shared accountability.

6. _____ The first step to improving America's business ethics is for top management to adopt and unconditionally support explicit codes of conduct.

7. _____ The best way to communicate to all employees that an ethics code is serious and cannot be broken is to back the program with timely action if rules are broken.

8. _____ Corporate social responsibility is the concern businesses have for their profitability.

9. _____ Corporate policy refers to the position a firm takes on social and political issues.

10. _____ In reality, it appears that people want to be socially responsible, but they can't define what being socially responsible means.

11. _____ One of the best ways to please customers is to hide product defects from them.

12. _____ Businesses have a responsibility to employees to create jobs.

13. _____ One of businesses' major responsibilities to the environment is not to pollute.

14. _____ One element of a business's social responsibility program includes such activities as local fund raising campaigns and donating executive time to nonprofit organizations.

15. _____ Ethical problems and issues of social responsibility are unique to the United States.

You Can Find It On the Net

Return to the Ben and Jerry's website at (www.benjerry.com). Go to the company's mission statement.

How does the company's mission statement demonstrate the company's sense of responsibility to its:

Customers?

Investors?

Society?

What are the three areas on which Ben and Jerry's focuses in terms of corporate philanthropy?

What is the purpose of the Ben and Jerry's Foundation?

ANSWERS

LEARNING THE LANGUAGE

1.	Compliance based ethics codes	6.	Corporate philanthropy
2.	Social audit	7.	Social responsibility
3	Corporate policy	8	Corporate responsibility
4.	Ethics	9.	Insider trading
5.	Integrity based ethics codes		

RETENTION CHECK

Managing Business Ethically and Responsibly

1. As the text states, many immoral and unethical acts are legal. Being legal means following the laws written to protect ourselves from fraud theft and violent acts. Ethical behavior requires more than simply following the law, and looks at behavior in terms of people's relations with one another.

2. Many Americans today have few moral absolutes, and seem to believe that what is right is whatever works best for the individual. Many decide whether it's all right to steal, lie or drink and drive based upon the situation, and think that each person works out for himself or herself the difference between right and wrong.

3. In some of the classic literature by Aristotle and others, basic moral values such as integrity, respect for human life, self-control, honesty, courage and self-sacrifice are taught to be right. Cheating, cowardice and cruelty are taught to be wrong.

4. A sense of personal ethics begins at home.

5. A recent study revealed that a majority of the American population reported never giving any time to their community. One third reported never giving to a charity. Business managers and workers cited low managerial ethics as a major cause of competitive woes for American businesses. Many students report cheating on exams. In other words, Americans are not especially "socially minded."

6. An ethical dilemma is a situation in which there may be no desirable alternative. You must choose between equally unsatisfactory alternatives when making a decision.

7.   Three questions to ask are:
   a.   Is it legal?
   b.   Is it balanced? (Am I acting fairly?)
   c.   How will it make me feel about myself?

Ethics is More Than an Individual Concern

8.   A sense of organizational ethics is instilled by the leadership and example of strong top managers.

9.   People learn their standards and values from observing what others do.

10.   The reasons to manage ethically are:
   a.   to maintain a good reputation
   b.   to keep existing customers
   c.   to attract new customers
   d.   to avoid lawsuits
   e.   to reduce turnover
   f.   to avoid government intervention
   g.   to please customers, employees and society
   h.   it's the right thing to do!

Setting Corporate Ethical Standards

11.   Two types of ethics codes are:
   a.   Compliance-based
   b.   Integrity-based

12.   *Compliance-based* ethics codes emphasize preventing unlawful behavior by increasing control and by penalizing wrongdoers. This type of ethics codes is based on avoiding legal punishment. *Integrity-based* ethics codes define the organization's guiding values, create an environment that supports ethically sound behavior and stress a shared accountability among employees.

13.   a.   Top management must adopt and support an explicit code of conduct.
   b.   Employees must understand that top management expects ethical behavior.
   c.   Managers and employees must be trained to consider ethical implications of business decisions.
   d.   Companies must set up an ethics office for employees to inquire about ethical matters.

e. Outsiders must be told about the ethics program.

f. The ethics code must be enforced.

14. An important factor to the success of enforcing an ethics code is to select an ethics officer. This person will set a positive tone, communicate effectively, and relate well with employees at every level.

Corporate Social Responsibility

15. Corporate social responsibility is the concern businesses have for the welfare of society.

16. a. Corporate philanthropy - charitable donations

b. Corporate responsibility - in all business decisions, such as hiring, pollution control and product decisions

c. Corporate policy - the position taken on social and political issues

17. Four stakeholder groups are:
a. Customers
b. Investors
c. Employees
d. Society

18. One responsibility of business is to satisfy customers by offering them goods and services that have a real value to the customer. One of the surest ways of failing to please customers is not being totally honest with them.

19. The payoff for socially conscious behavior could result in new business as customers switch from rival companies simply because they admire a company's social efforts. This can become a powerful competitive edge.

20. Ethical and socially responsible behavior is good for shareholder wealth and adds to the bottom line. In fact, many people believe it makes financial, as well as moral, sense to invest in companies that are planning ahead to create a better environment. By choosing to put their money into companies whose goods and services benefit the community and the environment, investors can improve their own financial health while improving society's health.

21. The responsibilities of businesses to employees include:

    a. a responsibility to create jobs

    b. an obligation to fairly reward hard work and talent

    c. a responsibility to maintain job security, or if layoffs are impossible to avoid, businesses have a responsibility to give employees warning.

22. When employees feel they have been treated unfairly many will strike back and get even in such ways as blaming mistakes on others, not accepting responsibility for decision making, manipulating budgets and expenses, making commitments they intend to ignore, hoarding resources, doing the minimum needed to get by, and making results look better than they are.

23. Three areas of responsibility to society are:

    a. to create wealth

    b. to promote social justice

    c. to make a contribution toward making the environment a better place

24. When companies believe they have a role in building a community, their contributions can include cleaning up the environment, providing computer lessons, supporting the elderly and children from low-income families, building community facilities, and other charitable acts.

25. The trick for companies is to find the right public good that will appeal to their target market.

26. A major problem of conducting a social audit is establishing procedures for measuring a firm's activities and their effects on society. The question is: What should be measured?

27. Examples of socially responsible business activities include:

    a. Community-related activities such as fund raising for local causes

    b. Programs designed to benefit employees such as flextime, improved benefits, equal opportunity programs, and others

    c. Taking a stand on such political issues as gun control, pollution control, and nuclear safety.

    d. Support of higher education, the arts, and non-profit agencies.

    e. Consumer education programs, honest advertising, prompt complaint handling and honest pricing policies.

28. A "net social contribution" is calculated by adding all positive social actions and then subtracting negative effects such as layoffs and pollution.

29. Four watchdog groups are:

   a. Socially conscious investors, who insist that companies extend the company's high standards to all their suppliers

   b. Environmentalists, who apply pressure by naming companies that don't abide by environmentalists' standards

   c. Union officials, who force companies to comply with standards to avoid negative publicity

   d. Customers who take their business elsewhere if a company demonstrates unethical and socially irresponsible practices.

International Ethics and Social Responsibility

30. No, ethical problems are not unique to the U.S. What is new about the moral and ethical standards by which government leaders are being judged is that the standards are much stricter now. In other words, government leaders are now being held to a higher standard than in the past.

31. Many American businesses are demanding socially responsible behavior from the international suppliers by making sure their suppliers do not violate U.S. human rights and environmental standards.

32. Examples of the questions surrounding the issues of international ethics are:

   Is it always ethical for American companies to demand compliance with our moral standards?

   Should the U.S. do business with countries where child labor is an accepted part of society?

   What about foreign companies doing business in the U.S.?

   What country's ethical standards should be followed?

   Should foreign companies expect American companies to comply with their ethical standards?

CRITICAL THINKING EXERCISES

1. This is a difficult problem, but ethically it's not really too hard to figure out what to do. The decision about going to the boss is an individual one, but using the secretary and the interns for personal business, particularly to the extent that Daryl is going, is probably unethical.

2. There is no "correct" answer to this question although there is probably a "most appropriate" mode of behavior. In this era of customer service and quality products in a competitive marketplace, these kinds of decisions are likely to come up frequently. Now is the time to think about how you would act. A helpful guide would be to ask yourself the questions the text proposes: a. Is it legal? b. Is it balanced? Would I want to be treated this way? Do I win at the expense of someone else? c. How will it make me feel about myself?

3. a. Integrity-based ethics code

   b. Compliance-based ethics code

4. a. Social responsibility includes providing a safe work environment, good benefits, a high quality product line, prompt complaint handling, and honest pricing policies. The result of a social audit would indicate that Mr. Furlong is running his business in a socially responsible manner, as far as he goes.

   b. Mr. Furlong's stakeholders would be his boss, the stockholders, employees, customers, competitors, suppliers and the general public.

   c. Although he would get fairly high scores from his employees in the area of social responsibility, Mr. Furlong doesn't appear to have any involvement with the community in which he operates. Of the three dimensions of corporate social performance, he addresses only the corporate responsibility issue; those of corporate philanthropy and corporate policy appear to be ignored. He could improve community relations (and even increase his customer base) by encouraging his employees to get involved in community related projects, donating time and/or money to local charities, developing a stand on local issues, improving employee-related benefits with job enrichment and employee development, and making opportunities for members of ethnic and minority groups.

5. Businesses are responsible to four general stakeholder groups: customers, investors, employees, and society in general. Being responsible to *customers* means offering them goods and services of real value. This includes being honest with customers about problems with products, and committing resources to solve the problems.

   Responsibility to *investors*, according to Milton Friedman, means making money for stockholders. This includes financial ethical behavior. Many believe that it makes financial, as well as moral sense to invest in companies that are planning ahead to create a better environment.

   Responsibility to *employees* means creating jobs, making sure that hard work and talent are fairly rewarded, and demonstrating respect for employees by treating them fairly.

   Responsibility to *society* means creating wealth, promoting social justice, giving back to communities, and helping to make the environment a better place.

6. In the past, officials of foreign firms have been judged by standards that were less harsh than those used in the United States. More recently, it seems that top leaders in some parts of the world are being judged by stricter standards. This could stem from the fact that American businesses have begun to demand more socially responsible behavior from international suppliers. As the business sector becomes increasingly globalized, international suppliers will be expected to conform to U.S. standards concerning ethics, human rights codes and the environment.

PRACTICE TEST

MULTIPLE CHOICE

1.	c	11.	b
2.	a	12.	b
3.	b	13.	d
4.	d	14.	b
5.	a	15.	d
6.	c	16.	c
7.	a	17.	c
8.	a	18.	a
9.	b	19.	d
10.	a		

TRUE/FALSE

1.	T	9.	T
2.	F	10.	T
3.	F	11.	F
4.	T	12.	T
5.	T	13.	T
6.	T	14.	T
7.	T	15.	F
8.	F		

LEARNING THE LANGUAGE

Listed here are important terms found in this chapter. Choose the correct term for each definition below and write it in the space provided.

Administrative agencies	Damages	Precedent
Bankruptcy	Deregulation	Product liability
Breach of contract	Express warranties	Statutory law
Business law	Implied warranties	Strict product liability
Common law	Involuntary bankruptcy	Taxes
Consideration	Judiciary	Tort
Consumerism	Negligence	Trademark
Contract	Negotiable instruments	Uniform Commercial Code (UCC)
Contract law	Patent	Voluntary bankruptcy
Copyright		

1.   Something of value, one of the requirements of a legal contract is _____.

2.   Government withdrawal of certain laws and regulations that seem to hinder competition is known as _____.

3.   Forms of commercial paper known as _____are transferable among businesses and individuals and represent a promise to pay a specified amount.

4.   Rules, statutes, codes, and regulations called _____are established to provide a legal framework within which business may be conducted and that is enforceable in court.

5.   The _____covers sales laws and other commercial law and has been adopted by every state in the United States.

6.   Specific representations by the seller regarding the goods sold are called _____.

7.   A(n) _____is a wrongful conduct that causes injury to another person's body, property, or reputation.

8.   The legal process of _____ is one by which a person or business, or government entity unable to meet financial obligations, is relieved of those obligations by having the court divide any assets among creditors, freeing the debtor to begin anew.

9.   A _____protects an individual's rights to materials such as books, articles, photos, and cartoons.

10.   State and federal constitutions, legislative enactment, treaties, and ordinances (written laws) are known as _____.

11.   _____are a guarantee legally imposed on the seller of goods.

12.   A social movement known as _____ seeks to increase the rights and strengths of buyers in relation to sellers.

13.   A _____means that one party fails to follow the terms of a contract.

14.   A legally enforceable agreement between two or more parties is a _____.

15.   A document called a _____gives inventors exclusive rights to their inventions for 20 years.

16.   The body of law known as _____ comes from judges' decisions; also known as "unwritten law."

17.   A set of laws called _____specify what constitutes a legally enforceable agreement.

18.   Legal procedures called _____are initiated by a debtor.

19.   The part of tort law known as_____ holds businesses liable for harm that results from the production, design, sale, or use of products they market.

20.   Institutions created by Congress with delegated power to pass rules and regulations within their mandated area of authority are _____.

21.   The branch of the government called the _____oversees the legal system through the court system.

22. A _____ is a legally protected name, symbol, or design that identifies the goods or services of one seller and distinguishes them from those of competitors.

23. Bankruptcy procedures filed by a debtor's creditors are _____.

24. The government raises money through _____.

25. The monetary settlement awarded to a person who is injured by a breach of contract is known as-_____.

26. Decisions judges have made in earlier cases, or _____, guide the handling of new cases.

27. Behavior is called _____ when it causes unintentional harm or injury.

28. Legal responsibility for harm or injury caused by a product regardless of fault is known as _____.

ASSSESSMENT CHECK

The Need for Laws

1. How is the court system in the United States organized?

2. What is the difference between statutory and common law?

3. What is "precedent" in law?

4.   What is meant by quasi-legislative, quasi-executive and quasi-judicial powers?

Tort Law

5.   What is the difference between an intentional tort and negligence?

6.   How is it that a company can be held liable for damages from a defective product even if the company didn't know of the defect? What type of liability is this?

7.   What has been the effect of strict product liability on businesses?

Laws Protecting Ideas

8.   What is required to file a patent?

9.   What are an inventor's chances of receiving a patent?

10. What is a business-method patent?

11. What is a submarine patent?

12. How long does a patent last compared to a copyright?

13. What are the rights of the holder of a copyright? What happens if a work is created by an employee in the course of a job?

14. How long does a trademark last?

Sales Law: The Uniform Commercial Code

15. What are two specific areas of sales law covered by the Uniform Commercial Code?

16. What is the difference between express and implied warranties?

17. What is the difference between a full and a limited warranty?

18. What are four conditions that must be met by a negotiable instrument?

   a. _____

   b. _____

   c. _____

   d. _____

Contract Law

19. List six conditions that must be met to make a contract legally binding.

   a. _____

   b. _____

   c. _____

   d. _____

   e. _____

   f. _____

20.   When does an offer become legally binding?

21.   What is the principle of mutual acceptance?

22.   How is competency determined?

23.   When does a contract become illegal and not enforceable?

24.   What kind of contracts must be put in writing?

25.   Identify three results of a breach of contract.

        a. _____

        b. _____

        c. _____

26. When can you sue for damages?

27. What are three elements that <u>must</u> be present in a contract?

   a. _____

   b. _____

   c. _____

Laws to Promote Fair and Competitive Practices

28. What are five important pieces of pro-competitive federal legislation?

   a. _____

   b. _____

   c. _____

   d. _____

   e. _____

29. What two things does the Sherman Act forbid?

30. What three "anticompetitive practices" does the Clayton Act prohibit?

31. What is

    a. exclusive dealing?

    b. a tying contract?

    c. an interlocking directorate?

32. What does the Federal Trade Commission Act prohibit?

33. What did the Wheeler-Lea Amendment do?

34. What does the Robinson-Patman Act prohibit?

Laws To Protect Consumers

35.   List four basic rights of consumers proposed by John F. Kennedy.

a. _____

b. _____

c. _____

d. _____

Tax Laws

36.   What are taxes used for?

37.   What is the purpose of a sin tax?

38.   What is a tax credit?

39.   What are three basic areas from which taxes are levied?

40. What will be a key tax issue in the early years of this century?

Bankruptcy Laws

41. Identify the two major amendments to the bankruptcy code. What do they say?

42. Why has the number of bankruptcies increased?

43. Distinguish between the two kinds of bankruptcy.

44. List the three most often used sections of the Bankruptcy Law.

   a. _____

   b. _____

   c. _____

45.   What are the provisions of a Chapter 7 bankruptcy?

46.   In what order are assets distributed among creditors in a Chapter 7 bankruptcy?

47.   What does Chapter 11 bankruptcy allow?

48.   What does a Chapter 13 bankruptcy permit? How does this compare to a Chapter 7? How does a Chapter 13 proceed?

Deregulation

49.   What prompted the move toward deregulation?

50. How has deregulation affected industries such as the airlines, telecommunications, and trucking in the United States? What appears to be the next target for deregulation?

CRITICAL THINKING EXERCISES

1. The types of laws governing business are varied. They include:

   Contract law   Bankruptcy law

   Sales law (Uniform Commercial Code)   Tort law

   Patent law

   Match the correct type of business law to each of the following situations.

   a. Firestone is being sued by the families of individuals injured by accidents caused by defects in the Firestone tires.

   b. A Sears Kenmore washer comes with a 12-month warranty.

   c. Planet Hollywood declares itself unable to meet its debt obligations, and filed for Chapter 11 reorganization.

   d. The formula for a woman's facial moisturizer is advertised as being protected from duplication until the year 2010.

   e. Bob and Dee Slone sue for damages when a building contractor fails to complete the building of their new home.

2. How has the definition of product liability changed and how has that affected manufacturers?

3.   A contract will be legally binding if it meets the following conditions:

An offer is made   Both parties are competent

There is voluntary acceptance of the offer   The contract is legal

Both parties give consideration   The contract is in proper form

Given the information below, determine whether each contract is legally binding (assuming other conditions are met) and why or why not.

a.   A resident of Tennessee signs an IOU to a casino in Las Vegas.

b.   You see a newspaper ad for a used car and after looking the car over, you agree to pay the owner $800 on the spot, with an oral contract.

c.   A 17-year-old puts a down payment on a new motorcycle.

d.   A student offers to buy your well-used Understanding Business textbook for $10, and you agree.

4. Three actions that can be taken when a breach of contract occurs are:

Specific performance

Payment of damages

Discharge of obligation

Indicate which action might be taken in each of the following breach of contract situations.

a. An actor fails to show up for a scheduled theater performance, without prior warning.

b. A typist working for an author finds that she doesn't have time to finish the manuscript, and quits.

c. An art dealer fails to deliver a piece of sculpture when promised for an art show.

5. Which of the following major pieces of federal legislation would be associated with each of the situations below?

Sherman Act	Robinson-Patman Act
Clayton Act	Federal Trade Commission Act
Wheeler-Lea Act	

a. Prohibits conspiracies in restraint of trade and attempts to monopolize.

b. A greeting card company unsuccessfully attempted to coerce its independently owned distributors into carrying only the products it manufactures.

c. The agency created by this act has conducted three times as many investigations and brought twice as many cases in the 1990s as it did in the 1980s. The legislation prohibits unfair methods of competition in commerce.

d. Prohibits several forms of price discrimination and applies to buyers as well as sellers.

e. This act gives the FTC even more power to prevent false and misleading advertising.

6. Using the list of consumer protection laws in Figure A-4 in your text identify the law associated with each of the following statements.

a. A coat label indicates that the coat is made from "various" wool products.

b. Baby cribs are required to have slats close enough together to prevent an infant's head from getting caught.

c. Fisher-Price was forced to recall a toy that had caused several injuries to young infants.

d. A car has a sticker price of $16,999.

e. The FDA has "food filth" allowances for such products as peanut butter and chocolate.

f. "Surgeon General's Warning: Cigarette Smoke Contains Carbon Monoxide."

g. Hot dogs are labeled as "all meat" or "all beef," but must contain only meat products.

h. The monthly statement on a Shell credit card indicates a periodic rate per month of 1.5% and an annual percentage rate of 18%.

i. The warranty for a Fisher-Price camera discloses that there is a three-year express warranty, and describes the conditions.

j. A bankruptcy filed several years ago will not show up on a credit report needed for a loan approval.

k. A tee-shirt label indicates that the shirt is 50% cotton and 50% polyester, and provides care instructions.

l. Marti Gilchrist purchases a fur coat that is part rabbit and part fox.

m. Apple Jacks cereal contains sugar, corn, wheat and oat flour, salt, dried apples, apple juice concentrate, and cinnamon. These ingredients must be accurately labeled.

n. A toy with a mechanical arm is packaged with a warning that it is intended only for children 8 years and older.

o. Indicates that flammable fabrics and wearing apparel can't be transported interstate.

p. Anheuser-Busch brought out Catalina Blond in 1998. The cans and bottles had to have a warning label in a visible place on the container. This is especially important as women are the target market.

q. When Judith Durham buys a box of Snack-Wells cookies, she knows exactly what ingredients are in the cookies and how much fat they contain.

7. When persons or businesses file for bankruptcy, they are relieved of their financial obligations by the courts.

Most bankruptcies are filed under one of the following three sections of the act:

Chapter 7   Chapter 11   Chapter 13

Which section of the bankruptcy law is being invoked in each of the following situations?

a. LTV Corporation filed for reorganization, and continued operations after declaring bankruptcy.

b. When the fast-food restaurant Jim S. owned failed, he filed for bankruptcy and sold all the assets to pay off his creditors, including his SBA loan.

c. Because of recent revisions in the bankruptcy law, a small dry cleaner was enabled to declare bankruptcy and set up a three year schedule for repayment to his creditors.

PRACTICE TEST

Multiple Choice – Circle the best answer

1. In Missouri, a law was passed to allow riverboat gambling. The law has been challenged in the legislature several times by different groups. This kind of law is an example of:

   a. common law.

   b. statutory law.

   c. tort law.

   d. liability law.

2. The fact that a company can be held liable for damages or injuries caused by a product with a defect even if the company did not know of the defect at the time of the sale is referred to as

   a. business law.

   b. negligence.

   c. strict product liability.

   d. implied warranty.

3. A _____ is a document that gives inventors exclusive rights to their inventions for 20 years.

   a. trademark

   b. copyright

   c. express warranty

   d. patent

4. The Uniform Commercial Code covers

   a. sales law.

   b. bankruptcy law.

   c. product negligence.

   d. contract law.

5. Which of the following is not a requirement for a contract to be legally enforceable?

   a. both parties must be competent
   b. an offer must be made
   c. there must be voluntary acceptance
   d. both parties must receive money

6. When John Pegg decided he wanted to buy a car, he went looking in the used car ads and found one in his price range of $400 from a private seller. John, who is 16, drove the car and decided he wanted to buy it. What needs to happen to make John's purchase an enforceable contract?

   a. the contract needs to be written up
   b. John needs to find a person older than he, like a parent, to make the contract for him
   c. the seller must wait for 3 days before he can sell it to John
   d. all of the above

7. The _____ prohibits exclusive dealing, tying contracts and interlocking directorates.

   a. Clayton Act
   b. Federal Trade Commission Act
   c. Robinson-Patman Act
   d. Interstate Commerce Act

8. Which of the following is not one of the rights of consumers outlined by President John F. Kennedy ?

   a. the right to safety
   b. the right to be informed
   c. the right to be heard
   d. the right to fair prices

9. Chapter _____ of the bankruptcy code allows businesses to continue operations while paying a limited portion of their debts.

   a. 7
   b. 11
   c. 13
   d. 22

10. How has deregulation affected business in the U.S.?

   a. some industries have become more competitive
   b. some companies must follow a stricter code of ethics
   c. many businesses are raising prices because the government is not controlling them anymore
   d. companies are becoming less ethical

True-False

1. _____ Government has reduced its control and enforcement procedures over the years.

2. _____ Common law is often referred to as unwritten law.

3. _____ A submarine patent is one that has not yet been granted.

4. _____ An express warranty is a specific representation by the seller that is relied upon by the buyer regarding the goods.

5. _____ Any contract for the sale of real property must be written.

6. _____ If a breach of contract occurs, the individual who breached the contract will always be required to live up to the contract eventually.

7. _____ The Sherman Act prohibits price discrimination.

8. _____ In a bankruptcy case, the first thing to be paid will be federal and state taxes.

ANSWERS

1. Consideration	11. Implied warranties	21. Judiciary
2. Deregulation	12. Consumerism	22. Trademark
3. Negotiable instruments	13. Breach of contract	23. Involuntary bankruptcy
4. Business law	14. Contract	24. Taxes
5. Uniform Commercial Code	15. Patent	25. Damages
6. Express warranties	16. Common law	26. Precedent
7. Tort	17. Contract law	27. Negligence
8. Bankruptcy	18. Voluntary bankruptcy	28. Strict product liability
9. Copyright	19. Product liability	
10. Statutory law	20. Administrative agencies	

RETENTION CHECK

The Need for Laws

1. The court system in the United States is organized at the federal, state, and local levels. At the federal and state levels, trial courts hear cases involving criminal and civil law. Both federal and state systems have appellate courts. These courts hear appeals of decisions made at the trial-court level brought by the losing party in the case.

2. Statutory law is written law, and includes state and federal constitutions, legislative enactment and so forth. Common law is the body of law that comes from decisions handed down by judges. It is often referred to as unwritten law.

3. Precedent is what judges have decided in previous cases. Precedent guides judges in the handling of new cases.

4. Some administrative agencies hold quasi-legislative, quasi-executive and quasi-judicial powers. This means an agency is allowed to pass rules and regulations within its area of authority, conduct investigations in cases of suspected rules violations, and hold hearings when it feels the rules and regulations have been violated.

Tort Law

5. An intentional tort is a willful act that results in injury. Negligence deals with *unintentional* behavior that causes harm or injury.

6. The rule of "strict liability" refers to product liability. It is the idea that a company can be liable for damages caused by placing a product on the market with a defect even if the company did not know of the defect at the time of the sale.

7.   The rule of strict product liability has caused serious problems for businesses. Several industries have lawsuits pending in the area of product liability. The gun industry, for example, has been accused of damages under the rules of strict product liability, and lawsuits have been filed on behalf of individuals affected by gun violence. Businesses and insurance companies have called for legal relief from huge losses that are often awarded in strict product liability suits.

Laws Protecting Ideas

8.   Filing a patent with the U.S. Patent office requires a search to make sure the patent is unique, followed by the filing of forms. The advice of a lawyer is usually recommended.

9.   Chances of receiving a patent are about 60 percent.

10.   Business-method patents involve different business applications using the Internet.

11.   Some inventors have been accused of intentionally delaying or dragging out a patent application, then waiting for others to develop the technology. The inventor surfaces to claim the patent, and demands large fees after others have developed the technology. This is a submarine patent.

12.   A patent lasts for 20 years. A copyright protects an individual's right to materials for the lifetime of the author or artist plus 50 years.

13.   The holder of an exclusive copyright may charge a fee to anyone who wishes to use the copyrighted material. If a work is created by an employee in the normal course of a job, the copyright belongs to the employer and lasts 95 years from publication or 120 years from creation, whichever comes first.

14.   A trademark belongs to the owner forever, so long as it is properly registered and renewed every 20 years.

Sales Law: The Uniform Commercial Code

15.   Article 2, which contains laws regarding warranties, and Article 3, which covers negotiable instruments.

16.   An express warranty is often enclosed with the product when purchased. It spells out the seller's warranty agreement. An implied warranty is legally imposed on the seller. It is implied that the product will conform to the customary standards of the trade or industry in which it competes.

17. A full warranty requires a seller to replace or repair a product at no charge if the product is defective. Limited warranties typically limit the defects or mechanical problems that are covered.

18. Negotiable instruments must be:
    a. Signed by the maker
    b. Made payable on demand at a certain time
    c. Made payable to the bearer or to order
    d. Contain an unconditional promise to pay a specific amount of money

Contract Law

19. To make a contract legally binding, these conditions must be met:
    a. An offer is made
    b. There is voluntary acceptance
    c. Both parties give consideration
    d. Both parties are competent
    e. The contract is legal
    f. The contract is in proper form

20. An offer is legally binding only when all conditions of a contract have been met.

21. The principle of mutual acceptance means that both parties to a contract must agree on the terms of the contract.

22. In order to be judged competent to enter into a contract, a person must not be under the influence of drugs or alcohol, be of sound mind and be of legal age.

23. A contract covering an illegal act is illegal.

24. An agreement for the sale of goods worth $500 or more must be in writing. Contracts that cannot be fulfilled within one year and contracts regarding real property must also be in writing.

25. A breach of contract may result in:
    a. Specific performance, i.e. the person may be required to live up to the agreement
    b. Payment of damages
    c. Discharge of obligation

26. An individual can sue for damages from someone when that person has not lived up to a contract. The amount for which one can sue is usually the amount they would lose from nonperformance.

27. A contract does not have to be complicated, but should have the following three elements
    a. It should be in writing
    b. mutual consideration is specified
    c. there is a clear offer and agreement

Laws to Promote Fair and Competitive Practices

28. Pro-competitive legislation includes:
    a. Sherman Act (1890)
    b. Clayton Act (1914)
    c. Federal Trade Commission Act (1914)
    d. Robinson-Patman Act (1936)
    e. Wheeler-Lea Act

29. The Sherman Act forbids (1) contracts, combinations or conspiracies in restraint of trade, and (2) actual monopolies or attempts to monopolize any part of trade or commerce.

30. The Clayton Act prohibits exclusive dealing, tying contracts, interlocking directorates and buying large amounts of stock in competing corporations.

31. a. Exclusive dealing is selling goods with the condition that the buyer will not buy goods from a competitor.
    b. A tying contract requires a buyer to purchase unwanted items in order to purchase the desired items.
    c. An interlocking directorate occurs when a board of directors includes members of the board of competing corporations.

32. The Federal Trade Commission Act prohibits unfair methods of competition in commerce.

33. The Wheeler-Lea Amendment gave the FTC additional jurisdiction over false or misleading advertising.

34. The Robinson-Patman Act prohibits price discrimination. It applies to both sellers and buyers who knowingly induce or receive an unlawful discrimination in price. It also stipulates that certain types of price cutting are criminal offenses.

Laws to protect consumers

35. a. The right to safety
    b. The right to be informed
    c. The right to choose
    d. The right to be heard

Tax Laws

36. Taxes have traditionally been used as a source of funding for government operations and programs. They have also been used as a method of encouraging or discouraging taxpayers from doing something.

37. If the government wants to reduce the use of certain types of products, it will pass a "sin tax." This is what has happened in the cigarette and alcohol industry.

38. A tax credit is an amount that can be deducted from a tax bill.

39. Three basic types of taxes are income taxes, property taxes, and sales taxes.

40. A key tax issue in the early part of the 21st century will revolve around Internet taxation, especially Internet transactions.

Bankruptcy Laws

41. Two major amendments to the bankruptcy code include the Bankruptcy Amendments and Federal Judgeships Act of 1984 and the Bankruptcy Reform Act of 1994. The 1984 legislation allows a person who is bankrupt to keep part of the ownership in a house, $1,200 in a car, and some other personal property. The Bankruptcy Reform Act of 1994 amends more than 45 sections of the bankruptcy code and creates reforms that speed up and simplify the process.

42. The number of bankruptcies increased in the 1990s primarily due to a lessening of the stigma of bankruptcy, the changing economy, an increase in understanding of bankruptcy law and the protection if offers, increased advertising by attorneys, and the ease with which consumers can get credit.

43. In voluntary bankruptcy cases, the debtor applies for bankruptcy, whereas in involuntary bankruptcy cases the creditors start legal procedures against the debtors.

44. The three most often used actions of bankruptcy law are:

    a. Chapter 7

    b. Chapter 11

    c. Chapter 13

45. Chapter 7 calls for straight bankruptcy, which requires the sale of nonexempt assets. Under federal exemption statures, a debtor may be able to retain up to $7,500 of equity in a home, up to $1,200 of equity in an automobile, up to $4,000 in household furnishings, and up to $500 in jewelry.

46. First, creditors with secured claims receive the collateral for their claims, or repossess the claimed asset. Then, unsecured claims are paid in this order

    a. Costs involved in the bankruptcy case

    b. Any business costs incurred after bankruptcy was filed

    c. Wages, salaries, or commissions

    d. Employee benefit plan contributions

    e. Refunds to consumers who paid for undelivered products

    f. Federal and state taxes

47. Chapter 11 allows a company to reorganize operations while paying only a limited portion of its debts. Under certain conditions, the company can sell assets, borrow money, and change officers to strengthen its market position. A company will continue to operate but has court protection against creditor's lawsuits while it tries to work out a plan for paying off its debts.

48. Chapter 13 bankruptcy permits individuals and small business owners to pay back creditors over a period of three to five years. Chapter 13 proceedings are less complicated and less expensive than Chapter 7 proceedings. The debtor files a proposed plan for paying off debts to the court. If the plan is approved, the debtor pays a court appointed trustee in monthly installments.

Deregulation

49. The move toward deregulation stemmed from a concern that there were too many laws and regulations governing business and that these laws and regulations were costing the public money.

50. The most publicized examples of deregulation have been in the airlines and the telecommunications industry. When restrictions were lifted in the airline industry, the airlines began competing for different routes and charging lower prices. New airlines were created to take advantage of new opportunities. In the telecommunications industry, deregulation gave consumers many more options in the telephone service market, and deregulation made the trucking industry more competitive as well.

The next targets of deregulation appear to be the electric power industry and other utilities. There is a call for new regulation in the banking and investment industries that would actually make them more competitive.

CRITICAL THINKING EXERCISES

1. a. Tort law
   b. Sales law (UCC)
   c. Bankruptcy law
   d. Patent law
   e. Contract law

2. At one time, the legal standard for measuring product liability was if a producer knowingly placed a hazardous product on the market. Today, many states have extended product liability to the level of strict liability. Legally this means without regard to fault. Therefore, a company could be liable for damages caused by placing a product on the market with a defect even if the company did not know of the defect at the time of the sale. This has subjected manufacturers to expensive lawsuits.

3. a Yes, this is a binding contract. Although the signer is a resident of Tennessee, he is in Nevada, where gambling is legal.
   b. No, this is not binding. Oral contracts are binding only when the value of the goods is less than $500. It's usually best to get a written contract for the protection of both parties.
   c. No, this is not a binding contract because a minor isn't legally competent to make a contract.
   d. Yes, this is a binding contract. The offer was voluntary, so was the acceptance and both parties received consideration.

4. a. Payment of damages
   b. Discharge of obligation
   c. Specific performance

5. a. Sherman Act (1890)
   b. Clayton Act (1914)
   c. Federal Trade Commission Act (1914)
   d. Robinson-Patman Act (1936)
   e. Wheeler-Lea Act

6. a. Wool Products Labeling Act
    b. Consumer Product Safety Act
    c. Child Protection Act
    d. Automobile Information Disclosure Act
    e. Food, Drug and Cosmetic Act
    f. Cigarette Labeling Act
    g. Pure Food and Drug Act
    h. Truth-in-Lending Act
    i. Magnuson-Moss Warranty-Federal Trade Commission Improvement Act
    j. Fair Credit Reporting Act
    k. Textile Fiber Products Identification Act
    l. Fur Products Labeling Act
    m. Fair Packaging and Labeling Act
    n. Child Protection and Toy Safety Act
    o. Flammable Fabrics Act (1953)
    p. Alcohol Labeling Legislation
    q. Nutrition Labeling and Education Act

7. a. Chapter 11
    b. Chapter 7
    c. Chapter 13

PRACTICE TEST

MULTIPLE CHOICE

1.	b	6.	b
2.	c	7.	a
3.	d	8.	d
4.	a	9.	b
5.	d	10.	a

TRUE/FALSE

1.	F	5.	T
2.	T	6.	F
3.	F	7.	F
4.	T	8.	F

CHAPTER 5
FORMS OF BUSINESS OWNERSHIP

LEARNING GOALS

After you have read and studied this chapter, you should be able to:

1. Compare the advantages and disadvantages of sole proprietorships

2. Describe the differences between general and limited partnerships and compare the advantages and disadvantages of partnerships.

3. Compare the advantages and disadvantages of corporations and summarize the differences between C corporations, S corporations and limited liability companies.

4. Define and give examples of three types of corporate mergers and explain the role of leveraged buyouts and taking a firm private.

5. Outline the advantages and disadvantages of franchises and discuss the opportunities for diversity in franchising and the challenges of international franchising.

6. Explain the role of cooperatives.

LEARNING THE LANGUAGE

Listed below are important terms found in this chapter. Choose the correct term for each definition and write it in the space provided.

Acquisition	General partner	Limited partnership
Conglomerate merger	General partnership	Master limited partnership
Conventional corporation	Horizontal merger	Merger
Cooperative	Leveraged buyout	Partnership
Corporation	Limited liability	S corporation
Franchise	Limited liability company (LLC)	Sole Proprietorship
Franchise agreement	Limited liability partnership (LLP)	Unlimited liability
Franchisee	Limited partner	Vertical merger
Franchisor		

1. The business proposition known as a _____ joins two firms in the same industry.

2. A company formed when two or more people legally agree to become co-owners of a business is called a _____.

3. A _____ is an arrangement whereby someone with a good idea for a business sells the rights to use the business name and to sell a product or service to others in a given territory.

4. In a(n) _____ one company buys the property and obligations of another company.

5. This means that limited partners are not responsible for the debts of a business beyond the amount they invest; so, limited partners and shareholders have _____

6   This unique government creation called a(n) _____ looks like a corporation but is taxed like sole proprietorships and partnerships.

7. A _____ is a business that develops a product concept and sells others the rights to make and sell the products.

8. A business proposition that joins firms in completely unrelated industries is called a(n) _____.

9. An agreement such as a(n) _____ is a partnership with one or more general partners and one or more limited partners.

10. A (n) _____ looks much like a corporation in that it acts like a corporation and is traded on the stock exchange like a corporation, but is taxed like a partnership and thus avoids the corporate income tax.

11. A(n) _____ is a legal entity with authority to act and has liability separate from its owners.

12. The result of two firms forming one company is a _____.

13. A _____ is a person who buys a franchise.

14. An individual is called a _____ when he has invested money in a business but does not have any management responsibility or liability for losses beyond the investment.

15. A new business entity which is similar to an S corporation, but without the special eligibility requirements is called a (n) _____.

16. An owner who has unlimited liability is called a _____ and is active in managing the firm.

17. A _____ is a business that is owned and controlled by the people who use it – producers, consumers or workers with similar needs who pool their resources for mutual gain.

18. A partnership is called a(n) _____ when all owners share in operating the business and in assuming liability for the business's debts.

19. An attempt by employees, management or a group of investors to purchase an organization primarily through borrowing is called a(n) _____.

20. A _____ is the right to use a business name and to sell a product or service in a given territory.

21. In the business venture known as a(n) _____, two companies join which are involved in different stages of related businesses.

22. A business that is owned, and usually managed, by one person is a _____.

23. The concept of _____ means that business owners are responsible for all of the debts of a business.

24. A _____ is one that limits partners' risk of losing their personal assets to only their own acts and omissions and to the acts and omissions of people under their supervision.

25. A state-chartered legal entity with authority to act and have liability separate from its owners is a _____.

ASSESSMENT CHECK

Learning Goal 1 **Basic Forms of Business Ownership**

1. What are three general forms of business ownership?

    a. _____

    b. _____

    c. _____

2. Which is the most common form of business ownership?

3. Which form of ownership is separate from its owners?

4. What are the advantages of a sole proprietorship?

    a. _____

    b. _____

    c. _____

    d. _____

    e. _____

    f. _____

5.   How are profits taxed in a sole proprietorship?

6.   What are the disadvantages of sole proprietorships

       a. _____

       b. _____

       c. _____

       d. _____

       e. _____

       f. _____

       g. _____

7.   How are the debts of a sole proprietorship handled?

Learning Goal 2   **Partnerships**

8.   What are the different forms?

       a. _____

       b. _____

       c. _____

       d. _____

9. What is the difference between a limited partner and a general partner? What is the minimum number of general partners required?

10. The Uniform Partnership Act (UPA) identifies what three key elements of a general partnership?

   a. _____

   b. _____

   c. _____

11. What are the advantages of a partnership?

   a. _____

   b. _____

   c. _____

12. What are the disadvantages of a partnership?

   a. _____

   b. _____

   c. _____

   d. _____

13. What is the benefit of a limited liability partnership?

14. What should be done in order to avoid problems when partners disagree?

Learning Goal 3   **Corporations**

15. Explain the following statement. "A corporation is separate from its owners." What is another name for the owners of a corporation?

16. What are the advantages of conventional "C" corporations?

   a. _____

   b. _____

   c. _____

   d. _____

   e. _____

   f. _____

   g. _____

17.   What is one way a corporation can raise money?

18.   Is there a benefit to the size of a large corporation? Does a company have to be large to be a corporation?

19.   What are the disadvantages of conventional "C" corporations?

a. _____

b. _____

c. _____

d. _____

e. _____

f. _____

g. _____

20.   What is meant by two tax returns and "double taxation?"

21. Illustrate the structure of a corporation

22. What are the advantages for an individual when they incorporate?

23. What criteria must be met in order to qualify as an "S" corporation?

    a. _____

    b. _____

    c. _____

    d. _____

24. Why would a company choose C corporation status over an S status?

25. What are the types of corporations, other than an "S"?

a. _____   f. _____

b. _____   g. _____

c. _____   h. _____

d. _____   i. _____

e. _____

26. What type of business ownership has been called the "business entity of the future"?

27. What are the advantages of limited liability companies?

a. _____

b. _____

c. _____

Learning Goal 4   **Corporate Expansion : Mergers and Acquisitions**

28. What is the difference between a merger and an acquisition?

29.   Identify the three types of corporate mergers

a. _____

b. _____

c. _____

30.   What does it mean to "take a firm private"?

31.   What happens in a leveraged buyout?

Learning Goal 5   **Special Forms of Business Ownership**

32.   What is the difference between a franchisor and a franchisee?

33.   What are four statistics that indicate the importance of franchising to the U.S. economy?

a. _____

b. _____

c. _____

d. _____

34.   List the advantages of owning a franchise

   a. _____

   b. _____

   c. _____

   d. _____

   e. _____

35.   Why does a franchisee have a greater chance of succeeding in business?

36.   How do some franchisors offer franchising assistance to franchisees?

37.   List the disadvantages of owning a franchise.

   a. _____

   b. _____

   c. _____

   d. _____

   e. _____

   f. _____

38. What is a royalty?

39. What is a recent change in franchising regarding management regulation of franchisees?

40. What is meant by the coattail effect?

41. How has the involvement of women and minorities in franchising changed?

42. What are some advantages of home franchising?

   a._____

   b._____

   c._____

   d._____

43. How has e-commerce affected franchising?

44.   What are some concerns regarding franchisee-sponsored websites?

45.   How has the Internet affected the relationship between franchisors and franchisees?

46.   What are some of the considerations of franchising in international markets?

Learning Goal 6   **Cooperatives**

47.   What are two kinds of cooperatives?

   a._____

   _____

   b._____

   _____

48.   What kind of involvement do members of cooperatives have?

CRITICAL THINKING EXERCISES

Learning Goal 1

1. Jeff Baker has his own business as the owner of a tanning salon in his hometown. He is talking with a good friend, Bill Jacobs, who is interested in going into business for himself. "After I had purchased the necessary equipment, all I had to do was fill out a form for the county and open my doors, easy as that" Jeff mentioned, over lunch one day. "The only problem is, now I owe a lot of money for this tanning equipment. I'll be in rough shape if we go under!" "You know", said Bill "I have company paid life and health insurance where I work now. I'm a little concerned about losing that." "Yeah, that's a concern," replied Jeff," but I can try things with this business that my old bosses would never have let me try. I can be really creative. I think we earned enough this year to open a second facility after we pay off the loans we have now. We're at our limit at the bank. But at least I can do what I want to with the profit, and not share it with anyone else." "What about the amount of time you spend at work? Any problem?" asked Bill. "Well... I usually get to the salon at 8 a.m. and don't leave until 10 or 11 p.m., if that's what you're asking" answered Jeff, "but you know, I don't mind, because this business is all mine, and it has been worth the hard work. Right now, though, I am having some problems finding a good person to help me out." "Listen", he continued, "I have to go. I've got an appointment with the accountant in 20 minutes. He saved me a lot of money last year, and I didn't owe anything. Great guy! My lawyer needs some information from him too. I 'm making a will to make sure the kids will get the business if anything happens to me. Hey Bill, good luck!"

    What advantages and disadvantages did Jeff mention about owning a sole proprietorship?

Learning Goal 2

2. Three basic types of partnerships are:

    general partnership   limited partnership   master limited partnership

    Using the information below, distinguish between each type of partnership

    a. Burger King is a type of partnership that is traded on a stock exchange _____

    b. When Joe Allen invested in his friend Jose's business, he didn't want to have any management responsibilities._____

c. Dave Pardo and his partner, Bettina Gregory, both stand to lose a lot of money if their business goes under, as they are both responsible for the debt the business has undertaken.
_____

d. Even though any of us could buy stock in Perkins Family Restaurant, the company is taxed like a partnership. _____

e. When Terry Esser invested in Dave and Bettina's company, she figured it was a minimal risk, because she (Terry) would only stand to lose what she invested if the company didn't make it. _____

f. Randy Ford and Marty Dietrich have agreed to spend equal time managing the business they have just started. _____

3. After thinking about it for a few days, Bill Jacobs decided he would ask Jeff Baker if he could become a partner in Jeff's business. "After all" Bill said to himself, "I've got some money, and Jeff does want to expand, and he's looking for someone to work for him. I'll just work with him, give him some free time. I'm a little nervous about taking on the debt, but the statistics say we're more likely to stay in business than a sole proprietorship is, so it shouldn't be too bad."

Bill went to Jeff and began to discuss becoming a partner in the business.

"Whoa…wait a minute" interrupted Jeff when he heard Bill's offer. "I have to think about this. I like making my own decisions, and I like keeping my profits! How do I know you'll work as hard as I do? Who will work when? What happens when I want to borrow money for some new equipment and you don't want to?" Bill had to admit these were things he hadn't thought of. "Well...if it doesn't work out, we can just split up, can't we?" said Bill. "It's just not that simple, Bill..."

What advantages and disadvantages of partnerships did Bill and Jeff discuss?

Learning Goal 3

4. Bill and Jeff eventually did form a partnership. Business has been very good. They have expanded their facility, rented some space to several hair stylists and added several product lines that compliment the tanning and hair salon area. They now have a total of three facilities and are wondering if they should incorporate their business, as they would like to expand even further,

perhaps franchising their idea someday. What can you tell them about the advantages and disadvantages of incorporation, and what would you suggest for them?

5. For a small business owner, what benefit does a corporation have over partnerships and sole proprietorships?

6. Types of Corporations

There are several terms used to describe different types of corporations

alien   quasi-public

domestic   professional

foreign   nonprofit

closed (private)   multinational

open (public)

Match the type of corporation to each of the following, using each term only once:

a. The stock of Maritz, Inc. is held by a small number of people and is not listed on a stock exchange. _____

b. Ralston-Purina has sold more than 200 million shares of stock._____

c. General Motors is incorporated in Delaware, but has its headquarters in Detroit, Michigan._____

d. You can have a Big Mac and fries in Three Rivers, Michigan, Paris, France, Sydney, Australia and Moscow._____

e. Toyota is incorporated in Japan, but has corporate offices located in the United States._____

f. Mainini Home Improvement is incorporated in Missouri, has its headquarters in Ellisville, Missouri and only does business in Missouri._____

g. The Red Cross sponsors a classic car show and auction every year to raise funds for disaster relief._____

h. Ameren U.E., an electrical service provider, must apply to a government agency when it wants to raise rates to its customers. _____

i. The City of Ann Arbor, Michigan sponsors a carnival each year and the city's recreation department runs a pool and baseball leagues for its residents. _____

7. Two forms of business ownership have received some attention recently, "S" corporations and limited liability companies. Which one is being described in the following?

a. This offers flexible ownership rules, and personal asset protection. _____

b. This type can tell the IRS how it wants to be taxed. _____

c. Looks like a corporation but is taxed like sole proprietorships and partnerships._____

d. New legislation will allow this type to own subsidiaries._____

e. This business may have no more than 75 shareholders. _____

f. This is the newest of the two types of ownership. _____

Learning Goal 4

8.	There are several types of corporate mergers and buyouts. Match the situation being described to the correct term. Use each term only once.

Acquisition　　　　　　　　Conglomerate merger

Vertical merger　　　　　　　Leveraged buyout

Horizontal merger　　　　　　Taking a firm private

a.	Tommy Hilfilger bought its Canadian distributor and its American licensee, Pepe Jeans USA, in order to own manufacturing and distribution rights._____

b.	When KK.R. bought out RJR Nabisco, they borrowed close to $25 billion. _____

c.	In the late 1990s, Boeing bought McDonnell Douglas. Subsequently, the McDonnell–Douglas Corporation ceased to exist. _____

d.	Two drug companies, Glaxo Wellcome PLC and SmithKline Beecham PLC began talks to merge their companies. _____

e.	Berkshire-Hathaway, which owns Samsonite Luggage and the Sara Lee corporation, also bought Helzberg Diamonds, a jewelry store chain in the Midwest._____

f.	When the management of Levi Strauss wanted to avoid a hostile takeover attempt, they formed a group to buy all the outstanding stock._____

Learning Goal 5

9.	KFC is a nationwide fast-food franchise. All prospective KFC franchise owners must go through an evaluation process, during which they must submit an application and site proposal for approval and submit to a personal interview in Louisville, Kentucky, KFC's headquarters. Upon approval, KFC offers the franchisee a training program covering management functions such as accounting, sales, advertising and purchasing. KFC pays a portion of this training program. KFC makes available to the franchisee an advertising and promotion kit, opening assistance, equipment layout plans and a choice of interior decor from a list they provide. In addition to standard menu items, a franchisee may offer other items upon approval from KFC management. KFC outlines the estimated cash requirements for opening for such things as equipment, insurance payments, utility down payments, as well as for the facility itself to give franchisees an idea of their cash needs. The franchise fee and the costs of the building and land are the responsibility of the franchisee. There is a royalty rate based on a percentage of gross sales, which is paid on a regular basis to KFC for continuing franchises.

KFC advertises on nationwide television on behalf of its franchisees, so local owners do not have to develop their own television advertising. The local owners do pay a percentage of their gross sales to KFC as a national advertising fee, and each franchisee is required to spend an additional percentage for local advertising.

Based on this description, identify some of the benefits and drawbacks of owning a franchise.

10.   How has technology helped franchisors and franchisees?

Learning Goal 1, 2, 3, 4

11.   There are many choices for business ownership. What option would you choose for these types of businesses? Why?

    a.   Landscape/lawn care service

    b.   Small manufacturer of a component part for automobiles

    c.   Fast food restaurant

    d.   Construction/Remodeling firm

PRACTICE TEST

Multiple Choice – Circle the best answer

1. Which of the following is not considered to be an advantage of sole proprietorships?

    a. It's easy to start and end
    b. You don't have to share the profits with anyone
    c. You get to be your own boss
    d. You have limited liability for debts and damages

2. One of the problems with a _____ is that there is no one to share the burden of management with.

    a. sole proprietorship
    b. limited partnership
    c. S corporation
    d. limited liability company

3. If you are interested in starting your own business, you want to minimize the hassle, and you don't want to have anyone tell you what to do, you should organize your business as a:

    a. S corporation.
    b. limited partnership.
    c. sole proprietorship.
    d. closed corporation.

4. At Sound Off!, a store that buys and sells used CD's, there is only one owner, Sonia.
    She spends all her time running the business, and makes all the decisions. Sonia's mother and brother put up money for her to buy the store, but they work full time at other jobs and have no management say in the running of Sound Off! This is an example of a:

    a. general partnership, with limited partners.
    b. master limited partnership.
    c. S corporation.
    d. a traditional corporation.

5. When going into a partnership, you should always:

   a. put all terms of the partnership into writing in a partnership agreement.
   b. make sure that you have limited liability while you are in charge.
   c. make sure all the profits are reinvested into the company.
   d. divide the profits equally.

6. Generally, one of the benefits a general partnership has over a sole proprietorship is:

   a. limited liability.
   b. more financial resources.
   c. easy to start.
   d. a board of directors to help with decisions.

7. The owners of a corporation are called:

   a. general partners.
   b. stockholders.
   c. limited partners.
   d. proprietors.

8. A _____ is one whose stock is not available to the general public through a stock exchange.

   a. alien corporation
   b. domestic corporation
   c. public corporation
   d. closed corporation

9. All of the following are advantages of a corporation except:

   a. unlimited liability.
   b. the amount of money for investment.
   c. the ease of changing ownership.
   d. ability to raise money from investors without getting them involved in management.

10. A form of ownership which can have only 75 shareholders, who must be permanent residents of the United States, is called a:

   a. limited liability company.
   b. closed corporation.
   c. domestic corporation.
   d. S corporation.

11. Which of the following is not considered an advantage of a limited liability company?

   a. limited number of shareholders
   b. personal asset protection
   c. choice of how to be taxed
   d. flexible ownership rules

12. When Jean-Marie Delacourt was born, her American grandmother bought her 10 shares of Disney stock. As Jean-Marie grows, so will her investment. However, if Disney should happen to go out of business:

   a. Jean-Marie will be responsible for some of the debt of Disney.
   b. Jean-Marie will have to go to court to show she has no involvement in the firm.
   c. Jean-Marie will only lose the value of her shares.
   d. Jean-Marie will have to borrow money from her grandmother to pay for the value of her shares.

13. Which of the following is not a form of corporate mergers?

   a. vertical merger
   b. horizontal merger
   c. conglomerate merger
   d. cooperative merger

14. When the May Company, which owns several department store chains, bought Lord & Taylor, another department store chain, so May could expand its product offerings, it was a:

   a. vertical merger.
   b. horizontal merger.
   c. conglomerate merger.
   d. cooperative merger.

15. The main reason for a conglomerate merger is that:

   a. the investors want more for their money.
   b. it ensures a constant supply of materials needed by other companies.
   c. it allows for a firm to offer a variety of related products.
   d. the business can diversify its business operations and investments.

16. When a major national bakery bought a smaller regional bakery in the east, it took over all their assets and their debt. This is an example of a(n):

   a. acquisition.
   b. merger.
   c. nationalization.
   d. appropriation.

17. In order to avoid a hostile takeover by a Kollmorgaen, managers at Pacific Scientific considered making a bid for all the company's stock themselves and taking it off the open market. This would be :

   a. a leveraged buyout.
   b. a conglomerate merger.
   c. taking the firm private.
   d. forming a master limited partnership.

18. When Pat Sloane bought a Tidy Maid franchise, she became a:

   a. franchisor.
   b. stockholder.
   c. venture capitalist.
   d. franchisee.

19. One of the advantages of a franchise is:

   a. receiving management and marketing expertise from the franchisor.
   b. fewer restrictions on selling than in other forms of businesses.
   c. lower start up costs than other businesses.
   d. you get to keep all the profits after taxes.

20. International franchising is:

    a. a successful area for both small and large franchises.

    b. costs about the same as domestic franchising.

    c. becoming increasingly difficult, and so is not growing.

    d. easy, because you really do not have to adapt your product at all.

21. In a _____, members democratically control the business by electing a board of directors that hires professional management.

    a. corporation

    b. cooperative

    c. franchise

    d. master limited partnership

True-False

1. _____ One of the benefits of a sole proprietorship is that you have easy availability of funds from a variety of sources.

2. _____ It is relatively easy to get in and out of business when you are a sole proprietor.

3. _____ A common complaint among sole proprietors is that good people to work for you are hard to find.

4. _____ It is best to form a limited partnership, because then there is no one individual who takes on the unlimited liability.

5. _____ In a partnership, one of the major disadvantages is the potential for conflict.

6. _____ A master limited partnership is much like a corporation because its stock is traded on a stock exchange.

7. _____ The owner of a corporation is called a director.

8. _____ One advantage of a corporation is the ability to sell stock to raise money.

9. _____ An S corporation avoids the double taxation of a conventional C corporation.

10. _____ An individual may not incorporate.

11. _____ A limited liability company can choose to be taxed either as a corporation or as a partnership.

12. _____ An example of a vertical merger is MCI Communications and WorldCom, another communications company.

13. _____ A conglomerate merger is the merger of two very large companies in related industries.

14. _____ A leveraged buyout is when the managers of a company buy all of the stock of a firm and take it off the open market.

15. _____ A franchise can be formed as a sole proprietorship, a partnership or a corporation.

16. _____ As a franchisee, you are entitled to financial advice and assistance from the franchisor.

17. _____ One of the disadvantages of a franchise is that if you want to sell, the franchisor must approve of the new owner.

18. _____ It is likely that women and minority participation in franchising will decline in the future.

19. _____ One of the advantages that a home-based franchisee has over a business owner who is not franchised but based at home is that the franchisee feels less isolated.

20. _____ One common element of a cooperative is for members to work a few hours a month as part of their duties.

You Can Find It On the Net

INC Magazine is dedicated to helping small businesses get off the ground. Visit their website at www.inc.com

What special hints are available to small business owners?

What kinds of advice does INC make available to entrepreneurs and small business owners?

Link into the Franchise Finder page. What kinds of opportunities are available.?

What companies are featured?

What business categories can you look into for franchises?

ANSWERS

LEARNING THE LANGUAGE

1. Horizontal merger	10. Master limited partnership	19. Leveraged buyout
2. Partnership	11. Corporation	20. Franchise
3. Franchise agreement	12. Merger	21. Vertical merger
4. Acquisition	13. Franchisee	22. Sole proprietorship
5. Limited liability	14. Limited partner	23. Unlimited liability
6. S Corporation	15. Limited liability company	24. Limited Liability partnership
7. Franchisor	16. General partner	25. Conventional corporation
8. Conglomerate merger	17. Cooperative	
9. Limited partnership	18. General partnership	

RETENTION CHECK

Basic Forms of Business Ownership

1.   a. sole proprietorship
       b. partnership
       c. corporation

2.   The sole proprietorship is the most common form of business ownership

3.   A corporation is the only form of ownership where the business is separate from the owners.

4.   a. Ease of starting and ending the business
       b. Being your own boss
       c. Pride of ownership
       d. Leaving a legacy
       e. Retention of profit
       f. No special taxes

5.   Profits of a sole proprietorship are taxed as the personal income of the owner.

6.   The disadvantages of sole proprietorships are:
      a.   Unlimited liability and the risk of losses
      b.   Limited financial resources
      c.   Management difficulties
      d.   Overwhelming time commitment
      e.   Few fringe benefits
      f.   Limited growth
      g.   Limited life span

7.   With a sole proprietorship, the debts or damages incurred by the business are your debts. You must pay them, even if it means selling your personal assets. This is the concept of unlimited liability.

Partnerships

8.   Three forms of partnerships agreements are:
      a.   general partnership
      b.   limited partnership
      c.   master limited partnership
      d.   limited liability partnership

9.   In a general partnership agreement, the partners agree to share in the operation of the business and assume unlimited liability for the company's debts. In a limited partnership, the limited partners do not have an active role in managing the business, and have liability only up to the amount invested in the firm. There must be at least one general partner in any partnership.

10.   Three key elements of a general partnership are:
      a.   Common ownership.
      b.   Shared profits and losses.
      c.   The right to participate in managing the operations of the business.

11.   Advantages of partnerships are:
      a.   More financial resources.
      b.   Shared management/pooled knowledge.
      c.   Longer survival.

12. Disadvantages of partnerships are:

    a. Unlimited liability.

    b. Division of profits.

    c. Disagreements between partners.

    d. Difficult to terminate.

13. The advantage of a limited liability partnership is that this form of ownership limits the liability of the general partners. The partners' risk is limited to losing their personal assets only from their own acts and omissions and the acts and omissions of people under their supervision.

14. To avoid problems when partners disagree, all the terms of the partnership should be spelled out in writing in a partnership agreement.

Corporations

15. The fact that a corporation is separate from its owners means that the owners are not liable for the debts or any other problems of the corporation beyond the money they invest. Another name for the owner of a corporation is a stockholder, or shareholder.

16. The advantages of a conventional "C" corporation include:

    a. More money for investment

    b. Limited liability

    c. Size

    d. Perpetual life

    e. Ease of ownership change

    f. Ease of drawing talented employees

    g. Separation of ownership from management

17. One way a corporation can raise money is to sell stock, or ownership, to anyone who is interested.

18. Because large corporations have the ability to raise large amounts of money to work with, corporations can build modern factories or software development firms with the latest equipment. They can hire experts or specialists, and buy other corporations to diversify their risk. In other words, they have the size and resources to take advantage of opportunities anywhere in the world. However, a company does not have to be large to be a corporation. Individuals and small companies can also incorporate.

19   The disadvantages of a conventional "C" corporation include:

    a. Initial cost

    b. Paperwork

    c. Two tax returns

    d. Size

    e. Difficulty of termination

    f. Double taxation

    g. Possible conflict with board of directors

20.   If an individual incorporates, he or she must file a corporate return and an individual tax return. Corporate income is taxed twice, because the corporation pays tax on income before it can distribute any to stockholders, then the stockholders pay tax on the income they receive from the corporation.

21.   The structure of a corporation looks like this:

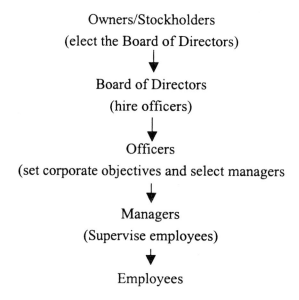

Owners/Stockholders
(elect the Board of Directors)

Board of Directors
(hire officers)

Officers
(set corporate objectives and select managers

Managers
(Supervise employees)

Employees

22.   The major advantage for individuals when they incorporate are limited liability and possible tax benefits.

23. An "S" corporation must:

 a. Have no more than 75 shareholders.

 b. Have shareholders that are individuals or estates and are citizens or permanent residents of the United States

 c. Have only one class of outstanding stock

 d. Not have more than 25% of income derived from passive sources such as rents, royalties, interest etc.

24. Since the top tax rate for S corporations is higher that the highest corporate rate, fast-growing small businesses, such as those in technology often choose C corporation status to avoid the higher tax rates. Because they don't pay owners dividends, they aren't subject to double taxation.

25. Types of corporations are:

 a. Alien

 b. Domestic

 c. Foreign

 d. Closed (private)

 e. Open (public)

 f. Quasi-public

 g. Professional

 h. Nonprofit

 i. Multinational

26. The limited liability company (LLC) has been billed as the business entity of the future. It is similar to an S corporation, but doesn't have the special eligibility requirements.

27. The advantages of a limited liability company are:

 a. personal asset protection

 b. choice to be taxed as a partnership or corporation

 c. flexible ownership rules

Corporate Expansion: Mergers and Acquisitions

28. An acquisition is one company buying the property and obligations of another company, while a merger is when two companies join and create one company. It's like the difference between a marriage (merger) and buying a house (acquisition).

29. The types of mergers are:
    a. Vertical mergers.
    b. Conglomerate mergers.
    c. Horizontal mergers.

30. When taking a firm private, a group of stockholders or management obtains all a firm's stock for themselves.

31. A leveraged buyout is an attempt by employees, management, or a group of investors to purchase an organization primarily through borrowing.

Special Forms of Business Ownership

32. A *franchisor* is someone with a good idea for a business who sells the right to use the business name to someone else, the *franchisee.*

33. Statistics that indicate franchising is important are:
    a. eight million people work in a franchise in the U.S.
    b. franchising accounts for 40 percent of the national retail sales
    c. one out of twelve American businesses is a franchise
    d. a new franchise opens every eight minutes each business day

34. The advantages of a franchise are:
    a. Management and marketing assistance
    b. Personal ownership
    c. Nationally recognized name
    d. Financial assistance
    e. Lower failure rate

35. A franchisee has a greater chance of succeeding because:
    a. they have an established product
    b. help with choosing a location
    c. help with promotion
    d. assistance in all phases of operation

36. Some franchisors offer to provide financing to potential franchisees. They also offer marketing and management assistance.

37. The disadvantages of franchising are:
    a. High start up cost
    b. Shared profit
    c. Management regulation
    d. Coattail effects
    e. Restrictions on selling
    f. Fraudulent franchisors

38. A royalty is a share of sales that must be paid to the franchisor by the franchisee.

39. One of the biggest changes in franchising in recent years is the banding together of many franchisees to resolve their grievances with franchisors rather than fighting their battles alone.

40. The coattail effect is a term used to describe the fact that if other franchisees fail, you could be forced out of business even if your particular franchise has been profitable.

41. Indications are that women and minorities will play a much larger role in franchising in the future than in previous years. Women have often turned to franchising to expand their businesses when financing was difficult, and so are participating in franchising as both franchisee and franchisor. The government is encouraging minorities to become involved in franchising through the Commerce Department's Federal Minority Business Development Agency.

42. Four advantages of home franchising are:
    a. relief from the time and stress of commuting
    b. extra time for family activities
    c. low overhead expenses
    d. home-based franchisees feel less isolated than home-based entrepreneurs

43. Today, Internet users all over the world are able to obtain franchises to open online retail stores fully stocked with merchandise made in all parts of the world. Many franchisees with existing brick-and-mortar stores are expanding their businesses online. Franchisees that started with a limited territory are branching out to customers throughout the world.

44. Many franchisors prohibit franchisee-sponsored websites. Conflicts between franchisors and franchisees can erupt if the franchisor then creates its own website. The franchisees may be concerned that the site will pull sales from their brick and mortar locations.

45. Many franchisors have used the Internet to meet the needs of both their customers and their franchisees. The Internet can help speed up communication, and gives immediate access to

subjects involving the franchise operation, including forms to complete. Franchisees can be kept up to date on company news via e-mail.

46.   One of the considerations of franchising in international markets is the cost, which can be high. Less competition and a fast growing market may counterbalance these high costs. Another consideration is the need to adapt products and services to the region into which the franchisor wants to expand.

Cooperatives

47.   Two kinds of cooperatives are:

a.   those which people have formed to meet their needs for such things as electricity, child care and food; these people who form these have similar needs and pool resources for mutual gain.

b.   cooperatives set up to give members more economic power than they would have as a group. An example is a farm cooperative.

48.   Some cooperatives ask members to work in the organization as part of their duties. Also, members democratically control these businesses by electing a board of directors that hires professional management.

CRITICAL THINKING EXERCISES

1.   Jeff and Bill covered most of the advantages and disadvantages of owning a sole proprietorship. Jeff mentioned the ease of starting the business, the fact that you are your own boss and how proud he seemed to be of what he had accomplished with his hard work. He also mentioned that his tax liability was reasonable (in other words, he didn't have to pay any special taxes), and that he was making a profit that was his to keep and do with as he pleased. Some of the disadvantages Jeff mentioned were that he worked long hours, and had some difficulty in finding financial sources beyond the bank. He was nervous about the unlimited financial liability, and agreed that few fringe benefits was a concern. He also noted that he's having a problem finding a good person to work for him as is common with sole proprietorships. Lastly, he noted one final disadvantage of sole proprietorship, the limited life span. He is making arrangements for his children to inherit the business and continue with it if something happens to him.

2.   a.   Master Limited Partnership (MLP)

b.   Limited partnership

c.   General partnership

d.   Master Limited Partnership (MLP)

e.   Limited partnership

f.   General partnership

3. It appears that Bill thought of most of the advantages and Jeff could only find disadvantages! Bill realized that he could give Jeff the financial resources he needed and could relieve Bill of the long hours he was spending at the business. He also recognized that statistics indicate that partnerships have a longer survival rate than partnerships. The one disadvantage Bill mentioned was the unlimited liability taken on by a general partner. Jeff was quick to point out the disadvantages of shared profits, potential disagreements and the difficulty of terminating a partnership.

4. There are a number of things to consider before Bill and Jeff decide to incorporate. If they are interested in expanding even further, incorporating would give them a wider source of funds for investment, because they could sell stock and keep the investors out of management for the most part. However, their business is small, and there is a question of how "marketable" their stock would be. A major advantage for them both is the aspect of limited liability. Expansion may require going into debt, and if they incorporate, Bill and Jeff would not be liable should something happen to the business. Another advantage for both of the partners is the perpetual life of a corporation. If something should happen to either Bill or Jeff, the remaining owners could still continue with the business. Further, if one of them decided to get out of the business, it is relatively easy, as they would simply have to sell their stock to the remaining owners.

    One major disadvantage of incorporating is the initial cost, which can be very high. It also requires a lot of additional paperwork, particularly regarding the accounting records. Bill and Jeff would have to file more tax returns, and they could be taxed twice, once on their earned income and additionally on any income they received from dividends.

    My advice to Bill and Jeff would be to incorporate, as it looks like the advantages may outweigh the disadvantages. Because they are a small company, they will become a closed corporation. That will eliminate the problem of having a market for their stock. They may also want to consider becoming an "S" corporation.

5. One of the primary advantages of a corporation over proprietorships and partnerships is unlimited liability for the owners. There are additional sources of revenue for a corporation and many times it is easier to attract talented employees because a corporation may be able to offer better benefits. Some corporations are very large, and so size becomes a distinct advantage in terms of facilities and the ability to hire specialties.

6. a. Closed
    b. Open
    c. Foreign
    d. Multinational
    e. Alien
    f. Domestic
    g. Nonprofit
    h. Quasi public
    i. Public

7. a. Limited liability
    b. Limited liability
    c. "S" corporation
    d. "S" corporation
    e. "S" corporation
    f. Limited liability

8. a. vertical merger
    b. leveraged buyout
    c. acquisition
    d. horizontal merger
    e. conglomerate merger
    f. taking a firm private

9. This description identifies several of the benefits of owning a franchise. One of the first in this case is the fact that KFC is a nationally recognized name, which almost guarantees an established customer base. That helps to reduce the risk of failing. KFC provides management training and pays for part of it. They offer advice with opening the store, advertising, layout and interior decor. They offer financial advice also and give the franchisee a feel for what the initial costs are going to be. The franchisee can take advantage of a national advertising campaign, while still advertising on a local basis so they are able to meet local needs.

    The drawbacks stem from the franchise fee which could be relatively high for a nationally recognized franchise, adding to the initial cost of opening. Further, a royalty rate must be paid on a regular basis to KFC, which takes away part of your profits, and the franchisee must contribute to a national advertising fund. Your menu items are limited to what the franchisor tells you, and you must get permission to offer anything different, so you are closely regulated in terms of the menu, and interior decor.

10. Franchisors are using the Internet to meet the needs of both customers and their franchisees. Franchisors have set up Web sites to streamline effective communication for employees, customers and vendors. Intranets are also being built to help franchisees communicate with one another, which has reduced paperwork. Using Web sites, franchisees have immediate access to every subject that involves franchise operations, including forms.

11. a. The landscape/lawn care firm could start out as a sole proprietorship or partnership. There may be no great need for capital to start out with, so there would be no need to incorporate. A partnership may be an advantage because of the amount of labor involved, in order to build the business and do more than one job in a day. Another possibility would be to be a sole proprietor and hire workers to help.
    b. A small manufacturer of component parts would likely do best as a corporation, primarily due to the capital investment required and the need for a variety of skills such as marketing,

manufacturing, engineering and so on. There is also the potential for liability in a manufacturing setting, and a corporate structure would protect the owners. This may initially be a closed corporation or even an "S" corporation.

c. If you want to get into the fast food business, one of the easiest ways would be to investigate owning a franchise. Some fast food franchises are among the fastest growing franchises in the country, and the industry is very competitive. A "guaranteed" market would be a definite plus! The drawback of course is the initial expense, but if you can come up with the money a franchise may be the best way to go.

d. The construction/remodeling business again could be a sole proprietorship or partnership. There is a definite need for several people to be working, so you could either hire workers to work for you, or find a partner who can help in the business. The investment in tools may be substantial which may be another indication of the need for a partner.

PRACTICE TEST

MULTIPLE CHOICE

1.	d	12.	c
2.	a	13.	d
3.	c	14.	b
4.	a	15.	d
5.	a	16.	a
6.	b	17.	c
7.	b	18.	d
8.	d	19.	a
9.	a	20.	a
10.	d	21.	b
11.	a		

TRUE/FALSE

1.	F	11.	T
2.	T	12.	F
3.	T	13.	F
4.	F	14.	F
5.	T	15.	T
6.	T	16.	T
7.	F	17.	T
8.	T	18.	F
9.	T	19.	T
10.	F	20.	T

CHAPTER 6

ENTREPRENEURSHIP AND STARTING A SMALL BUSINESS

LEARNING GOALS

After you have read and studied this chapter, you should be able to :

1. Explain why people are willing to take the risks of entrepreneurship; list the attributes of successful entrepreneurs, describe the benefits of entrepreneurial teams and intrapreneurs, and explain the growth of home-based and Web-based businesses.

2. Discuss the importance of small business to the American economy and summarize the major causes of small-business failures.

3. Summarize ways to learn about how small businesses operate.

4. Analyze what it takes to start and run a small business.

5. Outline the advantages and disadvantages of small businesses have in entering global markets.

LEARNING THE LANGUAGE

Listed here are important terms found in this chapter. Choose the correct term for each definition and write it in the space provided.

Active Corps of Executives (ACE)	Market
Business plan	Micropreneurs
Entrepreneurial team	Service Corps of Retired Executives (SCORE)
Entrepreneurship	Small Business
Incubators	Small Business Investment Companies (SBIC)
Intrapreneur	Venture capitalists

1. A _____ consists of people with unsatisfied wants and needs who have both the resources and willingness to buy.

2. Volunteers from industry, trade associations, and education who counsel small business make up a group known as _____.

3. A group of experienced people from different areas of business who join together as an _____ form a managerial team with the skills needed to develop, make, and market a new product.

4.	A _____ is independently owned and operated, not dominant in its field of operation, and meets certain standards of size in terms of employees or annual receipts.

5.	Individuals or companies known as _____ invest in new businesses in exchange for partial ownership of those businesses.

6.	Created by states to provide low-cost offices, _____ give small businesses basic business services such as accounting, legal advice and secretarial help.

7.	This SBA office known as _____ has 13,000 volunteers of retired executives who provide consulting services for small businesses free (except for expense).

8.	_____ is accepting the risk of starting and running a business.

9.	Creative people known as _____ work as entrepreneurs within corporations.

10.	A _____ is a detailed written statement that describes the nature of the business, the target market, the advantages the business will have in relation to competition, and the resources and qualifications of the owners.

11.	Private investment companies which the Small Business Administration licenses to lend money to small businesses are called _____.

12.	A _____ is an entrepreneur willing to accept the risk of starting and managing the type of business that remains small, lets them do the kind of work they want to do, and offers them a balanced lifestyle.

ASSESSMENT CHECK

Learning Goal 1	**The Age of the Entrepreneur**

1.	What are four reasons why people become entrepreneurs?

a. _____

b. _____

c. _____

d. _____

2.   What are five desirable attributes for entrepreneurs?

   a. _____

   b. _____

   c. _____

   d. _____

   e. _____

3.   What are the advantages of entrepreneurial teams?

4.   What is the difference between an entrepreneur and a micropreneur?

5.   List the reasons for the growth of home-based businesses

   a. _____

   b. _____

   c. _____

   d. _____

6. Identify 5 challenges faced by the owners of home-based businesses.

   a. _____

   b. _____

   c. _____

   d. _____

   e. _____

7. What are some suggestions for those wanting to get into a home-based business?

   a. _____

   b. _____

   c. _____

   d. _____

   e. _____

8. What is expected to happen in the area of Web based businesses over the next few years?

9.   What are some Internet sites suggested in the text that help entrepreneurs in setting up online stores?

a. _____   d. _____

b. _____   e. _____

c. _____   f. _____

10. What is the difference between an entrepreneur and an intrapreneur? What is the purpose behind intrapreneur?

11. What was part of the intention of the Immigration Act of 1990? What are investor visas?

12. What are the ways countries can encourage entrepreneurship?

13. What are incubators and what impact have they had on American business?

14.   What are three criteria used to classify a business as "small?"

   a. _____

   b. _____

   c. _____

15.   What is meant by "small is relative?"

16.   What are some statistics that illustrate the impact of small business on the American economy?

17.   How are women-owned and minority-owned businesses doing?

18.   Why do small business owners believe they have an advantage over big business?

19.   What is the failure rate of small business? Why are the statistics misleading?

20.   What are 2 general reasons for small business failure?

21.   In general, the easiest businesses to start are:

22.   In general, the easiest businesses to keep going are:

23.   In general, the businesses that can make you rich are:

Learning Goal 3   **Learning About Small-Business Operations**

24.   What are three ways to learn about small business?

    a. _____

    b. _____

    c. _____

25.   What is the "rule of thumb" about getting experience in small business?

26. Where do many new entrepreneurs come from? Why?

27. What are three factors used to determine the value of a business?

    a. _____

    b. _____

    c. _____

Learning Goal 4   **Managing a Small Business**

28. What two management functions are of primary concern when you are first starting your business? What three functions are of concern, when managing the business after the start-up?

29. What are the tips for small business owners who want to borrow money?

    a. _____

    b. _____

    c. _____

    d. _____

    e. _____

    f. _____

    g. _____

30. List the information that generally should be included in a business plan.

a. _____

b. _____

c. _____

d. _____

e. _____

f. _____

g. _____

h. _____

i. _____

j. _____

31. What are several sources of small business funding?

a. _____

b. _____

c. _____

d. _____

e. _____

f. _____

g._____

h._____

i._____

j._____

k._____

32.   Other than personal savings, what is the primary source of capital for entrepreneurs?

33.   What is an angel investor?

34.   What is one potential drawback with using venture capitalists?

35.   What are seven types of financial assistance provided by the Small Business Administration?

a._____

b._____

c._____

d._____

e. _____

f. _____

g. _____

36.   How does the microloan program award loans?

37.   What are Small Business Development Centers and how do they operate?

38.   What are the three important elements of small-business success regarding a market?

       a. _____

       b. _____

       c. _____

39. What three criteria are critical for a small business owner with regard to managing employees?

    a. _____

    b. _____

    c. _____

40. How do employees of small businesses feel about their jobs? Why?

41. In what area do most small business owners feel they need assistance the most?

42. How can an accountant help in managing a small business?

43. What are five areas in which you may need assistance as a small business owner?

    a. _____   d. _____

    b. _____   e. _____

    c. _____

44. In what ways can a lawyer help?

45. How can marketing research help?

46. What government-sponsored agencies does the text cover that help small business owners?

a. _____   b._____   c._____

Learning Goal 5   **Going International: Small-Business Prospects**

47. What are four hurdles small businesses face in the international market?

a. _____

b. _____

c. _____

d. _____

48. Identify five reasons for going international.

a. _____

b. _____

c. _____

d. _____

e. _____

49. List the advantages small businesses have over large business in the international market.

a. _____

b. _____

c. _____

d. _____

CRITICAL THINKING EXERCISES

Learning Goal 1

1. You have read in earlier chapters that many parts of Eastern Europe and developing countries n other parts of the world are trying to move to a free market system. How can these developing countries encourage entrepreneurship, and why is it important that entrepreneurship be supported and encouraged?

2. Eric is a young man with a vision. He sees himself as heading up a large corporation someday, a company that he has started and helped to grow. He has basically supported himself since he was fifteen, and has, at the age of 20, already started and sold two successful small businesses. Right now he is going to college full time because he feels that getting an education will be beneficial to him in the long run. He is supporting himself partially with the money he received from the sale of his last business. He intends to start yet another business as soon as he graduates.

Eric's most recent business was in a fairly competitive market in the area in which he lives, St. Louis. He says that while he received some encouragement from a few friends, for the most part they all said he was crazy to work as hard as he was working. But Eric says he just felt that he "had to do things my own way" and built his business to become the second largest of its type in the St. Louis area.

How does Eric portray the entrepreneurial attributes your text identifies?

Learning Goal 2, 3

3. Based on the information from the previous question, Eric seems to have beaten the odds already. What do you think Eric would tell you about success (or failure) and how to learn to be a successful small business owner?

4. Eric has graduated from school and is ready to start his new business. He has never applied for a bank loan, and has come to you for advice on how to beat the odds. What will you tell him?

5. Distinguish between the following types of SBA loans;

    Direct loan   Women's Financing Section

    Guaranteed loans   Women's Prequalification Pilot Loan

    Participation loans   Microloans

    MESBICs

    a. _____   Maria Araruiz received this loan for $100,000 because she owns 60% of the business she runs with her brother.

    b. _____   Terry Krull got a loan for his construction company partly from the SBA and partly from his bank. The SBA will guarantee repayment of the bank loan.

    c. _____   Dennis Franks is a painter, who was disabled several years ago. The SBA gave him a loan when Dennis had difficulty obtaining a conventional loan.

    d. _____   John Hoffman got a loan for his home automation business from his local bank, but the SBA will repay the loan if John stops making the payments.

e. _____ Janice Peterson is a single mother who started her own accounting business with this SBA loan for $5,000.

f. _____ John Rattler is an African-American who started a business writing software for small business application.

g. _____ Danielle Frontiere took out a loan for $35,000 to start her home business of importing lace from Ireland.

Learning Goal 3, 4

6.   After planning and financing, the functions necessary to be successful in running your small business include:

Knowing your market   Keeping efficient records

Managing employees   Looking for help

Read the following situation, keeping in mind what you have learned about successful small businesses. Do you think this small business will "beat the odds?"

Dave and Kevin worked together as sales representatives for a clothing manufacturer in Michigan. They were successful, but were interested in working on their own and started to develop a plan for a partnership as manufacturer's representatives selling clothing and hats to their current customers, using a supplier network they would develop. While they were working full time, Dave and Kevin spent six months finding backers, lining up suppliers, and identifying which of their current customers they could count on later. They casually consulted with an accountant and a lawyer.

Finally, they decided they were ready, and opened under the name of Premium Incentives, Inc. Here is the situation on the day Premium Incentives opened:

*   They each worked at home
*   They had promises, but no written contract, from two suppliers to lend them a total of $100,000 over a one-year period in return for all their business.
*   They decided not to do a business plan, because they already had financing
*   Dave's wife agreed to do the bookkeeping as a favor. She had a degree in business, but not in accounting. However, she had a full time job and a three-year-old child and was expecting another child in five months.
*   They hired sales representatives to help with sales outside their home state and planned to pay them on commission
*   They set up a price schedule designed to under-cut their competitors by a significant amount

After two months in business, Dave and Kevin were still hopeful, but disappointed. They had made $5,000 in sales, but hadn't yet been paid, as the product hadn't been delivered to the customers, and they had over $3,000 in start-up expenses. This would not have been a problem had the suppliers come through on their promises to finance Premium Incentives. However, one of the suppliers, after reconsidering, decided not to lend them any money, and the second dropped his offer down to $5,000 a month for six months with repayment beginning in the seventh month. Since Premium Incentives, Inc. did not have a written contract, they had no legal recourse. Dave and Kevin didn't worry too much about repaying the $60,000 loan, as they figured they still had four months to build up the business. The problem was, their customers weren't buying as much as Dave and Kevin had anticipated, and they weren't sure what to do to find new customers.

Dave's wife was having problems keeping up with the books, so Dave began spending several days a week working on that, in addition to trying to sell. His wife suggested they develop some way of billing a customer, then re-billing if they hadn't paid within 15 days. Dave and Kevin disagreed about what to do, and eventually did nothing. They did finally hire a bookkeeper after several months of doing the books themselves. They continued to struggle with not knowing when a customer was going to pay, and therefore had no idea how much income they were going to have each month.

What do you think? What did Dave and Kevin do right? What did they do wrong? What are their chances of success?

7.   "Small business people have learned, sometimes the hard way, that they need outside consulting advice early in the process."

A. List the types of consultants whose services you may need in starting and managing your small business.

a. _____

b. _____

c. _____

d. _____

e. _____

f. _____

g. _____

B. What are other sources of information available?

a._____   d._____

b._____   e._____

c._____   f._____

Learning Goal 5

8.   Chad Lane is the owner of a small software business based in California. Because there is so much competition in the U.S. he has begun to look for opportunities in global markets. What would you tell him as his advisor?

PRACTICE TEST

Multiple Choice – Circle the best answer

1. Entrepreneurs take the risk of starting a business for all of the following reasons except:

    a. they want independence.
    b. they like the challenge and the risk.
    c. they want to make money for themselves.
    d. they want to work less.

2. An entrepreneurial team is:

    a. a group of people who work within a corporation to launch new products.
    b. a group of experienced people who join together to develop and market a new product.
    c. a group from the Small Business Administration which consults with small business owners.
    d. a group of managers who get together to find creative solutions to problems.

3. Federiko Romero is a business owner who works from home as a freelance video producer. He really enjoys his work, but isn't looking to "set the world on fire" with his company. He just wants to make a good living and spend time with his family when he can. Federiko would be classified as a(n)

    a. entrepreneur.
    b. intrapreneur.
    c. micropreneur.
    d. venture capitalist.

4. Which of the following is a false statement about small business?

    a. The number of women owning small businesses is increasing
    b. The vast majority of non-farm businesses in the U.S. are considered small
    c. The first job for most Americans will probably not be in a small business.
    d. The majority of the country's new jobs are in small business.

5. A small business:

    a. must have fewer than 100 employees to be considered small.
    b. is considered small relative to other businesses in its industry.
    c. cannot be a corporation.
    d. should be an S corporation.

6. In general:

   a. the easier to start the business, the more likely it is to succeed.

   b. businesses that are more difficult to start are most likely to fail.

   c. the easier a businesses is to start the higher the growth rate.

   d. businesses that are difficult to start are the easiest ones to keep going.

7. Miriam Njunge wants to start a small business importing some products from her native Kenya. Before she starts, some good advice to Miriam would be:

   a. talk to others who have been or are in the import business.

   b. get a loan right away.

   c. find a business to buy as soon as possible.

   d. incorporate immediately.

8. In measuring the value of a small firm, which of the following would not be included?

   a. What the business owns

   b. What the business earns

   c. What makes the business unique

   d. What products the business makes

9. The primary concerns when first starting your business are:

   a. marketing and accounting.

   b. planning and human resources.

   c. financing and planning.

   d. financing and marketing.

10. A business plan for a new business does not need to include:

    a. a marketing plan.

    b. a discussion of the purpose of the business.

    c. a description of the company background.

    d. the name of the lending bank.

11. What are the primary sources of funding for entrepreneurs?

    a. personal savings and individual investors
    b. finance companies and banks
    c. the Small Business Administration and banks
    d. former employers and the Economic Development Authority

12. This program awards loans on the basis of belief in the borrower's integrity and the soundness of their business ideas.

    a. SBIC loan
    b Guaranteed loan
    c. Direct loan
    d. Microloan

13 For a market to exist, there must be potential buyers:

    a. and a product that is safe and inexpensive.
    b. who have a willingness and the resources to buy.
    c. and stores which are willing to carry the product.
    d. who are looking for a bargain.

14. Employees in small businesses generally

    a. are more satisfied with their jobs than counterparts in big business.
    b. are less satisfied with their jobs because there is less room for advancement.
    c. are generally only using the job as a springboard to get into a larger company.
    d. are most likely going to quit to find a company that accepts their ideas.

15. Small business owners often say that the most important assistance they need is in

    a. marketing.
    b. accounting.
    c. planning.
    d. manufacturing.

16. The Small Business Administration sponsors groups of volunteers who consult with small businesses for free or for a small free. These groups are:

   a. Venture capitalists and entrepreneurs.
   b. Retired executives and people currently in business.
   c. Stockholders and investors.
   d. Franchisors and bankers.

17. There are many reasons why small business owners don't go international. Which is not considered to be one of the reasons?

   a. They don't know how to get started.
   b. Financing is often difficult to find.
   c. Paperwork is often overwhelming.
   d. The market is expanding too rapidly.

18. Small businesses have an advantage over large business in international trade in all these ways except:

   a. They can begin shipping faster.
   b. They can provide a wide variety of suppliers.
   c. Overseas buyers like dealing with individuals rather than large bureaucracies.
   d. Their prices are usually lower.

19. Small business owners who want to explore the opportunities in international business will find that:
   a. There is not much information about exporting.
   b. Most small businesses still don't think internationally.
   c. There is usually no need to adapt products to foreign markets.
   d. It is more difficult for small businesses to enter international markets than for large businesses.

True-False

1. _____ It is important for an entrepreneur to be self-directed and self-nurturing.

2. _____ An intrapreneur is an individual who is a member of an entrepreneurial team.

3. _____ The Immigration Act of 1990 created investor visas which allow 10,000 people to come to the U.S. if they invest $1 million in an enterprise that creates 10 jobs.

4. _____ Taxes have little effect on entrepreneurship.

5. _____ The majority of new jobs in the private sector are created by small business.

6. _____ Many of the businesses with the lowest failure rates require advanced training to start.

7. _____ One of the ways to get information about starting a small business is by attending classes at a local college.

8. _____ A substantial percentage of small-business owners got the idea for their businesses from their prior jobs.

9. _____ An effective business plan should catch the reader's interest right away.

10. _____ The most important source of funds for a small business owner is bank loans.

11. _____ States have not been especially supportive of small business.

12. _____ The SBA offers a lot of advice but no financial assistance to small business owners.

13. _____ Finding funding for a small business is probably the easiest thing about starting a small business.

14. _____ A market is basically anyone who wants to buy your product.

15. _____ Employees of small businesses are often more satisfied with their jobs than counterparts in big business.

16. _____ Most small businesses can't afford to hire experts as employees, so they need to turn to outside assistance for help.

17. _____ It is best to stay away from other small business owners for counsel, as they are likely to use your ideas before you can get started.

18. _____ A relatively small number of firms accounts for over 80 percent of U.S. exports.

You Can Find It on the Net

If you are interested in starting your own small business, the Small Business Administration can help. Go the to Small Business Administration Web site (www.sbaonline.sba.gov) Find the following information about the SBA services available in your area.

1. What is the address and phone number of the SBA office nearest you?

2.	Are there any SBA sponsored special events scheduled in your area? If so, what are they?

3.	Is there a Small Business Development Center in your area? Where?

4.	Identify the lenders licensed to participate in the Small Business Investment Company (SBIC) program. If you needed to borrow $100,000 to start your business, which lender would you approach? Which would you approach to borrow $500,000?

5.	What does your state's small business profile tell you about the importance of small business to your state's economy? (Identify the percentage of businesses that are considered small businesses, the increase or decrease of business start-ups, the increase or decrease of business failures, the increase or decrease of new jobs and the percentage of new jobs in your state that are in small businesses.)

	Identify

	a.	the percentage of businesses that are considered small _____

	b.	the increase or decrease of business start ups_____

	c.	the increase or decrease of business failures _____

	d.	the increase or decrease of new jobs _____

	e.	the percentage of new jobs in your state that are in small business _____

ANSWERS

Learning the Language

1.	Market	7.	Service Corps of Retired Executives(SCORE)
2.	Active Corps of Executives (ACE)	8.	Entrepreneurship
3.	Entrepreneurial team	9.	Intrapreneurs
4.	Small business	10.	Business plan
5.	Venture capitalist	11.	Small Business Investment Company (SBIC)
6.	Incubators	12.	Micropreneur

ASESSMENT CHECK

The Age of the Entrepreneur

1.   Four reasons people become entrepreneurs are:
   a.   Opportunity
   b.   Profit
   c.   Independence
   d.   Challenge

2.   Desirable attributes for entrepreneurs are that they be:
   a.   Self-directed
   b.   Self-nurturing
   c.   Action-oriented
   d.   Highly energetic
   e.   Tolerant of uncertainty

3.   a.   A team can combine creative skills with areas (such as design) from the beginning.
   b.   A team can ensure coordination between functions of a business, and better cooperation.

4.   An entrepreneur is not all that different from a micropreneur. Actually, a micropreneur is a "kind "of entrepreneur who is interested in simply enjoying a better lifestyle and in having the opportunity of making a living doing the kind of work they want to do. An entrepreneur may be interested in "growing" their business.

5. Home-based businesses are growing because:
    a. Computer technology has leveled the playing field. This allows home based-businesses to look and act like their corporate competitors
    b. Corporate downsizing has made workers aware that job security is not a sure thing.
    c. Social attitudes have changed
    d. New tax laws have loosened restrictions regarding deductions for home offices

6. Challenges for home-based businesses include:
    a. Getting new customers
    b. Managing time
    c. Keeping work and family tasks separate
    d. Abiding by city ordinances
    e. Managing risk

7. Home-based business owners should focus on:
    a. opportunity, instead of security
    b. getting results instead of following a routine
    c. earning a profit instead of a paycheck
    d. trying new ideas instead of avoiding mistakes
    e. long-term vision instead of a short-term payoff

8. Web based businesses have experienced tremendous growth, and the growth is expected to continue. By 2003, the number of small businesses using the Internet is expected to grow to over 4 million.

9. Internet sites for entrepreneurs include:
    a. Hypermart.com
    b. Shownow.com
    c. Microsoft's LinkExchange
    d. Electronic Commerce Guide
    e. The E-Commerce Research Room
    f. Builder.com

10. Entrepreneurs are risk takers who have started their own businesses. Intrapreneurs are creative people who work as entrepreneurs within corporations. The idea is to use existing human, financial, and physical resources to launch new products and generate new profits.

11. Part of the idea behind the Immigration Act of 1990 was to encourage more entrepreneurs to come to the United States. The act created a category of "investor visas" that allows 10,000 people to come to the U.S. each year if they invest money in an enterprise that creates or preserves 10 jobs.

12. Countries can encourage entrepreneurship by offering investment tax credits and tax breaks to businesses and investing to build the nation's infrastructure to support business.

13. Incubators are centers that offer news businesses low cost offices with basic business services. The number of incubators in the U.S. has grown, and incubators have created nearly 19,000 companies that are still in business, and about 245,000 jobs.

Getting Started in Small Business

14. A small business is one that is:
    a. independently owned and operated
    b. not dominant in its field of operation
    c. meets certain standards of size in terms of employees or annual receipts

15. A small business is considered small relative to others in that industry. If it still meets the criteria listed in the previous question, a $22 million business would still be considered small.

16. Small business is very "big." Nearly 750,000 tax-paying, employee hiring businesses are started every year. Small businesses account for over 40% of GDP, produce 75% of new jobs, and employ more than the populations of Australia and Canada. About 80 percent of Americans find their first jobs in small businesses. There are about 24.5 million full and part-time home-based businesses in the United States.

17. The number of women- and minority-owned businesses has increased considerably.

    The number of small businesses owned by women has grown to nearly 6 million, which is more than one-third of all small businesses. Minority-owned businesses are one of the fastest-growing segments of the U.S. economy. This includes businesses owned by Asians, Hispanics, and African Americans.

18. Small businesses owners believe their advantages over large businesses are: more personal customer service and their ability to respond quickly to opportunities

19. Some believe that the failure rate for new businesses can be as high as 80 percent. The SBA reports a failure rate of 62 percent within 6 years. However, the statistics can be misleading because when small business owners went out of business to start new and different businesses,

they were included in the business failure statistics. Also, when a business changes its form of ownership from a partnership, for example, to a corporation, it was included in the statistics as were retirements.

20. Two general reasons for small business failure are managerial incompetence and inadequate financial planning

21. In general, the easiest businesses to start are the ones that tend to have the least growth and the greatest failure rate.

22. In general, the easiest businesses to keep going are the difficult ones to get started.

23. The ones that can make you rich are the ones that are both hard to start and hard to keep going.

Learning About Small Business Operations

24. Three ways to learn about small business are:
    a. learn from others
    b. get some experience
    c. take over a successful firm

25. The "rule of thumb" is to have three years of experience in a comparable business.

26. Many new entrepreneurs come from corporate management. They are tired of the big business life or have been laid off due to corporate downsizing.

27. Value is based on
    a. what the business owns
    b. what it earns
    c. what makes it unique

Managing a Small Business

28. The two management functions of primary concern are planning and financing. The three important functions after the startup are knowing your customers (Marketing) managing your employees (Human resource development) and keeping records (Accounting).

29. Tips for small business owners wanting to borrow money are:
   a. pick a bank that serves small businesses
   b. have a good accountant prepare a complete set of financial statements and personal balance sheet
   c. go to the bank with an accountant and all the necessary financial information
   d. make an appointment before going to the bank
   e. demonstrate good character
   f. ask for all the money you need
   g. be prepared to personally guarantee the loan

30. A business plan should include a:
   a. Cover letter
   b. Executive Summary of proposed venture
   c. Company background
   d. Management team
   e. Financial plan
   f. Capital required
   g. Marketing plan
   h. Location analysis
   i. Manufacturing plan
   j. Appendix which includes marketing research and other information about the product

31. Sources of small business funding include:
   a. Personal savings
   b. Relatives
   c. Former employers
   d. Banks
   e. Finance companies
   f. Small Business Administration
   g. Farmers Home Administration
   h. Economic Development Authority
   i. Potential suppliers
   j. SBIC (Small Business Investment Company)
   k. SBDCs (Small Business Development Centers)

32. Other than personal savings, individual investors themselves are the primary source of capital for most entrepreneurs.

33. Angel investors are individuals who invest their own money in potentially hot companies before they go public.

34. The potential drawback with venture capitalists is that they will often ask for as much as 60% ownership in your business.

35. The types of financial assistance from the Small Business Administration are:
    a. Direct loans
    b. Guaranteed loans
    c. Participation loans
    d. Loans from Minority Enterprise Small Business Investment Companies (MESBICs)
    e. Loans from the Women's Financing Section
    f. The Women's Prequalification Pilot Loan Program
    g. Microloans

36. Microloans are awarded on the basis of belief in the borrowers' integrity and the soundness of the business idea.

37. Small Business Development Centers are funded jointly by the federal government and individual states and are usually associated with state universities. SBDCs can help a small business owner evaluate the feasibility of their idea, develop the business plan, and complete the funding application, all of which is free of charge.

38. A market must have:
    a. people with unsatisfied wants and needs
    b. who have the resources and the willingness to buy
    c. once you have identified your market and its needs, you must fill those needs

39. Three criteria critical for a small business owner regarding managing employees are:
    a. hiring
    b. training
    c. motivating employees

40. Employees of small companies are often more satisfied with their jobs than their counterparts in big business. Often they find their jobs more challenging, their ideas more accepted, and their bosses more respectful.

41. Most small business owners say they need the most assistance in accounting.

42. A good accountant can help in setting up computer systems for record keeping such as inventory control, customer records, and payroll. He/She can also help make decisions such as whether to buy or lease equipment and whether to own or rent a building. Further, an accountant can help with tax planning, financial forecasting, choosing sources of financing, and writing requests for funds.

43. Small business owners have learned they need help with
    a. legal advice
    b. tax advice
    c. accounting advice
    d. marketing
    e. finance

44. Lawyers can help with such areas as leases, contracts and protection against liabilities.

45. Marketing research can help you determine where to locate, whom to select as your target market, and what would be an effective strategy for reaching those people.

46. Government agencies helping small business owners are:
    a. SBA
    b. SCORE
    c. ACE

Going International : Small Business Prospects

47. Four hurdles for small businesses in the international market are:
    a. Financing is difficult to find
    b. Many would-be exporters don't know how to get started
    c. Potential global business people do not understand cultural differences
    d. The bureaucratic paperwork can be overwhelming

48. Good reasons for going international are:
    a. most of the world's markets lie outside the U.S.
    b. exporting can absorb excess inventory
    c. exporting softens downturns in the domestic market
    d. exporting extends product lives
    e. exporting can spice up dull routines

49. Small businesses have advantages over big businesses in the international market, such as:
    a. Overseas buyers enjoy dealing with individuals rather than large corporate bureaucracies
    b. Small companies can begin shipping faster
    c. Small companies provide a wide variety of suppliers
    d. Small companies can give more personal service and more undivided attention

CRITICAL THINKING EXERCISES

1. Developing (and developed) countries have several options available to support entrepreneurship. Creating a system that makes it easy for investors to come into the country is an important step. The United States, for example, passed the Immigration Act of 1990 which created a special category of visa designed to lure entrepreneurs to the U.S.

   Many developing countries do not have the infrastructure to support a rapidly growing economy. Governments need to prioritize building the kind of infrastructure businesses need. Providing tax credits and tax breaks to businesses is another way to encourage entrepreneurship.

   Entrepreneurship creates jobs, and when people are working, and spending, that creates more jobs, and so the economy grows. Developing countries need the kind of programs that will encourage investments, which create jobs. Encouraging and supporting entrepreneurship is one way these countries can help their economies to grow, become self-sufficient, and to be participants in the emerging global economy.

2. The text mentions that desirable entrepreneurial attributes include being self-directed, self-nurturing, action-oriented, highly energetic, and tolerant of uncertainty. Eric demonstrates these characteristics in several ways. He is self-directed in that he had the discipline not only to build 2 businesses, but to leave those businesses when he decided that he wanted to go on to college. He has been self-supporting for a number of years, and so most likely is quite tolerant of uncertainty, and probably feels quite comfortable with that element of risk in starting his own businesses. He continued to work while his friends told him he was "crazy for working that hard" so it seems that he doesn't depend on other people's approval i.e. he's self-nurturing, and appears to be pretty energetic. He must be action oriented, because he was able to build his "dream into a reality" by taking an idea and creating a successful business.

3. Eric seems to lend validity to the questionable failure statistics mentioned in the text. He has beaten the odds twice, and it would seem that the odds of failure may have been lower than traditionally reported.

   Eric may tell you that you need to talk to people who have already started their own businesses and get their advice. They can give you valuable information about the importance of location, finding good workers, and having enough capital to keep you going.

He may also suggest that you work for an successful entrepreneur and get some experience in the fields in which you're interested.

Another idea is to take over a firm that has already been successful. (That's what the buyers of Eric's most recent firm decided to do!) A strategy may be to work for the owner for a few years, then offer to buy the business through profit sharing or an outright purchase.

4.   I would tell Eric to be prepared. First, have a business plan already prepared. Pick a bank that serves small businesses, have an accountant prepare complete financial statements, including a personal balance sheet and take all the financial information with you to the bank, with the business plan. Make an appointment with the loan officer, and ask for exactly what you need. Be prepared to personally guarantee the loan.

5.   a.   Women's Financing Section
       b.   Participation loan
       c.   Direct loan
       d.   Guaranteed loan
       e.   Microloan
       f.   MESBIC
       g.   Women's Financing Section

6.   Dave and Kevin followed one of the suggestions in the text for successfully starting a business, as they worked for someone else in the same field before starting out on their own. They knew their customers, and by all indications the market was there with the resources to buy what Dave and Kevin were selling. Other than Dave's wife they had no employees to manage, as they were using independent sales representatives. As is typical in some small business partnerships, Dave and Kevin couldn't agree on some issues.

Keeping efficient records seems to be a real weakness. Dave's wife didn't really have the skill or time to do the books. Hiring a bookkeeper was a good idea. Perhaps the bookkeeper can suggest an effective billing method.

Although Dave and Kevin had funding, it appears to have been very "casual," and not very well planned. They made no plan to repay the supplier's loan which was to come due in four months. They didn't look for any help, and so ran the risk of running into legal as well as financial problems. Since they decided not to do a business plan, they don't seem to have been very well organized. They had no marketing plan, and no effective strategy for reaching customers other than their original customers. They appear to have made many of the mistakes the text mentions being causes for small business failure, i.e. poor planning and inadequate financial management.

(Ed. note: The company "limped along" for about three years before Dave and Kevin began to disagree on how to proceed. They were sued by the supplier for non payment of the loan, and eventually the business dissolved. Each partner went out on their own. Neither is still in business.)

7. A. There are a number of outside consultants that a small business owner can go to for help in starting and managing their businesses, for example:
    a. Accountant
    b. Lawyer
    c. Marketing research service
    d. Commercial loan officer
    e. Insurance agent
    f. Other business owners
    g. Business professors

    B. Other sources of information include:
    a. Chambers of Commerce
    b. Better Business Bureau
    c. National and local trade associations
    d. Library business sections
    e. The Internet
    f. Computer bulletin boards

8. The international market can be a very lucrative and Chad is in a good business for that market, according to Figure 6-2. It may be a good idea for Chad if he has extra inventory or sees a softening in the domestic market. As a small business owner he has several advantages over larger businesses because he can deal with his customers personally and he can start providing his product immediately.

    There are several hurdles to overcome in the international market, especially if Chad is inexperienced. Cultural differences for the product may not be a problem, but sales techniques will vary from those in the United States. In addition, the paperwork in developing an international market can be overwhelming. Chad has several places available to him to find information, including the SBA, the Commerce Department, export management companies, and export trading companies.

PRACTICE TEST

MULTIPLE CHOICE				TRUE/FALSE			
1.	d	11.	a	1.	T	10.	F
2.	b	12.	d	2.	F	11.	F
3.	c	13.	b	3.	T	12.	F
4.	c	14.	a	4.	F	13.	F
5.	b	15.	b	5.	T	14.	F
6.	d	16.	b	6.	T	15.	T
7.	a	17.	d	7.	T	16.	T
8.	d	18.	d	8.	T	17.	F
9.	c	19.	b	9.	T	18.	T
10.	d						

CHAPTER 7
MANAGEMENT, LEADERSHIP, AND EMPLOYEE EMPOWERMENT

LEARNING GOALS

After you have read and studied this chapter, you should be able to:

1. Explain how the changes that are occurring in the business environment are affecting the management function.

2. Enumerate the five functions of management.

3. Relate the planning process and decision making to the accomplishment of company goals.

4. Describe the organizing function of management, including staffing and diversity management

5. Explain the differences between leaders and managers and describe the various leadership styles.

6. Summarize the five steps of the control function of management.

7. Differentiate the skills needed at each level of management.

LEARNING THE LANGUAGE

Listed below are important terms found in the chapter. Choose the correct term for the definition and write it in the space provided.

Autocratic leadership	Internal customers	Organization chart
Conceptual skills	Knowledge management	Participative (democratic) leadership
Contingency planning	Laissez-faire leadership	Planning
Controlling	Leading	Staffing
Decision making	Management	Strategic planning
Delegating	Managing diversity	Supervisory management
Empowerment	Middle management	SWOT analysis
Enabling	Mission statement	Tactical planning
External customers	Objectives	Technical skills
Goals	Operational planning	Top management
Human relations skills	Organizing	Vision

1.   Assigning authority and accountability to others while retaining responsibility for results is called _____.

2.   Individuals and units within the firm, called _____, receive services from other individuals or units.

3.   _____ are specific short- term statements detailing how to achieve goals.

4.   The process of _____ involves developing detailed, short-term statements about what is to be done, who is to do it, and how it is to be done.

5.   Finding the right information, keeping the information in a readily accessible place, and making the information known to everyone in the firm is known as _____.

6.   The level of management that includes general managers, division managers, and branch and plant managers who are responsible for tactical planning and controlling is called _____.

7.   The process of _____ means choosing among two or more alternatives.

8.   An individual who uses _____ makes managerial decisions without consulting others.

9.   The management function of _____ involves designing the structure of the organization, and creating conditions and systems in which everyone and everything work together to achieve the organization's goals and objectives.

10.   A _____ is a sense of why the organization exists and where it is trying to head.

11.   When an individual uses _____ managers and employees work together to make decisions.

12.   _____ is the process of determining the major goals of the organization and the policies and strategies for obtaining and using resources to achieve those goals.

13.   The management function of _____ includes hiring, motivating, and retaining the best people available to accomplish the company's objectives.

14. Skills that involve the ability to perform tasks in a specific discipline or department are

   _____.

15. When a manager is involved in _____ he or she is building systems and a climate that unite different people in a common pursuit without undermining their diversity.

16. The management function of _____ includes anticipating trends and determining the best strategies and tactics to achieve organizational objectives.

17. The highest level of management consisting of the president and other key company executives who develop strategic plans is called _____.

18. When a manager does _____ he or she is in the process of preparing alternative courses of action that may be used if the primary plans do not achieve the objectives of the organization.

19. When using _____ managers set objectives and allow employees to be relatively free to do whatever it takes to accomplish those objectives.

20. An _____ is a visual device which shows the relationship and divides the organization's work; it shows who is accountable for the completion of specific work and who reports to whom.

21. _____ is the process used to accomplish organizational goals through planning, organizing, leading and controlling people and other organizational resources.

22. Skills called _____ involve the ability to picture the organization as a whole and the relationship among its various parts.

23. A term that means giving employees the authority and responsibility to respond quickly to customer requests is _____.

24. The management function of _____ involves determining whether or not an organization is progressing toward its goals and objectives, and taking corrective action if it is not.

25. Creating a vision for the organization, and guiding, training, coaching, and motivating others to work effectively to achieve the organization's goals and objectives is called _____.

26. The level of management known as _____ includes managers who are directly responsible for assigning specific jobs to workers and evaluating their daily performance.

27. Broad, long-term statements known as _____ are accomplishments an organization wishes to attain.

28. An analysis of an organization's strengths, weaknesses, opportunities, and threats is called a _____.

29. _____ means giving workers the education and tools needed to assume their new decision making powers.

30. When a manager is doing _____ he or she is setting work standards and schedules necessary to implement the tactical objectives.

31. Dealers, who buy to sell to others and ultimate customers, or end users, who buy products for their own personal use are called _____.

32. The _____ is an outline of the fundamental purposes of the organization.

33. Skills that involve communication and motivation called _____, enable managers to work through and with people.

ASSESSMENT CHECK

Learning Goal 1   **The New Business Environment**

1. How has technological change affected management, the kinds of workers needed, and the buyer-seller relationship?

2. How are today's managers changing? Why?

3.   What are the four functions of management of the management process?

   a. _____

   b. _____

   c. _____

   d. _____

4.   Identify the activities performed in each of the four management functions.

   Function   Activities

   A. _____   a. _____

                                               b. _____

                                               c. _____

                                               d. _____

   B. _____   a. _____

                                               b. _____

                                               c. _____

                                               d. _____

   C. _____   a. _____

                                               b. _____

                                               c. _____

                                               d. _____

                                               e. _____

D. _____   a. _____

                                 b. _____

                                 c. _____

5.   What is the trend today in planning? In organizing? In leading?

Learning Goal 3   **Planning : Creating a Vision for the Organization**

6.   Distinguish between a "vision" and a goal:

7.   How does a mission statement relate to the goals of an organization?

8.   What is the difference between goals and objectives?

9.   What are three fundamental questions answered by planning?

      a. _____

      b. _____

      c. _____

10. Where does a SWOT analysis fit into the planning process?

11. What are four types of planning?

   a. _____   c. _____

   b. _____   d. _____

12. What is decided at the strategic planning stage? What is making strategic planning more difficult? What level of management is involved in strategic planning?

13. Describe tactical planning. At what level is tactical planning usually done?

14. What is operational planning? At what level of management is operational planning usually done?

15. Why is contingency planning important?

16. What are the "Seven D's" of the decision making process?

a. _____

b. _____

c. _____

d. _____

e. _____

f. _____

g. _____

Learning Goal 4   **Organizing: Creating a Unified System Out of Multiple Organizations**

17. What are the three levels of management?

a. _____   b. _____   c. _____

18. What positions will be found in top management?

19.   What are the primary responsibilities of a:

        CEO:

        COO:

        CFO:

        CKO:

20.   List some positions found in middle management.

21.   What is supervisory management?

22.   What has been the dominating question regarding organizing? Who are stakeholders?

23.   According to the text, what stakeholders have most influenced how companies are organized?

24. What has made the organizing task more complex today?

25. What is staffing, and what makes it so critical today?

26. Why is managing diversity important for businesses today?

Learning Goal 5   **Leading: Providing Continuous Vision and Values**

27. What is the difference between management and leadership?

28. What are four things leaders must do?

   a._____

   b._____

   c._____

   d._____

29. Describe three leadership styles.

a. _____

b. _____

c. _____

30. When is autocratic leadership effective?

31. What is the benefit of participative leadership and when is it successful?

32. When is laissez-faire leadership the most effective? What traits do managers need in organizations with laissez-faire leadership?

33. What leadership style is best?

34. How do traditional leaders differ from progressive leaders? How is a manager's role changing as a result?

35. What are the steps in developing a knowledge management system? What is the key to a successful knowledge management system?

Learning Goal 6   **Controlling**

36. List the five steps in the control process

a. _____

b. _____

c. _____

d. _____

e. _____

37. Standards must be:

a. _____   b. _____   c. _____

38. What are the criteria for measuring success in a customer-oriented firm?

39.   What is a corporate scorecard?

Learning Goal 7   **Tasks and Skills at Different Levels of Management**

40.   List three categories of skills managers should have.

a. _____

b. _____

c. _____

41.   Describe technical skills.

42.   What are human relations skills?

43.   Describe conceptual skills.

44. How do the various levels of management differ in the skills needed?

CRITICAL THINKING EXERCISES

Learning Goal 1

1. This chapter describes the new "breed" of worker as being more educated with a higher level of skill. This type of worker demands more freedom and a "different managerial style." How does the changing role of managers, described also in the introductory portion of this chapter, meet the needs of the new "breed" of workers?

Learning Goal 2

2. There are four functions of management:

   Planning   Leading

   Organizing   Controlling

   Read the following examples and identify which leadership function the manager is performing.

   a. Grant Wimmer is concerned about his newest employee, Peter Wong. In looking over his sales reports, Grant sees that Peter hasn't been performing well and has only met his sales goals once in the past 6 months. _____

   b. John Bradford is a manager for a firm in the technology industry. John feels it is vital for him to monitor the changes in the industry, and look for opportunities presented by those changes. If he sees a major trend emerging, John sets an objective to learn more about it and to determine ways for his company to participate in the trend. _____

   c. Elvira Mihalek is a manager who spends a lot of time with her employees helping them to attain their goals. She looks for ways to motivate them, makes sure they are trained well, and gives them a great deal of freedom to do their jobs in the best way for them, while still working to achieve the goals of the organization. _____

d. Phil Ardmore is focused on how his company can better serve their customers. He is constantly looking for ways he can design jobs and his department in the best way to be as flexible as possible to meet the needs of their customers. _____

Learning Goal 3

3.   Do you have an idea of what you want to be doing in 5 years? How about in a year?

On a sheet of paper, write out one of your long range (strategic) goals, one tactical objective which will help you to reach your long range goal, and one thing you could do within the next week or month which will get you one step closer to your goals.

Next, keep a time log for the next 48 hours. How did you spend your time? Did you spend some time doing the things which will help you reach those long term goals?

Strategic:

Tactical:

Operational:

Sample Tally of Time Spent

Hours spent:

Working

Studying

In class

Watching t.v.

Sleeping

Recreation

Commuting

SAMPLE TIME LOG

Day 1   Day 2

Out of bed – noon	

Noon – 6:00 p.m.	

6:00 p.m. to bed	

4. Strategic and Tactical planning provide the framework for the planning process. Contingency planning provides alternative plans of action.

Look back to Chapter 5, where we introduced Eric, the young man who wants to start his own business. Eric has decided to start a small manufacturing business, making a product he invented for the automotive industry. It's a component part, designed as a "built-in" carrier for tapes and CD's, which can be removed and taken with you when you get out of the car. The product is called "Music-stor." He wants to sell it to both auto manufacturers and auto parts stores. Can you write a mission statement for Music-stor and outline a strategic plan, tactical plan and a Contingency plan?

Mission Statement:

a. Strategic plan

b. Tactical plan

c. Contingency plan

5. Using the information in your text and in the Spotlight on Small Business, do a brief SWOT analysis for Music-stor. In other words, what do you believe may be the strengths, weaknesses, opportunities and threats for this company in the coming years?

6.   "When organizing, a manager develops a ...framework ....called the organization structure. This is called an organization chart."

Identify two individuals at your college or university at each level of management. Can you draw a simple organization chart?

a. Top managers   _____

_____

b. Middle   _____

_____

c. Supervisory   _____

_____

7.   We have read about changes occurring in business and in the marketplace in previous chapters. In this chapter we read about the changes in the structure of business, which is becoming customer-oriented. Businesses are forming partnerships with several firms, and creating systems of companies working together. Given what you know from previous chapters, why do you think this type of organizational structure has begun to evolve?

8.   Eric has hired you to be the supervisor in the Music-stor plant where they are going to make the tape/CD storage cases. Your workers are well educated and highly skilled. How do you intend to lead and organize these employees? How will your leading (or directing) differ from Eric's, the top manager?

9. Effective leadership styles range along a continuum based upon the amount of employee involvement in setting objectives and making decisions. The three leadership styles are called:

Autocratic   Participative democratic   Laissez-faire

Which of those styles are being illustrated in the following situations?

A. Production workers complain about having to punch a time clock each day.

    a. "Too bad, I'm not getting rid of it! _____

    b. "Let's get a committee together and see if we can come up with some alternatives to using the time clock." _____

B. A university sees a need for some action to be taken to reverse declining enrollment trends.

    a. "Let's form a committee of faculty and administrators to study the problem and give recommendations on how to solve the problem. _____

    b. "The objective for each division is to increase enrollment by 10% for the next school year. Each division is free to take whatever action is appropriate for their area in order to reach the objective. _____

C. A manager notices that an employee consistently turns in work past the deadline.

    a. "Bob, your work has been late three times this month. This is a problem. How can we work together to solve it?" _____

    b. "Bob, your work has been late three times this month. One more time and you will be disciplined. Two times and you're fired. Got it?" _____

10. What is meant by the statement "There is no one best leadership style?"

11.   "Music-Stor" has been in business for several months and you have just been assigned to re-organize the production department. Eric knows that he will need inventory if things go as planned, but production is very slow right now and there are already some orders to fill. Money, however, is tight. All the production workers are peers (none are supervisors), but there is one member of the group who appears to be the informal leader. The workers are paid by the hour, and they are well paid by normal standards.

You have some ideas about how to increase production without increasing costs. One idea, for example, is to change the method of paying workers from hourly to by how much they produce. The way you have it figured, the workers would have to produce more to make the same income. Another way is to set up individual workstations to cut down on the amount of socializing you have seen going on.

While you are confident these ideas, and others you have thought of, are the best solutions, you aren't sure how to implement the changes. You do know that this will be a test of your management and leadership skills.

a. How would you go about developing alternatives and implementing changes you believe are necessary to increase productivity and save money?

b   What leadership style do you think you used in developing your solution? Why?

c. Which of the twelve "golden" rules of leadership does your solution illustrate? Which of the seven "sins" of leadership?

12. You have been in your supervisory position for several months, and have found your boss to be a great person to work with. She speaks often about the kind of division she wants to create, one where all the employees feel a sense of loyalty to a team. She stresses customer service, high product quality, and fair treatment of her employees. If she makes a mistake, she is always up front about it. She insists on honesty from her employees, and you notice that all her employees are treated fairly and with respect. She expects a lot from you and her other subordinates but is sure to let you make your own decisions (as well as your own mistakes!) She encourages employee problem solving and is quick to implement changes, which will make the division more effective and efficient. How does your boss differ from the old style "manager" and demonstrate the leadership of today?

Learning Goal 6

13. "The control system's weakest link tends to be the setting of standards." Standards must be : specific, attainable and measurable.

   Rewrite the following vague standards:

   1. Increase sales _____

   2. Get a degree _____

   3. Be a better manager _____

14. There are many specific skills needed by various levels of management:

   Technical skills   Managing diversity

   Human relations skills   Decision-making

   Conceptual skills

   For each of the following situations, indicate the management level and the skills being used or described.

A. Alice Burling is concerned about Bob Mailing's sales performance. In their meeting, Alice and Bob agree there's a problem. Alice listens carefully to Bob while he explains the situation in his territory, and after asking some questions, Alice shows Bob how to handle things differently. After the meeting, Alice completes a schedule assigning new accounts to various salesmen in her department. Later, with one of the sales people, Alice makes a sales call to a particularly important customer.

    a. Management level _____

    b. Skills _____

B. In a typical week in her office, Tonya works on a long range forecast for a new product the company is considering, and decides to implement a new program to encourage communication and idea exchange between division heads. She appoints several division heads to formulate a plan for implementation. She includes someone from human resources who is in charge of the company's cultural diversity sensitivity training program. She schedules most meetings, but leaves time open for interruptions and unplanned meetings with subordinates.

    a. Management level _____

    b. Skills _____

C. In reviewing weekly production reports, Joel Hodes notices a drop in overall production from last month. He works for several days on an incentive plan he thinks will push production back up to the company's objectives and still maintain high morale. He then calls a meeting with the line supervisors. After getting their responses and suggestions, Joel revises and implements the plan in his plant.

    a. Management level _____

    b. Skills _____

PRACTICE TEST

Multiple Choice – Circle the best answer

1.   Workers in the future:

    a.   will be more closely supervised and highly skilled.
    b.   will require managers that will give them direction and give precise orders.
    c.   will be more educated, highly skilled and self directed.
    d.   will work more individually rather than in teams.

2.   Which of the following would not be included in a discussion of the four functions of management?

    a.   producing.
    b.   organizing.
    c.   leading.
    d.   controlling.

3.   Managers of the future

    a.   will closely supervise highly skilled workers who would like to "do their own thing."
    b.   will emphasize teamwork and cooperation, and will act as coaches, rather than "bosses."
    c.   will have to become specialists in one or two functional areas.
    d.   will have to function as intermediaries between workers and unions.

4.   Antoine Gaudette is doing a performance evaluation for one of his employees. Antoine is looking at the employee's performance for the past year and identifying areas where this employee could improve her performance. Antoine is performing the management function of:

    a.   planning.
    b.   organizing.
    c.   controlling.
    d.   leading.

5.   A(n) _____ is a specific short-term statement detailing how to achieve _____.

    a.   mission statement/ goals
    b.   goal/ objectives
    c.   goal/the mission statement
    d.   objective/goals

6. Maria Mainini is in the middle of setting her plan for the next year. She knows the company wants more market share in the Northeast, so she has developed a detailed plan for increasing the advertising budget for the next year, and adding at least one more sales person to cover the larger territories. Maria is involved in:

   a. Contingency planning.
   b. Operational planning.
   c. Strategic planning.
   d. Tactical planning.

7. Which of the following employees of the local hardware store, Hammerhead, would most likely be involved in strategic planning?

   a. Joe Hartley – department head
   b. Annelise Oswalt – advertising manager
   c. Elliot Nessy – President and CEO
   d. Manny Martinez – chief accountant

8. General managers, division managers, plant managers, and college deans are all a part of

   a. supervisory management.
   b. middle management.
   c. top management.
   d. first-line management.

9. Which of the following is a false statement?

   a. Companies are looking at the best way to be organized to respond to the needs of customers
   b. General consensus is that larger companies are more responsive to customer needs than smaller companies.
   c. Many large firms are being restructured into smaller, customer-focused units.
   d. Companies are organizing so that customers have more influence, than managers.

10. In the future
    a. Workers are more likely to be empowered to make decisions on their own.
    b. Firms will be less likely to establish close relationships with suppliers.
    c. Top managers will be allocating more of their time to giving more detailed instructions to workers.
    d. Small firms will stay away from each other as competition gets fierce.

11. Measuring performance relative to objectives and standards is part of _____.

    a. planning
    b. organizing
    c. leading
    d. controlling

12. Which step in the control process is considered to be the weakest?

    a. Setting clear standards
    b. Monitoring and recording results
    c. Communicating results to employees
    d. Taking corrective action

13. Which of the following objectives is stated most effectively as a control standard?

    a. Cut the number of finished product rejects.
    b. Empower employees to make more decisions next year.
    c. Praise employees more often this month.
    d. Increase sales of our top end product from 2000 in the first quarter to 3000 during the same period.

14. In measuring success in today's firms:

    a. Companies must focus primarily on satisfying the external customers.
    b. Traditional measures of success should be considered most important.
    c. Firms must go beyond financial measures and look at how to please all stakeholders.
    d. Companies must focus on satisfying the employees who deal most with customers.

15. Which of the following is not characteristic of an effective leader?

    a. A leader has a vision and rallies others around the vision.
    b. A leader will establish corporate values.
    c. A leader will emphasize corporate ethics.
    d. A leader will always attempt to keep things from changing.

16. H. Ameneggs is working on a project to determine his company's strengths and weaknesses by looking at the economy, technology, the competition, social and other changes that are affecting his firm. He is looking to identify some opportunities his company can take advantage of in the new economy. H. is also concerned about some things he has identified that inhibit his company's growth. H. is working on

   a. Setting objectives.
   b. A mission statement.
   c. A SWOT analysis.
   d. Contingency planning.

17. When a manager uses democratic leadership, he or she will

   a. make managerial decisions without consulting employees.
   b. set objectives and allow employees to be relatively free to do what it takes to accomplish them.
   c. give employees direction, and be sure that they are doing their job the way the manager wants them to.
   d. work with employees to make decisions together.

18. As the trend toward self-managed teams continues, managers will

   a. find their jobs will remain essentially the same.
   b. delegate more planning, organizing, and controlling to lower levels in the organization.
   c. use more autocratic styles of leadership.
   d. be empowering more individuals than teams.

19. The three basic categories of skills managers must have include all except:

   a. technical skills
   b. disciplinary skills
   c. human relations skills
   d. conceptual skills

20. The level of management most likely to need conceptual skills is

   a. supervisory.
   b. first-line.
   c. middle.
   d. top.

21. At Schwinn, the bicycle manufacturer, managers of the various new departments were told, " go out and shape the department the way you want. You have total freedom." That is an example of

   a. effective delegating.
   b. laissez-faire leadership style.
   c. decision making.
   d. technical skills.

True-False

1. _____ Accelerating change in business has increased the need for workers who are more highly educated and have higher skill levels.

2. _____ Today progressive managers are being educated to tell people what to do and to watch over these new type of workers.

3. _____ Organizing involves determining the best strategies and tactics to achieve the organization's objectives.

4. _____ A mission statement outlines a company's fundamental purpose.

5. _____ Planning answers the questions, "What is the situation now," and "Where do we want to go?"

6. _____ According to the text, the firms with the most innovative and creative workers can go from start-up to major competitor in a very short time.

7. _____ In today's organizations it is necessary to establish close relationships with suppliers and with retailers who sell our products.

8. _____ The planning function of management is the heart of the management system because it provides the feedback that enables managers and workers to make adjustments.

9. _____ The criteria for measuring success in a customer-oriented firm is customer satisfaction of both internal and external customers.

10. _____ The difference between managers and leaders is that a leader creates the vision, the manager carries it out.

11. _____ Generally, there is one best leadership style to which all leaders should adhere.

12. _____ Autocratic leadership is most effective in emergencies or when absolute followership is needed.

13. _____ The trend in the United States is toward placing more workers on teams, which are often self-managed.

14. _____ The skills needed by managers are different at different levels.

15. _____ Research has shown that homogeneous (similar) groups are more effective than heterogeneous (mixed) groups in the workplace.

You Can Find It On the Net

You may find it interesting to determine your ability to make appropriate supervisory decisions. Go to the Leadership Challenge part of the Positive Employee Relations Council Web site www.perc.net/Background.html). This simulation involves you in fictional but realistic situations. It is broken down into moves or steps. The objective is to finish with the least number of steps and a high score. You will discover that this simulation is a maze of related decisions and interacting problems. You will find that effective supervisory decisions bring you closer to the end of the challenge. Weaker decisions inhibit your efforts, require additional steps, and get you further involved. Print the scorecard to record your results.

How did you score?

Improve your score by taking the challenge again using what you learned on the first round to make better decisions.

ANSWERS

LEARNING THE LANGUAGE

1. Delegating	12. Strategic planning	23. Empowerment
2. Internal customers	13. Staffing	24. Controlling
3. Objectives	14. Technical skills	25. Leading
4. Tactical planning	15. Managing diversity	26. Supervisory management
5. Knowledge management	16. Planning	27. Goals
6. Middle management	17. Top management	28. SWOT
7. Decision making	18. Contingency planning	29. Enabling
8. Autocratic leadership	19. Laissez-faire leadership	30. Operational planning
9. Organizing	20. Organization chart	31. External customers
10. Vision	21. Management	32. Mission statement
11. Participative (democratic) leadership	22. Conceptual skills	33. Human relations skills

ASSESSMENT CHECK

The New Approach to Corporate Management

1. Technological change has increased the need for a new type of worker, who is more educated and has higher skill levels. These workers demand more freedom and different managerial styles. Because the workforce is becoming more educated and self-directed, many managerial and non-managerial jobs are being eliminated.

   The Internet has given consumers more power in the buyer-seller relationship. Consumers have more information available, and they demand the highest quality goods and the best prices, delivered as quickly as possible. Businesses also have more information about consumers and their needs, and these businesses can respond more quickly to consumer demands.

2. Traditional managers were called "bosses," and their job was to tell people what to do and watch over them to be sure the employees did what they were told. Today's managers are being educated to guide, train, support, motivate and coach employees rather than to boss them around. Modern managers will emphasize teamwork and cooperation. In many companies, managers are dressing more casually, are friendlier than bosses were in the past, and treat employees as partners rather than workers who have to be disciplined and watched over.

3. The four functions of management are:
   a. planning
   b. organizing
   c. leading
   d. controlling

4. | Function | Activities |
|---|---|
| A. Planning | a. Set goals |
| | b. Develop strategies to reach goals |
| | c. Determine resources needed |
| | d. Set standards |
| B. Organizing | a. Allocate resources, assign tasks and establish procedures |
| | b. Create structure |
| | c. Recruit, select, train, develop employees |
| | d. Effective placement of employees |
| C. Leading | a. Leading employees to work effectively |
| | b. Give assignments |
| | c. Explain routines |
| | d. Clarify policies |
| | e. Provide performance feedback |
| D. Controlling | a. Measure results against objectives |
| | b. Monitor performance relative to standards |
| | c. Take corrective action |

5.   The trend today in planning, is to have planning teams to help monitor the environment, find business opportunities, and watch for challenges. In organizing, many of today companies are being designed around the customer, to design the firm so that everyone is working to please the customer at a profit. In leading, the trend is to empower employees, giving them as much freedom as possible to become self-directed and self-motivated.

Planning: Creating a Vision for the Organization

6.   Goals are broad, long-term accomplishments that an organization wants to reach. A vision is greater than a goal; it is the larger explanation of why the organization exists and where its trying to head.

7.   A mission statement is the foundation for setting goals and selecting and motivating employees.

8.   Objectives are specific, short-term statements detailing how to achieve the goals that have been set. Goals are broad, long-term accomplishments that an organization wants to reach.

9.   a. What is the situation now?
   b. Where do we want to go?
   c. How can we get there from here?

10. The questions asked in the initial planning stage, such as what is the situation now? What is the state of the economy and other environments? What opportunities exist for meeting needs? What products are most profitable and so forth form part of the SWOT analysis. This analysis begins with an analysis of the business environment in general. The internal strengths and weaknesses are identified. Lastly, external opportunities and threats are identified.

11. Four types of planning are:
    a. Strategic
    b. Tactical
    c. Operational
    d. Contingency

12. At the strategic planning stage, the company decides which customers to serve, what products or services to sell, and the geographic areas in which the firm will compete. Strategic planning is becoming more difficult because changes are occurring so fast that plans set for even months in the future may quickly become obsolete. Top management is involved in the strategic planning process.

13. Tactical planning is the process of developing detailed, short-term strategies about what has to be done, who will do it and how it is to be done. Managers or teams of managers at lower levels of the organization do this type of planning.

14. Operational planning is the setting of work standards and schedules necessary to implement the tactical objectives. Operational planning focuses on specific supervisors, department managers, and individual employees. The operational plan is the department manager's tool for daily and weekly operations.

15. Contingency planning is important to do in the event that the primary plans don't achieve the organization's goals. The environment changes so rapidly that contingency plans are needed in anticipation of those changes. The idea is to stay flexible and to take opportunities when they present themselves, whether they were planned or not.

16. a. Define the situation
    b. Describe and collect needed information
    c. Develop alternatives
    d. Develop agreement among those involved
    e. Decide which alternative is best
    f. Do what is indicated (implement solution)
    g. Determine whether the decision was a good one and follow up

Organizing : Creating a Unified System Out of Multiple Organizations

17. The three levels of management are:
     a. supervisory or first-line
     b. middle
     c. top

18. Top management consists of the president and other key executives who develop strategic plans, such as the CEO (chief executive officer), COO (chief operating officer), and CFO (chief financial officer).

19. CEOs are responsible for introducing change into an organization. The COO is responsible for putting those changes into effect. His or her tasks include structuring, controlling, and rewarding to ensure that people carry out the leader's vision. The CFO is responsible for obtaining funds, budgeting, collecting funds, and other financial matters. The CKO or CIO is responsible for getting the right information to other managers.

20. Middle management positions include general managers, divisional mangers, branch managers, plant managers and college deans.

21. Supervisory or first-line management includes people directly responsible for supervising workers and evaluating their daily performance.

22. The dominating question of organizing in recent years has been how to best organize the firm to respond to the needs of customers and other stakeholders. Stakeholders include anyone who's affected by the organization and its policies and products. That includes employees, customers, suppliers, dealers, environmental groups, and the surrounding communities.

23. Companies today are organizing so that customers have influence. Most large firms are being restructured into smaller, more customer-focused units.

24. Today the organizing task is more complex because firms are forming partnerships and joint ventures, so the job becomes an effort to organize the whole system, not just one firm.

25. Staffing involves recruiting, hiring, and retaining the best people available to accomplish the company's objectives. Today recruiting good employees is critical, especially in the Internet and high-tech areas. Firms with the most innovative and creative workers can go from start-up to major competitor with leading companies in a very short time.

26. Diversity includes people from a wide variety of backgrounds. If people are to work on teams, they have to learn to work together with people who have different personalities, different

priorities, and different lifestyles. Research has shown that mixed groups are more productive than similar groups in the workplace. It is often quite profitable to have employees who match the diversity of customers so that cultural differences are understood and matched.

Leading: Providing Continuous Vision and Values

27.   The difference between leadership and management is that leadership is creating a vision for others to follow, while management is the carrying out of the vision.

28.
    a. Have a vision and rally others around the vision
    b. Establish corporate values
    c. Emphasize corporate ethics
    d. Embrace and create change

29.
    a. Autocratic involves making managerial decisions without consulting others
    b. Democratic or participative consists of managers and employees working together to make decisions
    c. Laissez-faire or free rein involves managers setting objectives and employees being relatively free to do what it takes to accomplish those objectives

30.   Autocratic leadership is effective when absolute followership is needed, and with new, unskilled workers who need more direction and guidance.

31.   Employee participation in decisions usually increases job satisfaction. Progressive organizations are highly successful at using a democratic style of leadership where traits such as flexibility, good listening skills, and empathy are dominant.

32.   Laissez-faire leadership is effective in professional organizations, where managers deal with doctors, engineers or other professionals. The traits needed by managers in laissez-faire organizations include warmth, friendliness, and understanding.

33.   Research indicates that successful leadership depends on who is being led and in what situation. Different leadership styles, ranging from autocratic to laissez-faire, may be successful depending on the people and the situation.

34.   Traditional leaders give explicit instructions to workers, telling them what to do to meet the goals and objectives of the organization. This is called directing. Progressive leaders are less likely than traditional leaders to give specific instructions to employees. They are more likely to empower employees the make decisions on their own. In cooperation with employees, managers will set up teams that will work together to accomplish goals.

35. The steps to developing knowledge management include determining what knowledge is most important, and then setting out to find answers to those questions. The key to success is learning how to process information effectively and turn it into knowledge that everyone can use to improve processes and procedures.

Controlling

36.
   a. Setting clear performance standards
   b. Monitoring and recording actual performance
   c. Comparing results against plans and standards
   d. Communicating results and deviations to the employees involved
   e. Providing positive feedback and taking corrective action when needed

37. Standards must be:
   a. specific
   b. attainable
   c. measurable

38. The criteria for measuring success in customer-oriented firms are customer satisfaction of both internal and external customers. Further, while traditional financial control measures are still important, others have been added which measure the success of the firm in pleasing customers, employees and other stakeholders. Other criteria may include the contribution the firm is making to society or improvements in the quality of the environment.

39. A corporate scorecard is a broad measurement tool that measures customer satisfaction, financial progress, return on investment and everything else that needs to be managed for a firm to be profitable.

Tasks and Skills at Different Levels of Management

40. Three categories skill managers must have are:
   a. technical skills
   b. human relations skills
   c. conceptual skills

41. Technical skills involve the ability to perform tasks of a specific discipline or department.

42. Human relations skills include skills such as communication and motivation, leadership, coaching, morale building, training and development, and being supportive.

43. Conceptual skills refer to a manger's ability to picture the organization as a whole and the relationship of various parts to perform tasks such as planning, organizing, controlling, decision making, problem analysis, coordinating and delegating.

44. Managers need to be skilled in all three skill areas. First-line managers spend most of their time on technical and human relations tasks, but they spend little time on conceptual tasks. Middle managers need to use few conceptual skills. Instead, almost all their time is devoted to human relations and conceptual tasks. Top managers use considerable time on conceptual skills and human relations tasks.

CRITICAL THINKING EXERCISES

1. As the book describes, at one time managers were "bosses" who directed the activities of their subordinates and generally kept a close watch over them. People who made mistakes or didn't perform according to the bosses' expectations were reprimanded, sometimes very sternly. This tends to be the "old school" of managing and certainly doesn't fit the new type of worker who is better educated and skilled in areas such as communication, teamwork and information technology. This type of worker is probably self-motivated and self directed, and needs little or no supervision or direction from a "boss." The new kind of manager is trained to guide and train, support, and motivate the new type of worker, emphasizing teamwork and cooperation. In other words, managers are working side by side with workers, rather than "above" them.

This makes better sense for workers who no longer need the kind of "boss" we used to know.

2. a. Controlling
   b. Planning
   c. Leading
   d. Organizing

3. Obviously, your answers will vary, depending upon your goals. An example might be:
   Strategic: Get a Bachelor's Degree in Business in the next 4 years
   Tactical: Take 12 hours next semester, 12 hours the following, and take at least one business course each semester
   Operational: Go to the registrar's office and get a catalog for next semester, or decide which courses you need to take, or if the timing is right, register!

   The time log will be different for each one of you. The big question will be whether or not you spent any time on the activities that will help you to reach the long-term goal you said you wanted to reach.

4. Eric has a big job ahead of him. There are many possible responses to this question, but some suggestions are:

Mission statement: Music-stor's mission is to make and develop products for the automotive industry. We are committed to helping our employees develop their potential and encourage their creativity and energy.

We intend to continually create value for our customers by forming long lasting partnerships with our customers and suppliers, and to exceed our customer's expectations.

a. Strategic plan - Become the major supplier of tape and C.D. storage cases for automobiles within the next 5 years, with a 15% market share.

b. Tactical - Contact the production and/or engineering managers of the major automobile manufacturers and sell them on the product within the next 12 months. Continue to look for other markets, by making 3 new contacts per month.

c. Contingency plan - If the automakers are not interested right now, begin focusing on the automotive after-market, to sell product as an add-on. Make 2 contacts in the after market by the end of the current fiscal year.

5.   A suggested SWOT analysis would contain:

    Strengths: Young, creative workforce

                        Energetic CEO

    Weaknesses: New company

                        Finding financing sources

    Opportunities: Growing popularity of CD players in cars, for all ages

    Threats: Competition from automakers adding their own carrying case

These are only suggestions. You may have come up with additional ideas!

6.   There are many variations for answering this question, depending upon your school. Some possibilities are :

a. Top Managers - Chancellor, President, Provost

b. Middle - Dean of Instruction, Executive Dean, Associate Dean

c. Supervisory - Lab supervisor, Department chair, Business manager

The organization chart may look like this:

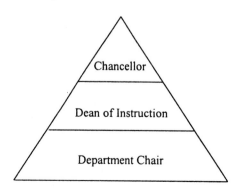

7.	In earlier chapters we have learned about the changing nature of U.S. business, increasing global competition, and continuing push for quality and increased productivity. These new structures are reflective of the need to focus on productivity, quality and the needs of the consumer in an increasingly competitive marketplace. For example, to be more productive we must cut costs, which interfirm relationships help to make possible. Further, to be more competitive, we must respond to customer demands by creating a "customer-oriented organization" with smaller, more customer-focused units.

8.	As a manager of the new "breed" of workers, you are less likely to be giving specific instructions to your employees. Instead, you may give them the authority to make decisions, which will allow them to respond quickly to any customer requests. In all likelihood, you will set up a team approach for the plant, using self-managed work teams if possible. Your job will be more that of a coach and team member, allowing for more participation in decision-making and more flexibility for the workers.

	Eric, as the top manager of the company, will be concerned with a broader view of where he wants the company to go. As a first line manager, your job will be more specific and your goals and objectives more specific than those Eric has outlined for the entire company. So your directions to subordinates, to the extent you will give them direction, will be more specific.

9.	A.	a.	Autocratic
		b.	Participative
	B.	a.	Participative
		b.	Laissez-faire
	C.	a.	Participative
		b.	Autocratic

10.	It is generally believed that there is no one leadership style which would be best in all situations. The most effective or successful manager will use a variety of leadership styles depending upon who is being led and upon the situation.

11.	Answers will vary, as you have your own individual style. However, review the material in this section of the chapter. Is there any opportunity to organize a self-managed team? Earlier in the study guide, the workers were described as the "new" breed of worker. Would a team-based approach be appropriate for this group? Could you use a participative management style? Did you consider getting opinions from the workers about what they see as a method to increase production without raising costs? In terms of the "Rules" and "Sins" of leadership, review them. Did you ask for advice? Did your solution inform them of the need for changing? Did you ask for new ideas?

12.	Leaders differ from managers is several ways. Effective leaders look at the four functions of management, planning, organizing, leading and controlling, from a much broader perspective. Planning is more global, the focus of organizing is on structuring the company to be more competitive in a global market, their leading involves creating a vision, and control means empowering people and holding them responsible.

Your boss appears to have those qualities. She has a vision of how she wants the division to operate. She trusts employees to make their own decisions, thus empowering them with control over their jobs. Her sense of corporate values is demonstrated by her concern for quality, customer service, and fair treatment of employees.

13.   a.   Increase sales of Product X by 10% in the next 6 months.

           b.   Get a Bachelor's Degree in Business in 4 years.

           c.   Spend 3 hours a week reading management articles or books. Praise employees twice a week.

14.   A. a.   Supervisory level

             b.   Human relations, technical skills

        B. a.   Top management

             b.   Managing diversity, decision making, conceptual skills

        C. a.   Middle management

             b.   Human relations skills, technical skills, decision making, conceptual skills

PRACTICE TEST

MULTIPLE CHOICE				**TRUE/FALSE**			
1.	c	12.	a	1.	T	9.	T
2.	a	13.	d	2.	F	10.	T
3.	b	14.	c	3.	F	11.	F
4.	c	15.	d	4.	T	12.	T
5.	d	16.	c	5.	T	13.	T
6.	d	17.	d	6.	T	14.	T
7.	c	18.	b	7.	T	15.	F
8.	b	19.	b	8.	F		
9.	b	20.	d				
10.	a	21.	a				
11.	d						

CHAPTER 8
ORGANIZING A CUSTOMER-DRIVEN BUSINESS

LEARNING GOALS

After you have read and studied this chapter, you should be able to:

1. Explain the organizational theories of Fayol and Weber.

2. Discuss the various issues connected with organizational design.

3. Describe line and staff organizations and their limitations.

4. Show how matrix-style organizations and cross-functional teams help companies become more customer oriented.

5. Defend the use of various organizational tools and techniques such as extranets, TQM and outsourcing.

6. Give examples to show how organizational culture and the informal organization can hinder or assist organizational change.

LEARNING THE LANGUAGE

Listed below are important terms found in the chapter. Choose the correct term for each definition and write it in the space provided.

Bureaucracy	Formal organization	Outsourcing
Centralized authority	Hierarchy	Real time
Competitive benchmarking	Informal organization	Reengineering
Continuous improvement	Inverted organization	Restructuring
Core competencies	Line organization	Span of control
Cross-functional teams	Line personnel	Staff personnel
Decentralized authority	Matrix organization	Total Quality Management (TQM)
Departmentalization	Networking	Transparency
Downsizing	Organizational culture	Virtual corporation
Economies of scale	Organizational design	

1. Groups of employees from different departments who work together on a semi-permanent basis are called _____.

2. A _____ is a system in which one person is at the top of the organization and there is a ranked or sequential ordering from top down of managers who are responsible to that person.

3. By using communications technology and other means of linking organizations, _____, allows working together on common objectives.

4. Redesigning organizations so that they can more effectively and efficiently serve their customers is known as _____.

5. Widely shared values within an organization, or the _____ provides coherence and cooperation to achieve common goals.

6. The _____ is the system of relationships and lines of authority that develop spontaneously as employees meet and form power centers; the human side of the organization that does not appear on any organization chart.

7. Those functions that the organization can do better than anyone else in the world are called _____.

8. A _____ is an organization with many layers of managers who set rules and regulations and oversee decision making.

9. When decision-making authority is maintained with the top level of management at the company's headquarters there is _____.

10. In an _____ contact people are at the top and the chief executive officer is at the bottom of the organization chart.

11. The _____ refers to the optimum number of subordinates a manager supervises or should supervise.

12. _____ is the structuring of workers so that they can best accomplish the firm's goals.

13. Employees known as _____ perform functions that contribute directly to the primary goals of the organization.

14. When a company is using _____ it is rating its practices, processes and products against the world's best.

15. When decision-making authority is delegated to lower-level managers more familiar with local conditions than headquarters' management, a company could be said to have _____.

16. When a company uses _____it is assigning various functions, such as accounting and legal work, to outside organizations.

17. A company is implementing _____ when it satisfies customers by ensuring quality from all departments in the organization.

18. By using _____ an organization is constantly improving the way it does things so that customer needs can be better satisfied.

19. Dividing organizational functions into separate units is called _____.

20. In the _____, the structure that details lines of responsibility, authority and position are shown on the organizational chart.

21. When a company is in the process of _____, it is rethinking and radically redesigning organizational processes to achieve dramatic improvements in critical measures of performance.

22. A _____ is an one in which specialists from different parts of the organization are brought together to work on specific projects but still remain part of a traditional line and staff structure.

23. Employees known as _____perform functions that advise and assist line personnel in performing their goals.

24. The concept of _____describes the fact that companies can produce goods more inexpensively if they can purchase raw materials in bulk and the average cost of goods goes down as production levels increase.

25. The process of eliminating managerial and non-managerial positions is called _____.

26. A _____ is one that has direct two-way lines of responsibility, authority, and communication running from the top to the bottom of the organization, with all people reporting to only one supervisor.

27. Using _____, data are available instantly because they are sent over the Internet to various organizational partners as they are developed.

28. When companies are so open to other companies working with them that the once-solid walls between them have become "transparent," and electronic information is shared as if the companies are one, there is a situation called _____.

29. A _____is a networked organization made up of replaceable firms that join the network and leave it as needed.

ASSESSMENT CHECK

Learning Goal 1   **The Changing Organization**

1. Why have organizations begun to change so much?

2. How were organizations designed in the past?

3. Why did the concept of "economies of scale" develop?

4.	Identify 10 of Fayol's "principles" of organizing

a._____	f._____

b._____	g._____

c._____	h._____

d._____	i._____

e._____	j._____

5.	How were organizations designed in the past, using Fayol's principles? What was the result of that design?

6.	Identify four characteristics of Max Weber's bureaucracy.

a._____

b._____

c._____

d._____

7.	What have firms done to resolve the problems created by a bureaucracy?

8.   How are companies changing their structure to make customers happy? Why are employees encouraged to form teams?

9.   What are some characteristics of bureaucratic organizations?

Learning Goal 2   **Issues Involved in Structuring and Restructuring Organizations**

10.   What are four organizational issues that have led to design changes?

        a._____   c._____

        b._____   d._____

11.   What is a "tall" organization? What was the result of tall organizational structures?

12.   What is a "flat" organizational structure? How is it different from a tall structure?

13. How does span of control vary in the organization? Why does it vary like this?

14. List eight factors used to determine the optimum span of control

a._____   e._____

b._____   f._____

c._____   g._____

d._____   h._____

15. What is the trend in span of control?

16. What are the advantages and disadvantages of departmentalization?

Advantages   Disadvantages
a._____   a._____

b._____   b._____

c._____   c._____

                                   d._____

                                   e._____

17. What are five methods of grouping, or departmentalizing, workers?

a. _____   d. _____

b. _____   e. _____

c. _____

18. What determines the decision about which way to departmentalize?

19. How has the Internet affected departmentalization, and ways for reaching customers?

20. What is the difference between centralized authority and decentralized authority?

Learning Goal 3   **Organization Models**

21. Name four types of organizational structures.

a. _____

b. _____

c. _____

d. _____

22. What are the disadvantages of a line organization for a larger organization?

23. What areas of a business are considered staff, and how do organizations benefit from staff personnel?

24. What disadvantage is common to both line and line-and-staff organizational structures? What benefits do both types of organizations have in common?

Learning Goal 4

25. What are the advantages and disadvantages of a matrix structure?

Advantages	Disadvantages
a._____	a._____
b._____	b._____
c._____	c._____
d._____	d._____

26.   What is a potential problem with the teams created by matrix management?

27.   Describe the trend today used to solve the problem mentioned in question 26.

28.   Describe the characteristics of self-managed, cross-functional teams.

Learning Goal 5   **Bringing the Voice of the Customer Into Organizations**

29.   How has the Internet changed the way information is shared between organizations, the structure of organizations, and organizational charts?

30.   How have "permanent ties" between organizations changed into "impermanent ties?"

31.   What is an extranet?

32.   What is an intranet?

The Restructuring Process and Total Quality

33.   What are "processes?" How does this relate to TQM?

34.   What is the difference between continuous improvement and reengineering?

35.   What is the difference between reengineering and restructuring?

36.   Illustrate an inverted organization.

37.   How do companies with an inverted structure support front-line personnel? How does this
        change the requirements for front-line personnel?

38. When will a company choose to go with outsourcing? When a company outsources, what term is used to describe the functions the company chooses to perform?

39. When a function is too important to outsource, what should a company do?

Learning Goal 6   **Establishing a Service-Oriented Culture**

40. How is the culture of an organization reflected?

41. Describe the kind of organizational cultures that the best organizations have.

42. What are two organizational systems that all companies have?

    a. _____   b. _____

43. What is a drawback of the formal organization? What is a benefit of the formal organization?

44.   What is the drawback of the informal organization? What is the benefit?

45.   What is at the center of the informal organization?

CRITICAL THINKING EXERCISES

Learning Goal 1

1.   Think about the organizational design of the school you are attending, or an organization with which you are familiar, like where you work. Can you identify the "hierarchy?" Identify how many layers of management come between the front-line workers and the highest level of management. Are there separate departments for various functions (instruction, bookstore, and so on)? Are there rules and regulations that seem to keep workers organized and are meant to make the organization run efficiently? (Hint - perhaps your instructor will have a copy of the organizational chart for your school, or your manager may have one for the company for which you work. There may be an organizational chart on the Web site of the organization you are describing.

2.   Can you find any evidence of restructuring, or changes that have helped the organization used in the previous question "more effectively and efficiently serve customers? Who are the customers of a college or university? How does the organization attempt to put the needs of its customers first?

3. Many organizations today have been organized around principles developed earlier in this century by Henri Fayol and Max Weber. Read the following and determine whose ideas are being described.

    a. Introduced several "principles" of organizing._____

    b. Believed workers should think of themselves as coordinated teams, and the goal of the team is more important than individual goals._____

    c. Promoted a bureaucratic organization._____

    d. Believed that large organizations demanded clearly established rules and guidelines, which were to be precisely followed. _____

    e. Wrote that each worker should report to only one boss._____

    f. Said that managers should treat employees and peers with respect _____

    g. Wrote that functions are to be divided into areas of specialization such as production, marketing and so on. _____

    h. Believed in written rules, decision guidelines, and detailed records._____

    i. Said that staffing and promotions should be based solely on qualifications._____

    j. Proposed that an organization should consist of three layers of authority: top managers, middle managers, and workers and supervisors. _____

    k. Believed the less decision-making employees had to do, the better. _____

    l. Believed that managers have the right to give orders and expect obedience. _____

4.   The factors to be considered in determining a span of control are:

Capabilities of the manager   Functional similarity

Capabilities of the subordinates   Need for coordination

Complexity of the job   Planning demands

Geographical closeness   Functional complexity

Read the following descriptions. Draw a simple organizational chart and indicate the span of control at each level and the reasons for your design.

a. A research lab, where a total of 10 chemists are working on several different types of research. All experiments are related to one particular disease. Often one experiment must be completed before another can be started, so coordination among the researchers is very important.

ORGANIZATION CHART

REASONS:

b. An assembly plant, consisting of five groups of six workers each. Each group has the responsibility of completing several stages of the assembly of the product before it moves on to the next group. In the plant, there are a total of three sections, all of which are working on the same product simultaneously. The finished product from the groups of all three sections goes to a separate and final quality control group, which checks out all products assembled in the plant.

ORGANIZATION CHART:

REASONS:

5. There are a number of ways companies have tried to departmentalize to better serve customers:

Function   Process Geographic location

Customer group Product

Match each of the following to the correct form:

A. General Motors has the Saturn, Chevrolet and Pontiac divisions, and the Buick, Oldsmobile divisions, each employing separate staffs for design, engineering, product development and so on. _____

B. At the highest corporate levels, G.E. has a corporate strategic planning staff, production staff, human resources staff, technical resources staff and finance staff.

_____

C. In manufacturing the Macintosh Computer System, Apple Computer begins with an assembly line that makes the logic board; another line makes the analog board. Once assembled, the boards go through diagnostic tests before being assembled into a computer unit. _____

D. When Wendy's made the decision to expand into the European market, the company created a separate European division. _____

E. Most banks have commercial loan officers who deal only with business customers and consumer loan specialists for personal loans. _____

6. Re-read the advantages and disadvantages of the traditional functional method of departmentalizing organizations. Apply what you know about changes in the global marketplace and in businesses to explain why companies are redesigning their structures.

7.   As companies are moving away from traditional methods of organizing, and taking different perspectives regarding span of control, how are companies changing in the area of centralization vs decentralization?

Learning Goal 3, 4

8.   There are 4 types of organizational structures:

Line   Matrix

Line and Staff   Cross-functional

Read below the brief descriptions of several companies and decide which form of organizational structure would be most suitable for each.

A. A small company, Dynalink, is in the biotechnology industry. Competition is fierce, and new product development is of highest importance. The field is changing and growing so rapidly that new product ideas must come fast and furious. The firm employs highly skilled, very creative people._____

B.   Another small firm is Cleanem Up, a dry cleaning establishment, with one owner and one store. They are located in a suburban area and have a loyal clientele. The store is known for its quality and courteous service. _____

C. Wells Industries is a medium sized firm employing about 1,500 people. Wells makes a variety of business- related products such as stationary, forms and so forth. They have a good sales force, who knows the product very well. While this is a fairly competitive industry, new product development happens as the need arises, such as when firms went from sophisticated word processing equipment to even more sophisticated computerized office management._____

D. Mitsubishi wants to develop a new luxury car to compete with Lexus, Infiniti, and others. Time is important as they want to enter the market within 18 months. _____

9.   How will cross-functional teams impact organizational designs of the future?

Learning Goal 5

10.   How does the inverted organizational structure relate to the other kinds of changes we have read about in this chapter, such as wider spans of control, decentralization, cross-functional teams, outsourcing, benchmarking, the Internet, and so on?

11.   Why does Gallo Winery, known for its wines, choose <u>not</u> to grow grapes?

Learning Goal 6

12.   What is the relationship between leadership style, the organizational structure, such as tall vs flat organizations, span of control, delegation, teams, and the creation of an organizational culture?

13.   How does the informal organization help to create the corporate culture?

Learning Goal 4, 5, 6

14.   Music-stor is in a growth state, and Eric, the founder, wants to be sure to build on a good foundation. You are already familiar with the product and have re-engineered the production area. Eric is now interested in the organizational design of the entire company. What suggestions can you give him, knowing what you already know about the company and its employees?

PRACTICE TEST

Multiple Choice – Circle the best answer

1.   In general, organizations today are:

   a.   eliminating managers and giving power to lower-level employees.
   b.   getting bigger, more international, and so are adding management layers.
   c.   becoming more bureaucratic.
   d.   managing employees more closely as they reduce the layers of management.

2.   Which of the following does not fit in when describing a bureaucratic organization?

   a.   many rules and regulations that everyone is expected to follow
   b.   people tend to specialize in many functions
   c.   communication is minimal
   d.   the organization is set up by function, with separate departments for marketing, engineering and so on

3.   When IBM changed its organizational design, the company gave more authority to lower level employees, to become more flexible in responding to customer needs. The company broke down barriers between functions, and ended top-down management. This process is best described as:

   a.   downsizing.
   b.   changing span of control.
   c.   restructuring.
   d.   becoming more bureaucratic.

4.   According to Henri Fayol, the principle of _____ means that each person should know to whom they report, and that managers should have the right to give orders and expect others to follow.

   a.   unity of command
   b.   division of labor
   c.   order
   d.   hierarchy of authority

5. Max Weber believed that

   a. large organizations demanded clearly established rules and guidelines.
   b. workers and supervisors should make decisions together.
   c. rules were to be considered only as guidelines, and employees should be flexible.
   d. there was no need for job descriptions.

6. Robin Banks is in a supervisor for a large, bureaucratic organization on the West Coast. According to the views of a bureaucratic organization held by Max Weber, this means that Robin should:

   a. be included on decision making when decisions affect her workers.
   b. have a wide span of control.
   c. try to get her workers organized into cross-functional teams.
   d. do her work and let middle and upper level managers do the decision making.

7. Reorganizing firms into smaller, less complex units is the result of:

   a. new technologies and international competition.
   b. employees rebelling against too many rules.
   c. upper level managers who were not good decision makers.
   d. bureaucrats changing their way of thinking.

8. Who Dunnit is a new firm which makes murder mystery games for sale in retail stores and through catalogs. The company is run by very few people, and almost everybody pitches in when they need to in order to get the job done. It is really a "team" effort, with very few layers of management. Who Dunnit is an example of a:

   a. tall organization.
   b. bureaucratic organization.
   c. centralized organization.
   d. flat organization.

9. A manager's span of control :

   a. can narrow as subordinates need less supervision.
   b. will narrow as the manager gets to higher levels in the organization and work becomes less standardized.
   c. will broaden as work is less geographically concentrated.
   d. will broaden as functions become more complex.

10. Dewey, Cheatum and Howe is a car company that makes four models, a sport utility, a sports car, a four door sedan and a compact car. Workers at Dewey basically work on only one type of vehicle, and separate marketing and product development processes are designed for each type of vehicle to better serve the customers for each type of vehicle. Dewey, Cheatum and Howe is departmentalized by:

    a. customer.
    b. function.
    c. process.
    d. product.

11. The form of organizational structure that is most flexible, and allows the organization to take on new projects without adding to the organizational structure is the:

    a. Line.
    b. Line and staff.
    c. Matrix.
    d. Cross-functional self managed team.

12. The line structure has the disadvantage of

    a. being too inflexible.
    b. being costly and complex.
    c. perceived loss of control for a manager.
    d. requiring self-motivated, highly trained employees.

13. The Daimler-Chrysler plant in suburban St. Louis is "connected" to its seat supplier in a way that the seat supplier has the information it needs to schedule its production to coordinate with the production of vans at the plant. The seat supplier knows, for example, that B. Goode's cherry red van with tan leather interior is scheduled for production so that it can make sure that the correct seats are in the process when the van is made. This type of communication is best explained as (an):

    a. Extranet.
    b. Virtual corporation.
    c. Transparency.
    d. Intranet.

14. Banana Computers is restructuring, and intends to implement cross-functional teams. All of the following *are likely to* serve on a cross-functional team except:

    a. a Banana engineer.
    b. an employee of Peelit, Inc. one of Banana's competitors.
    c. an employee of Monkeyshine, one of Banana's suppliers.
    d. a Banana salesperson.

15. Ima Doogooder works for Banana Computers and is very good at her job. However, Ima believes that there is always something she can do better, and she is constantly looking for better ways to satisfy customer needs. Ima is apparently a practitioner of:

    a. Reengineering.
    b. Restructuring.
    c. Continuous improvement.
    d. Benchmarking.

16. In an inverted organization, the managers' job is to:

    a. maintain direct contact with customers.
    b. direct and closely monitor employee performance.
    c. look for the best ways to outsource functions.
    d. assist and support sales personnel and other employees who work directly with customers.

17. When a firm is rating its processes and products against the best in the world, the firm is practicing:

    a. total quality management.
    b. outsourcing.
    c. their core competencies.
    d. competitive benchmarking.

18. Which of the following would not be used to describe a company with a positive corporate culture?

    a. emphasizes service to others, especially customers
    b. people enjoy working together to provide good products at reasonable prices
    c. less need for policy manuals, formal rules, and procedures
    d. closer supervision of employees

19.   The corporate structure shown on the organizational chart which details lines of responsibility is known as the :

   a.   informal structure.
   b.   bureaucratic structure.
   c.   formal structure.
   d.   grapevine.

20.   Sgt. Bilko is the one to see in the company when there is something you need. He will obtain what you need quickly, and can avoid the red tape that often delays action. Bilko is the one to see if you need advice or help. Bilko is an important member of the firm's:

   a.   purchasing department
   b.   informal organization
   c.   formal structure
   d.   bureaucratic structure

True-False

1.   _____   A typical hierarchy will consist of top management, middle managers, and supervisory, or first line managers.

2.   _____   A bureaucratic organizational system is a good when workers are relatively well educated and are trained to make decisions.

3.   _____   Henri Fayol and MaxWeber are best know for such organizational concepts as division of labor, unity of command and strict rules, guidelines and policies.

4.   _____   An organization with many layers of management, such as the U.S. Army or a large corporation, is a good example of a flat organization.

5.   _____   Companies that cut management layers are tending to create cross-functional and self-managed teams.

6.   _____   The more experienced a manager is, the broader the span of control can be.

7.   _____   One of the advantages of a functional structure is an ability to respond quickly to external changes.

8.   _____   Today's rapidly changing markets tend to favor centralization of authority, so decisions can be made quickly.

9.   _____   Safety, quality control and human resource management are examples of staff positions in a manufacturing firm.

10. _____ An extranet is a communication link within a specific company that travels over the Internet.

11. _____ Total quality management calls for continuous improvement of processes.

12. _____ When a company can't perform a certain function as well as the best, the company may outsource that function, in order to concentrate on the functions at which they are the best.

13. _____ Many firms are discovering that the key to long-term success in a competitive market is to empower front-line people to respond quickly to customer wants and needs.

14. _____ In general, an organizational culture cannot be negative.

15. _____ The informal organization in most organizations is not particularly powerful.

You Can Find It on the Net

There is a lot of information on the Internet about the topics covered in this chapter. To do a web search, try www.yahoo.com, and in the search box, type in cross-functional teams, self-managed teams, and view the results. You should find a significant number of resources listed. Try www.wilsonmar.com. teamdef.htm

What is the typical organizational chart?

What does the site have to say about continuous improvement, cross-functional teams, culture, and self-directed teams?

What is www.APAC.org?

Try www.onlinejournal.net/iri/RIM/1999/42/3/html/42_3_56.html

In "The Human Side," what does Michael Macoby have to say about developing cross functional capability? What should organizations have? What are the leadership needs? What should team members have?

ANSWERS

KEY TERMS AND DEFINITIONS

1. Cross-functional teams	11. Span of control	21. Reengineering
2. Hierarchy	12. Organizational design	22. Matrix organization
3. Networking	13. Line personnel	23. Staff personnel
4. Restructuring	14. Competitive benchmarking	24. Economies of scale
5. Organizational culture	15. Decentralized authority	25. Downsizing
6. Informal organization	16. Outsourcing	26. Line organization
7. Core competencies	17. Total quality management (TQM)	27. Real time
8. Bureaucracy	18. Continuous improvement	28. Transparency
9. Centralized authority	19. Departmentalization	29. Virtual corporation
10. Inverted organization	20. Formal organization	

RETENTION CHECK

Changing the Organizational Hierarchy

1. Much of the change in organizations today is due to the changing business environment – more global competition and faster technological change, especially challenges from the onset of Internet commerce. Consumer expectations have also changed, and consumers expect the highest quality products and fast, friendly service at a reasonable cost.

2. In the past, many organizations were designed more to facilitate management, rather than to please the customer. Managers could control workers though rules and regulations. Most organizations were rather small until the 20th century, and organizing workers was fairly easy.

3. With the introduction of mass production business organizations became complex and difficult to manage. The bigger the plant, the more efficient production became, or so it seemed. This concept was called economies of scale. This means that companies can produce goods more inexpensively if they can purchase raw materials in bulk, and the average cost of goods goes down as production levels increase.

4. a. Unity of command
    b. Hierarchy of authority
    c. Division of labor
    d. Subordination of individual interests to the general interest
    e. Authority
    f. Degree of centralization
    g. Clear communication channels
    h. Order

i. Equity

j. Esprit de corps

5. Organizations in the past were designed so that no person had more than one boss, lines of authority were clear, and everyone knew to whom they were to report. These principles tended to become rules and procedures as organizations became larger. This led to rigid organizations and a feeling among workers that they belonged to an inflexible system

6. a. Job descriptions

    b. Written rules, decision guidelines, and detailed records

    c. Consistent procedures, regulations, and policies

    d. Staffing and promotions based on qualifications

7. Many organizations today are attempting to rid themselves of bureaucracy because it slows the process of changing. When several layers of management have to be included in a decision, the decision can take weeks. In today's companies decisions often have to made within days or even minutes. So, many firms are eliminating many managerial and non-managerial positions and giving more authority and responsibility to those employees who deal directly with customers.

8. To make customers happy, organizations are giving employees more power to make decisions on their own. They don't have to follow strict rules and regulations. Rather, they are encouraged to please the customer no matter what. This has meant fewer layers of management. Since an individual employee may not have all the skills needed to please customers, employees have been encouraged to form small groups, or teams, so that someone in the group can be responsive to customer requests.

9. Some characteristics of a bureaucratic organization are: many rules and regulations which everyone is expected to follow, an organization set up by function in which people tend to specialize in one function, where communication among departments is minimal.

Issues Involved in Structuring and Restructuring Organizations

10. Organizational issues leading to design changes include:

    a. tall versus flat structures

    b. span of control

    c. departmentalization

    d. centralization versus decentralization

11. Tall organizational structures have many layers of management. The net effect of tall structures is a huge complex of managers, management assistants, secretaries, assistant secretaries, supervisors, and trainers. Costs of keeping all these managers is very high, the amount of paperwork was high, and communication and decision-making were inefficient.

12. A flat organization structure is one where there are few layers of management. Such structures are usually much more responsive to customer demands because power to make decisions may be given to lower-level employees and managers don't have to make so many decisions. This is unlike a tall structure where there are several layers of management, and decision making stays with managers.

13. Span of control narrows gradually at higher levels of the organization. Because work is standardized at lower levels, it is possible to implement a wider span of control. The number gradually narrows at higher levels of the organization because work is less standardized and there's more need for face-to–face communication.

14.
   a. Capabilities of the manager
   b. Capabilities of the subordinates
   c. Complexity of the job
   d. Geographical closeness
   e. Functional similarity
   f. Need for coordination
   g. Planning demands
   h. Functional complexity

15. The trend is to expand span of control as organizations get rid of middle managers and hire more educated and talented lower-level employees. This will be possible as employees become more professional, as information technology makes it possible for managers to handle more information and employees take on more responsibility for self-management.

16.
   Advantages
   a. Skills can be developed
   b. Coordination with the function
   c. Economies of scale

   Disadvantages
   a. Lack of communication
   b. Employees don't identify with the company as a whole
   c. Response to change is slow
   d. People trained too narrowly
   e. Groupthink

17.
   a. Geographic location
   b. Function
   c. Customer group
   d. Process
   e. Product

18. The decision about which way to departmentalize depends upon the nature of the product and the customers served.

19. The development of the Internet has created new opportunities for reaching customers directly. The company can interact with customers, ask them questions, and provide them with information they want. Companies must learn now to coordinate the efforts made by traditional departments and their Internet people to create an easy to use process for customers and the company to access information and to buy goods and services.

20. Centralized authority means that decision-making authority is maintained at the top level of management at headquarters. Decentralized authority means that decision-making authority is delegated to lower-level managers and employees.

Organization Models

21. a. Line organizations
    b. Line-and-staff organizations
    c. Matrix-style organizations
    d. Cross-functional, self-managed teams

22. In a large business, a line organization may have the disadvantages of being too inflexible, having too few specialists, having long lines of communication, and being unable to handle complex decisions necessary in a large organization.

23. Staff personnel perform functions that advise and assist line personnel, such as marketing research, legal advising and human resource management. Organizations benefit from the advice of staff personnel in such areas as safety, quality control, computer technology, and investment. Staff positions strengthen the line positions.

24. Both line, and line-and-staff structures have a certain amount of inflexibility, which is a disadvantage. However, both types of organizations have established lines of authority and communication and both work well in companies with a relatively unchanging environment and slow product development.

Matrix-style organizations and cross-functional teams

25. Advantages
    a. Flexible
    b. Encourages cooperation among departments
    c. Can produce creative solutions to problems
    d. Allows for efficient use of resources

    Disadvantages
    a. Costly and complex
    b. Can confuse employees
    c. Requires good interpersonal skills and cooperative managers and employees
    d. Temporary solution

26.   A potential problem with matrix management is that the project teams are not permanent. After a problem is solved or a product developed, the team breaks up, so there is little opportunity for cross-functional training.

27.   The trend is to develop permanent teams and to empower them to work closely with suppliers, customers, and others to quickly and efficiently bring out new, high quality products while giving great service.

28.   The permanent teams are often self-managed. They automatically have the freedom and authority to do what it takes to please a customer. The teams consist of groups of employees from different departments who work together on a semi permanent basis. The barriers between design, engineering, marketing, distribution and other functions fall when these inter-departmental teams are created.

Bringing the Voice of the Customer Into Organizations

29.   Organizations are so closely linked by the Internet that each organization knows what the others are doing, in real time. Since data is so readily available to organizational partners, companies are so open to one another that the solid walls between them have become transparent. Because of this integration, two companies can now work together so closely that they operate as two departments within one company. Many modern organizations are part of a vast network of global businesses. An organizational chart showing what people do within any one organization may not be complete because the company is actually part of a system of companies.

30.   Organizational structures tend to be flexible and changing. Experts from one company may work for one company one year, and another the next year. Organizations deal with each other on a temporary basis and the ties between organizations are no longer permanent. These are often called virtual corporations because they are made up of replaceable firms that join the network and leave it as needed.

31.   An extranet is an extension of the Internet that connects suppliers, customers, and other organizations via secure Web sites.

32.   An intranet is a set of communication links within one company that travel over the Internet.

The Restructuring Process and Total Quality

33.   Processes are sets of activities strung together for a reason, such as the process for handling a customer's order. Total quality management is the practice of striving for customer satisfaction by ensuring quality from all departments by constantly improving the way the organizations perform their processes so that customer needs can be better satisfied.

34.   Continuous improvement means constantly improving the way an organization does things. Reengineering is the fundamental rethinking and radical redesign of organizational processes to achieve dramatic improvements in critical measures of performance.

35.   Reengineering is more complex than restructuring. Restructuring involves making relatively minor changes to an organization in response to a changing environment.

36.

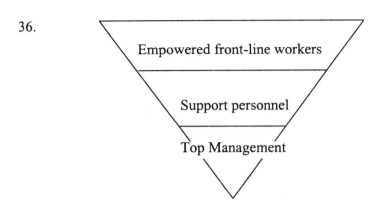

37   Companies based upon an inverted organization structure support front-line personnel with internal and external databases, advanced communication systems and professional assistance. This means that front line personnel have to be better educated, better trained and better paid than in the past.

38.   A company will use outsourcing if it can't perform a function as well as the best. The company will choose to perform those functions it can do as well or better than other organizations. These are its core competencies.

39.   When a function is too important to outsource, the company should use benchmarking on the best firms and restructure their own departments to try to be equally good.

Establishing a Service-Oriented Culture

40.   The culture of an organization is reflected in stories, traditions and myths.

41.   The best organizations have cultures that emphasize service to others; the atmosphere is one of friendly, concerned and caring people who enjoy working together to provide a good product at a reasonable price. Those companies have less need for close supervision of employees, policy manuals, organization charts and formal rules, procedures, and controls.

42.   All companies have a(n)
      a.   formal organization
      b.   informal organization

43. The benefit of a formal organization is that it provides helpful guidelines and lines of authority to follow in routine situations. The drawback of the formal organization is that it is often too slow and bureaucratic to enable an organization to adapt quickly.

44. The drawback of the informal organization is that it is often too unstructured and emotional to allow careful, reasoned decision-making on critical matters. But the informal organization is very effective in generating creative solutions to short-term problems and providing a feeling of camaraderie and teamwork among employees.

45. The center of the informal organization is the grapevine, the system through which unofficial information flows between employees and managers.

CRITICAL THINKING

1. There will obviously be many different answers to this question. A typical hierarchy in a community college for example may be President, Dean of Instruction, Associate Deans, Department Chairs, and faculty for instruction. For non-instruction areas, there may be Associate Deans, Directors, and non-management positions. There are often many layers of management between the lowest levels and the higher levels, and functional areas are well defined.

2. Colleges, for example, may have set up programs for providing high school students with admission and enrollment information; may have developed faculty-student "mentoring" programs, orientation programs; encouraged faculty to be accessible to students; made it easier to apply for financial aid and so forth. The college may hold classes in areas other than the main campus, to make it easier for students to enroll in and attend classes. Each college will have different programs.

3.
   a. Fayol   e. Fayol   i. Weber
   b. Fayol   f. Fayol   j. Weber
   c. Weber   g. Fayol   k. Weber
   d. Weber   h. Weber   l. Fayol

4. A. There could be multiple answers to this question. One suggestion for an organizational chart is:

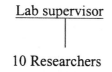

Lab supervisor

10 Researchers

The supervisor's span of control is 10. The reasons for this type of structure are that the researchers probably don't need much supervision, the functions, although complex, are similar in that they are all research related, and all the employees are in the same lab, so are geographically close. Because of the need for coordination of research projects, the supervisor would need to develop an effective communication system.

2.   Possible answer

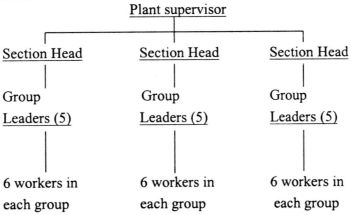

Span of control -   Plant supervisor -3
                      Section Heads - 5
                      Group Leaders - 6

Reason: Each group leader can coordinate the work of his group with the other groups in his section, and the section heads can coordinate their sections. The functions in each group are different, so there is a need for a narrower span of control.

NOTE! These are possible answers. Other structures could be utilized, such as self-managed teams.

5.   A. Product and function   D. Geographic location
        B. Function   E. Product and customer group
        C. Process

6.   In previous chapters we have learned about the global nature of our economy and of the business sector in particular. We have also read about the focus on productivity and the search for ways to make firms in the United States more efficient. With globalization comes competition from companies that have been focusing on those productivity issues for quite some time. Some of the disadvantages of the more traditional methods of departmentalization—the functional structure in particular—are lack of communication, slow response times to external changes and narrowly focused training. These disadvantages can hinder efforts to increase productivity to better serve an increasingly demanding customer base.

7. Changes in the areas we have been discussing are closely related to the changes we are seeing in the area of decision making. As spans of control widen, and non-traditional ways of grouping workers emerge, decision-making is being delegated to lower levels of management, or even to non-management levels. Self-managed teams, which are at the "lowest levels" of the organization, for example, are being given decision-making authority. Today's rapidly changing markets and differences in consumer tastes are favoring a more decentralized structure, with wider spans of control and a team based structure.

8. a. The best answer is most likely a matrix system.
    b. Line
    c. Line and staff/or matrix
    d. Cross-functional

9. Cross-functional teams will have a major impact on organizational designs of the future. Using extranets, companies will be linked with customers, suppliers, and distributors through these teams. They will serve to virtual corporations, an integrated system of firms working together to create products and services designed to exactly meet customers needs. Firms designed in such a manner will have a real competitive edge over corporations that are more traditional.

10. These organizational changes are focused on designing the organization with meeting the needs of the customer as the most important objective. Inverted organizations empower front-line workers, who deal directly with the customers, and provide them with the information and support to satisfy customers. Total quality management programs, such as continuous improvement, also focus on customer service and emphasize the firm's core competencies and call for outsourcing the functions at which the company is less proficient. Those functions that are not outsourced are benchmarked against the best in the world. The Internet makes it possible for firms to link with suppliers and customers to bring the "voice of the customer " into the organization. The common theme is customer service.

11. Gallo Winery chooses to stick to what it does best, which is the production and marketing of wine products. Gallo knows its core competencies and has the most up-to-date information and distributions systems to help them be the best at serving the wine market, without growing grapes.

12. The best organizations have positive corporate cultures that emphasize service to customers, have a relaxed atmosphere, and employ concerned employees who enjoy working together to provide the best product at the best price. Companies that have good organizational cultures have less need for close supervision of employees, organization charts and formal rules, procedures, and controls. That would indicate broad spans of control, empowered employees, flatter organizations, and a participative leadership style. Employees who need minimal supervision will flourish in self-managed teams, and there is mutual trust between workers and management.

13. The informal organization is the human side of a company that does not show up on the organization chart. It is the system of relationships that develop over time, in a company. At the center of the informal organization is the grapevine, the unofficial flow of information. In a company with a positive culture, the informal organization can help to create a spirit of cooperation between managers and employees. It can strongly reinforce a feeling of teamwork and cooperation and can be an invaluable asset that promotes harmony among workers. The informal organization can also be disruptive and negative, and powerful in influencing employees to resist management directives.

14. How you would design the organization is up to you. Many of the ideas presented in the chapter could be helpful. This is a small company so a line organization might be appropriate. We noted earlier that the workers are a "new breed," who don't need a lot of supervision, however, so close monitoring probably could prove to be counter-productive. There doesn't seem to be an immediate need for new product development so a matrix structure probably wouldn't be necessary. The emphasis on customer service has been apparent throughout the chapter so the focus should be on whatever design will most effectively help the company to meet customer needs. This will be accomplished with such tools as the Internet, to develop strong ties with both customers and suppliers.

PRACTICE TEST

MULTIPLE CHOICE

1.	a	11.	c
2.	b	12.	a
3.	c	13.	a
4.	d	14.	b
5.	a	15.	c
6.	d	16.	d
7.	a	17.	d
8.	d	18.	d
9.	b	19.	c
10.	d	20.	b

TRUE/FALSE

1.	T	9.	T
2.	F	10.	F
3.	T	11.	T
4.	F	12.	T
5.	T	13.	T
6.	T	14.	F
7.	F	15.	F
8.	F		

CHAPTER 9
OPERATIONS MANAGEMENT

LEARNING GOALS

After you have read and studied this chapter, you should be able to:

1. Define operations management.

2. Describe the operations management functions that are involved in both the manufacturing and the service sectors.

3. Discuss the problem of productivity in the service sector and how new technology is being used to make services more consumer friendly.

4. Explain process planning and the various manufacturing processes being used today.

5. Describe the new manufacturing techniques that have made U.S. companies more productive, including just-in-time inventory control, flexible manufacturing, computer aided design and manufacturing, and digital manufacturing.

6. Explain the use of PERT and Gantt charts.

LEARNING THE LANGUAGE

Listed below are important terms found in the chapter. Choose the correct term for each definition and write it in the space provided.

Assembly process	Form utility	Operations management
Competing in time	Gantt chart	Process planning
Computer aided design (CAD)	Goods	Process manufacturing
Computer aided manufacturing (CAM)	Intermittent process	Production
Computer integrated manufacturing (CIM)	ISO 9000	Program Evaluation and Review Technique (PERT)
Continuous process	ISO 14000	Purchasing
Critical path	Just in time inventory control	Robot
Enterprise resource planning (ERP)	Lean manufacturing	Quality control
Facility location	Mass customization	Services
Facility layout	Mass production	
Flexible manufacturing	Materials requirement planning (MRP)	

1.   A bar graph that shows production managers what projects are being worked on and what stage they are in on a daily basis is called a _____.

2.   Tangible products such as automobiles, shoes, and furniture are examples of _____.

3.   A computer based production and operations system called _____ links multiple firms into one integrated production unit.

4.   A production process called the_____ puts together components.

5.   Intangible products such as funerals, banking, and retailing are called _____.

6.   A computer-controlled machine called a(n) _____ is capable of performing many tasks requiring the use of materials and tools.

7.   The use of computers in the design of products is called _____.

8.   A concept known as _____means tailoring products to meet the needs of individual customers.

9.   A specialized area in management called _____converts or transforms resources into goods and services.

10. The function in a firm that searches for quality material resources, finds the best suppliers and negotiates the best price for goods and services is known as _____.

11. The process of _____ is the arrangement of resources to produce goods and services effectively and efficiently.

12. The use of computers in the manufacturing of products is _____.

13. In the function of _____ products and services are measured against set standards.

14. The value added by the creation of finished goods and services, such as the value added by taking silicon and making computer chips or putting services together to create a vacation package is known as _____.

15. The production process known as _____ physically or chemically changes materials.

16. The design of machines to do multiple tasks so that they can produce a variety of products is _____.

17. _____ is the production of goods using less of everything compared to mass production.

18. A _____ is the sequence of tasks in a PERT chart that takes the longest time to complete.

19. A computer based production management program called _____ uses sales forecasts to make sure that needed parts and materials are available at the right place and the right time.

20. Using computer-aided design with computer- aided manufacturing is called _____.

21. Production processes known as _____ have long production runs which turn out finished goods over time.

22. The common name given to quality management and assurance standards is _____.

23. _____ is the making of a limited variety of products at very low cost.

24. When a minimum of inventory is kept on the premises, and parts, supplies and other needs are delivered just in time to go on the assembly line, the company is using _____

25. The process of _____ is selecting a geographic site for a company's operations.

26. A method called _____ means analyzing the tasks involved in completing a given project, estimating the time needed to complete each task, and identifying the minimum time needed to complete the total project.

27. _____ is the creation of finished goods and services using the factors of production: land, labor, capital, entrepreneurship and knowledge.

28. A(n) _____ is one in which the production run is short and the machines are changed frequently to make different products.

29. Being as fast or faster than the competition in responding to consumer wants and needs and getting goods and services to the customer is called_____.

30. A collection of standards called _____ identifies the best practices for managing an organization's impact on the environment.

31. Choosing the best means for turning resources into useful goods and services is _____.

ASSESSMENT CHECK

Learning Goal 1   **America's Evolving production and Services Base**

1. What are 5 things U.S. manufacturers have done to regain a competitive lead in the world marketplace?

   a. _____

   b. _____

   c. _____

   d. _____

   e. _____

2. What is production management?

3. What is the difference between goods and services?

4. What is a service economy?

5. How have companies such as IBM, General Electric, and Dell changed what they do to grow and prosper?

6. What are Application Service Providers?

Learning Goal 2   **Operations Management Functions**

7. What are three functions of operations management?

    a. _____

    b. _____

    c. _____

8. What is the main idea of facilities location?

9. What do brick and mortar stores have to do to compete with services offered over the Internet?

10. What are three major reasons why firms shift facilities from one area to another?

   a. _____

   b. _____

   c. _____

11. What are some issues surrounding moving to foreign countries in search of low cost labor?

12. Why do companies such as Honda and Mercedes locate in the United States? What do U.S. firms look for when locating in foreign countries?

13. What kinds of developments have given firms flexibility in choosing locations while remaining competitive?

14. What might state and local governments do to provide incentives for companies looking to locate in their area?

15. What is important in terms of facilities layout for service businesses?

16. In manufacturing, what kind of layout is replacing the assembly line?

17. What is a fixed position layout, and when is it used?

18. How has the Internet affected operations management, and what kinds of companies are facilitating the process?

19. How has quality control changed from the earlier days of manufacturing in the United States? What is the major purpose of quality control?

20. How is a TQM program implemented?

21. What are the seven key areas in which a company must show quality in order to qualify for the Baldridge Awards?

a._____   e._____

b._____   f._____

c._____   g._____

d._____

22. Name the two major criteria for the Baldridge Awards.

a._____

b._____

23. What do the ISO 9000 standards require?

24.   Why is ISO certification so important for U.S. firms?

25.   What is the difference between ISO 9000 and ISO 14000?

26.   What are the requirements for ISO 14000 certification?

Learning Goal 3   **Operations Management in the Service Sector**

27.   According to the text, what has become the quality standard for luxury hotels, as well as for other service businesses?

28.   Where is the greatest productivity problem in the United States?

29. Why is productivity in the service sector difficult to measure?

30. What are some examples of how technology has begun to improve productivity in the service sector?

31. How is the Internet changing the service industry?

Learning Goal 4 **Operations Management in the Manufacturing Sector**

32. What are the three basic requirements of production, according to Andrew Grove?

   a. _____

   b. _____

   c. _____

33. What are two types of manufacturing processes?

   a. _____

   b. _____

34. What are two production processes?

a._____

b._____

35. What is the difference between a continuous production process and an intermittent process?

36. Why do most manufacturers today use intermittent processes?

37. What did materials requirement planning (MRP) do for manufacturers?

38. How is enterprise resource planning (ERP) different from materials requirement planning (MRP) and MRPII?

39. What is DNP?

40. Describe "sequential delivery "in manufacturing.

Learning Goal 5   **Modern Production Techniques**

41. What are 7 major developments that have radically changed the production process in the United States?

a. _____   e. _____

b. _____   f. _____

c. _____   g. _____

d. _____

42. How does a JIT program work? What is the benefit?

43. What does ERP, in combination with JIT systems, provide?

44. What are the responsibilities of the purchasing department?

45. What are three forms of Internet marketplaces?

a. _____

b. _____

c. _____

46. What benefits do flexible manufacturing systems provide to manufacturers?

47. What is the objective of lean manufacturing? How does a company become "lean?"

48. What has mass customization allowed manufacturers to do?

49. What is meant by "competing in time?"

50. What has CAD/CAM made possible?

51.   What is CIM and what does it do?

Learning Goal 6   **Control Procedures: PERT and Gantt charts**

52.   List the four steps in designing a PERT chart

     a. _____

     b. _____

     c. _____

     d. _____

53.   Where does the critical path fit in a PERT Chart?

54.   What is the difference between a Gantt Chart and a PERT Chart?

55.   How can a manager use a Gantt Chart?

CRITICAL THINKING EXERCISES

Learning Goal 1

1.   We have been reading throughout the text of the move toward a global marketplace and the need for U.S. firms to make changes to be competitive. How are production and productivity fundamental to the process?

Learning Goal 2

2.   Why has the term "production management" been changed to "operations management?" What are some examples of operations management?

3.   Businesses may choose to locate close to where the buying power for their product is located, where labor is inexpensive and/or skilled, where land and resources are inexpensive and readily available, or close to their markets.

Evaluate the area in which you live based on the site-selection criteria discussed in the text. Does your area have an advantage in the variables considered for site selection? If so, which ones? Are you located close to markets? What could you say to convince a producer or service business to locate in your area?

4.   How does the concept of facility layout help companies become more "customer focused" and more competitive?

5.   How has increased global competition forced U.S. firms to "rethink" quality?

6.   In the past, quality control in U.S. firms was often done at the end of the production line. How does the concept of "total quality" change the old way of thinking about quality?

Learning Goal 3

7.   Bob Sloan is concerned. He is up for promotion at General Dynamo where he has worked for several years. For the last three years, Bob was the general manager of the G.D. Service division. His counterpart, Gerry Franz, is also in line for the job Bob wants. Gerry is the general manager of a manufacturing division. Bob's concern is that while he has completely automated his division and has received recognition for high quality work, productivity in his division is only up one percent. Gerry's division, through automation, has increased productivity by over six percent. Bob is afraid he won't look as good as Gerry in performance reviews. What's the problem?

8.   In manufacturing, two types of manufacturing processes are:

a.   process manufacturing, changing materials

b.   an assembly process which is putting together components

In addition, production processes are either : continuous or intermittent

Match the correct type of production process to each of the following, according to the description:

a.   The steel industry never shuts down its ovens._____

b.   In the furniture industry, a store will sell custom designed furniture and pass the order on to the manufacturer, who then custom makes each piece. _____

c. The Macintosh computer is assembled piece by piece along an assembly line_____

d. In the steel industry, ore is melted down, poured into forms, then cooled. _____

9. Music-stor is beginning to really gear up for production. It has 2 main product lines: a component part, for built-in tape and CD storage, designed to be installed during the automotive assembly process, and an "after-market" product, to be sold in auto parts stores which can be installed by the consumer. Music-stor buys the raw material from a plastic supplier. They melt the plastic down and pour it into molds, which are then allowed to cool. During the process, color is added, color-coded to the colors offered by the car company they have contracted with. Later, clips and other parts are added which are needed for installation. The process is similar for both product lines with some alterations needed for the retail version. What type of production process is Music-stor likely to be using? How can the company ensure their product is available when the assembly plant needs it and when the retailer wants to sell it?

Learning Goal 4

10. How do flexible manufacturing systems, lean manufacturing, and mass customization reflect the customer orientation we have discussed in earlier chapters?

Learning Goal 5

11. Five radically different production techniques have emerged in recent years:

Just-in-time inventory control   Mass customization   Lean manufacturing

Flexible manufacturing   Competing in time

Distinguish the differences between each technique in the following by using each of the techniques given only once:

a. The Daimler-Chrysler plant in Fenton, Missouri receives shipments about every four hours from its seat supplier, (located in a neighboring town), and literally hundreds of other parts continually. There is virtually no storage space in the plant.
   _____

b. Volvo uses modular construction in their plants, where workers are grouped into autonomous teams working on mobile assembly platforms that carry the cars to the workers. Each worker has been trained to do a whole cluster of tasks. This system enabled Volvo to build quality cars with fewer workers in more space efficient plants and has reduced the number of hours need to assemble a car. _____

c. Because of increased competition from its Japanese counter-parts, Xerox implemented a program designed to cut its new product development time in half. _____

d. Levis markets a service which enables any customer to order a custom-made pair of jeans from any retailer at any time. The jeans cost $10 more than an "off-the-rack" pair._____

e. At Dynalink Industries, 15 machines are used to make, test, and package component parts for stereo and quadraphonic sound systems. The parts are never touched by human hands._____

12. How does CAD/CAM relate to mass customization?

13. You have learned in earlier chapters that one advantage small businesses often have over larger, less flexible companies is the ability to move quickly to serve the needs of their markets and provide more customized service. As increasing numbers of large businesses implement the modern production techniques discussed in this chapter, what potential impact could this have on small businesses?

Learning Goal 6

14. PERT, Critical Path, and Gantt charts are control measures used to ensure that products are manufactured and delivered on time.

Draw a PERT Chart for cooking and serving a breakfast of 3-minute eggs, buttered toast and coffee. Identify the critical path.

PRACTICE TEST

Multiple Choice – Circle the best answer

1. What statement does not fit in when describing the trend in manufacturing in the United States?

   a. Operations management has replaced "production " management.
   b. New manufacturing techniques have replaced more traditional forms.
   c. Rebuilding America's manufacturing base will be a major business issue in the future.
   d. Foreign competition has not affected U.S. manufacturers.

2. New production techniques have:

   a. been difficult and costly to implement and have been largely ignored.
   b. made it possible to custom-make products for individual buyers.
   c. have been implemented primarily by foreign manufacturers.
   d. have not been shown to be effective in making U.S. manufacturers competitive

3. Music-Stor is beginning to see some competition for their portable compact disc storage units. In order to remain competitive, Music-Stor must be sure to:

   a. replace all workers with automated equipment.
   b. move all manufacturing to foreign countries.
   c. train all salesmen in aggressive selling techniques.
   d. keep the costs of inputs down.

4. Which of the following is not considered a strong reason for companies to move production facilities from one area to another?

   a. availability of cheap labor
   b. cheaper natural resources
   c. the level of unemployment in a geographic area
   d. reducing the time it takes to deliver products to the market

5. What is the most important benefit manufacturers see in locating close to larger markets, according to the text?

   a. businesses can lower transportation costs and be more responsive to customers
   b. more availability of skilled labor
   c. guaranteed lower tax rates in the suburban areas
   d. cheaper natural resources

6.   One reason ISO 9000 standards are so important is that:

      a.   they must be met in order to win any quality awards.
      b.   most free trade agreements require that these standards be met.
      c.   meeting these standards will automatically increase worker productivity.
      d.   companies that want to do business with the EU must be certified by ISO standards.

7.   Measuring quality in the service sector:

      a.   has been easy using government standards.
      b.   has been facilitated by the Internet.
      c.   has become more complicated with the advent of computers.
      d.   has been difficult because productivity measurements don't capture improvements in quality.

8.   Boiling an egg is an example of:

      a.   an assembly process.
      b.   process manufacturing.
      c.   an analytic system.
      d.   continuous process.

9.   Tailoring products to meet the needs of individual customers is commonly called:

      a.   mass production
      b.   mass customization
      c.   mass marketing
      d.   mass process manufacturing

10.   Music-Stor wants to link its resource planning and manufacturing with its suppliers in order to
      develop a more integrated system. Music-Stor could use:

      a.   enterprise resource planning.
      b.   continuous process manufacturing.
      c.   PERT charts.
      d.   total quality control.

11. Tony Ruggali is in the process of opening a new restaurant. Tony wants to be sure that his new place The Fresh Place, always has the freshest ingredients and will always be known for being the "freshest place in town." He also wants to devote most of the space in the restaurant to tables for diners, not for storing produce. Tony could use:

    a. analytic production.
    b. Gantt charts.
    c. Just in time inventory.
    d. mass production.

12. Which of the following would not be included in a list of the types of Internet marketplaces that assist in the purchasing function of manufacturing?

    a. Internet-based materials requirement planning
    b. Trading exchange platforms
    c. Industry sponsored exchanges
    d. Net market makers

13. _____ enable manufacturers to custom-make goods as quickly as mass produced items once were.

    a. PERT techniques
    b. Flexible manufacturing systems
    c. Lean manufacturing
    d. Computer aided design

14. Quon Ho believes that there must be a way to cut down on the amount of resources his company uses in the production process. Quon feels that the company uses more space, tools and time to make their product than is necessary. Quon ideas are an example of:

    a. lean manufacturing.
    b. CAD/CAM.
    c. mass customization.
    d. competing in time.

15. A _____ is a bar graph that shows which projects are being worked on and how much has been completed.

   a. PERT chart
   b. flexible manufacturing system
   c Gantt chart
   d. CAD/CAM system

16. Walter Rhodes is a production supervisor at the local cucumber processing plant. Walter is looking at a chart that illustrates for him the sequence of tasks involved in processing the cukes. He is especially interested in the sequence of tasks that take the longest time to complete. Walter is interested in the:

   a. Gantt chart.
   b. total quality management process.
   c. critical path.
   d. lean manufacturing process.

17. Which of the following is not a part of the TQM process?

   a. continual employee evaluations
   b. analyzing the consumer to determine quality demands
   c. incorporating quality features into the product design
   d. ensuring quality standards are met during the entire production process

18. The U.S. award that recognizes firms that meet customer needs, produce high quality products and have high quality internal operations, is known as:

   a. ISO 9000 standards.
   b. The Customer Excellence Award.
   c. The Malcolm Baldrige National Quality Award.
   d. ISO 14000 standards.

True-False

1. _____ One thing U.S. manufacturers have done to regain a competitive edge has been to incorporate more rigid management styles.

2. _____ Operations management is a specialized area that converts resources into goods and services.

3. _____ Form utility is the value added by the creation of finished goods and services using raw materials, components, and other inputs.

4. _____ Many firms in the U.S. are moving to the Northeastern states in the search for inexpensive labor.

5. _____ Facility layout is not an important factor in the services industry.

6. _____ Eventually, suppliers will be linked with manufacturers and retailers in a completely integrated system to facilitate the smooth flow of goods to the consumer.

7. _____ Global competition has had little impact on U.S. manufacturers.

8. _____ Flexible manufacturing systems are so flexible that a special order, even a single item can be produced without slowing down the manufacturing process.

9. _____ It is likely that robots will totally replace manufacturing workers in the future.

10. _____ Computer integrated manufacturing allows computer aided design machines to "talk" to computer-aided manufacturing machines.

11. _____ A Gantt computer program will allow a manger to trace the production process minute by minute to determine which tasks are on time and which are behind.

12. _____ Enterprise Resource Planning is a way of integrating functions within a single firm.

13. _____ Competing in time means being as fast or faster than the competition in responding to consumer wants and needs.

14. _____ Government and businesses find it difficult to measure productivity gains in the service sector.

You Can Find It on the Net

We have studied some of the ideas of lean manufacturing in this chapter. To learn more, visit www.leanstrategies.com

What are the key strategies of "lean" companies?

What are "lean" customer relationships?" How do you create them?

What are the areas to consider in "lean" order fulfillment?

What do "lean" supply chains do, and what areas are important?

What must a company do to have "lean" product development?

ANSWERS

LEARNING THE LANGUAGE

1. Gantt chart	12. Computer aided manufacturing (CAM)	23. Mass production
2. Goods	13. Quality control	24. Just in time inventory control
3. Enterprise resource planning (ERP)	14. Form utility	25. Facility location
4. Assembly process	15. Process manufacturing	26. Program evaluation and review technique (PERT)
5. Services	16. Flexible manufacturing	27. Production
6. Robot	17. Lean manufacturing	28. Intermittent process
7. Computer aided design (CAD)	18. Critical path	29. Competing in time
8. Mass customization	19. Materials requirement planning (MRP)	30. ISO 14000
9. Operations management	20. Computer integrated manufacturing (CIM)	31. Process planning
10. Purchasing	21. Continuous process	
11. Facility layout	22. ISO 9000	

ASSESSMENT CHECK

America's Manufacturing Base

1.   Manufacturers today have:
   a.   Taken a customer focus.
   b.   Created cost savings through site selection.
   c.   Total quality management using ISO 9000 and ISO14000 standards.
   d.   Used new manufacturing techniques.
   e.   Relied on the Internet to unite companies.

2.   Production management is the term used to describe all the activities managers do to help their firms create goods.

3.   Goods are tangible products such as cars and furniture. Services are intangible products such as engineering services and the service you receive in retail stores.

4.   A service economy is one that is dominated by the service sector, such as financial and consulting businesses.

5. These companies have expanded operations management out of the factory and moved it closer to the customer,. They are providing services such as customer manufacturing, fast delivery, credit, installation and service repair.

6. Application Service Providers are companies that provide software services online so that companies do not have to buy their own software but can have instant access to the latest programs.

Operations Management Functions

7. a. facility location
   b. facility layout
   c. quality control

8. The main idea of facility location is to make it easy for consumers to access your service.

9. In order for bricks and mortar stores to compete with Internet shopping they have to choose good locations and offer outstanding service to those who come to the store.

10. Firms shift facilities from one site to another for these reasons:
    a. low cost labor or the right kind of skilled labor
    b. cheaper natural resources, and skilled, talented human resources
    c. reducing time-to-market

11. Low-cost labor is a key reason why less technologically advanced producers move their plants to foreign locations. This has caused problems for some firms, as they have been charged with using child labor and with providing substandard working conditions. It is important for firms to maintain the same quality standards and fair labor practices wherever they produce.

12. Companies choose to locate in foreign counties in order to get closer to international customers. By locating close to customers businesses lower transportation costs and can be more responsive to customer service needs. U. S. firms consider whether they are near to transportation facilities and quality of life issues.

13. New developments in information technology, such as computers, modems, e-mail, voice mail and so forth are enabling firms and employees to be more flexible in choosing locations while remaining competitive. These innovations have made telecommuting a major trend in business.

14. State and local governments may compete with one another by giving tax reductions and other support such as zoning changes and financial aid so that businesses will locate there.

15. Facilities layout depends on the processes that are to be performed. For services, the layout is designed to help the consumer find and buy what they need. Often this means helping consumers to find and buy things on the Internet.

16. In manufacturing, many companies are moving from an assembly line layout to a modular layout, where teams of workers combine to produce more complex units of the final product.

17. A fixed-position layout is where workers congregate around the product to be completed. This type of layout is used when working on a major project.

18. With the Internet, companies have been able to create new relationships with suppliers, so that operations management is becoming an interfirm process, where companies work together to design, produce and ship products to customers. To facilitate such transactions, companies called "e-hubs" have emerged to make the flow of goods among firms faster and smoother.

19. In the past quality control was often done at the end of the production line in the quality control department. Today, quality means satisfying customers by building in and ensuring quality from product planning to production, purchasing, sales, and service. Emphasis is placed on customer satisfaction so quality is everyone's concern, not just the people at the end of the assembly line

20. A TQM program begins by analyzing the market to see what quality needs to be established. Quality is then designed into products, and every product must meet those standards every step of the way in the production process.

21. To qualify for a Baldrige Award, a firm must show quality in:
    a. leadership
    b. strategic planning
    c. customer and market focus
    d. information and analysis
    e. human resources focus
    f. process management
    g. business results

22. The two major criterion for the Baldrige Awards are
    a. whether customer wants and needs are met
    b. customer satisfaction ratings better than the competition

23. ISO 9000 standards require that a company must determine what customer needs are, including regulatory and legal requirements. There must also be communication arrangements to handle issues like complaints. Other standards involve process control, product testing, storage, and delivery.

24. ISO certification is important for U.S. firms because the European Union is demanding that companies that want to do business with the EU be certified by ISO standards.

25. ISO 9000 is the name given to quality management and assurance standards. ISO 14000 is a collection of the best practices for managing an organization's impact on the environment. It does not prescribe a performance level like ISO 9000 does.

26. The requirements for ISO 14000 include having an environmental policy, having specific improvement targets, conducting audits of environmental programs, and maintaining top management review of the processes.

Operations Management in the Service Sector

27. The quality standard for luxury hotels and for other service businesses has become anticipating customer needs and delighting customers.

28. The greatest productivity problem in the United States is reported to be in the service economy.

29. The increase in productivity in the service sector has been in quality, not in quantity, and quality increases are hard to measure with traditional productivity measurements.

30. Technology has changed productivity in the service sector in a number of ways. ATMs have made banking easier, and the new system of universal product codes has allowed computerized retail checkout so the process goes much faster. In the airline industry, computers are used to process reservations with the use of prepackaged meals on board, handling luggage, serving passengers and so on.

31. The Internet and the World Wide Web are revolutionizing services. Interactive services are already available from banks, stockbrokers, travel agents, and all kinds of information providers.

Production Processes

32. a. Build and deliver products in response to demands of a customer at a scheduled delivery time
    b. Provide an acceptable quality level
    c. Provide everything at the lowest possible cost

33. Two types of manufacturing processes are:
    a. process manufacturing
    b. assembly process

34. Two types of production processes are:
    a. continuous
    b. intermittent

35. A continuous process is one in which long production runs turn out finished goods over time. An intermittent process is an operation where the production run is short and the machines changed frequently to produce different products.

36. Most new manufacturers use intermittent processes because the use of computers, robots, and flexible manufacturing processes make it possible to make custom-made goods almost as fast as mass-produced goods were once made.

37. Materials requirement planning allowed manufacturers to make sure that needed parts and materials are available at the right place and the right time.

38. ERP is the newest version of MRP. Enterprise resource planning is a computer-based production and operations system that links multiple firms into one integrated production unit. MRP II is a system that monitors systems within a single firm. ERP is much more sophisticated than MRP II because it monitors processes in multiple firms at the same time.

39. Dynamic performance monitoring, or DNP, enables plant operators to monitor the use of power, chemicals and other resources and to make needed adjustments.

40. Sequential delivery is a system where suppliers provide components in an order sequenced to the customer's production process.

Modern Production Techniques

41. These developments have changed the production process in the U.S.
    a. just-in-time inventory control   f. mass customization
    b. purchasing over the Internet   g. competing in time
    c. flexible manufacturing   h. computer-integrated design and manufacturing
    d. lean manufacturing

42. In a JIT program, a manufacturer sets a production schedule using enterprise resource planning or a similar system, and determines what parts and supplies will be needed. It then informs its suppliers of what will be needed. The supplier delivers the goods just in time to go on the assembly line. The supplier becomes more like another department in the firm because it is linked to the manufacturer by computer. The benefit is lower costs, as only a bare minimum of inventory is needed.

43. ERP in combination with JIT make sure the right materials are at the right place at the right time, at the cheapest cost to meet customer needs and production needs. This is the first step in modern production innovation.

44. The purchasing department is responsible for finding suppliers, negotiating long-term contracts with them, and getting the best price possible.

45. Three forms of Internet marketplaces are:
   a. trading exchange platforms
   b. industry sponsored exchanges
   c. net market makers

46. Flexible manufacturing systems enable manufacturers to custom-make goods as quickly as mass-produced items were once made. This enables producers to more closely meet the wants and needs of customers.

47. The objective of lean manufacturing is to use less human effort, less manufacturing space, less investment in tools, and less engineering time to develop a new product. A company becomes lean by continuously increasing the capacity to produce more, higher quality products with fewer resources.

48. Mass customization has allowed manufacturers to meet the needs of individual customers with virtually customized products.

49. Competing in time means being as fast or faster than the competition in responding to consumer wants and needs and getting goods and services to them.

50. CAD/CAM has made it possible to custom-design products to meet the needs of small markets with very little increase in cost. A producer can program the computer to make a simple design change, and that change can be incorporated directly into the production line.

51. Computer integrated manufacturing is software that enables machines involved with computer-aided design to "talk" with machines involved with computer-aided manufacturing.

Control Procedures: PERT and Gantt charts

52.   Steps involved in developing a PERT chart include:

   a.   Analyze and sequence tasks that need to be done

   b.   Estimate the time needed to complete each task

   c.   Draw a PERT network illustrating the two previous steps

   d.   Identify the critical path

53.   The critical path in a PERT chart identifies the sequence of tasks that takes the longest time to complete. It is the last step in the development and is critical because a delay in the time needed to complete this path would cause the project or production run to be late.

54.   A PERT chart analyzes the tasks involved in completing a given project, estimating the time needed to complete each task, and identifying the minimum time needed to complete the total project. A Gantt chart is more basic and is used to measure production progress using a bar chart that shows what projects are being worked on and how much has been completed.

55.   With a Gantt chart, a manager can trace the production process minute by minute to determine which tasks are on time and which are behind so that adjustments can be made to stay on schedule.

CRITICAL THINKING EXERCISES

1.   Production is the creation of finished goods (output) using the factors of production, (inputs) while productivity measures how <u>efficiently</u> the output has been created. To be competitive in world markets, manufacturers must keep the cost of production (inputs) low while output must be relatively high. The fundamental question is: How does a producer keep costs low and still produce more? In other words, how do manufacturers increase productivity?

2.   The term production has changed to operations to reflect the fact that the United States has become a service based economy, and the term "operations" reflects both goods and services production. Operations management is a specialized area of management, and includes inventory management, quality control, production scheduling, and more. An example of operations management in goods manufacturing is an automotive plant, where operations management transforms raw materials, human resources, parts, supplies, and other resources into automobiles. In a college, operations management takes inputs such as information, professors, supplies, buildings and so on to create a process of education.

3.   The area in which you live may meet a number of important criteria. Look for a population that may be willing to work hard for less pay, such as new immigrants. What kind of skilled labor is available in your area? Is your state a "right to work" state or a heavily unionized state? That affects labor costs. Are you in a rural, suburban or urban area? That affects the availability and costs of land.

If you live in a large urban area, such as Chicago, New York, or much of California, businesses may be attracted because that's where their customers are. However, land is more expensive so a large production facility may not be built there. There may be lots of opportunity for a service-based business to locate in that area. Government support will vary from one area to another, in the form of tax incentives and zoning laws.

4.   Most of the decisions about facilities layout revolve around finding the most benefit for the customer. In services, facilities layout is usually designed to help the consumer find and buy things. Manufacturing plants have been redesigned to reduce cost, increase productivity, simplify the production process and speed things up. That benefits the consumer in the form of lower prices, and lower time to market.

5.   If U.S. firms want to remain competitive in today's global environment, they must focus on quality issues the same way that European and Asian countries have done. As we have read in earlier chapters, these countries are often able to produce high quality goods at low prices. Further ISO standards have provided a common denominator of business quality around the world. U.S. firms have begun to realize that in order to be competitive, they must not only compete with, but also cooperate with, international firms to continue to serve global markets with the highest quality products and services at the lowest possible prices.

6.   Total quality means satisfying customers by building in and ensuring quality from product planning to production, purchasing, sales, and service. In essence, the customer is ultimately the one who determines what the standard for quality should be, so emphasis is placed on customer satisfaction and the fact that quality is everyone's concern. A total quality management program begins by analyzing what the consumer expects in terms of quality and then continues by designing that level of quality into the products. Every product must meet those standards every step of the way in the production process. So, the focus on quality is no longer just at the "end of the line."

7.   Bob's concern stems from how productivity gains are measured. Productivity increases measure the increase in output using the same amount of labor, thus reducing costs. Service productivity, which is the area Bob is concerned with, is difficult to measure because services are labor intensive, and increases often come not in the form of higher quantity, but higher quality, which is much more difficult to measure. A measurement system will favor Bob's friend Gerry, because he works in manufacturing.

8.   a.   continuous
        b.   intermittent assembly process
        c.   assembly process
        d.   process manufacturing

9.   It sounds like Music-stor uses the process manufacturing system to create the product. This would most likely be an intermittent process, as the machines or molds may need to be changed

when they go from producing the retail version to the built-in version when they change colors according to manufacturer.

Music-stor needs to keep track of its own inventory, as well as that of the auto assembly plants and their retail customers. Enterprise resource planning is a sophisticated computer-based operations system that would link Music-stor with their suppliers, as well as with their customers. With this system, Music-stor could track the availability of the plastic they need from their supplier. They could monitor their own inventory to ensure adequate stock at crucial times and be sure that their customers have what they need when they need it to keep production flowing smoothly and sales at the retail level from slacking off.

10. Flexible manufacturing systems, lean manufacturing and mass customization are all ways companies have available to put customer needs first. Manufacturers can custom-make goods at a very low cost very quickly, which is exactly what consumers want!

11.   a. Just-in-time inventory control   d. Mass customization
        b. Lean manufacturing   e. Flexible-manufacturing system
        c. Competing in time

12. CAD/CAM is the integration of computers into the design and manufacture of products. This process has enabled manufacturers to tailor products to meet the needs of individual consumers at very little or no extra cost. A simple design change can be incorporated directly into the production line. It is what has enabled the Levi Strauss Company to offer "custom made" jeans at very little additional cost. CAD/CAM systems have revolutionized the production process and have essentially <u>created</u> and allowed for the concept of mass customization.

13. As bigger businesses increase the use of sophisticated manufacturing technology, they will be able to meet the changing needs of their markets much more quickly. This weakens one advantage small businesses have had, which has been the ability to adapt quickly to changing customer markets. Additionally, big businesses are now able to customize their product, enabling them to meet the needs of smaller target markets, traditionally a stronghold for smaller businesses.

14. To cook a breakfast of 3-minute eggs, buttered toast, and coffee, a PERT chart may look like this:

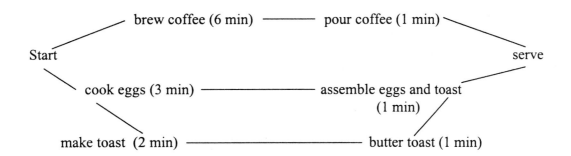

The critical path is the brewing and pouring of the coffee, as it takes the longest time to complete.

PRACTICE TEST

MULTIPLE CHOICE

1.	d	10.	a
2.	b	11.	c
3.	d	12.	a
4.	c	13.	b
5.	a	14.	a
6.	d	15.	c
7.	d	16.	c
8.	b	17.	a
9.	b	18.	c

TRUE/FALSE

1.	F	8.	T
2.	T	9.	F
3.	T	10.	T
4.	F	11.	T
5.	F	12.	F
6.	T	13.	T
7.	F	14.	T

CHAPTER 10
MOTIVATING EMPLOYEES AND BUILDING SELF-MANAGED TEAMS

LEARNING GOALS

After you have read and studied this chapter, you should be able to:

1. Explain Taylor's scientific management.

2. Describe the Hawthorne studies and relate their significance to human based management.

3. Identify the levels of Maslow's hierarchy of needs and relate its importance to employee motivation.

4. Differentiate among Theory X, Theory Y, and Theory Z.

5. Distinguish between motivators and hygiene factors identified by Herzberg.

6. Explain how job enrichment affects employee motivation and performance.

7. Identify the steps involved in implementing a management by objectives (MBO) program.

8. Explain the key factors involved in expectancy theory.

9. Examine the key principles of equity theory.

10. Explain how open communication builds teamwork and describe how managers are likely to motivate teams in the future.

LEARNING THE LANGUAGE

Listed below are important terms found in the chapter. Choose the correct term for each definition and write it in the space provided.

Equity theory	Intrinsic reward	Maslow's Hierarchy of needs
Expectancy theory	Job enlargement	Motivators
Extrinsic reward	Job enrichment	Principle of motion economy
Goal-setting theory	Job rotation	Scientific management
Hawthorne effect	Job simplification	Time-motion studies
Hygiene factors	Management by objectives (MBO)	

1. Elements of a job called _____ cause dissatisfaction if missing, but do not motivate if increased.

2. The process of _____ produces task efficiency by breaking down the job into simple steps and assigning people to each of those steps.

3. _____ are studies of the tasks performed to complete a job and the time needed to do each task.

4. A(n) _____ is the good feeling you have when you have done a job well.

5. A system of goal setting and implementation known as _____ involves a cycle of discussion, review, and evaluation of objectives among top and middle-level managers, supervisors, and employees.

6. A strategy known as _____ combines a series of tasks into one assignment that is more challenging and interesting.

7. A(n) _____ is something given to you by someone else as recognition for good work, including pay increases, praise, and promotions.

8. A motivational strategy that emphasizes motivating the workers through the job itself is called_____.

9. Factors known as _____ cause employees to be productive and give them satisfaction.

10. The theory of _____ is that setting specific, attainable goals can motivate workers and improve performance if the goals are accepted, accompanied by feedback and facilitated by organizational conditions.

11. The _____ refers to the tendency for people to behave differently when they know they are being studied.

12. _____ is a job enrichment strategy involving moving employees from one job to another.

13. Victor Vroom's _____ indicates that the amount of effort employees exert on a specific task depends on their expectations of the outcome.

14. The study of workers to find the most efficient way of doing things and then teaching people those techniques is known as _____.

15. _____ proposes that employees try to maintain perceived balance between inputs and outputs compared to others in similar positions.

16. _____ is the theory that every job can be broken down into a series of elementary motions.

17. The motivation theory called _____ places different types of human needs in order of importance, including basic physiological needs to safety, social, esteem, and self-actualization needs.

ASSESSMENT CHECK

Learning Goal 1   **The Importance of Motivation**

1. What is the difference between an intrinsic reward and an extrinsic reward?

2. Who is known as the Father of Scientific Management? What was his goal?

3. What three elements were basic to Taylor's Scientific Management?

a. _____

b. _____

c. _____

4.   What did Taylor believe was the way to improve productivity?

5.   What is Gantt best known for?

6.   What contribution to scientific management was made by Frank and Lillian Gilbreth?

7.   What view of workers was held by proponents of scientific management?

Learning Goal 2   **The Hawthorne Studies (Mayo)**

8.   What did the Hawthorne Experiments originally intend to test?

9.   What was the problem with Mayo's initial experiments?

10. Why did the experimenters believe the Hawthorne Experiments were a failure after the second series of experiments?

11. List three conclusions drawn from the Hawthorne Experiments

   a. _____

   _____

   b. _____

   _____

   c. _____

   _____

12. What is the Hawthorne effect?

13. How did research assumptions change after the Hawthorne Experiments?

14.   What did Maslow believe about motivation?

15.   Identify the five need levels on Maslow's Hierarchy?

   a. _____

   b. _____

   c. _____

   d. _____

   e. _____

16.   According to Maslow, what kinds of needs are people motivated to satisfy? What happens when
        a need is satisfied?

17.   What must U.S. firms do with regard to motivation, in order to successfully compete?

18.   According to Andrew Grove, where does motivation come from? What kind of people are
       achievers, according to Grove?

Learning Goal 4   **McGregor's Theory X and Theory Y**

19.   List the assumptions of a Theory X manager.

       a._____

       b._____

       c._____

       d._____

20.   How do the attitudes of a Theory X manager affect his/her behavior?

21.   What are the assumptions of a Theory Y manager?

       a._____

       b._____

       c._____

       d._____

       e._____

f. _____

g. _____

22. How does this theory Y manager's attitude affect his/her behavior toward employees?

23. What steps should management follow in order to use "empowerment" as a motivator?

a. _____

b. _____

c. _____

24. What is the management trend in today's companies? Why?

25. List the major elements of Ouchi's "Type J" management approach.

a. _____

b. _____

c. _____

d. _____

e. _____

f. _____

g. _____

26.   How do the ideas of Type J contrast with Ouchi's "Type A?"

27.   What is the difference between a Type J firm and a Type A firm?

28.   What is Theory Z, and what are the major elements?

29.   How is the Japanese management system changing? Why?

30.   What did Herzberg's research find were the most important factors that motivate workers?

a. _____   h. _____

b. _____   i. _____

c. _____   j. _____

d. _____   k. _____

e. _____   l. _____

f. _____   m. _____

g. _____   n. _____

31.   Based upon this list, what did Herzberg note about workers with regard to what motivates them and what doesn't motivate them?

32.   Identify Herzberg's motivators.

a. _____

b. _____

c. _____

d. _____

e. _____

33.   List Herzberg's hygiene factors.

a. _____

b. _____

c. _____

d. _____

e. _____

34.   What impact do motivating factors have on workers? What about hygiene factors?

35.   What conclusions come from combining McGregor's Theory Y with Herzberg's motivating factors?

36.   Is money the number one motivator for most people? Why or why not?

Learning Goal 6   **Job Enrichment**

37.   How is job enrichment implemented?

38.   List the five characteristics of work important in affecting individual motivation and performance. Include a brief description of each.

a. _____

b. _____

c. _____

d. _____

e. _____

39.   What is the difference between job enlargement and job rotation?

Learning Goal 7   **Goal-Setting Theory and Management By Objectives**

40.   What is the basic principle of goal-setting theory?

41. What four things does a manager do in an MBO program?

42. What are the six steps in an MBO program?

a. _____

b. _____

c. _____

d. _____

e. _____

f. _____

43. What is the difference between helping and coaching?

Learning Goal 8   **Meeting Employee Expectations : Expectancy Theory**

44. According to expectancy theory, what are three questions employees ask before exerting maximum effort to a task?

45.   What are the steps to improving employee performance, according to expectancy theory?

a. _____

b. _____

c. _____

d. _____

e. _____

Learning Goal 9   **Treating Employees Fairly : Equity Theory**

46.   What is the basic principle of equity theory, and what role do perceptions play in equity theory?

47.   What do people do when they perceive an inequity?

48.   What's a key point to remember about equity theory, and how might organizations address the challenge?

49.   What are two things companies with highly motivated work forces have done?

50.   What are things companies can do to encourage open communication?

a. _____

b. _____

c. _____

d. _____

51.   What is meant by "re-inventing work?"

52.   Describe the lessons learned about motivation from the Miller Brewing Company and the Mary Kay examples.

a. _____

b. _____

c. _____

53. How will managers of tomorrow motivate workers? Why?

54. How will generational differences between baby boomers and Generation X affect motivation?

CRITICAL THINKING EXERCISES

Learning Goal 1

1. Early management studies were conducted by:

   Frederick Taylor - Scientific Management

   Frank and Lillian Gilbreth - Motion economy

   H.L. Gantt - Gantt charts

   Elton Mayo – Hawthorne Experiments

   Read the following and indicate which ideas are being described.

   a. Conducted a series of experiments designed to measure the effect of working conditions on worker productivity. _____

   b. These studies became the basis for human-based management._____

   c. Developed "therbligs."_____

   d. Created time-motion studies to measure output over time._____

   e. Discovered that worker productivity could increase despite adverse conditions._____

f. Believed the way to improve productivity was to scientifically study the most efficient way to do things, then teach people those methods._____

g. Developed a chart plotting employees' work a day in advance._____

h. The principle of motion economy was based on his theory._____

i. Developed the principle of scientific management._____

j. Discovered that when workers are involved in planning and decision-making, productivity tends to increase. _____

k. Found that workers were motivated in an informal atmosphere where they could interact with supervisors._____

l. Believed people would be motivated primarily by money._____

m. Identified the tendency for people to behave differently when they know they are being studied._____

n. Developed the idea that every job could be broken down into a series of elementary motions, which could then be analyzed to make it more efficient. _____

o. The findings led to new assumptions about employees, including the idea that pay is not the only motivator for workers. _____

Learning Goal 1, 2

2. How did Taylor and other proponents of Scientific Management view workers?

How does that compare to Mayo's Hawthorne Studies?

3.   The principle behind Maslow's ideas is that only unmet needs are motivators and that needs could be arranged in a hierarchy.

Complete the illustration shown below, and give two examples for each need level, where appropriate.

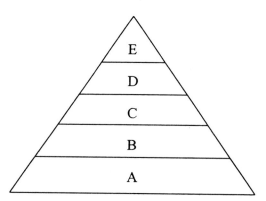

A. _____   D._____

    1._____   1._____

    2._____   2._____

B. _____   E._____

    1._____   1._____

    2._____   2._____

C._____

    1._____

    2._____

4. Read the following statements and determine which need on Maslow's Hierarchy is being described.

   a. Ryan Raley gets home from school and immediately raids the refrigerator _____

   b. Jan Stahl joins as many campus organizations as she can fit into her schedule. _____

   c. Bill Cook wins "Zone Manager of the Month" in his sales office in recognition of his outstanding performance. _____

   d. Wendy Armstrong, a 33-year-old student with severe cerebral palsy, receives her bachelor's degree, a lifelong dream._____

   e. A union contract negotiator makes sure that layoffs will be made on the basis of seniority. _____

5. In developed countries, people seek to fill social, self-esteem, and self-actualization needs at work. Give two actions that a company or a manager could take to fill each of these higher level needs. What would motivate you?

   a. Social

   b. Self-esteem

   c. Self-actualization

6. McGregor observed that managers had two different attitudes toward workers which led to different management styles. He called these styles Theory X and Theory Y.

   Which type of manager would make each of the following statements?

   a. "Joe is pretty good at solving these kinds of problems. Let's get his input on this."_____

   b. "Ann, I know you'd like that promotion. Keep up the good work, and I think you'll be the next new product manager." _____

c. "Tell that secretary that if she values her job, she'll keep those coffee breaks down to 15 minutes!" _____

d. "I think that secretary takes long coffee breaks because she gets her work done so quickly and then doesn't have much to do. She's been asking about working on the new product project. I'll talk to her about it and see what she thinks." _____

e. " Ann, new product managers have to work a lot of weekends and evenings. If you think you want that job, you'll have to prove to me you're willing to work those extra hours."

_____

7. What kind of leadership style would a Theory X manager use most often?

Theory Y? Why?

8. How does empowerment fit into Theory X/Y?

Learning Goal 5

9. Workers at Universal Industries are among the best paid in the industry. Their factories are clean and workers seem to get along well with one another. "The bosses are okay" one worker is quoted as saying, "but they sure do hang around us a lot." The union has made sure that everyone has a secure position. Management at Universal is aware that their competitive position is in jeopardy, as several foreign firms have been making inroads into their market. Management is also aware that while there doesn't seem to be any problems with the workers, they don't seem to be motivated. Using Herzberg's theory of motivators and hygiene factors, discuss what the problem may be.

10. Make your own personal ranking of the 14 job related factors listed in the text. Relate them to a job you have had, or currently have, to explain why you were or were not motivated!

1._____   8._____

2._____   9._____

3._____   10._____

4._____   11._____

5._____   12._____

6._____   13._____

7._____   14._____

Learning Goal 4, 5, 6

11. Using the outline below, illustrate the relationship between Maslow, Herzberg and where McGregor's X and Y managers would fall.

MASLOW   HERZBERG   MCGREGOR

12. What kind of leadership (or management) style would the theories of Maslow, Herzberg and McGregor indicate is best for motivating employees?

Learning Goal 6

13. Four job design strategies are;

    job enrichment   job enlargement

    job simplification   job rotation

    Which of the following is being illustrated in each of the following examples? Use each strategy only once.

    a. Employees at Published Image, a financial newsletter, are combined into a team so that one team has the entire responsibility of selling, writing, proofing, editing, and distributing the newsletter to their own group of clients. While each member will specialize in a certain area, each member of the team knows enough about all the jobs to get the product out.

    b. New zone managers at Ford Motor Company move from one job to another during their training program to familiarize themselves with the operations of the district sales office.

    c. At the Pasta House Company restaurant, you are either an expediter, a host, a busser, or a server. The job lines don't cross and are distinct from one another.

    d. At the Hosin Manufacturing Company, production is such that each worker makes an entire motor, instead of working only on separate parts.

14. Keeping in mind the five characteristics of work important in affecting motivation and performance, design an "enriched" job for publishing campus newsletters or for another area with which you are familiar.

15.   How does job enrichment relate to Herzberg and Maslow?

16.   Things have really been happening at Music-stor. Lots of changes have been made and it would
       seem like things ought to be going smoothly. However, there are problems with the workers,
       and you just can't figure out what's wrong. People don't seem to be motivated, although they are
       being paid well. You have been in charge, made the decisions you thought were best for the
       company and the workers, and have even pitched in and shown people how you want things done
       from time to time. Everybody has his/her own job, and they know exactly how it's supposed to
       be done. You have heard some people complain that their job is boring, but you know that the
       way you have shown them is the best way to get things done. People come in late, and
       sometimes seem to actually resent your help! You would really like the employees of this
       company to feel like they are a team. How will you solve this problem?

       Re-read your answer - Are you a Theory X or a Theory Y manager?

Learning Goal 7

17.   Review the six steps of implementing an MBO program described in the text. How does an
        MBO program fit into the ideas of Maslow and Herzberg? Why is the third step a key step in the
        program?   What are some potential problems with MBO?

18.   Think about expectancy theory and how it works for you. What is something you really want? How likely is it that you can reach the goal? Will the hard work be worth the effort? For example:

What do you need to do to accomplish the goal? Is it possible if you exert the effort?

What intrinsic and extrinsic benefits will you get from accomplishing the goal?

19.   Hal Yard is in marketing with a major manufacturer of sailboats. He has been happy with his job since he started there 3 years ago. He has received several raises, and has always gotten very good reviews. He is in line for a good promotion, which he should know about soon. Hal recently went to lunch with a new co-worker, Donna Telli. Donna just got her degree at night school, and this is her first "real" job. During the course of their conversation, Donna mentioned her starting salary, which is only $50 per month lower than Hal's!

How would you feel if you were Hal? Why? What would you do? What theories of motivation may come into play here?

20.   If you are currently working, think about the ways that your company encourages, or discourages, open communication. If you aren't working, ask the same questions of someone you know who is working.

PRACTICE TEST

Multiple Choice – Circle the best answer

1. Time and motion studies, methods of work and rules of work were all part of the ideas of

   _____.

   a. Maslow's hierarchy of needs
   b. Herzberg's two factor theory
   c. Taylor's scientific management
   d. the Hawthorne Experiments

2. Which of the following was not a part of the Hawthorne Experiments?

   a. Workers enjoyed the atmosphere of their special room
   b. The workers thought of themselves as a social group
   c. The workers expected to be involved in the planning of the experiment
   d. Workers felt their ideas were respected

3. Frederick Taylor believed the best way to improve worker productivity was to:

   a. scientifically determine the most efficient way to do things and then teach people those steps.
   b. design jobs to be interesting and challenging.
   c. determine people's needs at work and find ways to meet those needs.
   d. give people the authority to make decisions.

4. Which of the following is not included as one of Maslow's needs?

   a. self-actualization
   b. social
   c. physical
   d. esteem

5. Harry Leggins has worked for Shavem Up for a number of years. He has just been passed over for promotion again, and is considering leaving his employer because it seems that his managers don't appreciate his abilities. The only problem is that he really likes his co-workers, and they need him as a member of their undefeated softball team. Harry is concerned with filling:

   a. esteem needs.
   b. social needs.
   c. self-actualization needs.
   d. safety needs.

6. Douglas McGregor believed that managers with a Theory X attitude believed:

   a. workers prefer to be directed.
   b. people seek responsibility.
   c. people will use imagination in problem solving.
   d. workers like work.

7. At Flo Valley Manufacturing workers are encouraged to find their own solutions to problems, and to implement their solutions when practical. They work with little supervision because management feels they are committed workers and that the workers are pretty creative. Flo Valley reflects a _____ attitude about workers.

   a. Theory Z
   b. autocratic
   c. scientific
   d. Theory Y

8. _____ emphasizes life-time employment, collective decision making, and individual responsibility for the outcome of decisions.

   a. Theory Z
   b. Theory X
   c. Theory Y
   d. Theory M

9. Herzberg motivators include:

   a. job security.
   b. salary.
   c. working conditions.
   d. recognition.

10. According to Herzberg, workers felt that good pay and job security

    a. are the most important motivators for most workers.

    b. were important for participative management.

    c. provided a sense of satisfaction, but did not motivate them.

    d. were the best way to keep jobs interesting and to help them achieve their objectives.

11. Which statement does not fit with the ideas of Herzberg and McGregor regarding the most effective way to motivate workers?

    a. Employees work best when mangers assumes employees are self-motivated.

    b. The best way to motivate employees is to make sure they know exactly what to do and how to do it.

    c. Interesting jobs is one of the best ways to motivate workers.

    d. It is important to recognize achievement through advancement and added responsibility.

12. The strategy of making work interesting and motivating employees by moving them from one job to another is called:

    a. job enlargement.

    b. job simplification.

    c. job rotation.

    d. job enrichment.

13. The degree to which a job has a substantial impact on the work of others in the company is called:

    a. skill variety.

    b. task identity.

    c. autonomy.

    d. task significance.

14. At the NOVA car manufacturing company, workers are grouped into self-managed teams, which are responsible for completing a significant portion of the automobile. Unlike the typical assembly plant, the car stops along the way, and the team completes their portion of the car before the vehicle moves on. The team is given the freedom to decide who does which job, and they receive constant feedback from the company. NOVA is using a job strategy of:

   a. job rotation.
   b. job enlargement.
   c. job enrichment.
   d. job simplification.

15. Management by Objectives calls for managers to do all of the following except:

   a. set a date for employees to turn in their goals to management.
   b. commit employees to those goals.
   c. use two way communication.
   d. reward accomplishment.

16. Which of the following is not one of the questions employees will ask themselves before committing a maximum effort toward a task?

   a. Can I accomplish this task?
   b. Is the reward worth the effort?
   c. Will I have help in accomplishing this task?
   d. If I do accomplish the task, what is the reward?

17. According to equity theory, when workers perceive an inequity, they will

   a. try to reestablish an equitable feeling
   b. always reduce their efforts in the future
   c. always increase their effort in the future
   d. generally be mistaken in their perceptions

18. According to the text, companies with highly motivated workers usually have

   a. high pay scales and good benefits
   b. good managers who tell employees exactly what to do and how to do it
   c. open communication systems and self-managed teams
   d. autocratic leadership and bureaucratic structures

19. To create an atmosphere of "us working together" and encourage open communication, managers should do everything but:

    a. provide feedback.

    b. eliminate separate facilities for managers.

    c. develop precise job descriptions so that everyone knows what to do.

    d. reward all upward communication, even if the discussion is negative.

20. The experiences of Mary Kay and Miller Brewing Company tell us:

    a. the future of industry and business depends upon advanced technology.

    b. motivation is best provided by managers.

    c. the first step to a motivation program is open communication.

    d. workers are primarily motivated by money and job security.

True-False

1. _____ The problem with the initial experiments of the Hawthorne Study was that the productivity of the experimental group actually decreased when lighting was changed.

2. _____ The satisfaction you feel when you have finished a term paper and done a good job is an example of an extrinsic reward.

3. _____ Frank and Lillian Gilbreth developed the principle of motion economy and therbligs.

4. _____ The Hawthorne Experiments led to new assumptions about workers, including that pay was not the only motivator.

5. _____ According to Maslow, people will always try to satisfy higher level needs before they focus on lower level needs.

6. _____ Maslow believes that in developed countries, basic needs such as those for food and shelter dominate workers' motivation.

7. _____ A Theory X manager believes that employees should be involved in both defining problems and in designing the solutions.

8. _____ Theory Z principles have been widely adopted by American companies.

9. _____ Herzberg's research results showed that the most important factors that motivate workers were a sense of achievement and earned recognition.

10. _____ Goal-setting theory is based on the notion that managers and employees together should set specific goals to be reached.

11. _____ The basic principle of expectancy theory is that workers try to maintain equity when they compare what they expect to gain to people in similar situations.

12. _____ The concept of re-inventing work involves respecting workers, rewarding good work, developing worker skills, and decentralizing authority.

You Can Find It On the Net

Sometimes we wonder what companies can do to create a motivated workforce in the "real world." Go to the Fortune Magazine web site www.fortune.com. Link to the magazine's list of America's Most Admired Companies, the top 100 companies to work for in the United States.

What do you think makes these companies good places to work?

What is their turnover rate?

Are the starting salaries exceptionally high?

Do they offer benefits that are unique or unusual?

Continue on to the accompanying story on America's Top Employers.

What does the article indicate about the companies on the list? Why are their workers so happy to work there?

ANSWERS

LEARNING THE LANGUAGE

1. Hygiene factors	7. Extrinsic reward	13. Expectancy Theory
2. Job simplification	8. Job enrichment	14. Scientific management
3. Time-motion studies	9. Motivators	15. Equity theory
4. Intrinsic reward	10. Goal setting theory	16. Principle of motion economy
5. Management by objectives	11. Hawthorne effect	17. Maslow's hierarchy of needs
6. Job enlargement	12. Job rotation	

ASSESSMENT CHECK

The Importance of Motivation

1. An intrinsic reward is a good feeling after having done a job well. It comes from within. An extrinsic reward is something given to you by someone else as recognition for good work

2. Frederick Taylor is known as the Father of Scientific Management. His goal was to increase worker productivity so that both the firm and the worker could benefit from higher earnings.

3. a. time

   b. methods

   c. rules of work

4. The way to improve productivity according to Taylor was to scientifically study the most efficient way to do things, determine the one best way, and then teach people those methods.

5. Gantt is best known for charts which managers use to plot the work of employees a day in advance down to the smallest detail.

6. Frank and Lillian Gilbreth used Taylor's ideas to develop the principle of motion economy, which showed that every job could be broken down into a series of elementary motions called a therblig.

7. Scientific management viewed people largely as machines that needed to be programmed. There was little concern for psychological or human aspects of work.

The Hawthorne Studies (Mayo)

8. Elton Mayo and his colleagues wanted to test the degree of lighting associated with optimum productivity.

9. The problem with the initial experiments was that productivity of the experimental group compared to other workers doing the same job went up regardless of whether the lighting was bright or dim.

10. The second series of experiments added a number of other environmental factors to the experiment, such as temperature and humidity. Productivity went up with each experiment. No matter what the experimenters did, productivity went up thus proving the initial ideas were invalid.

11. a. People in work groups think of themselves as a social group
    b. Involving employees in decision making motivates them
    c. Job satisfaction increases with a friendly atmosphere and additional compensation

12. The Hawthorne Effect refers to the tendency for people to behave differently when they know they're being studied.

13. After the Hawthorne Experiments, the emphasis of research shifted away from Taylor's scientific management to a new human-based management.

Motivation and Maslow's Hierarchy of Needs

14. Maslow believed that motivation arises from needs.

15. a. Physiological   d. Self-esteem
    b. Safety   e. Self-actualization
    c. Social

16. Maslow believed that people are motivated to satisfy unmet needs. When one need is satisfied another, higher level need emerges, and a person will attempt to satisfy that need. Needs that have been satisfied do not provide motivation.

17. To compete successfully, U.S. firms must create a work environment that motivates the best and brightest workers. This means establishing a work environment that includes goals such as social contribution, honesty, reliability, service, quality, dependability, and unity.

18. According to Andrew Grove, all motivation comes from within. People who are "self-actualized" are achievers.

McGregor's Theory X and Theory Y

19.   a. The average person dislikes work and will avoid it if possible.

       b. The average person must be forced, controlled, directed or threatened with punishment to make them work.

       c. The average worker prefers to be directed, wants to avoid responsibility, has little ambition and wants security.

       d. Primary motivators are money and fear.

20. A Theory X manager will hang over people, telling them what to do and how to do it. Motivation will take the form of punishment for bad work, rather than reward for good work.

     Workers are given little responsibility, authority, or flexibility.

21.   a. The average person likes work, and feels it is as natural as play or rest.

       b. The average person naturally works toward goals to which they are committed.

       c. How committed a person is to goals depends on the rewards for achieving them.

       d. Under certain conditions, the average person accepts and seeks responsibility.

       e. People are capable of creativity, cleverness, and imagination.

       f. The average person's intellectual potential is only partially used in industry.

       g. People are motivated by a variety of rewards, unique to each worker.

22. A Theory Y manager will emphasize a more relaxed atmosphere, in which workers are free to set objectives, be creative, be flexible, and go beyond the goals set by management. A key factor in this environment is empowerment, which gives employees the ability to make decisions and the tools to implement the decisions they make.

23.   a. Find out what problems people think are in the organization.

       b. Let them design the solutions

       c. Get out of the way and let them put the solutions into action

24. The trend today is toward a Theory Y management style. One reason for this is that many service industries are finding Theory Y is more conducive to dealing with on the spot customer problems.

25. The elements of Type J management include:
    a. life-time employment
    b. consensual decision making
    c. collective responsibility
    d. slow promotion and evaluation
    e. implicit informal control
    f. nonspecific career paths
    g. holistic concern for employees

26. The type A, American management, approach differs significantly from the Type J. Type A involves short-term employment, individual decision-making, individual responsibility for the outcomes of decisions, rapid evaluation and promotion, explicit control mechanisms, specialized career paths and segmented concern from employees.

27. Type J firms are based on the culture of Japan, a focus on trust and intimacy within the group and family. Similarly, Type A firms are based on the culture of America. But our cultures are different and the American culture focuses on individual rights and achievements.

28. Theory Z blends the characteristics of Type J and Type A. This approach involves long-term employment, collective decision-making, individual responsibility for the outcome of decisions, slow evaluation and promotion, moderately specialized career paths, and a holistic concern for the employee, including the family. Theory Z emphasizes participative decision-making and views the organization as a family that fosters cooperation and organizational values.

29. Negative economic growth, demographic and social changes, and fierce global competition are forcing Japanese managers to reevaluate the way they conduct business. Japanese managers and firms need more dynamic ways to become more efficient in order to compete more effectively in today's changing global economy. Companies such as Hitachi have, for example, eliminated the ritual morning exercises. Managers felt that these morning exercises symbolized doing the same thing the same way, and reinforces that employees don't take risks or think for themselves.

Herzberg's Motivating Factors

30.
    a. sense of achievement
    b. earned recognition
    c. interest in the work
    d. opportunity for growth
    e. opportunity for advancement
    f. importance of responsibility
    g. peer and group relationships

    h. pay
    i. supervisor's fairness
    j. company policies and rules
    k. status
    l. job security
    m. supervisor's friendliness
    n. working conditions

31. Herzberg noted that the factors that motivated workers clustered around job content. Workers like to feel that they contribute. They want to earn recognition and feel their jobs are important. They want responsibility and want recognition for that responsibility by having a chance for growth and advancement. They also want their jobs to be interesting.

   Herzberg also noted that factors having to do with job environment were not considered motivators by workers. This includes pay, which workers feel gives them a sense of satisfaction, but does not motivate.

32. Herzberg's motivators are:
   a. The work itself
   b. Achievement
   c. Recognition
   d. Responsibility
   e. Growth and advancement

33. Hygiene factors are:
   a. Company policy and administration
   b. Supervision
   c. Working conditions
   d. Interpersonal relations
   e. Salary, status, job security

34. Motivators cause employees to be productive and gave them a great deal of satisfaction. Workers felt that the absence of hygiene factors, such as good pay, job security, friendly supervisors, and the like could cause dissatisfaction, but the presence of those factors did not motivate them; they just provided satisfaction and contentment in the work situation.

35. Employees work best when management assumes that employees are competent and self motivated. Theory Y calls for a participative style of management. The best way to motivate employees is to emphasize motivators by making the job interesting, helping employees to achieve their objectives, and by recognizing that achievement through advancement and added responsibility.

36. Surveys conducted to test Herzberg's theories have supported the findings that money is not the number one motivator, but rather a sense of achievement and recognition for a job well done. The reason for this is that most organizations review an employee's performance once a year, and allocate raises once a year. To inspire and motivate employees to perform their best, achievements and progress toward goals must be recognized more than once a year.

Job Enrichment

37. In a program of job enrichment, work is assigned to individuals so that they have the opportunity to complete an identifiable task from beginning to end. They are held responsible for successful completion of the task.

38.   a. Skill variety—the extent to which a job demands different skills

           b. Task identity—the degree to which the job requires doing a task with a visible outcome

           c. Task significance—the degree to which the job has a substantial impact on the lives or work of others

           d. Autonomy—the degree of freedom, independence, and discretion in scheduling work and determining procedures.

           e. Feedback—the amount of direct and clear information that is received about job performance.

39.   Job enlargement combines a series of tasks into one assignment that is more challenging, interesting, and motivating. Job rotation also makes work more interesting, but does so by moving employees from one job to another.

Goal-Setting Theory and Management by Objectives

40.   Goal-setting theory is based on the notion that setting specific but attainable goals will lead to high levels of motivation and performance if goals are accepted, accompanied by feedback, and facilitated by organizational conditions.

41.   Management by Objectives calls on managers to formulate goals in cooperation with everyone in the organization, to commit employees to those goals, to monitor results and to reward accomplishment.

42.   a. Managers set goals in cooperation with subordinates and provide the means to meet them

           b. Objectives are set for each department, including deadlines

           c. Individual objectives are set by managers and the individual, in writing.

           d. Constant two-way communication and review to show employees progress

           e. Results are evaluated

           f. Reward employees for achieving the goals

43.   Helping means working with the subordinates and doing part of the work if necessary. Coaching means acting as a resource, teaching, guiding, and recommending, but not participating or actively doing the task.

Meeting Employee Expectations : Expectancy Theory

44.   Before exerting maximum effort employees will ask:

           a. Can I accomplish the task?

           b. If I do accomplish it, what's my reward?

           c. Is the reward worth the effort?

45. To improve employee performance, based on expectancy theory managers should:
    a. determine what rewards are valued by employees
    b. determine the employee's desired performance standard
    c. ensure performance standards are attainable
    d. guarantee rewards are tied to performance
    e. be certain rewards are considered adequate

Treating Employees Fairly: Equity Theory

46. The basic principle of equity theory is that workers try to maintain equity between inputs and outputs compared to people in similar positions. It is based on the perceptions of fairness and how those perceptions affect employees' willingness to perform.

47. When workers perceive an inequity, they will try to make the situation more equitable. They may change their behavior or rationalize the situation in some way.

48. A key element to equity theory is that equity, or inequity, is based upon *perception* of reality. Workers often overestimate their own contributions, and so they are often going to feel that there is a lot of inequity. Sometimes organizations try to deal with this by keeping salaries secret, but that can make things worse. The best remedy is clear and frequent communication.

Building Teamwork Through Open Communication

49. Companies with highly motivated work forces have established open communication and implemented self-managed teams.

50. a. Top management must create an organizational culture that rewards listening by being listeners themselves, and by facilitating discussion.
    b. Train supervisors and managers in listening.
    c. Get rid of barriers to open communication, such as separate offices, parking spaces bathrooms, and other facilities for various levels of management and workers.
    d. Make efforts to facilitate open communication, with such things as large tables in lunch areas, conference rooms, picnics, company athletic teams and so on.

51. Re-inventing work means respecting workers, providing interesting work, rewarding good work, developing workers' skills, allowing autonomy and decentralizing authority.

52. The lessons learned from Miller and Mary Kay are:
    a. the future growth of industry and business in general depends on a motivated productive work force.
    b. motivation is largely internal, generated by the workers themselves.
    c. the first step in any motivation program is to establish open communication among workers and managers so that the feeling is one of cooperation and teamwork.

53. The managers of tomorrow will not be able to use any one formula for all employees. Instead, they will have to get to know each worker personally and tailor the motivational effort to the individual. This is true because different employees respond to different managerial and motivational styles. This is further complicated by the increase in global business and the fact that managers now work with employees from many different cultures.

54. Baby boomer managers will need to learn to be flexible with their Generation X employees, or risk losing them. Generation X employees will need to use their enthusiasm for change and streamlining to their advantage.

CRITICAL THINKING EXERCISES

1. a. Hawthorne Experiments   i. Taylor
    b. Hawthorne Experiments   j. Hawthorne Experiments
    c. Gilbreth   k. Hawthorne Experiments
    d. Taylor   l. Taylor
    e. Hawthorne Experiments   m. Hawthorne Experiments
    f. Taylor   n. Gilbreth
    g. Gantt   o. Hawthorne Experiments
    h. Taylor

2. Taylor and the other proponents of scientific management viewed people largely as machines which, properly programmed, could perform at a high level of effectiveness. Time and motion specialists studied every move a worker made, and standardized every motion. The most important tools were a stopwatch and observation.

    Although the Hawthorne studies grew out of Taylor's research, they came to a very different conclusion. Mayo began by studying environmental effects on worker productivity, with the idea of determining the degree of lighting associated with optimum productivity. When productivity increased regardless of the amount of illumination, a second series of experiments was conducted. When those, too, failed, Mayo guessed that some human or psychological factor was involved. When workers were interviewed about their feelings Mayo recognized that people were motivated at work by a relaxed atmosphere, being involved in decision-making, and by being in a social group as well as by additional compensation.

The Hawthorne Studies, then, recognized the human and psychological factors that impact worker productivity. This was different from scientific management, which ignored the human aspect of work.

3. Your answers may vary. Here are some examples.

A. Physiological
   1. Food
   2. Rest

B. Safety
   1. Locks on your doors
   2. Job security

C. Social
   1. Belonging to a club
   2. Family life

D. Self-esteem
   1. Winning an award
   2. Getting a desired promotion

E. Self-actualization
   1. Accomplishing a goal
   2. Getting an "A" in a difficult class

4. a. Physiological
   b. Social
   c. Self-esteem
   d. Self-actualization
   e. Safety

5. a. Here are some examples: To fill social needs, companies could sponsor baseball teams, hold picnics, implement self-managed work teams.

   b. Esteem needs can be met by recognition programs, recognizing an employee's achievement in a company newsletter, allowing employees to participate in decision-making.

   c. To help fill self-actualization needs, companies could offer tuition assistance programs, provide job training, allow people to set their own goals, implement self-managed work teams, provide appropriate rewards for accomplishing objectives.

6. a. Y   e. Y
   b. Y   f. X
   c. X

7. A Theory X manager would most likely use an autocratic style of leadership. When a manager believes that workers prefer to be told what to do, and do not want to assume responsibility, they are not likely to involve workers in decision making. A Theory X manager will make decisions, then announce the decision to his/her workers.

A Theory Y manager is more likely to use a more democratic or participative leadership style. Employee input will be important to a Y manager, who believes that people are creative and seek responsibility. A Theory Y manager may also lean toward a laissez-faire leadership style.

8. Empowerment means giving employees the right to make decisions and the tools to implement those decisions. Theory Y emphasizes a "freer" managerial style where workers are free to set goals and reach them. In essence Theory Y empowers employees to reach their potential.

9. From Herzberg's perspective, it looks like management and the union both have been concentrating on hygiene factors, while ignoring those factors that would motivate workers to greater productivity. The workers are apparently satisfied, as there are no problems, according to management. This means that the workers are content with pay, supervision, working conditions and interpersonal relations, as is indicated throughout the story. If management wants motivated workers, they should continue what they are doing now, but also find ways to give workers a sense of achievement, make the work more interesting, give workers more responsibility, a chance for growth and advancement. According to Herzberg, these are factors which will motivate workers.

10. The way you have ranked the 14 job-related factors Herzberg researched will be unique to you. Look, however, to see which type of things you ranked near the top, and near the bottom. Are motivators more important to you? or, did you focus on those factors Herzberg listed as hygiene factors? If the motivators ranked highest, you may want to look at firms which are using the "new" approach to management. If hygiene factors ranked highest, you may be happier in a more traditional organizational setting.

11. Comparing Maslow, Herzberg and McGregor

MASLOW	HERZBERG	MCGREGOR
	Motivators	
self-actualization	challenge	Theory Y
	work itself	
self-esteem	achievement	Participative management
	recognition	style
	responsibility	
	growth	
	Hygiene	
social	interpersonal relations	
safety	company policy	Theory X
	supervision	Autocratic management
	working conditions	style
physiological	salary	

12. Generally, these theories indicate that a participative or democratic management style is most effective in motivating most employees. Employees work best when management assumes that employees are competent and self motivated.

13. a. job enrichment   c. job simplification
     b. job rotation   d. job enlargement

14. An "enriched" job would include skill variety, task identity, task significance, autonomy and feedback. For publishing a newsletter, you could create self-managed teams, with each team member trained to do all the jobs necessary to get the newsletter out on deadline: editing, proofing, research, layout, selling advertising, fielding questions. The team members will be responsible for deciding which member will do what job will establish what the deadline needs to be, coordinate with the other teams, and will they evaluate their own performance. This meets all the criteria identified.

15. With job enrichment, work is assigned to individuals or groups so that they have the opportunity to complete an identifiable task from beginning to end. They are held responsible for successful completion of the task. The motivation comes from the opportunities for personal achievement, challenge and recognition, which are Herzberg's motivators, and which meet the higher level needs on Maslow's hierarchy.

16. How you would solve these problems is really up to you. It's a matter of personal style. However, there are some suggestions. You may want to sit down with these people and find out exactly what they think the problem is, or even if they recognize that there is a problem. It will help to listen to them, ask for their suggestions about how to solve the problems and implement those suggestions.

     It sounds like you have been making most of the decisions yourself, and not generally trusting these workers to be responsible. In other words, sounds like you have used a Theory X approach focusing on Herzberg's hygiene factors as a way to increase productivity. This may be appropriate in some instances, but you recall from previous chapters that these are the "new breed" of workers who may prefer less direction and "bossing" and more "coaching." You can act as a resource, teaching, guiding, and recommending but not actively participating in doing work. Allow them to decide the most appropriate way of designing their jobs. Programs such as job enlargement may be appropriate, or job rotation. You may also consider self-managed teams. Many of the programs and theories described in this chapter suggest the solutions to your problems.

17. MBO programs fill upper level needs on Maslow's hierarchy and serve as motivators in Herzberg's terms by giving workers responsibility, a chance for growth and help in meeting their own personal goals. The third step is a key one because it focuses on the participative management aspects of MBO, the type of leadership or management style these theories support.

Problems with MBO can arise when management uses it as a strategy to force managers and workers to commit to goals that are not mutually agreed on, but set by top management.

18. The answer to this question will depend on what your goals are and how hard you are willing to work to reach them. The level of motivation you feel will be determined, according to expectancy theory, by how strongly you value what you say your goals are, and whether or not you feel like you can "make the grade" or get the kind of job you want. And lastly, your motivation will be determined by whether or not you feel that the effort would actually be worth it.

19. If you were Hal, you may feel like there is an inequity in your level of compensation compared to Donna's. This is equity theory at work! After all, she is new, and you have been a good employee for three years. What you would do will depend upon your own view of how big the inequity is. You may choose to talk to your boss, work harder to get promoted and recognized, work a little less for a while, rationalize the inequity in some way, or take the afternoon off!

20. In the end, it is really the individual who motivates him or herself. The manager's job is to understand that all workers are different and respond to different motivational styles. Managers will have to get to know each worker as an individual and fit the "reward" to each individual. Rewards will come from the job itself rather that from external rewards. Managers need to give workers what they need to do a good job: the right tools, the right information, and the right amount of cooperation.

PRACTICE TEST

MULTIPLE CHOICE

1.	c	11.	b
2.	c	12.	c
3.	a	13.	d
4.	c	14.	c
5.	a	15.	a
6.	a	16.	c
7.	d	17.	a
8.	a	18.	c
9.	d	19.	c
10.	c	20.	c

TRUE/FALSE

1.	F	7.	F
2.	F	8.	F
3.	T	9.	T
4.	T	10.	T
5.	F	11.	F
6.	F	12.	T

CHAPTER 11
HUMAN RESOURCE MANAGEMENT

LEARNING GOALS

After you have read and studied this chapter, you should be able to:

1.   Explain the importance of human resource management and describe current issues in managing human resources.

2.   Summarize the six steps in planning human resources.

3.   Describe methods that companies use to recruit new employees and explain some of the problems that make recruitment challenging.

4.   Outline the six steps in selecting employees.

5.   Illustrate the use of various types of employee training and development methods.

6.   Trace the six steps in appraising employee performance.

7.   Summarize the objectives of employee compensation programs and describe various pay systems and fringe benefits.

8.   Explain scheduling plans managers use to adjust to workers' needs.

9.   Describe the ways employees can move through a company: promotion, reassignment, termination, and retirement.

10.   Illustrate the effects of legislation on human resource management.

LEARNING THE LANGUAGE

Listed below are important terms found in the chapter. Choose the correct term for the definition and write it in the space provided.

Affirmative action	Human Resource Management	Off-the-job training
Apprenticeship programs	Job analysis	On-the- job training
Cafeteria-style fringe benefits	Job description	Performance appraisal
Compressed workweek	Job sharing	Recruitment
Contingent workers	Job simulation	Reverse discrimination
Core time	Job specifications	Selection
Employee orientation	Management development	Training and development
Flextime plans	Mentor	Vestibule training
Fringe benefits	Networking	

1.	The set of activities called _____ are used to obtain a sufficient number of the right people at the right time to select those who best meet the needs of the organization.

2.	The written summary of the minimum qualifications required of a worker to do a particular job is called the _____.

3.	Work schedules known as _____give employees some freedom to adjust when they work, as long as they work the required number of hours.

4.	Employment activities designed to "right past wrongs " by increasing opportunities for minorities and women are known as _____ activities.

5.	Programs known as a(n) _____ involve a period during which a learner works alongside an experienced employee to master the skills and procedures of a craft.

6.	The process of _____is the training and educating employees to become good managers and monitoring the progress of their managerial skills over time.

7.	Known as _____ these include sick-leave pay, vacation pay, pension plans, and health plans that provide additional compensation to employees.

8.	Discrimination against whites or males in hiring or promoting is called
_____.

9.	An experienced employee, called a_____ supervises, coaches and guides selected lower-level employees by introducing them to the right people and groups and generally being their organizational sponsors.

10.	The process of evaluating human resource needs is called _____, which involves finding people to fill those needs, and getting the best work from each employee by providing the right incentives and job environment, all with the goal of meeting organizational objectives.

11.	A(n)_____is a work schedule that allows an employee to work a full number of hours per week but in fewer days.

12.	A(n) _____is a study of what is done by employees who hold various job titles.

13. The process of_____ involves establishing and maintaining contacts with key managers in one's own organization and in other organizations and using those contacts to weave strong relationships that serve as informal development systems.

14. The process of gathering information and deciding who should be hired, under legal guidelines, for the best interests of the individual and the organization is known as _____.

15. A program known as _____ occurs away from the workplace and consists of internal and external programs to develop a variety of skills and to foster personal development.

16. A(n) _____ is a summary of the objectives of a job, the type of work to be done, the responsibilities and duties, the working conditions, and the relationship of the job to other functions.

17. _____ refers to the period when all employees are present at their job stations.

18. An arrangement known as _____ is one whereby two part-time employees share one full-time job.

19. The program known as _____ is one where the employee immediately begins his or her tasks and learns by doing, or watches others for a while and them imitates them, right at the workplace.

20. _____ includes all attempts to improve employee performance by increasing an employees ability to perform.

21. The activity known as _____ initiates new employees to the organization, to fellow employees, to their immediate supervisors; and to the policies, practices and objectives of the firm.

22. A _____ is an evaluation in which the performance level of employees is measured against established standards to make decisions about promotions, compensation, and additional training.

23. A type of training known as _____ is done in schools where employees are taught on equipment similar to that used on the job.

24. A program called _____ is a fringe benefits plan that allows employees to choose the benefits they want up to a certain dollar amount.

25.   A training method that uses equipment that duplicates job conditions and tasks so that trainees can learn skills before attempting them on the job is called _____.

26.   Workers known as _____ do not have the expectation of regular, full-time employment.

ASSESSMENT CHECK

Learning Goal 1   **Working With People is Just the Beginning**

1.   Identify the six functions of human resource management.

a. _____   d. _____

b. _____   e. _____

c. _____   f. _____

2.   How has the role of human resource management changed in recent years?

3.   Why has human resource management received increased attention in recent years?

4. What are the challenges facing the human resources area?

a. _____

b. _____

c. _____

d. _____

e. _____

f. _____

g. _____

h. _____

i. _____

j. _____

k. _____

l. _____

Learning Goal 2   **Determining Your Human Resources Needs**

5. List the steps in human resource planning

a. _____   d. _____

b. _____   e. _____

c. _____   f. _____

6.   What information is included in a human resources inventory?

7.   What's the difference between a job description and job specifications?

8.   What affects future demand for employees?

9.   What is likely to happen regarding supply of future employees?

Learning Goal 3   **Recruiting Employees From a Diverse Population**

10.   What are some reasons recruiting has become more difficult?

    a._____

    b._____

    c._____

11. What are three activities in recruiting?

    a. _____

    b. _____

    c. _____

12. What are two general sources for recruiting?

    a. _____

    b. _____

13. What are some internal methods of recruiting?

    a. _____

    b. _____

    c. _____

14. What are some external sources of recruiting?

    a. _____

    b. _____

    c. _____

    d. _____

    e. _____

    f. _____

    g. _____

15. What are some of the newest tools used to recruit employees?

Learning Goal 4   **Selecting Employees Who Will Be Productive**

16. Why is the selection process such an important element in the human resources program?

17. List the six steps in selecting employees

a. _____

b. _____

c. _____

d. _____

e. _____

f. _____

18. How do legal issues make the steps in the selection process more challenging?

19.   What are employment tests used to measure? What is the important element of employment tests?

20.   What is the benefit, to the firm, of a trial period?

21.   What types of workers are included in the definition of "contingent workers?"

22.   When do firms hire contingent workers?

23.   What are the ups and downs of being a contingent worker?

24.   What is the difference between training and development?

25.   What are three steps in the process of creating training and development programs?

   a. _____

   b. _____

   c. _____

26.   Identify seven types of training programs.

   a. _____   e. _____

   b. _____   f. _____

   c. _____   g. _____

   d. _____

27.   Identify the activities in an employee orientation program.

28.   In what type of situation is on-the- job training effective? How have intranets affected on the job training programs?

29. What types of jobs would you train for in an apprenticeship? What job classification comes after apprenticeship? How will apprenticeship programs change?

30. What is another name for Internet training?

31. When is vestibule training used?

32. What kinds of jobs use job simulation type training?

33. List four types of training included in management training programs.

   a. _____

   b. _____

   c. _____

   d. _____

34. What are three reasons for companies to develop mentoring and networking programs for women and minorities in the workplace?

   a. _____

   b. _____

   c. _____

Learning Goal 6   **Appraising Employee Performance**

35. What decisions are based upon a performance appraisal?

36. What are the steps followed in a performance appraisal?

   a. _____

   b. _____

   c. _____

   d. _____

   e. _____

   f. _____

37. What three characteristics must performance standards have?

a. _____

b. _____

c. _____

38. Describe the latest form of performance appraisal.

Learning Goal 7   **Compensating Employees**

39. Why are compensation and benefit packages being given special attention today?

40. List several objectives that can be accomplished by a carefully managed compensation and benefit program.

a. _____

b. _____

c. _____

d. _____

e. _____

41.	Identify the various types of pay systems

a._____		e._____

b._____		f._____

c._____		g._____

d._____

42.	In looking at team compensation, what is the problem when pay is based strictly on individual performance?

43.	What are the two most common compensation methods for teams?

44.	Describe a skill based pay system for teams.

45.	What are two problems with skill-based pay systems?

46.   Describe a profit sharing, or gain sharing, system of compensation for teams.

47.   Where does individual compensation fit into these team-based plans?

48.   What are some of the things included in a fringe benefits package? How big a part of companies' compensation plans are fringe benefits?

49.   What are "soft benefits?"

50.   Why have companies implemented cafeteria-style benefits packages? What is the key to offering these types of plans?

Learning Goal 8 **Scheduling Employees**

51.   What are 4 alternatives for job scheduling?

a._____   c._____

b._____   d._____

52.   What are some benefits to flextime? What are some disadvantages?

53.   What is a disadvantage of a compressed work week?

54.   What are the benefits to working at home for workers? For employers?

55.   What are four benefits to job sharing?

a._____

b._____

c._____

d._____

56.   What are some disadvantages to job sharing for employers?

Learning Goal 9   **Moving Employees Up, Over, and Out**

57.   What are four ways of moving employees through the organization?

a. _____   c. _____

b. _____   d. _____

58.   What are the benefits of promotion from within a company?

59.   What events have created a need for managers to manage layoffs and firings?

60.   Why are companies hesitant to re-hire permanent employees?

61.   What is the doctrine of "employment at will?" How has the "employment at will" doctrine changed?

62.   What are two tools used to downsize companies?

63.   What are two advantages of early retirement programs?

Learning Goal 10   **Laws Affecting Human Resource Management**

64.   What are six laws enacted to prevent discrimination in the workplace?

        a. _____

        b. _____

        c. _____

        d. _____

        e. _____

        f. _____

65.   What does Title VII of the Civil Rights Act of 1964 prohibit?

66.   What is the EEOC? What powers does the EEOC have?

67.   What was the purpose of affirmative action programs?

68.   How did affirmative action programs result in charges of reverse discrimination?

69.   What did the Civil Rights Act of 1991 do?

70.   Who does the Vocational and Rehabilitation Act of 1973 protect?

71.   What does the ADA require?

72. What do companies now believe "accommodation" means, and what do accommodations in the workplace include?

73. What did the Age Discrimination in Employment Act do?

74. Identify four important aspects of the impact of legislation on human resource management.

   a._____

   b._____

   c._____

   d._____

CRITICAL THINKING EXERCISES

Learning Goal 1

1. Six functions of human resource management are:

Human resource planning	Training and development
Recruitment	Evaluation
Selection	Compensation

   You have read in previous chapters of the changing structure of American business and about population trends occurring in the United States. In this chapter, we read about the challenges in human resource management.

For each of the following, identify at least one area of human resource management that could be affected, and how companies are affected or how companies could respond to the change.

	AREA AFFECTED	COMPANY RESPONSE
a. Shortages of trained workers	_____	_____
		_____
		_____
b. An aging workforce	_____	_____
		_____
		_____
c. Increases in single parent and two-income families	_____	_____
		_____
		_____
d. Changing attitude toward work	_____	_____
		_____
		_____
e. Complex laws	_____	_____
		_____
		_____
f. Concern over work environment and equality	_____	_____
		_____
		_____

Learning Goal 2

2. Six steps in human resource planning are:

Forecast of human resource needs   Assess future demand

Current human resource inventory   Assess future supply

Job analysis, description, specification   Establish a strategic plan

Match the correct step to each of the following:

a. A large West Coast two-year college recently required its clerical staff to identify all the tasks involved in their jobs and to show how each job related to the other areas of their department. _____

b. Ford periodically requests employees to update information in their personnel file, for such things as recent courses taken, recent training programs, and other employee information.

_____

c. Diamler Chrysler anticipates that its plant managers will need to develop updated skills in new management techniques as technology changes._____

d. Daimler Chrysler makes arrangements with a local college for on-site training for its plant managers and arranges to retrain workers at state-sponsored retraining programs.

_____

e. The human resources manager of a large East Coast firm gets statistics on the educational background of the graduating MBA classes of several East Coast colleges, including two schools with a large minority enrollment and two high tech schools._____

f. Based on a five-year strategic plan, a small business owner determines that he will need at least three additional sales people within the next two years, and one more office person with a computer background._____

Learning Goal 3

3. Be observant! Look around you and observe how many ways you can notice that firms are using to recruit employees. Newspapers, radio, signs in windows, college placement office? What ways would you use to look for a job and "be recruited" to apply? Can you find at least 3 Internet recruiting sites?

Learning Goal 4

4.   A typical selection process may involve six steps

Complete application   Background investigations

Initial and follow-up interviews   Physical exams

Employment tests   Trial periods

Match each of the following to the correct step in the selection process:

a.   Contributes to the high cost of turnover but enables a firm to fire incompetent employees after a certain period of time. _____

b.   Helps a firm to determine the information about an employee that is pertinent to the requirements of the job. Legal guidelines limit what companies can ask.

_____

c.   An investigation of previous work records, school records, and follow-up on recommendations._____

d.   These have been criticized because of charges of cultural discrimination. They are most often used to measure specific job skills._____

e.   Used to screen applicants after the application form has been reviewed. Gives the company an opportunity to assess communication skills. _____

f.   A major controversy in this step is pre-employment drug testing to detect drug or alcohol abuse and AIDS screening._____

Learning Goal 1, 2, 3, 4

5.   Music-stor needs the human resources manager to begin developing some job descriptions, that identify the various skills needed to perform the different jobs in the company, and to start to develop a recruitment and selection process. Select at least one job that will be a part of Music-stor's organization, write a job description, job specifications, and develop a plan for recruiting and selecting job candidates.

6.   Firms have several types of training programs available: Use each type only once.

Employee orientation   Vestibule training

On-the-job training   Job simulation

Apprentice programs   Online training

Off-the-job training

Match the correct type of training program to each situation described:

a. Before Tom Hershberger went to work for a construction firm, he had a lot of training on how to use the heavy equipment he was assigned to operate._____

b. Bill Martin is a plumber. Before he became a journeyman, he had to work for several years alongside another plumber to learn the skills and procedures for the job. _____

c. Maria Alvarez went on a sales call her second day on the job. She basically "learned by doing." _____

d. Scott Toblin is learning to fly the newest and largest commercial aircraft, a 797. Before he takes it up in the air, he will work the control panel, and "land" on the runways of virtually every airport in the United States, all while staying right on the ground.

_____

e. Bernie Breen spent three weeks learning effective communications and human relations skills for his job as a middle manager in a major corporation. Bernie didn't have to leave his office to "attend" class; his computer served as the classroom, as he was connected over the Internet._____

f. In his first day on the job, Hong Nyu was introduced to several department managers, studied a corporate brochure describing all the company's products, and saw a video of the history of his company. He was even assigned a mentor.

_____

7.   The text discusses networking, and its importance in business. How could networking become even more important in the future, and how can you start now to develop a "network?"

Learning Goal 6

8. You are the newly appointed sales manager for Music-stor, and your job is to develop a new appraisal system that is effective and objective. This is the first real test of your skills as a manager. What, specifically, do you think you should do? In other words, what kinds of things will you include on an appraisal form, and then what will you do after that's completed?

9. Right now at Music-stor, you have a salesperson who doesn't seem to be performing adequately. You know something must be done. This is the second real test of your management skills. What will you do?

Learning Goal 7

10. In today's competitive environment , compensation and fringe benefit packages are being given special attention. A good program can accomplish several benefits for an organization.

    Basic pay systems include:

    Salary systems   Commission plans

    Hourly wage   Bonus plans

    Piecework   Profit-sharing

    Give a suggested pay system for each situation described below. Your suggestion can be a combination of systems:

    a. A sales job that includes a variety of non selling functions such as advising, keeping records and setting up displays. _____

    b. An assembly line operation in which each worker completes several tasks before the product moves to the next station._____

c. An office manager just starting out with new office equipment designed to increase productivity. _____

d. The president of a small firm that makes computer chips. _____

e. A worker in a garment factory, making shirts. _____

11. How can a company ensure that their benefits programs meet the needs of a changing workforce? Why is that important?

Learning Goal 8

12. Changing workforces mean changing schedules for many companies and their employees. Some alternative work schedules are:

Job sharing   Compressed work weeks

Flextime plans   In-home work

What kind of program is being described:

a. This type of program can give an employee a break and lets them sleep in once in a while!
_____

b. At Readers Guide, employees work 35 hours in 4 days for each week in May, giving everyone a three day weekend. _____

c. At St. Lukes Hospital, Julie Andersen fills a full-time position by working as an accountant every morning, and Mary Krull takes over each afternoon.
_____

d. Felicia Hill has a fax, modem, and a computer that she carries with her wherever she goes, but she doesn't have an office! _____

e. Some of the benefits of this schedule include a reduction in absenteeism and tardiness, because people can handle their other duties in off hours._____

f. With this program, Juan and Elena Morena can schedule their days so that one of them is home to see their children off in the morning, and the other is home when the children come home from school._____

g. One of the disadvantages of this program is the need to hire, train and supervise twice as many people._____

h. Gil Pfaff likes this schedule, because it allows him to work his full day, and still avoid the heavy morning traffic during his commute to work. _____

i. Manager David Whitsell likes this program because he has found workers who take advantage of it are often more productive and it is easier for him to schedule people into peak demand periods for his department._____

j. Debbie Rhodes schedules doctor's appointments on days when she comes in early and leaves early._____

13. How have the changes in the workforce and in the workplace, discussed in this and other chapters, affected the ways companies move employees around?

14. How have changes in the "make-up" of the workforce (more immigrants, more minorities, more women, and so on) affected corporations from a legal perspective?

PRACTICE TEST

Multiple Choice – Circle the best answer

1.   Human resource management does not include:

    a.   leading.
    b.   evaluation.
    c.   recruitment.
    d.   selection.

2.   Which of the following would not be included in a discussion of the challenges faced by human resource managers?

    a.   Shortages of people trained to work in growth areas
    b.   A growing population of workers who need retraining
    c.   Challenges from an overseas labor pool available for lower wages
    d.   Fewer older workers, and too many of them who want to retire, making it difficult to fill their jobs

3.   A human resource inventory will provide information about:

    a.   what is done by various employees who fill different job titles.
    b.   whether or not the labor force is paid adequately.
    c.   the strategic plan for recruiting, selecting training and development.
    d.   education, capabilities, training, and specialized skills to determine if the company' s labor force is technically up-to-date.

4.   "Clerical worker, with responsibilities of answering phones, greeting clients, filing for human resources department. Some weekends required." This is an example of a:

    a.   job analysis.
    b.   job specification.
    c.   job description.
    d.   job evaluation.

5. According to the text, the greatest advantage of hiring from within is:

   a. it is quick.
   b. it requires less training.
   c. it helps maintain employee morale.
   d. it keeps the firm from having an oversupply of workers trained in certain areas.

6. Which of the following is not included in a list of reasons why recruiting has become difficult?

   a. sometimes people with necessary skills aren't available
   b. the number of available recruiting tools has begun to shrink
   c. the emphasis on participative management makes it important to hire people who fit in with the corporate culture
   d. some companies have policies which make it difficult to recruit.

7. What is the first step in the selection process?

   a. obtaining a completed application form
   b. contacting an employment agency
   c. background investigation
   d. interviews

8. Background investigations:

   a. are no longer legal.
   b. help weed out candidates that are less likely to succeed.
   c. include an investigation of skills.
   d. are not good predictors of who will be successful.

9. The use of contingent workers

   a. is more expensive that hiring full time workers.
   b. is appropriate when jobs require minimum training.
   c. is declining.
   d. is not a good way to find good employees.

10. Internal and external programs to develop a variety of skills and to foster personal development away from the job is called:

    a. off-the-job training.
    b. vestibule training.
    c. an apprentice program.
    d. employee orientation.

11. _____is a type of training that exposes managers to different functions of the organization by giving them assignments in a variety of departments.

    a. Understudy positions
    b. On-the-job coaching
    c. Job enlargement
    d. Job rotation

12. In developing a performance appraisal, standards should have all of the following characteristics except:

    a. they should be specific.
    b. they should be subject to measurement.
    c. they should be easily attainable.
    d. they should be reasonable.

13. The latest form of performance appraisal requires feedback from up, down, and around the employee and is called a:

    a. 360-degree review.
    b. turnaround review.
    c. complete feedback review.
    d. total review.

14. Ima Gogetter is interested in making a lot of money! He is a very good salesperson. People tell him he could sell sand to Saudi Arabia! He is a very hard worker, and is willing to work a lot of hours to make the kind of money he wants. Ima should most likely look for the kind of job that is paid :

   a. on salary with overtime.
   b. hourly.
   c. with profit sharing.
   d. on commission.

15. Studies of compensation for teams have shown that:

   a. it is recommended that pay should be based on team performance.
   b. team based pay programs are pretty well developed and need not be changed.
   c. team members should be compensated as individuals.
   d. skill based pay programs are relatively easy to apply.

16. A program that gives employees freedom to adjust when they work, as long as they work the required number of hours is called:

   a. job sharing.
   b. flextime.
   c. a compressed workweek.
   d. home based work.

17. Which of the following is not a benefit of job sharing?

   a. reduced absenteeism
   b. ability to schedule people into peak demand periods
   c. a high level of enthusiasm and productivity
   d. less supervision

18. The effect of downsizing on human resources management has been that:

   a. fewer layers of management make it more difficult for employees to be promoted to higher levels of management.
   b. companies are now scrambling to re-hire those workers who were laid off.
   c. a decrease in the level of complexity of managing human resources.
   d. less need to adhere to employment law.

19. Affirmative action programs:

 a. are no longer legal and have had to be thrown out.
 b. were designed to "right past wrongs" endured by females and minorities.
 c. came into being as a result of the ADA.
 d. refer to problems experienced with reverse discrimination.

20. Title VII of the Civil Rights Act:

 a. requires that disabled applicants be given the same consideration for employment as people without disabilities.
 b. prevents businesses from discrimination against people with disabilities on the basis of their physical or mental handicap.
 c. prohibits discrimination in hiring, firing, and other areas on the basis of race, religion, creed, sex, or national origin.
 d. gives the victims of discrimination the right to a jury trail and punitive damages.

True-False

1. _____ Qualified labor is more scarce today, which makes recruiting and selecting more difficult.

2. _____ Job descriptions are statements about the person who does the job.

3. _____ The newest tools used to recruit employees are Internet online services.

4. _____ The application form and the initial interview are good ways for a company to find out about an applicant's family and religious backgrounds.

5. _____ It can be more cost effective for a company to hire contingent workers rather than hire permanent employees when more workers are needed.

6. _____ In an apprentice program, a worker immediately begins his or her tasks and learns by doing.

7. _____ In a mentoring program, an older, more experienced worker will coach and guide a selected lower level manager by introducing him or her to the right people and groups.

8. _____ Decisions about promotions, compensation, additional training, and firing are based upon performance evaluations.

9. _____ While compensation and benefits packages are important to keep employees, these programs play little role in attracting qualified employees.

10. _____ Most companies have found that compensating teams is a relatively straightforward issue.

11. _____ Some companies have found that telecommuting has helped the company to save money.

12. _____ Legislation to prevent employer abuse in firing workers has restricted management's ability to terminate workers as it increased workers' rights to their jobs.

13. _____ While early retirement programs are a more expensive strategy of downsizing than laying off employees, it can increase the morale of remaining employees.

14. _____ Legislation and legal decisions have had little effect on human resource management.

15. _____ The EEOC is charged with enforcing affirmative action programs.

You Can Find It On the Net

The Web site www.workforceonline.com is a comprehensive Human Resources site which provides a considerable amount of information about a wide variety of topics. These topics will vary over time.

What "Features" topics did you find?

What topics were in the "News" portion?

What topics are listed under the following areas:

Compensation and Benefits

HR Management

Recruiting and Staffing

Training and Development

ANSWERS

KEY TERMS AND DEFINITIONS

1. Recruitment	10. Human resource management	19. On-the-job training
2. Job specifications	11. Compressed work week	20. Training and development
3. Flextime plans	12. Job analysis	21. Employee orientation
4. Affirmative action	13. Networking	22. Performance appraisal
5. Apprenticeship Programs	14. Selection	23. Vestibule training
6. Management development	15. Off-the-job training	24. Cafeteria-style benefits
7. Fringe benefits	16. Job description	25. Job simulation
8. Reverse discrimination	17. Core time	26. Contingent workers
9. Mentor	18. Job sharing	

RETENTION CHECK

Working With People Is Just the Beginning

1.
   a. Human resource planning   d. Training and development
   b. Recruitment   e. Evaluation
   c. Selection   f. Compensation

2.   Historically firms assigned the functions of human resources management, such as recruiting, selecting, training and so on to various functional departments. "Personnel" was viewed mostly as a clerical function responsible for screening applications, keeping records, processing payroll and finding people when necessary. Today the job of human resource management has taken on a new role in the firm. It has become so important that it is a function of all managers.

3.   Human resource management has received greater attention recently because in the past, labor, or "human resources" was plentiful, and there was little need to nurture and develop the labor force. If you needed qualified people, all you had to do was hire them. If they didn't work out, you could simply hire others. Qualified labor is scarcer today, and that makes the whole area of human resource management more challenging.

4.
   a. Shortages of people trained to work in growth areas.
   b. Large numbers of workers from declining industries who need retraining.
   c. A growing population of new workers who are poor and undereducated
   d. A shift in the age composition of the work force, including older workers and baby boomers.
   e. Complex laws in human resource management.

f. Increasing number of single parent and two-income families who need programs like day care, job sharing and family leave

g. Changing employee attitudes toward work with leisure having a greater priority

h. Downsizing, its effect on morale and need for contingency workers.

i. Challenges from an overseas labor pool.

j. Increased demand for benefits tailored to the individual.

k. Growing concern for issues such as health care, elder care and employment for people with disabilities.

l. Decreased sense of employee loyalty resulting in increased employee turnover and increased costs of replacing lost workers.

Determining Your Human Resources Needs

5. a. Forecast human resource needs.

b. Prepare an inventory of current human resource information.

c. Prepare job analyses, job descriptions, and job specifications.

d. Assess future demand, including what training programs may be needed.

e. Assess future supply of human resources with needed skills.

f. Establish a strategic plan for recruiting, selecting, training, evaluating and scheduling.

6. A human resources inventory includes ages, names, education, capabilities, training, specialized skills and other information pertinent to the organization, such as languages spoken. This information reveals whether or not the labor force is technically up to date and thoroughly trained.

7. A job description specifies the objectives of the job, the types of work to be done, responsibilities and duties, working conditions and the relationship of the job to other functions. Job specifications specify the qualifications of the individual needed to fill the job. In other words, the job description is about the job, and job specifications are about the person who does the job.

8. The demand for employees will be affected by changing technology: often training programs must be started long before the need is apparent.

9. There are likely to be increased shortages of some skills in the future, like computer and robotic repair workers and an oversupply of other types of skills, like assembly-line workers.

Recruiting Employees From a Diverse Population

10. Recruiting has become difficult because:
    a. Sometimes people with the right skills are not available and must be hired and trained internally.
    b. The emphasis on culture, teamwork, and participative management makes it important to hire the right kind of people.
    c. Some organizations have policies that demand promotion from within or other situations that make recruiting and keeping employees difficult.

11. a. finding
    b. hiring
    c. training

12. a. internal sources
    b. external sources

13. a. Transfers
    b. Promotions
    c. Employee recommendations

14. a. Advertisements
    b. Public and private employment agencies
    c. College placement bureaus
    d. Management consultants
    e. Professional organizations
    f. Referrals
    g. Walk in applicants

15. Some of the newest tools used to recruit employees are Internet online services, such as Career Mosaic, The Monster Board, and Jobtrak.

Selecting Employees Who Will Be Productive

16. The selection process is so important because the cost of selecting and training employees has become so high.

17. a. Obtaining a complete application form   d. Background investigations
     b. Initial and follow-up interviews   e. Physical exams
     c. Employment tests   f. Trial periods

18. Legal issues affect the selection process in a number of ways. Today, legal guidelines limit the kinds of questions one can ask on an application or in an interview. Employment tests have been challenged because of discrimination, so tests must be directly related to the job. Some states will only allow physical examinations after an offer of employment has been accepted, and such tests must be given to everyone applying for the same position. Conditional employment, where a company gives an employee a trial period, have made it easier to fire inefficient or problem employees.

19. Employment tests measure basic competencies in specific job skills and help evaluate applicants' personalities and interests. It is important that the employment test be related to the job.

20. During a trial period, a person can prove his or her worth to the firm. After the trial period, a firm has the right to discharge an employee based upon performance evaluations, so it is easier to fire inefficient employees.

21. Contingent workers are workers who do not have the expectation of regular, full-time employment. These workers include part-time workers, seasonal workers, temporary workers, independent contractors, interns and co-op students.

22. Firms have contingent workers when there is a varying need for employees, full time employees are on leave, there is a peak demand for labor, and quick service to customers is a priority.

23. Contingent workers are often offered full-time positions, but as contingent workers they receive few health, vacation, and pension benefits. They also earn less than permanent workers.

Training and Developing Employees for Optimum Performance

24. Training is short-term skills oriented while development is long-term career-oriented.

25. a. Assessing the needs of the organization and the skills of the employees to determine training needs.
     b. Designing the training activities to meet the needs.
     c. Evaluating the effectiveness of the training.

26.   a. Employee orientation   e. Online training
      b. On-the-job training   f. Vestibule training
      c. Apprenticeship programs   g. Job simulation
      d. Off-the-job training

27.   During an employee orientation program, new employees will be introduced to fellow employees and to their immediate supervisors, and learn about the policies, practices and objectives of the firm. Orientation programs included everything from informal talks to formal activities that last a day or more and include visits to various departments and required reading of selected handbooks.

28.   On the job training is the easiest kind of training to implement, and can be effective where the job is easily learned, such as clerking in a store, or performing repetitive physical tasks. Technology such as Intranets are leading to cost-effective forms of on-the-job training programs that are available 24 hours a day, all year long.

29.   As an apprentice, you would train for a craft, such as a bricklaying or plumbing. Workers who successfully complete an apprenticeship earn the classification of journeyman. In the future, there are likely to be more but shorter apprenticeships programs to prepare people for skilled jobs in changing industries.

30.   Another name for Internet training is distance learning, or online training.

31.   Vestibule training is used when proper methods and safety procedures must be learned before using equipment on the job.

32.   Job simulation is the use of equipment that duplicates job conditions and tasks so trainees can learn skills before attempting them on the job. It differs from vestibule training in that simulation attempts to duplicate the *exact* conditions that occur on the job.

33.   a. On-the-job coaching   c. Job rotation
      b. Understudy positions   d. Off-the-job courses and training

34.   Companies taking the initiative to develop female and minority mangers understand that:
      a. grooming women and minorities for management position is a key to long term profitability.
      b. the best women and minorities will become harder to attract and retain in the future.
      c. more women and minorities at all levels means that businesses can serve female and minority customers better.

Appraising Employee Performance

35.   Decisions about promotions, compensation, additional training or firing are all based on performance evaluations.

36.
    a. Establish performance standards
    b. Communicate the standards
    c. Evaluate performance
    d. Discuss results with employees
    e. Take corrective action
    f. Use the results to make decisions

37.   Performance standards must be:
    a. understandable
    b. subject to measurement
    c. reasonable

38.   The latest form of performance appraisal is called the 360 degree review, because it calls for feedback from superiors, subordinates, and peers.

Compensating Employees

39.   Compensation and benefits packages have become a main marketing tool used to attract qualified employees. At the same time, employee compensation is one of the largest operating costs for many organizations, and the firm's long-term survival may depend on how well it can control employee costs, while still attracting and keeping qualified personnel.

40.
    a. Attracting the kind of people the organization needs.
    b. Providing employees with incentives
    c. Keeping valued employees from leaving
    d. Maintaining a competitive position in the marketplace
    e. Assuring employees a sense of financial security through insurance and retirement benefits

41.   a. Salary systems   e. Bonus plans
        b. Hourly wage or daywork   f. Profit sharing plans
        c. Piecework   g. Stock Option plans
        d. Commission plans

42.   The problem with paying members of a team based on individual performance is that it erodes team cohesiveness and makes it less likely that the team will meet its goals as a collaborative effort.

43.   Two types of pay systems for teams are skills-based pay and profit sharing.

44.   Skill-based pay is related to the growth of the individual and of the team. Base pay is raised when team members learn and apply new skills.

45.   The drawbacks of the skill-based pay system are the complexity and the difficulty of correlating skill acquisition to bottom-line gains.

46.   In a profit sharing, or gain sharing system, bonuses are based on improvements over a previous performance baseline.

47.   Outstanding team players that go beyond what is required and make an outstanding individual contribution to the firm should be separately recognized for their additional contribution. A good way to avoid alienating recipients who feel team participation was uneven is to let the team decide which members get what type of individual award.

48.   Fringe benefits include sick-leave pay, vacation pay, pension plans, and health plans. They can also include everything from paid vacations to health-care programs, recreation facilities, company cars, country club memberships, day care services and executive dining rooms, dental care, eye care, elder care, legal counseling, mental health care and shorter workweeks. Fringe benefits account for approximately one-third of payrolls today.

49.   "Soft benefits" are such things as on-site haircuts and shoe repair, concierge services and free breakfasts that help workers maintain the balance between work and family life .

50.   Firms have begun to offer cafeteria-style benefits to counter the growing demand for different kinds of benefits. Today employees are more varied and need different kinds of benefits. The key to cafeteria-style benefits is flexibility, where individual needs can be met.

Scheduling Employees

51.   a. flextime   c. home based (telecommuting)
         b. compressed work week   d. job sharing

52.   Flextime plans are designed to allow employees to adjust to demands on their time, and to have freedom to adjust when they work, as long as they work the required number of hours.

One disadvantage of flextime is that it doesn't work in assembly-line processes where everyone must work at the same time. In addition, managers often have to work longer days to be able to assist and supervise employees. Flextime can make communication more difficult, as certain employees may not be at work when you need to talk to them. Further, some employees could abuse the system, and that could cause resentment.

53.   A disadvantage to a compressed work week is that some employees get tired working such long hours, and productivity could decline.

54.   Workers who work at home can choose their own hours, interrupt work for childcare and other tasks, and take time out for personal reasons.

Telecommuting can be a cost saver for employers, can increase productivity and can broaden the available talent pool.

55.   Benefits to job sharing can be;
     a. employment opportunities to those who cannot or prefer not to work full-time
     b. a high level of enthusiasm and productivity
     c. reduced absenteeism and tardiness
     d. ability to schedule people into peak demand periods

56.   The disadvantages to job sharing include having to hire, train, motivate and supervise twice as many people and to prorate some fringe benefits.

Moving Employees Up, Over and Out

57.   a. Promotion & reassignments   c. Retirements
      b. Termination   d. Losing employees

58.   Many companies find that promotion from within the company improves employee morale. Promotions are also cost-effective because the promoted employees are already familiar with the corporate culture and procedures.

59. Downsizing and restructuring, increasing customer demands for value, the pressure of global competition, and shifts in technology have made human resource managers struggle.

60. Companies are hesitant to rehire permanent employees because the cost of terminating employees is so high. Managers choose to avoid the cost of firing by not hiring in the first place. Instead, companies are using temporary employees or outsourcing.

61. "Employment at will" is an old doctrine that meant that managers had as much freedom to fire workers as workers had to leave voluntarily. Most states now have written employment laws that limit the "at will" doctrine to protect employees from wrongful firing. This has restricted management's ability to terminate employees as it increased workers' rights to their jobs.

62. Two tools used to downsize are to offer early retirement benefits and laying off employees.

63. Two advantages of early retirement programs are increased morale of surviving employees and greater promotion opportunities for younger employees.

Laws Affecting Human Resource Management

64. a. Civil Rights Act of 1964
     b. Equal Employment Opportunity Act
     c. Civil Rights Act of 1991
     d. Vocational Rehabilitation Act
     e. Americans with Disabilities Act
     f. Age Discrimination Act

65. The Civil Rights Act of 1964 - Title VII prohibits discrimination in hiring, firing, compensation, apprenticeships, training, terms, conditions, or privileges of employment based on race, religion, creed, sex, national origin, or age.

66. The EEOC, the Equal Employment Opportunity Commission is a regulatory agency created by the Civil Rights Act in 1964. The EEOC has the power to enforce programs put forth by various legislation. More specifically, the EEOC has the power to issue guidelines for acceptable employer conduct in administering equal employment opportunity, enforce mandatory record-keeping procedures, and insure that mandates are carried out.

67. The purpose of affirmative action was to "right past wrongs" endured by females and minorities in the administration of human resources management.

68. Charges of reverse discrimination occurred when companies have been perceived as unfairly giving preference to women or minority groups in hiring and promoting, when following affirmative action guidelines.

69. The Civil Rights Act of 1991 expanded the remedies available to victims of discrimination. Now victims have the right to a jury trial and punitive damages.

70. The Vocational Rehabilitation Act of 1973 extended protection from discrimination, in all areas of human resource management, to people with disabilities.

71. The Americans with Disabilities Act of 1990 requires that disabled applicants be given the same consideration for employment as people without disabilities. Companies must make "reasonable accommodations" to people with disabilities including modifying equipment or making structural changes.

72. Employers today believe accommodation means that they must treat different people differently. Accommodations include putting up barriers to isolate people readily distracted by noise, reassigning workers to new tasks, and making changes in supervisors' management styles.

73. The Age Discrimination in Employment Act outlawed mandatory retirement in most organizations before the age of 70.

74.
   a. Employers must be sensitive to the legal rights of all groups in the workplace
   b. Legislation affects all areas of human resource management
   c. It is clear that it is sometimes legal to go beyond providing equal rights for minorities and women to provide special employment and training to correct past discrimination
   d. New court cases and legislation change human resource management almost daily.

CRITICAL THINKING EXERCISES

1.

		AREA	COMPANY RESPONSE
a.	Shortages of trained workers	Training Recruitment	Training programs, aggressive recruiting programs
b.	Aging work force	Compensation Planning	Demand for good retirement programs will change benefits packages. Companies will also need to plan for replacement of workers in the future. Also family leave programs needed for workers to care for older parents
c.	Increases in single-parent and two income families	Compensation	Companies will need to look at income, offering day care, and continued cafeteria style benefits will be especially important as companies experience shortages of trained workers.
d.	Changing attitudes about work	Planning`	Need to look at flextime, and compressed work weeks to meet needs of future workers.
e.	Complex laws	Selection Recruitment Compensation	These laws will require companies to look at their policies regarding hiring, promotion and termination.
f.	Concern over work environment and equality	Planning Compensation	Companies will begin to offer programs to help employees deal with issues regarding eldercare and access at the work place for disabled workers

2.
   a. Job analysis
   b. Human resource inventory
   c. Assess future demand
   d. Establish a plan
   e. Assess future supply
   f. Forecast future human resource needs

3. You will probably notice a number of ways that companies are trying to recruit new employees. One good reason to develop a "network" is that employers often use current employees to find new hires. The newspaper, especially on Sundays, may have several pages of employment opportunities. On your college campus, there may be signs in windows, ads in the college newspaper, and ads on electronic bulletin boards are among a myriad of other ways that companies are using to look for qualified employees.

4.
a. Trial periods
b. Complete application
c. Background investigations
d. Employment tests
e. Initial and follow up interviews
f. Physical exams

5. Your answer will depend upon what kind of job you have chosen. There are many different jobs which will be a part of Music-stor : Sales, production, marketing, accounting, and clerical, to name a few. For a sales job, a job description may be: Sales for a small manufacturing company, calling on automotive manufacturers and/or automotive after market dealers. Sales territory will be primarily based on geographic location. Duties will include sales calls, follow up reports, working directly with production manager, direct input into marketing program development. Compensation will be salary plus commission.

Skills required include familiarity with electronic communication equipment, teamwork skills, good oral and written communications skills, presentation skills, and a Bachelor's degree, preferably in marketing or a related area.

You may make use of any of the recruiting tools listed in the text. Good sources may include current employees, local colleges, a local professional marketing organization, or simply advertising. The selection process should include several interviews, in particular with the people with whom the sales person will work, the production manager, other marketing people, and other members of the team he/she will work with.

6.
a. Vestibule training
b. Apprenticeship
c. On-the-job training
d. Job simulation
e. Management development
f. Employee orientation

7. As corporations downsize, and layers of management "thin out" your network of co-workers, friends and professional associations could become especially important. To get the kind of job that meets your needs, you may have to do a lot of searching. To "move up the ladder" in the face of declining numbers of management positions, you may have to find the right mentor.

In college, you can begin to develop a network in a number of ways. If there are student chapters of professional business organizations, such as The American Marketing Association or The American Management Association for example, you could take advantage of student membership rates, attend monthly meetings, and meet people already working in the field. Your professors may have contacts in your area of interest. Further, you could begin a series of "informational interviews." Make appointments with managers in corporations where you may have an interest in working, and find out exactly what kind of skills they seek, what kinds of jobs they think will be available in the future, and a little bit about the company. Lastly, network with your fellow students. You never know who may be the future CEO of the company where you're dying to work.

8. The first thing you need to do in developing this appraisal system is decide exactly what elements of the salespeople's' jobs will be included in the system. For example, you will probably include: sales volume, number of sales calls, number of sales compared to number of sales calls (called the closing ratio), dollar amount per sale, number of units per sale, sales expenses, average dollar volume per customer, and so on, as well as what time frame will be used for evaluations, six months or a year, for example. After that, you will want to decide what is an acceptable and reasonable standard for each of those areas - i.e. how many sales calls per month is enough? What's an acceptable dollar amount per sale? What is an acceptable sales volume in the given period?

    Lastly, these standards must be communicated to each salesperson, explained clearly, and precisely. Each individual must know exactly what is expected of them.

9. How you would deal with an employee who is not performing well is a matter of individual style. However, there are a number of suggestions to make the process more effective. The most important thing to do first is to discuss the problem with the employee and determine what is causing the problem. There may be a problem in the territory, family problems that took her away from work or inadequate support from the company. Figure 11-4 gives you some specific suggestions about conducting an effective appraisal. It will be important to get agreement from the employee that there is a problem, and suggestions about how to take corrective action. It may be a good idea to give a period of time to improve, and then re-evaluate.

10. These are some suggested answers:
    a. Salary or salary plus commission
    b. Hourly wages plus profit sharing
    c. Salary plus bonus for meeting objective
    d. Salary plus profit sharing, or bonus for meeting profit objective
    e. Piecework, plus profit sharing

11. To counter growing demands for more individualized benefits, companies have begun to offer cafeteria-style benefits. The key to this type of program is providing enough choices so that employees can meet their varied needs, while still maintaining cost effectiveness. These types of programs are particularly important in light of the predicted difficulty in finding skilled employees.

12.
a.	Flextime	f.	Flextime
b.	Compressed work week	g.	Job sharing
c.	Job sharing	h.	Flextime
d.	In home work	i.	Job sharing
e.	Job sharing	j.	Flextime

13.   As downsizing has created flatter organizational structures, there are fewer opportunities for employees to be promoted. To keep morale from sagging, and to keep employees productive, it is common today for companies to reassign workers rather than promote them. This kind of transfer allows employees to develop and display new skills. Downsizing has also forced companies to struggle with layoffs and terminations. Many companies are reluctant to rehire permanent workers because of the high cost involved. Legislation has also made firing more difficult, in light of wrongful discharge lawsuits, and some companies find it more cost effective to use part time workers to replace permanent workers when the need arises.

As an alternative to layoffs, companies have offered early retirement to entice older employees to resign, and allow younger workers to move up. As the workforce gets older, these programs will enable companies to reduce the number of older, more expensive workers. However, if skilled workers are in short supply, companies may need experienced workers, and could reconsider offering early retirement plans.

14.   As the workforce becomes more culturally diverse, laws protecting minorities from discrimination will be carefully monitored. These areas have become very complex, and a diverse workforce makes enforcement even more complex. However, as more women and minorities with the necessary skills enter the workforce, compliance with these laws may actually become less an issue than in the past.

A major issue has been providing equal opportunity for people with disabilities. Companies are finding that making structural accommodations is less difficult than understanding the difference between the need to be accommodating and the need to be fair to all employees. As the workforce ages, age discrimination may become more of an issue.

PRACTICE TEST

MULTIPLE CHOICE

1.	a	11.	d
2.	d	12.	c
3.	d	13.	a
4.	c	14.	b
5.	c	15.	a
6.	b	16.	b
7.	a	17.	d
8.	b	18.	a
9.	b	19.	b
10.	a	20.	c

TRUE/FALSE

1.	T	9.	F
2.	F	10.	F
3.	T	11.	T
4.	F	12.	T
5.	T	13.	T
6.	F	14.	F
7.	T	15.	T
8.	T		

CHAPTER 12

DEALING WITH EMPLOYEE-MANAGEMENT ISSUES AND RELATIONSHIPS

LEARNING GOALS

After you have read and studied this chapter, you should be able to:

1.   Trace the history of organized labor in the United States and discuss the major legislation affecting labor unions.

2.   Outline the objectives of labor unions.

3.   Describe the tactics used by labor and management during conflicts and discuss the role of unions in the future.

4.   Explain some of the controversial employee-management issues such as executive compensation; comparable worth; child care and elder care; AIDS testing, drug testing, and violence in the workplace; and employee stock ownership plans (ESOPs).

LEARNING THE LANGUAGE

Listed below are important terms found in the chapter. Choose the correct term for the definition and write it in the space provided.

Agency shop agreement	Decertification	Primary boycott
American Federation of Labor (AFL)	Employee Stock Ownership Plans (ESOPs)	Right-to-work laws
Arbitration	Givebacks	Secondary boycott
Bargaining zone	Grievance	Sexual harassment
Certification	Industrial unions	Shop steward
Closed-shop agreement	Injunction	Strike
Congress of Industrial Organizations (CIO)	Knights of Labor	Strikebreakers
Collective bargaining	Lockouts	Unions
Comparable worth	Mediation	Union Security Clause
Cooling-off period	Negotiated labor management agreement	Union shop agreement
Craft Union	Open shop agreement	Yellow-dog contracts

1. The _____ is the range of options between the initial and final offer that each party will consider before negotiations dissolve or reach an impasse.

2. A time known as the _____ is a period when workers in a critical industry return to their jobs while the union and management continue negotiations.

3. The process known as _____ is one in which workers take away a union's right to represent them.

4. A charge by employees that management is not abiding by the terms of the negotiated labor agreement is called a(n) _____.

5. This tactic, known as a(n) _____, occurs when management puts pressure on unions by closing the business.

6. A tactic called a(n) _____ occurs when the union encourages its members and the general public not to buy the products of a firm involved in a labor dispute.

7. Employee organizations known as _____ have the main goal of representing members in employee-management bargaining about job-related issues.

8. A clause in a labor-management agreement whereby employers may hire nonunion workers who are not required to join the union but must pay a union fee is called a(n) _____.

9. The issue of _____ is the concept that jobs requiring similar levels of education, training and skills should receive equal pay.

10. Under _____ a third party, called a mediator, encourages both sides of a contract dispute to continue negotiating and often makes suggestions for resolving the dispute.

11. _____ results in unwelcome sexual advances, requests for sexual favors, and other conduct of a sexual nature.

12. A _____ was an agreement in which employees had to agree not to join a union as a condition of employment.

13. A _____ is a labor official who works permanently in an organization and represents employee interests on a daily basis.

14. A provision in a negotiated labor-management agreement known as a _____ stipulates that employees who reap benefits from a union must either join or pay dues to the union.

15. An organization known as the _____ consisted of craft unions that championed fundamental labor issues.

16. Concessions made by union members to management or gains from labor negotiations which are given back to management to help employers remain competitive and save jobs are called _____.

17. Under this type of agreement, known as an _____ workers in right to work states have the option to join or not join the union, if one exists in their workplace.

18. Workers who are hired to do the jobs of striking employees until the labor dispute is resolved are called _____.

19. The process of a union's becoming recognized by the NLRB as the bargaining agent for a group of employees is called _____.

20. Labor organizations called _____ consist of unskilled workers in mass production-related industries such as automobiles and mining.

21. This clause in a labor-management agreement called a(n)_____, indicates that workers do not have to be members of a union to be hired, but must agree to join the union within a prescribed period.

22. The process known as _____ is where union representatives agree upon a labor-management agreement for workers.

23. The name of the first national labor union was the _____.

24. A _____ is an attempt by labor to convince others to stop doing business with a firm that is the subject of a primary boycott.

25. The agreement to bring in an impartial third party to render a binding decision in a labor dispute is called _____.

26. The clause in a labor-management agreement known as a _____ specified that workers had to be members of a union before being hired.

27. A program called a(n) _____ is one whereby employees can buy part or total ownership of the firm.

28. A(n) _____ is a settlement which sets the tone and clarifies the terms under which management and labor agree to function over a period of time.

29. Legislation that gives workers the right, under an open shop, to join or not join a union if it is present are called _____.

30. A union strategy known as a _____ means that workers refuse to go to work to further their objectives after an impasse in collective bargaining.

31. The _____ is the union organization of unskilled workers that broke away from the AFL in 1935 and rejoined it in 1955.

32. A labor organization of skilled specialists in a particular craft or trade is a _____.

33. An _____ is a court order directing someone to do something or to refrain from doing something.

ASSESSMENT CHECK

Learning Goal 1   **Employee-Management Issues**

1. What triggered the growth of unions?

2. How long have labor unions existed in the United States?

3. What impact did the Industrial Revolution have on the economic structure of the U.S.? What impact did it have on workers?

4. What was the first national labor organization? What was the intention of this labor union?

5. What was the AFL?

6. Why did the AFL limit membership?

7. What was the CIO? Why was it formed?

8. How did the AFL-CIO form?

Labor Legislation and Collective Bargaining

9.   Name five major pieces of labor-management legislation.

a. _____

b. _____

c. _____

d. _____

e. _____

10.   What are the major elements of the Norris LaGuardia Act?

11.   What did the Wagner Act provide for?

12.   What does the NLRB do?

13.   What is the Fair Labor Standards Act?

14. What did the Taft-Hartley Act provide for?

15. What is a "right to work" state?

16. What was the Landrum-Griffin Act?

Learning Goal 2   **Objectives of Organized Labor**

17. What were the objectives of organized labor, and how have they changed?

18. List the general topics covered in labor-management agreements.

a. _____   g _____

b. _____   h. _____

c. _____   i. _____

d. _____   j. _____

e. _____   k. _____

f. _____

19. Identify four different forms of union contracts.

a. _____   c. _____

b. _____   d. _____

20. What will be the focus of union negotiations in the future?

21. What are three methods used to resolve labor-management disputes?

a. _____

b. _____

c. _____

22.   What are generally the sources of grievances?

a. _____   d. _____

b. _____   e. _____

c. _____

23.   When does mediation become necessary? What does a mediator do?

24.   How does arbitration differ from mediation?

Learning Goal 3   **Tactics Used in Labor-Management Conflicts**

25.   What are the tactics used by labor in labor-management disputes?

a. _____   c. _____

b. _____   d. _____

26.   What are the effects of a strike?

27. What are workers doing when they picket? What is the purpose?

28. What is the difference between a primary boycott and a secondary boycott?

29. What are the tactics available to management in labor-management disputes?

   a._____   c._____

   b._____

30. What will unions have to do in order to grow in the future?

31. In what kinds of activities will unions be involved in the future?

Learning Goal 4   **Controversial Employee-Management Issues**

32.   Identify several controversial non-union employee-management issues.

a. _____

b. _____

c. _____

d. _____

e. _____

f. _____

g. _____

33.   What does management consultant Peter Drucker say regarding the level of executive compensation?

34.   How does the pay of U.S. executives compare to executive pay in other countries? What may be an explanation for the difference?

35.   How does comparable worth differ from "equal pay for equal work?"

36.   What explains the disparity between women's pay and men's pay?

37.   A person's conduct on the job could be considered sexually harassing if:

a. _____

b. _____

38.   What is the concept of a "hostile workplace?"

39.   How important is the issue of sexual harassment in the workplace? What is a problem with
       harassment policies?

40.   Why is the issue of child care important to employers today?

41.   Identify two questions surrounding the child care debate.

        a. _____

        b. _____

42.   List five kinds of programs companies are providing to help with child care concerns.

        a. _____   d. _____

        b. _____   e. _____

        c. _____

43.   Why has the issue of elder care become important in today's workplace?

44.   Why is HIV and AIDS a concern to employers?

45.   What is a controversial employee-management policy regarding HIV/AIDS?

46.   Identify the kinds of costs which could be incurred by an employer of an AIDS afflicted employee.

    a._____   c._____

    b._____   d._____

47.   What is the loss to business due to substance abuse? What have companies done in response?

48.   What is the second leading cause of fatalities in the workplace?

49.   Why don't many companies provide formal training for dealing with violence in the workplace?

50.   What is the theory behind employee stock ownership programs?

51. What are the expected benefits from ESOPs?

a. _____

b. _____

c. _____

d. _____

e. _____

52. List the potential problems with ESOPs.

a. _____

b. _____

c. _____

d. _____

CRITICAL THINKING EXERCISES

Learning Goal 1

1. What were the issues that concerned the early crafts unions, before and during the Industrial Revolution? How do those issues compare with modern day work issues?

2. Five major pieces of legislation which have had an impact on the development of labor unions are:

Norris-LaGuardia Act 1932

National Labor Relations Act (Wagner Act) 1935

Fair Labor Standards Act 1938

Labor-Management Relations Act (Taft-Hartley Act) 1947

Labor-Management Reporting and Disclosure Act (Landrum-Griffin Act) 1959

Identify which act is being discussed in each of the following:

a. Texas, Florida, Georgia, Iowa, Kansas and 16 other states have passed right-to-work laws under this act. _____

b. The AFL-CIO and Teamsters file financial reports every year with the U.S. Department of Labor. _____

c. Union members picketed the Price Chopper grocery stores to protest the stores' use of non-union labor. _____

d. A retail store in Michigan is prevented from getting an injunction against a worker who is trying to organize a union. _____

e. Workers at a General Motors plant in Ohio went on strike, forcing closings at another plant that needed parts supplied by the striking plant. _____

f. A grocery store in Illinois carries products produced by a company the AFL-CIO is striking. Under this law, the AFL-CIO cannot call for a boycott of the grocery store. _____

g. Voter fraud was alleged in the election of a UAW union official, and is being investigated._____

h. In an attempt to avoid a strike, union and management officials in the automotive industry begin negotiating a year in advance of the end of the current contract.

_____

i.   In the mid-1990s Congress raised the minimum wage to $5.15 per hour.
_____

3.   There are four types of union contracts

closed shop   union shop

agency shop   open shop

Identify each of the following:

a.   When Tom Oswalt worked in an automotive factory for the summer in Michigan, he chose not to join the local union. However, he was still required to pay a fee to the union under a union-security clause. _____

b.   After the Wagner Act was passed, unions sought security with this type of agreement. With passage of the Taft-Hartley Act in 1947, however, these types of shops were made illegal.
_____

c.   When Peter Tobler went to work at Tyson Foods in Springdale, Arkansas, he was not required to join the union, and did not have to pay any fees to the union.
_____

d.   Gary Reese took a job with the Saint Louis plant of Anheuser-Busch in August. He had until October to join the union. _____

Learning Goal 2, 3

4.   Several years ago, the National and American League baseball players went on strike and ended the baseball season for the year. While player representatives continued to negotiate with team owners, (sporadically) the strike was still not resolved by the opening of the season in the spring of the following year. Even President Bill Clinton could not convince the owners and players to come to the bargaining table and talk to one another. What options are available to labor and management for resolving agreements, which could have been used before the players went on strike, or while they were on strike?

5. When the collective bargaining process breaks down, both management and labor have specific tactics available to them to reach their objectives.

Management	Labor
Injunction	Strike
Lockout	Picketing
Strikebreakers	Primary boycotts
	(Secondary boycotts)

Match the tactic being used in each of the following descriptions;

a. In the past, members of various unions have mounted campaigns to persuade consumers not to buy Coors Beer, because Coors does not use union labor._____

b. When contract negotiations broke down, the owners of the national hockey clubs refused to allow players to play, and delayed the start of the season by several weeks. _____

c. While the hockey players were being prevented from working, the baseball players were refusing to work! _____

d. In order to start a season anyway, the baseball club owners hired replacement players, bringing many up from the minor leagues. _____

e. During a strike against AT&T, union members attempted to raise public awareness and sympathy for their cause by gathering outside their places of employment carrying signs outlining their grievances. _____

f. To prevent a sympathy strike by its machinists, United Airlines obtained a court order making it illegal for the machinists to strike during a strike by the flight attendants._____

g. Although they are illegal, the employee of an airline threatened this action against the railways. _____

6. How do unions fit into the concepts we have discussed in previous chapters, such as self-managed teams, continuous improvement, and so on?

Learning Goal 4

7. What justifications can you name for the high level of executive pay in the United States?

8. What are the negative aspects of the high level of executive pay in the United States?

9. The issue of comparable worth centers on comparing the value of jobs traditionally held by women with the value of jobs traditionally held by men. What do comparisons of "men's jobs" with "women's jobs" show? How are things changing?

10. As more women have entered the workforce, the issue of sexual harassment has become increasingly visible. What are the problems surrounding this issue, and what are companies doing about it?

11.	What are the issues surrounding:

Eldercare

AIDS

Drug testing

Violence in the workplace

12.	How do ESOP programs fit into the changes in the workplace we have studied about in earlier chapters?

PRACTICE TEST

Multiple Choice – Circle the best answer

1. Most historians agree that today's union movement is an outgrowth of:

   a. the Great Depression.
   b. the Civil War.
   c. the Industrial Revolution.
   d. the Revolutionary War.

2. The first national labor organization was the

   a. Knights of Labor.
   b. American Federation of Labor.
   c. Congress of Industrial Organizations.
   d. United Mine Workers.

3. The minimum wage and maximum hours for workers requirements were established by the:

   a. Norris-LaGuardia Act.
   b. Taft-Hartley Act.
   c. Landrum-Griffin Act.
   d. Fair Labor Standards Act.

4. When Joe Kerr began working at his local bakery, he felt there was a need for the workers to sit down with management and talk about some of the problems facing the workers at their job. Joe found out there was a union for the bakery workers, but that management didn't take them seriously, and refused to sit down with the union and negotiate. After some research Joe found out that under the _____, workers had the right to expect management to negotiate with them.

   a. Norris-LaGuardia Act
   b. Wagner Act
   c. Fair Labor Standards Act
   d. Taft-Hartley Act

5.	When Dave Sutton went to work for a printing shop, he thought he was going to have to join the union representing the shop. However on his first day of work he was told that while there was a union representing the workers, he was not *required* to join, and he didn't have to pay any dues to the union if he chose not to join. Dave works in a(n) _____ shop.

a.	union
b.	agency
c.	closed
d.	open

6.	When baseball players went on strike, an individual was brought in to help resolve the dispute between management and players. This third party was involved to make suggestions, and did not make any decisions about how the players dispute should be settled. This is an example of:

a.	arbitration.
b.	grievance.
c.	mediation.
d.	a bargaining zone.

7.	When organized labor encourages its members not to buy products made by a firm in a labor dispute, it is encouraging a:

a.	strike.
b.	primary boycott.
c.	lockout.
d.	injunction.

8.	Which of the following is not a tactic used by management in a labor dispute?

a.	lockout
b.	injunction
c.	use of strikebreakers
d.	secondary boycott

9.	For unions to grow in the future, they will have to:

a.	continue to grant givebacks to management.
b.	begin to organize foreign workers.
c.	adapt to a more culturally diverse, white collar workforce.
d.	take up the fight against continuous improvement and employee involvement.

10. When compared to their European and Japanese counterparts, U.S. corporate executives:

   a. are making considerably more than executives in other countries
   b. are being paid much less that their counterparts, considering how much more they work
   c. are compensated better when times are good, but worse when the company isn't doing as well
   d. are at about the same level in terms of compensation

11. The issue of comparable worth deals with:

   a. paying equal wages to men and women who do the same job
   b. equal pay for different jobs that require similar levels of training and education or skills
   c. assuring that men and women have equal opportunity in the job market
   d. ensuring that executive pay is not more than 20 times the pay of the lowest paid worker

12. Which of the following is not included in a discussion of behavior which would be considered sexually harassing?

   a. an employee must submit to behavior as a condition of employment
   b. submission or rejection of behavior is used as a basis for employment decisions
   c. behavior interferes with job performance or creates a hostile working environment
   d. reporting of behavior results in job dismissal

13. Which of the following is not true regarding the issue of child care for workers?

   a. Federal child-care assistance has declined significantly and is expected to continue to do so
   b. Workplace changes have taken place with the Family and Medical Leave Act
   c. The number of companies providing some kind of child- care services is growing
   d. Parents have made it clear they will compromise on the issue of child- care

14. Companies have responded to requests for assistance in child-care with all of the following except:

   a. discount arrangements with national child care chains
   b. vouchers that offer payment toward the kind of child-care the employee prefers
   c. on-site child-care centers
   d. increases in the number of allowable sick leave days for employees to use when a child is ill

15. One of the more controversial employee-management policies concerns

    a. sexual harassment policies.
    b. policies against violence in the workplace.
    c. mandatory testing for the AIDS antibody.
    d. offering ESOPs to all employees.

16. Employee stock ownership programs allow employees to:

    a. gain a voice in running the company thorough voting.
    b. buy ownership in the company.
    c. gain permanent job security.
    d. have a secure path to file grievances.

17. A bargaining zone is:

    a. the location in which negotiations take place.
    b. a type of legislation that gives workers the right to join or not join a union.
    c. a contract that requires employees to agree not to join a union as a condition of employment.
    d. the range of options between the initial and final offer that each party will consider before negotiations dissolve.

18. The sources of grievances are generally

    a. overtime rules, promotions and layoffs.
    b. money and company policies.
    c. hours worked, other employees and contract negotiations.
    d. items to be included in contract negotiations.

True-False

1. _____ During the Industrial Revolution issues such as low wages and the use of child labor made the workplace ripe for the emergence of national labor unions.

2. _____ The CIO, Congress of Industrial Organizations, grew out of the Knights of Labor.

3. _____ Yellow dog contracts, preventing workers from joining a union as a condition of employment, were outlawed by the Fair Labor Standards Act.

4. _____ In arbitration, an impartial third party will make a binding decision in a labor dispute.

5. _____ Strikebreakers are often used by management to replace strikers during a prolonged strike until the dispute is resolved.

6. _____ Unions have begun to take a leadership role in encouraging cooperation of employees in employee involvement programs.

7. _____ In the past, the primary explanation for the disparity between men and women's pay has been that women often aren't as educated as men.

8. _____ Women file the majority of sexual harassment cases.

9. _____ The issue of elder care is expected to decline in importance in coming years.

10. _____ Many companies and executives don't take workplace violence seriously.

You Can Find It on the Net

Let's take a look at the issues unions are considering in the 21st century. Visit the AFL-CIO website at www.aflcio.org/home.htm

What are some of the issues featured on this website? How do those issues reflect what you have read in this chapter?

Find out how much the pay gap between men and women will cost you by clicking on that link.

Go to the link that will show you how much your pay would be if you were a CEO. How much would you be making today if you were the CEO? Pick a company and find out what the CEO of that company made.

What are some of the reasons that women are paid less than men according to this website?

What does the union say about training partnerships for the new economy?

What are the major concerns of working women according to this site?

ANSWERS

LEARNING THE LANGUAGE

1. Bargaining zone	12. Yellow dog contract	23. Knights of Labor
2. Cooling off period	13. Shop steward	24 Secondary boycott
3. Decertification	14. Union security clause	25. Arbitration
4. Grievance	15. American Federation of Labor (AFL)	26. Closed shop agreement
5. Lockout	16. Givebacks	27. Employee stock ownership plan (ESOPs)
6. Primary boycott	17. Open shop agreement	28. Negotiated labor management agreement
7. Unions	18. Strikebreakers	29. Right-to-work laws
8. Agency shop agreement	19. Certification	30. Strike
9. Comparable worth	20. Industrial unions	31. Congress of Industrial Organizations (CIO)
10.Mediation	21. Union shop agreement	32. Craft union
11.Sexual harassment	22. Collective bargaining	33. Injunction

ASSESSMENT CHECK

Employee-Management Issues

1. Most historians agree that the union movement of today is an outgrowth of the economic transition caused by the Industrial Revolution. The workers who worked in the fields suddenly became dependent upon factories for their living. Over time, workers learned that strength through unions could lead to improved job conditions, job security and better wages.

2. Labor unions have existed in the United States since as early as 1792, when shoemakers met to discuss the work issues of pay, hours, working conditions, and job security.

3. The Industrial Revolution changed the economic structure of the United States. Productivity increases from mass production and job specialization made the U.S. a world economic power. However, this growth brought problems for workers in terms of expectations, hours of work, wages, and unemployment.

4. The first national labor union was the Knights of Labor. The intention of the Knights of Labor was to gain significant political power and eventually restructure the entire U.S. economy.

5. The American Federation of Labor, AFL, was an organization of craft unions that championed fundamental labor issues.

6.   The AFL limited membership to skilled workers assuming they would have better bargaining power in getting concessions from employers.

7.   The Congress of Industrial Organizations, CIO was formed to organize both craftspeople and unskilled workers.

8.   The AFL and the CIO merged in1955 after each organization struggled for leadership for several years.

Labor Legislation and Collective Bargaining

9.   a.   Norris-LaGuardia Act 1932
     b.   National Labor Relations Act (Wagner Act) 1935
     c.   Fair Labor Standards Act 1938
     d.   Labor Management Relations Act (Taft-Hartley Act) 1947
     e.   Labor Management Reporting and Disclosure Act (Landrum-Griffin Act)1959

10. The major elements of the Norris-LaGuardia Act are that it prohibited courts from issuing injunctions against nonviolent union activities and it outlawed yellow dog contracts.

11. The Wagner Act gave employees the right to form or join labor organizations and the right to collectively bargain with employers. It also gave workers the right to engage in strikes, picketing, and boycotts. The act prohibited certain unfair labor practices by management and established the National Labor Relations Board.

12. The NLRB provides guidelines and offers legal protection to workers that seek to vote on organizing a union to represent them in the workplace.

13. The Fair Labor Standards Act set a minimum wage and maximum basic hours for workers.

14. The Taft-Hartley Act amended the Wagner Act. It permitted states to pass right-to-work laws and set up methods to deal with strikes affecting national health and security. The act also prohibits secondary boycotts, closed- shop agreements, and featherbedding.

15. In a "right-to-work" state, workers are required to work under the open shop agreement and have the option to join or not join a union if one is present.

16. The Landrum-Griffin Act amended the Taft-Hartley Act and the Wagner Act. It guaranteed individual rights of union members in dealing with their union and required annual financial reports to be filed with the U.S. Department of Labor.

Objectives of Organized Labor

17. The primary objectives of labor unions in the 1970s were additional pay and additional benefits. Later the focus was on job security and on global competition and its effects.

18.
   a. Management rights
   b. Union recognition
   c. Union security clause
   d. Strikes and lockouts
   e. Union activities and responsibilities
   f. Wages
   g. Hours of work and time-off policies
   h. Job rights and seniority principles
   i. Discharge and discipline
   j. Grievance procedures
   k. Employee benefits, health and welfare

19.
   a. Union shop
   b. Agency shop
   c. Closed shop
   d. Open shop

20. In the future unions will focus on child and elder care, worker retraining, two-tiered wage plans, employee empowerment, and integrity and honesty testing.

21.
   a. Grievance
   b. Mediation
   c. Arbitration

22. Sources of grievances are:
   a. overtime rules
   b. promotions
   c. layoffs
   d. transfers
   e. job assignments

23. Mediation becomes necessary if labor-management negotiators aren't able to agree on alternatives within the bargaining zone. The mediator encourages both sides to continue negotiating and often makes suggestions for resolving a work dispute.

24. In arbitration, an impartial third party will render a binding decision in the labor dispute. A mediator can only make a suggestion.

Tactics Used in Labor-Management Conflicts

25.
   a. Strikes
   b. Pickets
   c. Primary boycotts
   d. Secondary boycotts

26.   A strike provides public focus on a labor dispute and at times causes operations in a company to slow down or totally shut down.

27.   When strikers picket, they walk around the outside of the organization carrying signs and talking with the public and the media about the issues in a labor dispute. Unions also use picketing as an informational tool. The purpose is to alert the public about an issue that is stirring labor unrest even though no strike has been voted.

28.   A primary boycott is when labor encourages its membership not to buy the products of a firm involved in a labor dispute. A secondary boycott is an attempt to convince others to stop doing business with a firm that is the subject of a primary boycott.

29.   a. Lockouts   c. Strikebreakers
        b. Injunctions

30.   For unions to grow, they will have to adapt to a work force that is increasingly culturally diverse, white collar, female, foreign born, and professional.

31.   In the future unions may help management in training workers, redesigning jobs, and assimilating the new workforce. They will recruit and train foreign workers, unskilled workers, former welfare recipients, and others who may need special help in adapting to the job requirements of the 21st century.

Controversial Employee-Management Issues

32.   a. Executive compensation   e. Elder care
        b. Comparable worth   f. AIDS, drug testing and violence
        c. Sexual harassment   g. Employee stock ownership plans
        d. Child care

33.   Management consultant Peter Drucker suggests that CEOs should not earn much more than 20 times as much as the company's lowest paid employee.

34.   American CEOs typically earn two to three times as much as executives in Europe and Canada. In Japan, the CEO of a large corporation makes about 40 times what the average factory worker makes, compared to 475 times for the American CEO. At some companies, the number is even higher. For example, a typical hot dog vendor at Disney World would need 52,327 years to make what Disney's CEO earned in 1998.

35.   Equal pay for equal work requires that men and women doing the same job should be paid the same. Comparable worth centers on comparing the value of jobs traditionally held by women

with jobs traditionally held by men. The idea is equal pay for different jobs that require similar levels of education, training, or skills.

36. In the past the primary explanation for the pay disparity between men and women was that women only worked a portion of their available years once they left school, whereas men worked all of those years. This has changed. Now the explanation is that many women try to work as well as have families, and so fall off the career track. Other women opt for lower paying jobs.

37. Conduct can be considered sexually harassing if:
   a. an employee's submission to such conduct is made either explicitly or implicitly a term of employment.
   b. the conduct interferes with a worker's job performance or creates an unhealthy atmosphere.

38. A hostile workplace implies a work atmosphere or behavior that would offend a reasonable male or female.

39. Managers and workers are much more sensitive to comments and behavior of a sexual nature than in the past. However, the EEOC reports that sexual harassment is the fastest growing area of employee complaints. A major problem is that workers and managers often know that a policy exists but have no idea what it says.

40. The issue of childcare is important to employers today because a sizable percentage of today's working women will have children during their working years. It is estimated that child-care related absences already cost American businesses billions of dollars each year, so the potential for these kinds of losses to continue is very high.

41. Two questions surrounding child care are
   a. who should provide child-care services
   b. who should pay for them

42. Companies have responded to the need for safe, affordable day care by providing:
   a. Discount arrangements with national child-care chains
   b. Vouchers that offer payments toward whatever child care the employee chooses
   c. Referral services that help identify quality child-care facilities
   d. On-site child-care centers
   e. Sick-child care

43. The issue has become important because the number of households with at least one adult providing elder care has tripled in the past ten years. It is expected that over the next five years, 18 percent of the U.S. workforce will be involved in the task of caring for an aging relative.

44. These illnesses are a concern for employers because HIV and AIDS are a leading cause of death for Americans between the ages of 25-44, a group which represents almost half of the nation's workforce.

45. One of the more controversial employee-management policies concerns the mandatory testing for the AIDS antibody.

46.
   a. insurance
   b. losses in productivity
   c. increased absenteeism
   d. employee turnover

47. Individuals who use drugs are three and a half times more likely to be involved in workplace accidents and five times as likely to file a worker's compensation claim. Illegal drug use costs U.S. companies between $60 billion and $110 billion annually, according to the Institute for a Drug-Free Workplace. The National Institutes of Health estimate that each drug abuser costs an employer approximately $7000 a year.

48. The U.S. Department of Labor cites homicide as the second leading cause of job-related fatalities.

49. Many executives and managers don't take workplace violence seriously and believe it is media hype. This is why many companies don't provide formal training for dealing with violence in the workplace.

50. The theory behind the ESOP programs is that no matter how hard workers fight for better pay, they will never become as wealthy as people who actually own the company.

51. Expected benefits from an ESOP include:
   a. Increased employee motivation
   b. Shared profitability through shared ownership of the firm
   c. Improved management /employee relations
   d. Higher employee pride in the organization
   e. Better customer relations

52. Potential problems with ESOPs include
    a. Lack of employee stock voting rights within the firm
    b. Lack of communication between management and employees
    c. Little or no employee representation on the company board of directors
    d. Lack of job security assurances

CRITICAL THINKING EXERCISES

1.   The development of crafts unions, beginning in 1792, came about to discuss work issues such as pay, hours, working conditions, and job security. The Industrial Revolution led to changes, and problems for workers in terms of productivity, hours of work, wages, and unemployment. If you failed to produce, you lost your job. Hours worked increased to as many as 80 hours per week. Wages were low and the use of child labor was common.

    The issues unions face today are similar in many was to those that concerned the early labor unions. However, union negotiators today have also begun to address such issues as global competition, drug testing, benefits such as day care and elder care, violence in the workplace, and employee stock ownership programs.

2.   a. Taft-Hartley   f. Taft-Hartley Act
     b. Landrum-Griffin   g. Landrum-Griffin
     c. Wagner Act   h. Wagner-Act
     d. Norris-LaGuardia   i. Fair Labor Standards Act
     e. Wagner Act

3.   a. Agency shop   c. Open shop
     b. Closed shop   d. Union shop

4.   There are three options available for resolving these disputes. The players union could have filed grievances against the owners before going on strike, in an attempt to resolve their differences without putting an end to the season. Either side could have brought in a mediator, before or during the strike. The mediator's job is to make suggestions for resolving the dispute. Lastly, arbitration could have been used. In arbitration, the parties agree to bring in a third party to make a binding decision, a decision that both parties must accept. The arbitrator must be acceptable to both parties. In fact, an arbitrator was discussed between the players and the owners, but neither side could agree on the choice of an arbitrator!

5.   a. Primary boycott   e. Picketing
     b. Lockout   f. Injunction
     c. Strike   g. Secondary boycott
     d. Strikebreakers

6. The role of unions is likely to be much different from that of the past. Union leadership is aware of the need to be competitive with foreign firms. Unions have taken a leadership role in introducing such concepts as continuous improvement, constant innovation and employee involvement programs. In the future, unions will help management in training, work design and in recruiting and training foreign workers, unskilled workers and others.

7. U.S. executives are responsible for billion dollar corporations. They often work 70 or more hours per week. Many can show stockholders that they have turned potential problems into profitable success. Further, many top performers in sports, movies, and entertainment are paid large sums, so is it therefore out of line that CEOs of major corporations should be compensated in the same way? The high level of executive pay creates incentives for lower level managers to work hard to get those jobs.

8. The drawbacks of the high level of pay are most noticeable when an executive makes staggering sums, while the financial performance of the company may be lagging. Some question the compensation paid to a departing CEO whose performance forced them to resign their job involuntarily. Stakeholders should certainly question these practices in a business. In comparison to our global competitors, U.S. executives earn substantially more than their counterparts. In the U.S. the average CEO earns 209 times what the average factory worker earns, while in Japan the CEO of a large corporation makes about 40 times the average factory worker. American CEOs typically earn two to three times as much as executives in Europe and Canada.

9. A comparison of jobs traditionally held by men like truck drivers with jobs traditionally held by women, like librarians would show that women earn about 75 percent of what men earn, thought the differences vary by profession, job experience and tenure and the person's level of education. In the past, disparities could be explained by the fact that women only worked 50 to 60 percent of their available years after they left school, whereas men worked all of those years. As fewer women left the work force for an extended period, this changed. Another explanation for the disparity may be that many women try to work as well as care for families, and thus do not move ahead in their careers as quickly as men. Others opt for lower paying jobs that are less demanding.

   In today's knowledge based economy, it appears that women will compete more successfully with men, financially, in such areas as health care, telecommunications, and knowledge technology.

10. The major question surrounding the issue of sexual harassment is the fact that while managers and workers may know that their company has a sexual harassment policy, they don't know what it says. The definition of sexual harassment is unwelcome sexual advances, requests for sexual favors, and other conduct of a sexual nature. The conduct becomes illegal when: 1) an employee's submission to such conduct is made either explicitly or implicitly a term of employment, or an employee's submission to or rejection of such conduct is used as the basis of employment decisions affecting the worker's status or 2) the conduct interferes with a worker's job performance or creates an unhealthy atmosphere. Companies are becoming more sensitive to

comments and behavior of a sexual nature. Suggestions are more management training, mandatory sexual harassment workshops for all employees and a revamping of the human resource department, if necessary, to ensure compliance.

11.   The <u>elder care</u> issue has arisen because the workforce of the U.S. is aging. Older workers are more likely to be concerned with finding care for elderly parents than with finding day care for children. Businesses do not seem to be responding to the need for elder care as quickly as they could, even though it is estimated that elder-care givers cost employers billions of dollars in lost output and replacement costs.

<u>Because of the spread of AIDS</u>, businesses are directing their attention to this serious problem. The most controversial employee-management policy concerns the mandatory testing for the AIDS antibody, as more firms are insisting upon that testing. A major reason for the testing is the cost to an employer that an AIDS afflicted employee can incur in terms of insurance, losses in productivity, increased absenteeism, and employee turnover. Many firms have gone beyond pre-employment testing and suggest that all employees should be tested for the antibody.

Some companies feel that <u>alcohol and drug abuse</u> is an even more serious problem than AIDs, because so many more workers are involved. Drug testing is growing at a rapid pace.

<u>Violence in the workplace</u> is a growing trend. Still, many companies don't offer formal training for dealing with prevention of violence in the workplace, because managers are not taking the issue seriously.

12.   In previous chapters we have studied ways that employers have begun to use forms of participative management to motivate workers and meet the needs of employees who are more self-directed. ESOP programs extend the power of employee decision making even further, allowing for, in theory, employee input, at the highest level, that of "owner." So, theoretically, ESOPs are a natural extension of empowerment programs and a great way to increase employee job satisfaction. Unfortunately 85% of all ESOP plans don't allow for employee voting rights, so there is still a long way to go.

PRACTICE TEST

MULTIPLE CHOICE

1.	c	10.	a
2.	a	11.	b
3.	d	12.	d
4.	b	13.	a
5.	d	14.	d
6.	c	15.	c
7.	b	16.	b
8.	d	17.	d
9.	c	18.	a

TRUE/FALSE

1.	T	6.	T
2.	F	7.	F
3.	F	8.	T
4.	T	9.	F
5.	T	10.	T

CHAPTER 13
MARKETING: BUILDING CUSTOMER AND STAKEHOLDER RELATIONSHIP MANAGEMENT

LEARNING GOALS

After you have read and studied this chapter, you should be able to:

1. Explain the marketing concept.

2. Give an example of how to use the four Ps of marketing.

3. Describe the marketing research process and how marketers use environmental scanning to learn about the changing marketing environment.

4. Explain various ways of segmenting the consumer market.

5. List several ways that the business to business market differs from the consumer market.

6. Show how the marketing concept has been adapted to fit today's modern markets.

7. Describe the latest marketing strategies, such as stakeholder marketing and customer relationship management.

LEARNING THE LANGUAGE

Listed below are important terms found in the chapter. Choose the correct term for the definition and write it in the space provided.

Benefit segmentation	Market	Product
Brand name	Market segmentation	Promotion
Business to business market (B2B)	Marketing	Psychographic segmentation
Consumer market	Marketing concept	Stakeholder marketing
Customer relationship management	Marketing management	Target marketing
Demographic segmentation	Marketing mix	Test marketing
Environmental scanning	Marketing research	Volume segmentation
Focus group	Mass marketing	
Geographic segmentation	Niche marketing	
Green product	One-to- one marketing	

1.	A word, letter or group of words or letters is a _____ that differentiates the goods and services of a seller from those of a competitor.

2.	All the techniques sellers use to motivate people to buy products or services is called _____.

3.	Dividing the market by geographic area is _____.

4.	All individuals and organizations that want goods and services to produce other goods and services or to sell, rent or supply goods to others is known as the _____.

5.	The process known as _____ is when an organization tests products among potential users.

6.	The process called _____calls for planning and executing the conception, pricing, promotion, and distribution of ideas, goods and services to create mutually beneficial exchanges.

7.	A _____is any physical good, service or idea that satisfies a want or need.

8.	The process of _____is dividing the market by age, income, and education level.

9.	A three-part business philosophy called the _____involves (1) a consumer orientation, (2) a service orientation, and (3) a profit orientation.

10.	A _____is a small group of people who meet under the direction of a discussion leader to communicate their opinions about an organization, its products, or other given issues.

11.	The process known as _____calls for finding small, but profitable, market segments and designing custom-made products for those groups.

12.	Establishing and maintaining mutually beneficially exchange relationships over time, or _____, is done with all the stakeholders of the organizations.

13.	The ingredients that go into a marketing program are the _____ and include product, price, place, and promotion.

14.	A product is called a _____ when the production, use, and disposal don't damage the environment.

15. The process known as _____ is marketing toward those groups and organizations a firm decides it can profitably serve.

16. The process called _____ is used to determine opportunities and challenges and to find the information needed to make good decisions.

17. The process of _____ means dividing the market by determining which benefits of our product we talk about.

18. The _____ consists of all the individuals or households who want goods and services for personal consumption or use.

19. The process of _____ is determining customer wants and needs and then providing customers with goods and services that meet or exceed their expectations.

20. A _____ consists of people with unsatisfied wants and needs who have both the resources and the willingness to buy.

21. The process of dividing the total market into several groups whose members have similar characteristics is called _____.

22. Developing products and promotions to please large groups of people is known as _____.

23. Learning as much as possible about customers, and doing everything you can to satisfy customers or even delight them with goods and services over time is called _____.

24. The process of _____ is identifying the factors that can affect marketing success.

25. Dividing the market by using a group's values, attitudes and interests is _____.

26. _____ is dividing market by usage (volume of use).

27. Developing a unique mix of goods and services for each individual customer is called _____.

ASSESSMENT CHECK

Learning Goal 1   **A Brief History of Marketing**

1.   Describe the three parts of the marketing concept.

2.   What is the idea of customer relationship management?

3.   What is the goal of the marketing process?

Learning Goal 2   **Marketing Management and the Marketing Mix**

4.   What are the 4 Ps of marketing?

     a._____   c._____

     b._____   d._____

5.   What does a marketing manager do?

6. List the eight steps in the marketing process

a. _____

b. _____

c. _____

d. _____

e. _____

f. _____

g. _____

h. _____

7. What is meant by "concept testing?"

8. What are prototypes?

9. What are marketing intermediaries?

10. What are six promotion techniques?

a. _____ d. _____

b. _____ e. _____

c. _____ f. _____

Learning Goal 3 **Providing Marketers with Information**

11. What are three things which marketing research helps to determine?

a. _____

b. _____

c. _____

12. Who should market researchers pay attention to?

13. What are the four steps of the marketing research process?

a. _____

b. _____

c. _____

d. _____

14. What is the difference between primary and secondary data?

15. What is the benefit of secondary data?

16. What is the observation method of collecting data?

17. What are six general sources of secondary data?

   a. _____   d. _____

   b. _____   e. _____

   c. _____   f. _____

18. What are some of the most common types of surveys?

19. How have company web sites improved the market research process?

20. What are the factors included in an environmental scan?

    a._____   d._____

    b._____   e._____

    c._____

21. What is the most dramatic global change? Why?

22. What have been the most dramatic technological changes? Why?

23. What are some social trends that marketers must monitor?

24. How has the Internet affected competition?

25. How would marketing change with a change in the economy?

Recognizing Different Markets: Consumer and Business to Business

26. What are two major markets in marketing?

27. What determines if a product is a business to business product or a consumer product?

Learning Goal 4 **The Consumer Market**

28. Why do companies use market segmentation?

29. What are the ways in which the consumer market can be segmented?

a. _____ d. _____

b. _____ e. _____

c. _____

30. What kind of segmentation is being used when we:
    a. Segment by what qualities a customer prefers?
    b. Segment by where people live?
    c. Segment by how much a customer uses?
    d. Segment by a group's values, attitudes, or interests?
    e. Segment by age, income, or education?

31.   What has made "niche marketing" possible?

32.   How does a mass marketer "operate?"

33.   What is the goal of relationship marketing?

34.   How is a "community of buyers" established?

35.   What are the steps in the consumer decision-making process?

a. _____

b. _____

c. _____

d. _____

e. _____

36.   List the four types of influences on the consumer decision-making process.

a. _____

b. _____

c. _____

d. _____

37.   In market research, what is:
a.   learning
b.   a reference group
c.   culture
d.   subculture
e.   cognitive dissonance

Learning Goal 5   **The Business-To-Business Market (B2B)**

38.   Why does business-to-business marketing differ from consumer marketing?

39.   What are six factors that differentiate business-to-business marketing from consumer marketing?

a. _____

b. _____

c. _____

d. _____

e. _____

Updating the Marketing Concept

40. What are the three basic elements of the marketing concept?

    a. _____

    b. _____

    c. _____

41. What does it mean to have a " customer orientation?" How have businesses done in this area?

42. How do companies perform the process of "competitive benchmarking?"

43. How do companies maintain a profit orientation?

Establishing Relationships with All Stakeholders

44. How does the traditional marketing concept differ from modern marketing? What must be balanced?

45. How have companies responded to the environmental movement? How does this demonstrate stakeholder marketing?

46. What is the "80/20" rule?

47. Why is customer relationship management so important?

CRITICAL THINKING EXERCISES

Learning Goal 1

1. Todd Whitman was a full-time student at a community college in the St. Louis area. In addition to going to school, Todd also worked for a company out of Idaho (Todd's home state) that made ice cream. As Todd tells it:" Alan Reed owns a potato farm in Idaho. He was looking for another market for his potatoes when he realized that the chemical make up of the potato was such that it could be used in making a tasty ice cream without using any sugar - i.e. a sugar free ice cream. He figured there had to be a market for that kind of product, one made without any artificial products to sweeten, so he made a few batches and tried it on his friends, without telling them it was made from potatoes." He called the ice cream Al and Reed's. This is where Todd came in. While in St. Louis, Todd's job was to attempt to get the product sold to St. Louisans. His employer shipped him a few gallons (as much as he could hold in his home freezer). Todd started trying to sell Al and Reed's to local grocery store chains, and ultimately got one of them to carry the ice cream in a couple of stores on a trial basis. He also brought some samples to his Introduction to Business class, after persuading his teacher to allow a taste test. The product went over well, until the students found out it was made from potatoes!

   Todd continued his promotional efforts with grocery stores, calling on them whenever he could. He left promotional pamphlets that explained the concept and production of ice cream made from potatoes, and offered the stores discounts for buying in volume.

a. Did Todd and Alan Reed use the marketing concept? Did Alan "find a need and fill it?" Explain.

b. What steps in the marketing process did Todd and Alan Reed take?

c. What potential problem might they encounter with this product? How could Todd and Alan use the last step of the marketing process to overcome the problem?

d. Identify the product, promotion and place variables in this situation. What price do you think they should charge? Why?

2. We read in earlier chapters about the "revolutionary" concepts of organizational design such as cross-functional, self managed teams, and such concepts as continuous improvement. What do these have to do with marketing?

Learning Goal 3, 4

3. We have been "creating" Music-stor, and its product throughout several chapters. Now is the time to begin developing a marketing plan for our product. We will become more specific in the following chapters. Generally,

a. What need did Eric see when he came up with the idea of Music-stor?

b.   Who/what do you think should be Music-stor's customers?

c.   How could concept testing have helped Eric?

d.   How do the various elements of the marketing environment affect Music-stor?

e.   Could Music-stor make use of mass customization?

4.   Marketing research is conducted to determine the needs of the market and the best ways to fill those needs.

Using the four steps outlined in your book, suggest a market research project that might be of use to Music-stor;

a. _____

b. _____

c. _____

d. _____

5.   Determine whether the following describes a consumer or a business-to-business product.

a.   Monsanto buys apples to sell in its company cafeteria. _____

b.   Jeff Walter buys a lawn mower for his lawn mowing business. _____

c. Darlene Knott buys a lawn mower to mow her lawn. _____

d. Marti Galganski buys apples for her daughter's lunch. _____

Learning Goal 4

6. The major segmentation variables are:

Geographic   Psychographic   Volume

Demographic   Benefit

Listed below are various products. Identify a target market for each product, then list the segmentation variable that could be used to identify that target market. There could be more than one target market for some products.

Example:

Head and Shoulders Shampoo:

Target market: People with dandruff

Variables: Benefit, health

a. Ford Focus automobile

b. Nike footwear

c. McDonald's

d. Campbell's nacho cheese soup

7. Harry Allen turned on his c.d player to listen to music while he was studying, and all he heard was a loud buzzing coming from his speakers. "Oh no! Now what?" thought Harry. Well Harry found the problem and realized that the system was shot. "Well, we've got to have music for the party coming up in two weeks, so I'm going to have to get a new player" Harry said to his roommate on the way to class. Harry looked through the ads in the Sunday paper and saw several sales at a couple of different stores. He spent part of the weekend, and part of a few days the following week looking at different component pieces, comparing each for price and sound quality and talking to sales people about which system was the best value. A couple of friends gave Harry their opinions of the brands, based on their experience with the specific brand Harry was considering. Harry knew this brand was a good one because his sister had purchased it last year. He bought the new stereo system the following weekend, before the sale ended. He felt somewhat uneasy at how much he had spent, but when he saw an ad for that same system in an upscale magazine for $100 more, he felt better.

Identify the steps in the decision making process that Harry took, and what factors influenced his decision, using the figure in your text.

Learning Goal 5

8.   Would you classify Music-Stor's product as a consumer good or as a business good? What characteristics of the business-to-business market will affect Music-stor's marketing efforts? How?

9.   Let's continue helping Music-stor to develop a marketing plan:

   a.   Who would you choose as Music-stor's target market?

   b.   If you were to choose the consumer market, what are some variables that you would want to consider?

   c.   How would marketing your product to an industrial market differ from marketing the product to the consumer market?

Learning Goal 6

10.   How has technology enabled companies to go from mass marketing to a modern version of the marketing concept?

PRACTICE TEST

Multiple Choice – Circle the best answer

1. The basis of marketing is to:

    a. find a need and fill it.
    b. produce as many products as possible.
    c. look for a market, then make a product.
    d. find a good product and make it available at a reasonable price.

2. When McDonald's considered adding pizza to their menu, the company made pizza available in some of their typical markets, to determine customer reactions. That process is called:

    a. promotion.
    b. test marketing.
    c. outsourcing.
    d. concept testing.

3. Which of the following would not be included in a discussion of the marketing concept?

    a. A customer orientation
    b. Service orientation
    c. Profit orientation
    d. A product orientation

4. Learning as much as possible about customers and doing everything you can to satisfy them or even delight them with goods and services is called:

    a. customer relationship management.
    b. marketing management.
    c. market segmentation.
    d. promotion.

5. Marketing research helps determine all but which of the following?

    a. how customer needs will change
    b   what customers have purchased in the past
    c. what changes have occurred to change what customers want
    d. what customers are likely to want in the future

6.   What is the first step in the marketing research process?

   a.   analyze data
   b.   collect data
   c.   define the problem
   d.   develop potential solutions

7.   The factors included in an environmental scan include all of the following except:

   a.   technological factors.
   b.   competitive factors.
   c.   management factors.
   d.   economic factors.

8.   Curious George went to the library to look up government statistics on the amount of bananas imported into the U.S. during the previous year. Curious was making use of:

   a.   primary data.
   b.   secondary data.
   c.   the observation method.
   d.   focused research.

9.   At one time, companies developed products and promotions to please large groups of people, and tried to sell as many products to as many people as possible. This is known as

   a.   relationship marketing.
   b.   a consumer orientation.
   c.   forming a community of buyers.
   d.   mass marketing.

10.   Which of the following products would be considered as the "business to business" market?

   a.   Classes at a university for a college freshman
   b.   Pens and pencils for that student
   c.   Books for the class, purchased by the student
   d.   A computer for the instructor to use while teaching the class

11. Which of the following is not considered to be one of the marketing mix variables?

a. Producing a want satisfying product
b. Promoting the product
c. Minimizing the cost of producing the product
d. Setting a price for the product

12. Alonzo Wilder has just been hired in marketing management for the L. Ingalls farming co-op. In his job as marketing manager, Alonzo's primary responsibility will be to

a. make sure the product is priced reasonably.
b. manage the primary sales force.
c. monitor production and make sure the product is in the right place at the right time.
d. manage the marketing mix variables to ensure an effective marketing program.

13. Which of the following is not a requirement for a "market"

a. people who have the authority to buy.
b. people with unsatisfied wants and needs.
c. people who have the resources to buy.
d. people who have the willingness to buy.

14. We FlyU Anywhere is a travel agency that specializes in creating exotic trips to unusual destinations for their clients. They will create a "designer" vacation just for you. The most accurate description for the kind of marketing this travel agency is doing would be:

a. Niche marketing.
b. One-to-one marketing.
c. Customer Relationship marketing.
d. Stakeholder marketing.

15. Kelly Butler is out looking for a new car. Kelly is an aspiring lawyer, and she is looking for a car that will help her to project that "lawyer " image. Kelly is influenced by

a. a cultural influence.
b. a reference group.
c. cognitive dissonance.
d. the consumer market.

16. After Kelly bought her car, she realized just how much money she had spent! She spent some time wondering if she had made the right decision. Kelly seems to be suffering from:

   a. cognitive dissonance.
   b. consumer behavior.
   c. self-doubt.
   d. psychological influences.

17. The company that makes the Nautica brand licensed with the Stride-Rite company to make an athletic shoe to compete with Nike. The company wants the shoe to be used for athletics, not worn just for style. Nautica is making use of :

   a. market analysis.
   b. market segmentation.
   c. niche marketing.
   d. one-to-one marketing.

18. The Saturn car company has parties for their buyers every year, and Harley Davidson has their HOGs (Harley Owners Group) . These companies have:

   a. formed a strong market segment.
   b. performed niche marketing.
   c. created communities of buyers.
   d. used focus groups.

19. Johnson and Johnson targets children with Sesame Street bandages, and GM targets women for their Chevy Blazer vehicle. These are examples of:

   a. benefit segmentation.
   b. volume segmentation.
   c. psychographic segmentation.
   d. demographic segmentation.

20. Which of the following is not descriptive of the business to business market?

   a. there are relatively few customers in the industrial market
   b. industrial customers are relatively large
   c. industrial buyers are generally more rational that consumer buyers
   d. industrial markets tend to be geographically scattered

21. Balancing the wants and needs of all a firm's stakeholders, such as employees, suppliers, dealers and the community is known as

    a. a consumer orientation.
    b. stakeholder marketing.
    c. mass marketing.
    d. forming a community of buyers.

True-False

1. _____ The role of marketing is to make a good or service and then make sure people want to buy it.

2. _____ Marketing middlemen are organizations that traditionally are in the middle of a series of organizations that distribute goods from producers to consumers.

3. _____ According to the text, most organizations have reached the goal of delighting customers.

4. _____ Coupons, rebates, and cents-off deals are part of the promotion variable of the marketing mix.

5. _____ In general, non profit organizations do not make use of marketing techniques.

6. _____ The four marketing mix variables are product, price, packaging, and promotion.

7. _____ Relationship marketing leads away from mass production toward more custom-made goods and services.

8. _____ To minimize costs, it is best to use secondary data first, when possible, in the market research process.

9. _____ If the economy begins to fall on hard times, about the only thing marketers can do is to cut production and wait for better times.

10. _____ The process of dividing the total market into several groups is called target marketing.

11. _____ The reason for distinguishing between consumer markets and the business-to-business market is because the strategies for reaching the markets are different, because the buyers are different.

12. _____ Business to business sales tend to be less direct than consumer sales because business buyers use more middlemen.

You Can Find It on the Net

Rollerblade's Web site contains a lot of information about a variety of areas. Visit this site at www.rollerblade.com

Does Rollerblade's Web site help the company strengthen the relationship it has with its customers? How does the site attempt to create new relationships with new customers?

How do the elements of Rollerblade's Web site reflect their target market? Be specific.

Does Rollerblade invite comments from visitors to its Web site? If so, how does this affect its attempt to build positive relationships with its customers?

ANSWERS

KEY TERMS AND DEFINITIONS

1. Brand name	10.Focus group	19. Marketing
2. Promotion	11.Niche marketing	20. Market
3. Geographic segmentation	12. Stakeholder marketing	21. Market segmentation
4. Business to business market	13. Marketing mix	22. Mass marketing
5. Test marketing	14. Green product	23. Customer relationship management
6. Marketing management	15. Target marketing	24. Environmental scanning
7. Product	16. Marketing research	25. Psychographic segmentation
8. Demographic segmentation	17. Benefit segmentation	26. Volume segmentation
9. Marketing concept	18. Consumer market	27. One-to-one marketing

ANSWERS

ASSESSMENT CHECK

A Brief History of Marketing

1. The marketing concept had three parts. The first is a customer orientation, which is to find out what customers want and provide it for them. Secondly, a service orientation, making sure everyone in the organization has the same objective of customer satisfaction. And lastly, a profit orientation, which is marketing the goods and services that will earn the firm profit and enable it to survive and expand.

2. The idea of customer relationship management is to get close to your customers and spend time with them, rather than to continually seek out new customers.. It is important to learn as much as possible about customers and do everything you can to satisfy them or delight them with goods and services over time.

3. The goal of the marketing process is to find a need and fill it.

Marketing Management and the Marketing Mix

4. a. product   c. promotion
    b. price   d. place

5. A marketing manager designs a marketing program that effectively combines the ingredients of the marketing mix in order to please customers. Marketing management is the process of planning and executing the conception, pricing, promotion, and distribution of goods and services to create mutually beneficial exchanges.

6.   a. Find a need

b. Conduct research

c. Design a product to meet the need, based upon research results

d. Test the product

e. Determine brand name, design packaging and set a price

f.   Select a distribution system

g. Design a promotional program

h. Build a relationship with your customers

7.   In concept testing, an accurate description of a product is developed, and then people are asked whether the concept appeals to them.

8.   Prototypes are samples of the product that you take to consumers to test their reactions.

9.   Marketing intermediaries or middlemen are organizations that specialize in distributing products. They are called middlemen because they're in the middle of a series of organizations that distribute goods from producers to consumers.

10.   a. advertising   d. publicity

b. personal selling   e. word of mouth

c. public relations   f. sales promotion

Providing Marketers with Information

11.   Marketing research helps to determine

a. what customers have purchased in the past

b. what situational changes have occurred to change what customers want

c. what they're likely to want in the future

12.   Market researchers should pay attention to what employees, shareholders, dealers, consumer advocates, media representatives, and other stakeholders have to say.

13.   a. Define the problem and determine the present situation

b. Collect data

c. Analyze the research data

d. Choose the best solutions

14.   Primary data are statistics and information not previously published that you gather on your own through observation, surveys, and personal interviews or focus groups. Secondary data are

published reports and research from journals, trade associations, the government, information services and others. Secondary data would be used before primary whenever possible.

15. The benefit of secondary data is that it is less expensive to gather information that has already been researched by others.

16. In the observation method, data are collected by observing the actions of potential buyers.

17.
a. Government Publications
b. Commercial Publications
c. Magazines
d. Newspapers
e. Internal sources
f. Internet searches

18. The most common methods of gathering survey information are telephone surveys, online surveys, mail surveys, and personal interviews.

19. Company web sites have improved the market research process because customers can now continuously interact with the company and other consumers to improve products and services.

20. The factors included in an environmental scan include global, technological, social, competitive, and economic factors.

21. The most dramatic global change is the growth of the Internet. Now a company can reach many of the consumers in the world relatively easily, and can carry on a dialogue about what consumers want.

22. The most important technological changes also involve the Internet and the growth of consumer databases. Using these, companies can develop products and services that more closely match the needs of consumers.

23. Marketers must monitor social trends such as population growth, and changing demographics such as the growing population of older people and the shifting ethnic nature of the American population.

24. Brick and mortar companies must be aware of new competition from the Internet. Consumers can now search literally all over the world for the best prices through the Internet.

25. If the economy were to slow or fall on hard economic times, marketers would have to adapt by offering products that are less expensive or more tailored to a slow-growth economy.

Recognizing Different Markets: consumer and Business to Business

26.   The two major markets in marketing are the consumer market and the business-to-business market.

27.   The buyer's reason for buying and the end use of the product determine whether a product is considered a consumer product or an industrial product.

The Consumer Market

28.   Consumer groups differ in age, education level, income and taste, and a business can't usually fill the needs of every group. So the company must decide what groups to serve, and develop products and services specially tailored to meet their needs.

29.   a. geographic   d. benefit
        b. demographic   e. volume
        c. psychographic

30.   a. benefit   d. psychographic
        b. geographic   e. demographic
        c. volume

31.   New manufacturing techniques make it possible to develop specialized products for small market groups. This is called niche marketing.

32.   The mass marketer tries to sell products to as many people as possible, using mass media, such TV, radio, and newspapers.

33.   The goal of relationship marketing is to retain individual customers over time by offering them products that exactly meet their requirements.

34.   When developing a community of buyers, a company begins by establishing a database so that every contact with consumers results in more information about them. Over time, the seller learns enough about the consumer to establish a community of buyers. This can be done in a variety of ways, including interactive Web sites, clubs, newsletters, meetings, rallies, and other events.

35. a. Problem recognition

 b. Information search

 c. Alternative evaluation

 d. Purchase decision

 e. Postpurchase decision (cognitive dissonance)

36. a. Marketing mix influences—product, price, promotion, place

 b. Sociocultural influences—Reference groups, family, social class, culture, subculture

 c. Situational influences—Type of purchase, social surroundings, physical surroundings, previous experience

 d. Psychological influences—Perception, attitudes, learning, motivation

37. a. Learning involves changes in an individual's behavior resulting from previous experiences and information.

 b. A reference group is the group that an individual uses as a reference point in the formation of his or her beliefs, attitudes, values or behavior.

 c. Culture is the set of values, attitudes, and ways of doing things that are passed down from one generation to another in a society.

 d. Subculture is the set of values, attitudes and ways of doing things that result from belonging to a certain ethnic group, religious group, racial group or other group with which one identifies.

 e. Cognitive dissonance is a type of psychological conflict that can occur after a purchase, particularly a major purchase.

The Business-To-Business Market (B2B)

38. The basic principle of business to business marketing is still "find a need and fill it," but the strategies differ from consumer marketing, because the nature of the buyers is different.

39. a. The number of customers in the industrial market is relatively few.

 b. The size of industrial customers is relatively large.

 c. Industrial markets tend to be geographically concentrated.

 d. Industrial buyers generally are more rational than ultimate consumers.

 e. Industrial sales tend to be direct.

 f. There is more emphasis on personal selling.

Updating the Marketing Concept

40. a. A consumer orientation

 b. Customer service orientation

 c. A profit orientation

41. A customer orientation is to please or delight customers by providing products that exactly meet their requirements or exceed their expectations. Most organizations have not reached the goal of delighting customers.

42. Competitive benchmarking means that companies compare their processes and products with those of the best companies in the world to learn how to improve them.

43. In pursuing a profit orientation a firm must make sure that everyone in the organization understands that the purpose behind pleasing customers and uniting organizations is to ensure a profit for the firm. Using that profit, the organizations can then satisfy other stakeholders of the firm.

Establishing Relationships with All Stakeholders

44. The traditional marketing concept emphasized giving customers what they want. Modern marketing goes further by recognizing the need to please other stakeholders as well. The firm must balance the needs and wants of all the firm's stakeholders, such as employees, customers, suppliers, dealers, stockholders, media representatives and the community.

45. Organizations have responded to the environmental movement when designing and marketing green products. Organizations that adopt stakeholder marketing take the environmental community's needs in mind when designing these green products.

46. The 80/20 rule says that 80 percent of your business is likely to come from just 20 percent of your customers.

47. Customer relationship management is so important because it is far more expensive to get a new customer than to strengthen a relationship with an existing one.

CRITICAL THINKING EXERCISES

1. a. From the story, it doesn't sound as if Al found a need for a sugar free ice cream and then found a way to develop it, which would be the first part of the marketing concept. There also doesn't appear to be a concern for customer satisfaction, other than to make sure the consumers liked the product. It sounds more like he had extra potatoes and needed to find a novel way to sell them!

    b. Alan recognized the need for a sugar free ice cream. (Step 1). At least he thought he did. We don't know how much research he did on the actual demand for a sugar free ice cream. He did test the concept (2) by making small batches and testing it with his friends. He made the product in small batches (3) at first. Todd did some research in his business class. You could say the concept testing was combined with the test marketing stage (4), or that St. Louis served as a test market. The brand name (5) stemmed from the originator's name, Alan Reed

(Al and Reed's). The marketing middlemen (6) are Todd, and then the grocery stores which finally agreed to sell the product through Todd's efforts. Promotion (7) was done primarily through pamphlets and personal selling by Todd. There is no mention made of any effort to build a relationship with the customer.

c. Probably the biggest potential problem is the negative reaction to the product. It could be that consumers will not be attracted to ice cream made from potatoes and would wonder about the taste. (The students actually liked the taste of the ice cream until they found out it was made from potatoes!) By talking with consumers, and grocery store managers (who are consumers, too, and must be convinced) Todd and Alan may have found ways to overcome the perception that ice cream made from potatoes must taste terrible.

d. Product – sugar free ice cream made from potatoes

Promotion – personal selling, such as Todd taking the ice cream to the grocery store. They also offered discounts to the grocers, which could be seen as a form of promotion.

Place – Todd's efforts were to place the product in the grocery store

Price – how much would you pay for this product? Would it be considered a premium product? Often sugar free versions of products are a little higher in price than the regular product. Would you pay $5 per gallon?

2. It has become clear that everyone in a firm has to work together to delight and satisfy customers. Companies have begun to see that employees will not provide first-class goods and services to customers unless they receive first-class treatment from their employer. Therefore, we have seen changes in organizational design, and a focus on the "internal" customer. Cross functional teams, discussed in previous chapters, are practicing continuous improvement and uniting employees in a joint effort to produce goods and services which will both please customers and assure a profit for the firm. Continuous improvement in processes are also focused on satisfying the customer while competing with speed, better higher quality products and lower prices.

3. a. Eric may have seen that more people are listening to tapes and compact discs in their cars. Compact discs especially are growing in popularity. When people want to listen to their own music in the car, a convenient place to store several tapes or CDs would be a real benefit.

b. There is a potential for two types of customers, the automotive manufacturers, for installation as an option in new cars, and the after-market dealers, like auto supply stores, for people who want to install their own.

c. Asking people if they need a product such as this would have given Eric a feel for what demand might have been. He would have to be sure to ask the right questions of the right people to get an accurate idea. He could have given prototypes to friends, or potential customers for use to "field test" or test market the product.

d. The Social environment consists of trends and population shifts. The trend toward installing compact disc players in autos, for example, contributes to a positive outlook for Music-stor's product. As the population ages, more people may prefer to listen to music they bring along, rather than the radio. It may also provide an opportunity for a different kind of storage device, video tapes, since there is a trend now to include tape players in many automobiles. Since that type of equipment comes only in certain kinds of cars, economic factors such as disposable income, and unemployment, would affect demand for the cars, thus for Music-stor's product. With a rapidly expanding global market, there may be possibilities outside the United States, as well as potential competition. Technology has affected Music-stor simply by virtue of the fact that c.d. players are a fact of life in cars today. Further, new high-tech production techniques will help Music-stor to produce more products with fewer people at a lower cost.

e. Can Music-stor adopt customized marketing? Basically, the product must be made to suit many different models of car with different interior shapes, different interior colors. The product is "custom made" for "customized marketing."

4. a. Music-stor may want to determine what kind of demand there will be for their product in the next five years. They may want to find out if their primary market should be younger or older drivers, and relate that to the type of car being driven. They may also want to determine if there are other markets they could enter. For example, over-the-road truckers could make use of this product, but it may have to be of a different size and shape to fit into the cab of a semi. Music-stor may want to look into potential demand for a portable storage case for video tapes.

b. Collecting secondary data for the automotive market may be easily done to determine potential demand for autos and their product in the automotive market. Trade journals and government publications would provide sales forecasts for the type of cars Music-stor is targeting. The truck market may require some primary research, such as focus groups or some kind of survey, possibly distributed through the mail, or directly to truckers in some way.

c. Analysis of the data may indicate there is a bigger market for the product for truckers than for the automotive market. Alternatively, it may indicate that sales are predicted to go flat for the kinds of cars Music-stor has targeted, indicating that the company may want to target a different car segment or another market altogether.

d. Choosing the best solution would be to choose the market that will be the most profitable for Music-stor and still meet the needs of their stakeholders.

5.   a. Business   c. Consumer
      b. Business   d. Consumer

6.   Sample Answers:
      a. Ford Focus
          Target market - Young drivers, may be buying their first car
          Variables – Could be demographic, such as age, income, family life cycle
      b. Nike
          Target market – Teenagers, boys and girls, interested in sports
          Variables – Demographic – sex, age and Psychographic – interests, self image
      c. McDonald's
          Target market – Families with young children
          Variables – Demographic – family life cycle, age, income, and Psychographic – lifestyle
      d. Campbell's nacho cheese soup
          Target market – Consumers in the west and southwest
          Variables – Geography – region, Demographic – nationality, or Culture

7.   Problem recognition came when Harry realized his system couldn't be fixed! Harry searched for information through the newspaper ads, and also by going to the stores and talking to salespeople. He was evaluating the alternatives by comparing each component piece for value and sound. When he finally made his purchase, he felt "cognitive dissonance," uneasy as to how much he spent, until he saw an ad for the same brand at a more expensive price.

      Along the way, several factors influenced Harry's decision. He spoke to friends, which could be considered a reference group. Family may have been an influence, as Harry's sister has the same brand. There was a cultural influence as well, just from the fact that Harry felt the importance of having a new CD system for his party, rather that using a less expensive alternative. The price variable of the marketing mix was an influence, as the system was on sale. You could consider the psychological influence of learning, as Harry's friends had learned that this was a good brand through experience, and passed that information along. You may have thought of other influences as well.

8.   Music-stor's product could be classified as both a consumer product and a product for the business to business market. If Eric sells the storage case through after-market auto equipment retailers, the product would be considered a consumer good, in general. In attempting to reach the automotive manufacturers, Eric is developing a business-to-business marketing relationship. The characteristics of the business-to-business market listed in your book will affect Music-stor in a number of ways. First, the primary market is the automotive industry, so there will be relatively few customers compared to the consumer market. Those car manufacturers are very large corporations, among the largest in the world, each with significant buying power. The domestic car market, at least, is concentrated in one geographic area. If Eric were to try to appeal to buyers for foreign manufacturers, he would have to do some more traveling. These buyers will consider Eric's product based on the "total product offer," including how much more

marketable Music-stor will make their product, in addition to factors such as quality and price. If the customer is the auto industry, Eric won't need to use wholesalers or retailers. He will sell directly to the car companies. For the consumer market, he will have to use at least a retail distribution center.

9. Keep in mind these are suggested answers, and you may come up with a totally different plan!

    a. We have often mentioned two target markets for Music-stor - the original equipment automotive market, to be installed as cars are assembled, and a consumer market, through auto parts stores perhaps for people who want to install the product later. You may have decided on another way to approach the market.

    b. If you chose the consumer market, variables could include: Income, because cars with installed CD players may be more high end; or with research you may find out that large numbers of younger drivers install their own CD players in their cars, so age would be a consideration. This is where research can really come in handy.

    c. To market to the industrial market, Music-stor must focus on personal selling, in a very concentrated market. The automotive industry has few domestic producers, but there are several foreign manufacturers with production facilities here in the United States. You would have to focus on quality, be able to meet the volume required to sell to the industrial market, and meet delivery requirements that may include dealing with just-in-time inventory control systems. This would require a sophisticated production and delivery system on the part of Music-stor.

10. With sophisticated information technology, marketers are able better than ever to find out what customers are buying, and what they will want to buy in the future. With such programs as CAD/CAM, flexible manufacturing, and mass customization, companies can more readily meet smaller, more individualized markets. With new production and information technology, companies will be able to both establish and maintain long-term relationships with customers.

PRACTICE TEST

MULTIPLE CHOICE

1.	a	12.	d	
2.	b	13.	a	
3.	d	14.	b	
4.	a	15.	b	
5.	a	16.	a	
6.	c	17.	b	
7.	c	18.	c	
8.	b	19.	d	
9.	d	20.	d	
10.	d	21.	b	
11.	c			

TRUE/FALSE

1.	F	7.	T
2.	T	8.	T
3.	F	9.	F
4.	T	10.	F
5.	F	11.	T
6.	F	12.	F

LEARNING GOALS

After you have read and studied this chapter, you should be able to:

1.   Explain the concept of a value package.

2.   Describe the various kinds of consumer and industrial goods.

3.   List and describe the six functions of packaging.

4.   Give examples of a brand, a brand name, and a trademark, and explain the concepts of brand equity and loyalty.

5.   Explain the role of brand managers and the six steps of the new-product development process.

6.   Identify and describe the stages of the product life cycle and describe marketing strategies at each stage.

7.   Give examples of various pricing objectives and strategies.

8.   Explain why nonpricing strategies are growing in importance.

LEARNING THE LANGUAGE

Listed below are important terms found in the chapter. Choose the correct term for the definition and write it in the space provided.

Brand	Generic name	Product screening
Brand association	High-low price strategy	Shopping goods and services
Brand awareness	Industrial goods	Skimming price strategy
Brand equity	Knockoff brands	Specialty goods and services
Brand loyalty	Manufacturers' brand names	Target costing
Brand manager	Penetration pricing strategy	Total fixed costs
Break-even analysis	Price leadership	Trademark
Commercialization	Product analysis	Unsought goods and services
Concept testing	Product differentiation	Value
Convenience goods and services	Product life cycle	Value package
Dealer (private) brands	Product line	Value pricing
EDLP	Product mix	Variable costs
Generic goods		

1.   The process used to determine profitability at various levels of sales is called _____.

2.   The method of pricing known as a _____ is when a product is priced low to attract more customers and discourage competitors.

3.   The strategy of _____ involves setting prices that are higher than EDLP stores, but having many special sales where the prices are lower than competitors.

4.   A _____ consists of everything that consumers evaluate when deciding whether to buy something.

5.   The degree to which customers are satisfied, like the brand, and are committed to further purchases is called _____.

6.   The four-stage theoretical model called the _____ shows what happens to sales and profits for a product class over time.

7.   A strategy known as a _____ is a method of pricing in which a new product is priced high to make optimum profit while there is little competition.

8.   A brand that has been given exclusive legal protection for both the brand name and the pictorial design is called a _____.

9.   The linking of a brand to other favorable images is called _____.

10.   Products called _____ are used in the production of other products.

11.   Conducting a _____ is making cost estimates and sales forecasts to get a feeling for the profitability of new ideas.

12.   A strategy known as _____ means providing consumers brand name goods and services at fair prices.

13.   A _____ is a name, symbol, or design that identifies the goods or services of one seller or group of sellers and distinguishes them from those of competitors.

14.   The process of _____ calls for taking a product idea to consumers to test their reactions.

15. Products called _____ are products that consumers want to purchase frequently with a minimum of effort.

16. The name for a product category is a _____.

17. Products called _____ do not carry the manufacturer's name, but carry the name of a distributor or retailers instead.

18. Products that have a special attraction to consumers who are willing to go out of their way to obtain them are called _____.

19. How quickly or easily a given brand name comes to mind when a product category is mentioned is _____.

20. A group of products known as the _____ are physically similar or are intended for a similar market.

21. Nonbranded products called _____ usually sell at a sizable discount from national or private brands.

22. Designing a product so that it satisfies customers and meets the profit margins desired by the firm is called _____.

23. Products known as _____ are products that consumers are unaware of, haven't necessarily thought of buying, or find that they need to solve an unexpected problem.

24. Consumers buy _____ only after comparing value, quality, and price from a variety of sellers.

25. A combination of factors called _____ includes awareness, loyalty, perceived quality, images, and emotion people associate with a brand name.

26. The brand names of manufacturers that distribute a product nationally are called _____.

27. Costs known as _____ change according to the level of production.

28. Consumers want a good quality product at a fair price, so they calculate the _____ of a product by looking at the benefits, and subtracting the costs to see if benefits exceed the costs.

29. Illegal copies of national brand-name goods are known as _____, and include goods such as Polo shirts or Rolex watches.

30. A _____ has direct responsibility for one brand or one product line.

31. The process of _____is designed to reduce the number of new-product ideas being worked on at any one time.

32. Known as _____ these are all the expenses that remain the same no matter how many products are sold.

33. Promoting a product to distributors and retailers to get wide distribution and developing strong advertising and sales campaigns to generate and maintain interest in the product among distributors and consumers is called _____.

34. The creation of real or perceived product differences are called _____.

35. The practice of _____ is setting prices lower than competitors and then not having any special sales.

36. The term _____ is used to describe the combination of product lines offered by a manufacturer.

37. The procedure of _____ is one by which one or more dominant firms set the pricing practices that all competitors in an industry follow.

RETENTION CHECK

Learning Goal 1   **Product Development and the Value Package**

1. What must marketers do today to satisfy customers? What must managers do?

2.	What are the factors that make up the "value package" of a product?

a._____		g._____

b._____		h._____

c._____		i._____

d._____		j._____

e._____		k._____

f._____

3.	What is a way that businesses can keep customers, according to the text?

4.	What is the difference between a product line and a product mix?

Learning Goal 2	**Product Differentiation**

5.	How does a marketer create product differentiation?

6.   List the four different classes of consumer goods and services. Give an example of each kind.

    a. _____

    b. _____

    c. _____

    d. _____

7.   What are three variables important to marketers of convenience goods?

    a. _____

    b. _____

    c. _____

8.   Where are shopping goods found? Why? What can marketers of shopping goods emphasize?

9.   How are specialty goods marketed?

10.   What's the best way to market convenience goods?

    a. _____

    b. _____

11. What are the best appeals for promoting shopping goods?

a._____

b._____

c._____

12. What do makers of specialty goods rely on to appeal to their markets?

13. What forms of marketing do unsought goods rely on?

14. What determines how a good is classified? Can a consumer good be classified in several ways?

15. What distinguishes a consumer good from an industrial good? Can a good be classified as both? How would the marketing be different?

16. Describe the categories of industrial goods

Learning Goal 3   **Packaging Changes the Product**

17. How can packaging change a product?

18. How has the importance of packaging changed?

19. Identify the functions of packaging.

   a. _____

   b. _____

   c. _____

   d. _____

   e. _____

   f. _____

Learning Goal 4   **Building Brand Equity**

20.   What are four categories of brands?

a._____   c._____

b._____   d._____

21.   How can a brand name become a generic brand?

22.   List the important elements of brand equity.

a._____

b._____

c._____

d._____

e._____

23.   How important is brand loyalty to a firm?

24.   Why is perceived quality an important part of brand equity?

25.   How can a company create brand associations?

Brand Management

26.   What benefit does a brand name have for a buyer? For the seller?

27.   What are four reasons for product failure?

a._____   c._____

b._____   d._____

28.   Identify the steps in the new product development process.

a._____   d._____

b._____   e._____

c._____   f._____

29.   What are the four most important sources of new product ideas for consumer products?

a._____   c._____

b._____   d._____

30. What are four sources of new product ideas for industrial goods?

    a._____   c._____

    b._____   d._____

31. What are the criteria needed for product screening?

32. What are product concepts?

33. What are the activities involved in concept testing?

34. What are two important elements for commercialization?

    a._____

    b._____

35. What must U.S. firms do with the new product development process to compete internationally?

36.   What are the four stages of the product life cycle?

a. _____

b. _____

c. _____

d. _____

37.   What's important about the product life cycle?

38.   Identify the strategies for the Marketing Mix variables in each stage of the Product Life Cycle by completing the following chart:

	Product	Price	Promotion	Place
Introduction				
Growth				
Maturity				
Decline				

Learning Goal 3   **Competitive Pricing**

39.   What are six pricing objectives?

a. _____   d. _____

b. _____   e. _____

c. _____   f. _____

40.   What influences pricing objectives?

41.   Name three ways used to set prices.

a. _____   c. _____

b. _____

42.   In the long run, who or what determines price? What is included in the price of a product in addition to costs?

43.   How does target costing work?

44.   What is the best way to offer value prices and not go broke?

45.   How do service industries use the same pricing strategies as goods producing firms? Give an example.

46.   What is a break-even point?

47.   What is the formula for determining a break-even point?

48.   What are some of the expenses included in fixed costs? Variable costs?

49.   What happens when sales go above the break-even point?

50.   At what level is price set in a skimming strategy? Why?

51.   At what level are prices set in a penetration strategy? Why?

52.   What is the idea behind EDLP?

53.   What is the idea behind high-low pricing? What is the problem with this type of pricing strategy?

54.   What is demand oriented pricing?

55.   What is competition oriented pricing? What will price depend upon with this type of pricing?

56.　How is the Internet affecting pricing?

57.　How do firms compete using something other than price?

58.　Describe three strategies for avoiding price wars?

a. _____

b. _____

c. _____

CRITICAL THINKING EXERCISES

Learning Goal 1

1.　In chapter 13 you read about the importance of the marketing process. Explain the relationship of the marketing concept to the importance of developing new products, as it is described in the text.

2. When people buy a product, they evaluate and compare on several dimensions: For each product below, identify some of the dimensions that may influence the buyer.

    a. Bicycle _____

    _____

    b. Toothpaste _____

    _____

    c. A new suit _____

    _____

3. Identify 3 product lines that General Motors sells, and a specific item in each line. What other products may make up their product mix?

    Product line _____   Item _____

    Product line _____   Item _____

    Product line _____   Item _____

Learning Goal 2

4. The two major product classifications are consumer goods and services and industrial goods and services.

    a. Classify the following products

       1. Milk _____

       2. Steel _____

       3. Tickets to the Olympics_____

4. Dry cleaners _____

5. Diesel engines _____

6. Flashlight batteries_____

7. Auto repair _____

8. Heart surgeon_____

9. Manufacturing consultant _____

10. Winter coat _____

b. Consumer goods and services are further classified as either: convenience, shopping, specialty or unsought. Indicate the correct class for each of the consumer items you identified above.

1. _____   5. _____

2. _____   6. _____

3. _____   7. _____

4.. _____

5. Marketing strategies will change depending upon the category of the product. Identify the most appropriate way to market:

a. a new car -

b. a marketing consulting firm -

c. banking services -

Learning Goal 3

6.   Packaging is carrying the promotional burden for products more than ever, and performs a number of functions: attract attention, describe contents, explain benefits, provide information, indicate price, value and uses, and protect goods. Evaluate the importance of packaging, which function(s) may be the most important, and how well the packaging performs those functions for the following:

a. Lunch meat (like bologna) _____

_____

b. Children's cereal (like Froot Loops) _____

_____

c. Potato chips (like Ripples) _____

_____

Learning Goal 1, 2, 3

7.   You are in conference with the marketing manager of Music-stor, and are still in the process of developing a marketing plan. In evaluating the disc and tape storage product to be produced by Music-stor, you want to know what dimensions customers might consider in purchasing Music-stor from a retailer. Are the same things going to be important if the main customers are the auto manufacturers? What additional or different dimensions might manufacturers consider?

Just before your meeting, you jotted down some other questions that you feel need to be answered in order to create an effective marketing plan:

a. What is the total product offer? _____

_____

b. How can we differentiate the product? _____

_____

c. How would Music-stor be classified? _____

_____

d. Will packaging be an important consideration for Music-stor? _____

_____

Learning Goal 4

8.   Brand categories include national brands and private brands. Some brand names have become generic, and have come to describe an entire product category.

   a.   Identify a national brand and a private brand for each of the following:

NATIONAL BRAND   PRIVATE BRAND

a. Orange juice _____   _____

b. Soft drinks _____   _____

c. Small tools _____   _____

d. Peanut butter _____   _____

e. Blue jeans _____   _____

f. Pain reliever _____   _____

   b.   How do you think customer perception of these products differs by the brand name? Why is this important?

c. What is the problem with a brand name becoming a generic name?

d. What are the important elements of brand equity, and how can brand equity be built?

Learning Goal 5

9. You have just been named as a product manager for the new company formed by the merger of Nestle and Ralston-Purina. Your manager has told you that your primary objective is to develop new products and bring them to market. This is your first day on the job! How will you accomplish the objectives your boss has given you?

Learning Goal 1

10. The product life cycle is a model of what happens to classes of products over time. It consists of four stages. Label the following illustration.

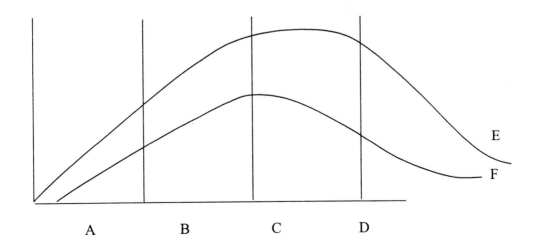

a. _____   d. _____

b. _____   e. _____

c. _____   f. _____

11.   There are different marketing strategies used in each stage of the product life cycle. Using your text, give a specific example of a marketing strategy from one of the four P's that could be used for the following products.

MARKETING STRATEGY

a. Introduction   Global Positioning   _____

                     Systems   _____

                                           _____

b. Growth   D.V.D players   _____

                                           _____

                                           _____

c. Maturity   Fast food   _____

                                           _____

                                           _____

d. Decline   Black and white T.V. _____

                                           _____

Learning Goal 7

12. Among the objectives that firms use in setting prices are:

Achieve a target profit   Increase sales

Build traffic   Create an image

Achieve greater market share   Social objectives

Match the correct pricing objective to each of the following statements.

a. Kroger's advertises eggs at 10 cents a dozen. _____

b. Ralston Purina changes a price that gives them a 25% profit on dog food, higher than they need. Consumers are willing to pay the high price for this particular dog food. _____

c. Farmers in Arkansas receive subsidies on their grain products, so they can keep their prices artificially low. This keeps prices on derivative products low enough for a larger market to purchase. _____

d. Retailers, facing several dismal Christmas seasons in a row, slashed prices on a wide variety of merchandise several years in a row. _____

e. "Polo Crest," a cologne for men by Ralph Lauren, costs $45 for a small bottle in most upscale retail stores. _____

f. If you go to Midas Muffler with a bid from a competitor, Midas will meet that price in order to keep your business. _____

13. a. How many units will Music-stor have to sell to break even if their costs are $800,000 and the revenue from each unit is $25? _____

b. How much profit will Music-Stor make if they sell 45,000 units? _____

c. What would the break-even point (the number of units which need to be sold in order to break even) be if Music-stor revenue increased to $40? _____

d. The marketing department has said that at increased revenue of $40, Music-stor would be able to sell about 19,000 units. Should they raise their price? Why or why not?

14. After determining which pricing objectives fit with the firm's objectives, a business can use any of several different strategies.

Skimming   Price leadership

Penetration   Competition oriented

Demand oriented

Match the correct pricing strategy to each of the following:

a. Home theater systems can run as high as $100,000 or more and there are only a few companies offering the systems. _____

b. Hotel and motel prices at Disney World are lower from September to Thanksgiving, from January to March, and from April to June, times which Disney defines as their "off" seasons. _____

c. The sticker price of similarly equipped Lexus, Infiniti and Acura automobiles is just about the same. _____

d. Carl Godwin is just starting out in the home remodeling and construction business. When he makes a bid, it is generally significantly lower than the bids of any of his competition, because Carl wants the business. _____

e. During the summer months, and at other peak times, the price of gasoline at most retail stations goes up, and virtually all stations charge the same price for a gallon of gas. _____

15. Many companies will try to sell their products by promoting something other than price. Identify three types of products in the marketplace that are promoted using nonprice competition. What are the companies using to promote their products?

a._____

b._____

c._____

PRACTICE TEST

Multiple Choice – Circle the best answer

1.   Which of the following would not be included in the overall value package of benefits consumers consider when they purchase a product?

   a.   Price
   b.   Image created by advertising
   c.   Brand name
   d.   Buyer's income

2.   Ford Motor Company produces cars, trucks, and SUVs and provides financing. These products are part of Ford's

   a.   product mix.
   b.   product depth.
   c.   product width.
   d.   product line.

3.   A company that distributes bottled water, like Evian or Naya, have the challenge of making a product that looks the same from one company to another, appear to have qualities unique to that brand. Companies create these perceived differences using

   a.   consumer goods classification.
   b.   the product life cycle.
   c.   the product mix.
   d.   product differentiation.

4.   Small businesses often have an advantage in product differentiation because

   a.   they have fewer products, so they can spend more time working on them.
   b.   they are more flexible in adapting customer wants and needs.
   c.   larger businesses aren't interested in getting close to the consumer.
   d.   larger businesses don't have to differentiate their products.

5. Which of the following is not one of the classifications of consumer products?

    a. convenience goods and services
    b. unsought goods and services
    c. shopping goods and services
    d. desired goods and services

6. Which of the following would be considered a shopping good?

    a. toothpaste
    b. funeral services
    c. washing machine
    d. bank

7. When a manufacturer buys a personal computer for use at work, the computer would be considered a:

    a. business good.
    b. specialty good.
    c. consumer good.
    d. shopping good.

8. The Jolly Green Giant, the Rams head representing the St. Louis Rams football team and Toucan Sam from Froot Loops are examples of

    a. brand name s.
    b. generic names.
    c. trademarks.
    d. knockoff brands.

9. Rollerblade is working to make sure that when people refer to inline skating, they don't use the name Rollerblade to refer to the sport. Rollerblade is afraid that their brand name will become a

    a. generic name.
    b. knockoff brand.
    c. private brand.
    d. trademark.

10. Because products are often being sold in self-service outlets, rather than by salespersons:

    a. brand names have become less important.

    b. packaging has become more important, as a way to promote the product.

    c. the popularity of generic products has declined.

    d. packaging has become less important, because consumers want to see what they are buying.

11. The first step in the product development process is

    a. development.

    b. product screening.

    c. commercialization.

    d. idea generation.

12. Which of the following is not an important criteria for screening products?

    a. how the product fits with current products

    b. profit potential

    c. personnel requirements

    d. ease of production

13. The process of taking a product idea to consumers to test their reactions is known as

    a. test marketing.

    b. concept testing.

    c. product screening.

    d. business analysis.

14. In order for the U.S. to remain competitive in the new product development process,

    a. managers must limit new ideas to test.

    b. companies must look at what foreign competitors are offering.

    c. managers must go out into the market and interact with dealers and customers.

    d. the new product development process must be shortened.

15. Which of the following is not one of the stages of the product life cycle?

    a. introduction
    b. growth
    c. maturity
    d. saturation

16. The importance of the product life cycle is that

    a. different stages in the product life cycle call for different marketing strategies.
    b. most brands follow the same pattern in the product life cycle.
    c. all products go through the product life cycle in the same length of time.
    d. in the growth stage, marketers will differentiate their product from competitors.

17. During the _____ stage of the product life cycle, marketers will keep the product mix limited, adjust the price to meet competition, increase distribution, and emphasize the brand name and product benefits in their advertising.

    a. introduction
    b. growth
    c. maturity
    d. decline

18. Which of the following is not included in a list of pricing objectives?

    a. increasing sales
    b. increasing market share
    c. create an image
    d. beat the competition

19. The pricing strategy of determining what the market will pay and then designing a product to fit the price is known as

    a. demand oriented pricing.
    b. cost-based pricing.
    c. target costing.
    d. value pricing.

20. If fixed costs are $100,000, variable cost per unit is $40 and the selling price is $60, how many units must be sold for the firm to break even?

    a. 10,000

    b. 1,000

    c. 2500

    d. 5000

21. When the Japanese entered the videotape recorder market, they priced the product lower than the U.S. makers in order to capture a large share of the market quickly.

    This strategy is called a

    a. skimming strategy.

    b. EDLP.

    c. high-low pricing strategy.

    d. penetration strategy.

True-False

1. _____ In today's market, marketers must learn to listen to consumers and adapt to a constantly changing market.

2. _____ An organization can use a high price to create an attractive value package.

3. _____ It is often easier for larger companies to establish a close relationship with customers because they have representatives in most parts of the country.

4. _____ An example of a convenience good would be a candy bar.

5. _____ One function of packaging is make sure a product fits well in a display area.

6. _____ Brand loyalty means that your product comes to mind when a product category is mentioned.

7. _____ The Internet has become an important variable in the commercialization step of the new product development process.

8. _____ An important element in making the new product development process effective is to go out into the market and interact closely with dealers, as well as with customers.

9. _____ A firm may have several pricing strategies all at once.

10. _____ Pricing objectives generally will have no effect on the other marketing mix variables.

11. _____ The break-even point is the point where sales revenue is equal to profits.

12. _____ When movie theaters charge lower rates for children, and companies give discounts to senior citizens, they are using demand oriented pricing.

13. _____ Most pricing depends upon what the competition is charging.

14. _____ Marketers won't generally compete on product attributes other than price.

You Can Find It On the Net

Joe Boxer wants to know if you are wearing clean underwear! The Web seems to be a natural way for this wacky underwear manufacturer. The company even has their own gigantic, interactive, electronic outdoor billboard in Times Square, in the heart of New York City. Selected consumers from all over the world can send messages on the 100-foot long electronic message strip. Visit the Joe Boxer web site at www.joeboxer.com

How does the web site reinforce the Joe Boxer brand name and image? Give examples to support your answer.

How does Joe Boxer appear to differentiate their product from Hanes? (www.hanes.com)

Compare the Hanes web site to Joe Boxer's. Are they targeting the same market? Why or why not?

Where do you think Joe Boxer is on the Product Life Cycle. How could they extend their product life cycle?

ANSWERS

LEARNING THE LANGUAGE

1. Break even analysis	14. Concept testing	27. Variable costs
2. Penetration pricing strategy	15.Convenience goods and services	28. Value
3. High-low price strategy	16. Generic name	29. Knockoff brands
4. Value package	17. Dealer brands (private brands)	30. Brand manager
5. Brand loyalty	18. Specialty goods and services	31. Product screening
6. Product life cycle	19. Brand awareness	32. Total fixed costs
7. Skimming price strategy	20. Product line	33. Commercialization
8. Trademark	21. Generic goods	34. Product differentiation
9. Brand association	22. Target costing	35. EDLP
10.Industrial goods	23. Unsought goods and services	36. Product mix
11. Product analysis	24. Shopping goods and services	37. Price leadership
12.Value pricing	25. Brand equity	
13.Brand	26. Manufacturer's brand name	

RETENTION CHECK

Product Development and the Value Package

1. To satisfy consumers, marketers must learn to listen and to adapt constantly to changing market demands and to price challenges from competitors. Managers must learn to manage change, in particular, new-product change.

2.
   a. Price
   b. Package
   c. Store surroundings
   d. Image created by advertising
   e. Guarantee
   f. Reputation of the producer
   g. Brand name
   h. Service
   i. Buyers' past experience
   j. Speed of delivery
   k. Accessibility of marketer (e.g. on the 'net)

3. One way to keep customers is to establish a dialogue with them and keep the information they provide in a database. One of the easiest ways to do this is to establish a Web site where consumers can ask questions, get information, and chat with others.

4. A product mix is the combination of products that a company has available for sale. The product mix consists of a company's product lines. Product lines are groups of products that are similar or are intended for a similar market.

Product Differentiation

5. Marketers use a mix of pricing, advertising and packaging to create a unique attractive image to differentiate their products.

6. Answers will vary. These are examples.
    a. Convenience - bread
    b. Shopping – furniture
    c. Specialty - Rolex watch
    d. Unsought – emergency car towing

7. a. location
    b. brand awareness
    c. image

8. Shopping goods are sold largely through shopping centers so that consumers can shop around. Marketers of shopping goods can emphasize price differences, quality differences, style and value, or a combination of these factors.

9. Specialty goods are often marketed through specialty magazines and through interactive Web sites.

10. The best way to market convenience goods is:
    a. make them readily available
    b. create the proper image

11. The best appeals for promoting shopping goods are
    a. price
    b. quality
    c. service

12. Makers of specialty goods rely on advertising and the Internet to reach specialty markets

13. Unsought goods rely on personal selling and certain kinds of advertising.

14. Whether a good or service falls into a particular class depends on the individual consumer. For example, what is a shopping good for one consumer could be a specialty good for another. So any good can conceivably be classified into any of the categories.

15. Consumer goods are purchased for personal consumption, while industrial goods are products used in the production of other products. A product can be classified as both an industrial and/or an consumer good depending upon the end use of the product. If a computer, for example, is bought as a consumer good, it would be sold through a store, whereas if it was bought by a business for business uses, the computer would likely be sold through personal selling or the Internet. The marketing varies by how the good is classified.

16. The categories of industrial goods are production goods and support goods.

    <u>Production</u> goods include raw materials, component parts and production materials.

    <u>Support</u> goods include Installation, like buildings, equipment and capital items; accessory equipment, like tools and office equipment; supplies like paper clips and other office supplies; service, like maintenance and repair.

Packaging Changes the Product

17. Packaging changes the product by changing its visibility, usefulness, or attractiveness.

18. Packaging is carrying more of the promotional burden than in the past. Many products that were once sold by sales persons are now being sold in self service outlets, and the package has been given more sales responsibility.

19. a. Protect the product from damage, be tamperproof and yet be easy to open and use
    b. Attract the buyer's attention
    c. Describe the contents of the product
    d. Explain the benefits of the product
    e. Provide information on warranties and any warnings
    f. Give an indication of price, value, and uses

Building Brand Equity

20. a. Manufacturers' brands   c. Knockoff brands
    b. Private brands   d. Generic "brands"

21. A brand name can become generic when a name becomes so popular, so identified with the product that it loses its brand status and becomes the name of the product category. Examples include aspirin, nylon, escalator, and zipper.

22.   a. Brand loyalty

       b. Perceived quality

       c. Brand awareness

       d. Feelings and images

       e. Emotions people associate with a brand name

23.   A loyal group of consumers can represent substantial value to a firm.

24.   Perceived quality is an important part of brand equity because a product that is perceived as better quality than its competitors can be priced higher.

25.   Brand associations can be created by linking your brand to other product users, to a popular celebrity, to a particular geographic area, or to competitors.

Brand Management

26.   For the buyer, a brand name assures quality, reduces search time, and adds prestige to purchases. For the seller, brand names facilitate new product introductions, help promotional efforts, add to repeat purchases, and differentiate products so that prices can be set higher.

27.   a. products that don't deliver what they promise

       b. poor positioning

       c. not enough differences from competitors

       d. poor packaging

28.   a. Idea generation

       b. Screening

       c. Product analysis

       d. Development

       e. Testing

       f. Commercialization

29.   a. analysis of the competition

       b. company sources other than research and development

       c. consumer research

       d. research and development

30.   a.   company sources other than research and development

          b.   analysis of the competition

          c.   research and development

          d.   product users

31.   Product screening is designed to reduce the number of ideas being worked on at any one time. Criteria needed for screening include whether the product fits in well with present products, profit potential, marketability, and personnel requirements.

32.   Product concepts are alternative product offerings based on the same product idea that have different meanings and values to consumers.

33.   Concept testing involves taking a product idea to consumers to test their reactions. Questions include: Do customers see the benefit of this product? How frequently would they buy it? At what price? What features do they like and dislike? What changes would they make? Different samples are tested using different packaging, branding, ingredients, and so forth until a product emerges that's desirable from both production and marketing standpoints.

34.   a.   promoting the product to distributors and retailers to get wide distribution

          b.   developing strong advertising and sales campaigns to generate and maintain interest

35.   To stay competitive in world markets, U.S. businesses must develop an entirely new product development process. Keeping products competitive requires continuous, incremental improvements in function, cost, and quality. Attention must be given to developing products in cooperation with their user. Managers must go out into the market and interact closely with their dealers and their ultimate customers. Changes are made over time to make sure that the total product offer exactly meets customer needs.

The Product Life Cycle

36.   a.   Introduction

          b.   Growth

          c.   Maturity

          d.   Decline

37.   The product life cycle is important because different stages in the product life cycle call for different strategies.

38.

	Product	Price	Promotion	Place
Introduction	Offer market-tested product	High price	Selective distribution	Primary advertising sales promotion
Growth	Improve product	Adjust to meet competition	Increase distribution	Competitive advertising
Maturity	Differentiate to satisfy different segments	Reduce price further	Intensify distribution and differences	Emphasize brand name and product benefits
Decline	Cut product mix	Consider developing new products	Drop some distributors	Reduce advertising outlets

Competitive Pricing

39.　　a.　Achieve a target profit　　　　d.　Increase sales

　　　　b.　Build traffic　　　　　　　　　　e.　Create an image

　　　　c.　Achieve a greater market share　　f.　Social objectives

40.　　Pricing objectives should be influenced by other marketing mix variable decisions, such as product design, packaging, branding, distribution, and promotion.

41.　　a.　Cost-based pricing　　　c.　Target costing

　　　　b.　Value pricing

42.　　In the end, the market determines what the price of a product will be. Pricing should take into account all costs, but should also include the expected costs of product updates, the objectives for each product and competitor prices.

43.　　Target costing makes cost an input to the development process. To use target costing, the firm will estimate the selling price people would be willing to pay for a product and subtract the desired profit margin. The result is the target cost of production.

44. The best way to offer value prices and not go broke is to redesign products from the bottom up and to cut costs whenever possible. The idea is to sell brand name items at low prices.

45. Service industries can use the same pricing tactics as goods-producing firms by cutting costs as much as possible. Then they determine what services are most important to customers. Those services that aren't important are cut. One example is cutting meal service on airlines. The idea is to give the consumer value.

46. The break-even point is the point where revenues from sales equal all costs.

47. Break even point = Fixed costs
                    Price per unit - variable cost per unit

48. Expenses included in fixed costs include rent and insurance. Variable costs include expenses for materials and the direct cost of labor used in making goods.

49. When sales go above the break-even point, the firm makes a profit.

50. A skimming price strategy sets initial prices high to make optimum profit while there is little competition.

51. A penetration strategy sets prices low, which attracts more buyers and discourages competitors. This enables the firm to penetrate or capture a large share of the market quickly.

52. The idea of EDLP is to set prices lower than competitors and then not have any special sales. Then consumers will come to those stores whenever they want a bargain and not wait until there is a sale, as they often do with department stores.

53. When a firm uses high-low pricing, regular prices are higher than EDLP stores, but a store will have many special sales where the prices are lower than competitors. The problem with this type of strategy is that it teaches consumers to wait for sales, and that can cut into profits.

54. Demand-oriented pricing is used when price is set on the basis of consumer demand rather than cost or some other calculation. An example is movie theaters with low rates for children or during certain times of the day.

55. Competition-oriented pricing is a strategy based on what all the other competitors are doing. In this type of pricing, the price will depend on customer loyalty, perceived differences, and the competitive climate.

56.   Customers can now compare prices of many goods and services on the Internet, and can get lower prices on items such as airline tickets. You can also buy used items online if you are unwilling to accept the prices of new goods. Price competition is going to heat up with the Internet, as more customers have access to price information from around the world.

57.   Firms using nonprice competition will stress product images and consumer benefits such as comfort, style, convenience, and durability.

58.   a. Add value
       b. Educate consumers
       c. Establish relationships

CRITICAL THINKING EXERCISES

1.   The initial stages of the marketing process include finding a need, conducting research and designing a product to meet the need. Knowing consumer preferences is crucial to the new product development process. Companies must constantly monitor the marketplace to determine customer preferences and how they are changing. To continually satisfy customers, marketers must adapt their products to meet the needs they identify in the marketplace. The marketing process and new product development process it would seem, go hand in hand, and are on going functions of marketing.

2.   a. In the purchase of a bicycle, a consumer may evaluate the product in terms of price, guarantee, reputation of the producer, brand name, past experience, and service the retailer may provide.
      b. In buying toothpaste, a purchaser may look at price, package, image created by advertising, brand name and the buyers' past experience.
      c. For a new suit, the dimensions may be price, store surroundings, image of the store, brand name, guarantee, and past experience.

3.   Possible answers
      Product line - Chevrolet   Item - Cavalier
      Product line - Pontiac   Item - Grand Am
      Product line -Saturn   Item - Saturn VUE

4.   a. 1. Consumer   6. Consumer
          2. Industrial   7. Consumer
          3. Consumer   8. Consumer
          4. Consumer   9. Industrial
          5. Industrial   10. Consumer

b. 1. Milk - Convenience
    2. Tickets to the Olympics - Specialty
    3. Dry Cleaners - Probably convenience service but could be shopping service
    4. Flashlight batteries- Convenience
    5. Auto repair - Unsought
    6. Heart Surgeon - Unsought
    7. Winter coat - Shopping

5. a. A car is a shopping good, so the best way to market this product would be to ensure customers that they are getting a good quality product at a good price. A car dealer may want to promote the services they offer customers, such as extended hours for getting a car serviced or free oil changes for the life of the car.

    b. A marketing consulting firm sells a specialty service. This type of service would best be marketed through a business oriented magazine, or a newspaper such as the Wall Street Journal. A good website will also be important.

    c. Banking services are considered to be convenience service. A bank will need to be conveniently located, near potential customers. It is important for the bank to make services available on the Internet while still ensuring privacy and safety for its customers.

6. a. For lunchmeat like bologna, the primary consideration would be protecting the product from spoiling, and enabling the buyer to see what they are getting. The price or uses won't be listed on the package, but the package may need to attract the buyer's attention, as there are many varieties. The main problem with the package is that once it is opened, most lunchmeat packages don't easily close, so the product gets stale quickly.

    b. For a children's cereal, the most important variable would be attracting the children's attention! For the parent, nutrition information would be important to include on the package. Further, keeping the product fresh would be important. For the most part, most kids' cereals do a great job of attracting children's attention and, by law, must provide nutrition information on each box. As with the lunchmeat, the problem with most of these packages is that once they are opened, they are difficult to re-close, and the cereal can turn stale quickly.

    c. One of the considerations for potato chips is protection from damage, as chips break easily. In fact, that consideration was one of the factors Proctor & Gamble looked at when they introduced Pringles. The package needs to attract attention, to distinguish the product from the competition. Most companies have not found a good way of keeping chips from breaking, and the same old problem arises: once they are opened, the package doesn't close very well, and the product can get stale quickly.

7. a. Total product offer is convenience, image, and the kind of store in which the product is sold, in addition to such product considerations as the size and fit of Music-stor, and color.

    Customers may look at price, image, guarantee, and service. The retailer will be an important variable in this combination. Will the retailer install the case? Will the store take it back if it breaks?

    b. Music-stor could differentiate the product by giving it an image of not only convenience, but of the "ultimate" kind of auto accessory that everyone needs to have in today's cluttered world. You could create the perception that this product isn't merely a luxury, but a necessity. Advertising could be aimed at the end consumer, with the idea of people asking for the product when they go to the dealership to buy the car.

    The main consideration for an auto manufacturer will be price, how much it will add to the sticker price of the car, guarantee, and speed of delivery and reputation of Music-stor. The ease of installation will also be a factor—where does it fit into the car? Color will also be a consideration.

    c. Music-stor would be classified as a consumer good, and could be marketing as either a shopping good or a specialty good. It is also an industrial good, when it is marketed to manufacturers for direct installation on the assembly line.

    d. Packaging could be an important variable for Music-stor for the consumer portion of the market. We may want to attract attention to our product on the shelf, give consumers an idea of what it is, and to protect it from being scratched or broken. These decisions depend upon our perception of the product as a shopping good or as a specialty good. The package will be less important for the industrial market, the focus being primarily on protection during shipping and handling.

8. a. Sample answers - The private brand name will vary by city, area, or region. These examples come from the Saint Louis area

		NATIONAL BRAND	PRIVATE BRAND
a.	Orange juice	Tree Sweet	President's choice
b.	Soft Drinks	Coca-Cola	Super S
c.	Small tools	Black & Decker	Craftsman
d.	Peanut butter	Jif	Schnuck's brand, Safeway brand
e.	Blue jeans	Levi's	Arizona
f.	Pain reliever	Tylenol	Good Sense

    b. Customer perception of brand names often affects their purchase decision. People are often impressed by certain brand names, although they may realize that there may be little or no difference between brands. This makes it important for a producer to create brand recognition and develop positive associations with their brand.

    c. The problem with a brand name becoming generic is that the producer must then come up with a new brand name and begin the process of developing brand awareness and brand loyalty all over again.

d. The important elements of brand equity are brand loyalty, brand awareness, perceived quality image and brand association. Brand equity can be built by creating a good relationship with your customers, for a start, and encouraging brand loyalty. Further, advertising can be used to build strong brand awareness, as well as other kinds of sales promotion designed to keep your name in front of the public. Creating a quality product, and communicating the message of quality to your consumers is also important. Further associating your product with other favorable images reinforces the image of your product in the consumer's mind.

9. A possible answer:

As a new product manager, I will need to start with generating ideas from many different sources. I would investigate my competitors, and try to generate ideas from our own company personnel.

Once enough ideas have been generated, I would then have to screen them for profitability and potential. Any product ideas not meeting the criteria we have set will be dropped from further analysis.

The next step will be to develop a product concept. If we develop a new premium pet food for example, as a concept, then we need to create a prototype to test with consumers and their pets. During that step we would make sure pets like the product, determine how much people might be willing to pay for a premium pet food, how people will view this product, and what flavors the pet prefers.

If the product tests well, we would take it to market through our traditional retailers, or perhaps through the Internet. We may choose to offer the product through pet stores rather than the grocery stores, to reinforce the idea of a premium product.

10. a. Introduction   d. Decline
    b. Growth   e. Industry product sales
    c. Maturity   f. Industry profits

11. Possible answers
    a. High price; Promote as a necessity for driving safety in upscale publications
    b. Change advertising to change product image; Add distribution outlets; Decrease price, or give price "deals."
    c. Add new menu items, such as healthier versions of standard items; Look for new target markets
    d. Reduce advertising; Limit the product variations; Reduce the number and kind of distribution outlets

12. a. Build traffic   d. Increase sales
    b. Achieve a target profit e. Create an image
    c. Social objectives   f. Achieve a greater market share

13.   a. The number of units Music-stor would have to sell to break even is 32,000.
       b. If they sold 45,000 units, profit would be $325,000.
       c. If Music-stor raised their price to $40, the break-even point would be 20,000 units.
       d. No, they should not raise their price to $40. If they will break even at 20,000 units, but can only sell 19,000 units at that price, they will be losing money. They should, then, price below $40, at some point where they can sell enough units to make a profit.

14.   a. Skimming
       b. Demand oriented
       c. Price leadership
       d. Penetration
       e. Competition oriented

15.   There are multiple answers. Some examples would be:

     Cosmetics -   Promoted by showing how the product enhances looks
     Food items -   Promoted by emphasizing flavor, freshness, convenience
     Gasoline -   Promoted by emphasizing quality or service.

PRACTICE TEST

MULTIPLE CHOICE

1.	d		12.	d
2.	a		13.	b
3.	d		14.	d
4.	b		15.	d
5.	d		16.	a
6.	c		17.	c
7.	a		18.	d
8.	c		19.	c
9.	a		20.	d
10.	b		21.	d
11.	d			

TRUE/FALSE

1.	T		8.	T
2.	T		9.	T
3.	F		10.	F
4.	T		11.	F
5.	F		12.	T
6.	F		13.	F
7.	T		14.	F

CHAPTER 15
DISTRIBUTING PRODUCTS EFFICIENTLY AND COMPETITIVELY: SUPPLY CHAIN MANAGEMENT

LEARNING GOALS

After you have read and studied this chapter, you should be able to:

1.   Explain the concept of marketing channels and the value of marketing intermediaries.

2.   Give examples of how intermediaries perform the six utilities.

3.   Describe the various wholesale organizations that assist in the distribution system.

4.   Explain the ways that retailers compete and the distribution strategies they use.

5.   Explain the various kinds of nonstore retailing.

6.   Discuss how a manufacturer can get wholesalers and retailers in a channel system to cooperate by the formation of systems.

7.   Describe some supply-chain management problems and how they are solved.

8.   Review the various distribution modes and their benefits and how they tie in with the materials handling and storage function.

LEARNING THE LANGUAGE

Listed below are important terms found in the chapter. Choose the correct term for the definition and write it in the space provided.

Administered distribution system	Freight forwarder	Retail sale
Brokers	Information utility	Selective distribution
Cash and carry wholesalers	Intensive distribution	Service utility
Category killer stores	Intermodal shipping	Supply chain
Channel of distribution	Marketing intermediaries	Supply chain management
Contractual distribution system	Materials handling	Telemarketing
Corporate distribution system	Merchant wholesalers	Time utility
Drop shippers	Place utility	Utility
E-tailing	Possession utility	Wholesaler
Exclusive distribution	Rack jobber	Wholesale sale
Form utility	Retailer	

1.   The sale of goods and services to businesses and institutions for use in the business or to wholesalers or retailers for resale is a _____.

2.   The economic term _____ refers to the value or want-satisfying ability that is added to goods or services by organizations when the products are made more useful or accessible to consumers than before.

3.   A marketing intermediary known as a _____ sells to other organizations.

4.   An _____ is a distribution system in which producers manage all the marketing functions at the retail level.

5.   The movement of goods within a warehouse factory or store is _____.

6.   The concept of _____ means taking raw materials and changing their form so that they become useful products.

7.   The distribution strategy known as _____ puts products into as many retail outlets as possible.

8.   The sale of goods and services by telephone is called _____.

9.   A firm adds _____ to products by having them where people want them.

10. The use of _____ includes multiple modes of transportation to complete a single long distance movement of freight.

11. The sequence of linked activities that must be performed by various organizations to move goods from the sources of raw materials to ultimate consumers is called _____

12. The distribution strategy known as _____ sends products to only one retail outlet in a given geographic area.

13. Providing fast, friendly service during and after the sale and by teaching customers how to best use products over time is called _____.

14. Marketing intermediaries in the _____ are wholesalers and retailers who join together to transport and store goods in their path from producers to consumers.

15. A _____ is an organization that sells to ultimate consumers.

16. A distribution system called a _____ is one in which all the organizations in the channel of distribution are owned by one firm.

17. A distribution strategy that sends products to only a preferred group of the available retailers in an area is called _____.

18. An organization adds value to products called _____ by opening two-way flows of information between marketing participants.

19. Organizations called _____ assist in the movement of goods and services from producer to industrial and consumer users.

20. A wholesaler known as a _____ furnishes racks or shelves full of merchandise to retailers, displays products, and sells on consignment.

21. A _____ is an organization that puts many small shipments together to create a single, large shipment that can be transported more cost-efficiently to the final destination.

22. A wholesaler called a _____ solicits orders from retailers and other wholesalers and has the merchandise shipped directly from a producer to a buyer.

23. A wholesaler that serves mostly smaller retailers with a limited assortment of products is a _____ wholesaler.

24. Marketing intermediaries called _____ bring buyers and sellers together and assist in negotiating an exchange but they don't own goods.

25. Adding value to products by making them available when they are needed is called _____

26. The idea of _____ is doing whatever is necessary to transfer ownership from one party to another, including providing credit, delivery, installation, guarantees, and follow-up service.

27. The sale of goods and services to consumers for their own use is a _____

28. In a _____ members are bound to cooperate through contractual agreements.

29. Independently owned firms called _____ take title to the goods they handle.

30. Large stores called _____ offer wide selections at competitive prices.

31. Selling goods and services to ultimate consumers online is known as _____.

32. The _____ consists of all the organizations that move goods and services from the source of raw materials to the final consumer.

ASSESSMENT CHECK

Learning Goal 1   **The Importance of Channels of Distribution**

1. What are two types of marketing intermediaries?

   a. _____   b. _____

2. What do channels of distribution ensure?

3. Why do we have marketing intermediaries?

4. What activities *don't* brokers perform? What are some kinds of brokers?

5.   How do marketing intermediaries add efficiency to the distribution system?

6.   How has the Internet affected distribution?

7.   What is the value versus the cost of intermediaries?

8.   What are three important points to remember about intermediaries?

      a. _____

      b. _____

      c. _____

Learning Goal 2   **Utilities Created by Intermediaries**

9.   List six utilities created by intermediaries.

      a. _____   d. _____

      b. _____   e. _____

      c. _____   f. _____

10.   Who creates form utility? How is it created?

11.   How does an intermediary add time utility?

12.   How do intermediaries add place utility?

13.   How do intermediaries provide possession utility?

14.   How do intermediaries add information utility?

15.   How is service utility provided?

16. Which of these is becoming the most important utility for retailers? Why?

Learning Goal 3 **Wholesale Intermediaries**

17. What is the difference between a "retail sale" and a "wholesale sale?"

18. Identify two types of merchant wholesalers and the difference between them.

19. List four types of limited-function wholesalers.

   a._____   c._____

   b._____   d._____

20. How does a rack jobber operate? What types of items do they sell?

21. How does a cash and carry wholesaler function?

22.   How does a drop shipper operate?

23.   Who uses a freight forwarder, and what does a freight forwarder do?

24.   How is a lot of B2B wholesaling being done?

Learning Goal 4   **Retail Intermediaries**

25.   What are five ways retailers compete?

a. _____   d. _____

b. _____   e. _____

c. _____

26.   How is the Internet affecting price competition?

27. What is involved in service competition?

28. How do services compete using location competition?

29. How is competition changing with regard to category killer stores?

30. How do smaller retailers compete with category killers?

31. How do brick and mortar stores offer entertainment competition?

32.   Name three retail distribution strategies.

   a. _____

   b. _____

   c. _____

33.   What types of products are sold using each of these three distribution strategies?

Learning Goal 5   **Nonstore Retailing**

34.   What are six types of non-store retailing?

   a. _____   d. _____

   b. _____   e. _____

   c. _____   f. _____

35.   What are the "battles," or challenges, of e-tailing?

36.   What are some of the customer service problems e-tailing sites have experienced?

37.   What are the latest trends in e-commerce? What will be needed in the future?

38.   What are the benefits of vending? Of kiosks and carts?

39.   What is direct selling?

40.   How does multilevel marketing work?

41.   What are an "upliner" and a "downliner" in multilevel marketing?

42.   What are two attractions of multilevel marketing?

       a. _____

       b. _____

43.   What are four forms of direct marketing?

a._____

b._____

c._____

d._____

Learning Goal 6   **Building Cooperation in Channel Systems**

44.   Identify four types of distribution systems

a._____

b._____

c._____

d._____

45.   What are three types of contractual distribution systems?

a._____

b._____

c._____

46.   Identify the characteristics of the three types of contractual distribution systems.

47. Why do retailers cooperate with producers in an administered distribution system?

48. How does a supply chain compare to a channel of distribution?

Learning Goal 7   **Supply Chain Management**

49. What is meant by "inbound logistics?"

50. What are factory processes?

51. What is "outbound logisitics?"

52. What is materials handling?

53.   What poses the biggest problem for the new online retailers?

Learning Goal 8   **Choosing the Right Distribution Mode and Storage Units**

54.   What is the primary concern of supply-chain managers?

55.   What does "piggyback" mean, in distribution? How about fishyback?

56.   List five transportation modes used in physical distribution, in order of volume.

a._____   d._____

b._____   e._____

c._____

57.   Name six criteria used to evaluate transportation modes.

a._____   d._____

b._____   e._____

c._____

58.   What is intermodal shipping? What is an intermodal marketing company?

59.   How much of the cost of physical distribution comes from storage? What does the cost include?

60.   What are two kinds of warehouses?

61.   What is the difference between the two kinds of warehouses?

CRITICAL THINKING EXERCISES

Learning Goal 1

1.   What is the relationship between the first two "P's" in the marketing mix, product and price, and the third "P," place, or distribution?

2.   Illustrate the channel of distribution for:

a.   cars

b.   soft drinks

c.   business forms (like blank invoices)

3.   Joe Dell and his friend Woody were complaining as they were shopping for suits about how expensive they seemed to be. "Man" said Joe, "if we just had one of those outlet malls where we could avoid the "middleman" we'd be better off. That outlet store down at the Lake of the Ozarks is always advertising about how much lower their prices are because they get shipments direct from the manufacturer. Wouldn't it be a better deal if we just didn't have to deal with these expensive stores!" Woody replied "Well Joe, I understand what you mean, but in my marketing class we've talked about marketing intermediaries, or middlemen, and they're not as bad as you think! Besides, if you go to an outlet store, you're still using a middleman!" What did Woody mean?

Learning Goal 2

4.   Marketing intermediaries add value to products by creating five utilities. The sixth utility, form utility, is mostly added by producers. The five utilities added by intermediaries include:

Time   Possession   Service

Place   Information

Match the correct response to each example:

a.   St. Lukes Hospital sponsors a "pediatric party" every Saturday for its young patients to show what will happen while they are in the hospital for surgery. _____

b . Although it is a division of a larger retailing company, Target offers their own credit card .

_____

c.   Many colleges are offering classes in the late afternoon and on weekends to meet the needs of a diverse student body. _____

d.   McDonald's restaurants can be found in some Wal-Mart superstores, where you can order your meal from the Wal-Mart check-out counter. _____

e.   St. Louis Community College offers classes on three different campuses, as well as on the Internet, to provide convenience for their students. _____

Learning Goal 1, 2, 3

5.   Music-stor is looking at the distribution function. You and the marketing manager must make a proposal soon. In general, what kind of marketing intermediaries should we consider? How does the classification of Music-stor as either a convenience good, shopping good, or a specialty good affect the answer to this question? What would the channel of distribution look like? Is there a need for a marketing intermediary if we target primarily the automotive manufacturers? What kind of utilities will our customers find most important?

6. There are several types of merchant wholesalers:

    Rack jobbers   Drop shippers

    Cash and carry wholesalers   Freight forwarders

    Identify the correct type of wholesaler with the following:

    a. These wholesalers have begun selling to the public in larger stores, and have begun to allow their customers to use credit cards, although traditionally customers were required to pay cash._____

    b. L'Eggs hosiery products are displayed in the store on a rack. When the product is sold, the company shares the profit with the retailer._____

    c. Peabody Coal will sell their product to this wholesaler, who will then make arrangements for the coal to be shipped from the mine to an Ameren facility in southern Missouri.

        _____

    d. Davidson's Trucking will add the shipments of many smaller companies to create a larger shipment that is more cost effective for the manufacturer. _____

Learning Goal 4

7. Fast Eddy's is a retailer going downhill fast! Eddy has turned to you to help him turn the store around and make it profitable again. Fast Eddy's has been selling general merchandise for years, with the gimmick of using sales associates on roller skates, to provide "fast service." The store looks a little run down. Eddy knows he has to do something about that, but he just can't seem to figure out what to do to compete "with the big guys." How can you advise him about how to compete?

8. The three types of retail distribution strategies are intensive, selective, and exclusive. Which strategy would likely be used for:

a. Chewing gum_____

b. Athletic shoes_____

c. Potato chips _____

d. Tickets to the Olympics _____

e. Rolex watches _____

f. winter coats _____

9. There are several types of nonstore retailing:

E-tailing   Direct selling

Telemarketing   Multilevel marketing

Vending machines, kiosks and carts   Direct marketing

Determine which is being described in each of the following:

a. Catalogs, telemarketing, and on-line shopping all help to make this form of retailing very convenient for consumers. _____

b. In Japan, everything from bandages and face cloths to salads and seafood are sold in machines located in airports, movie theaters, and other public places.

_____

c. Lingerie, artwork, baskets, jewelry, and plastic bowls are sold at "parties" held at a customer's home or work place. _____

d. Companies "reach out and touch someone" using this form of marketing, to supplement or replace in-store selling. _____

e. Retailers like this form, as it lends an outdoor marketplace atmosphere to the mall in which they are located._____

f. Using this form of retailing, a new salesperson's job is to sell the products provided by the company and to recruit several people who will use the product and recruit others to sell and use the product. _____

g. Traditional "brick and mortar" stores are beginning to use this type of non-store retailing.
_____

Learning Goal 6, 7

10. A further look at Music-stor's distribution shows the need to consider the kind of cooperation necessary for us to create an efficient system.

In what kind of distribution system (corporate, contractual, or administered) will Music-stor take part ? Can you describe what their supply chain might look like? What are the important aspects of Music-stor's supply chain management?

Learning Goal 8

11. Five basic modes of transportation are:

Railroad   Ship (water)

Truck   Airplane

Pipeline

A. Using the figure in your text, determine which mode of transportation would likely be used in the following situations when:

1. Speed of delivery is the most important criterion, and cost is not a essential element.
_____

2. There is a need to serve multiple locations fairly quickly. _____

3. Products are bulky, cost is a major consideration, and speed of delivery is not an essential element. _____

4. There is a need for constant or steady delivery to a minimal number of locations; speed of delivery is not important. _____

5. There are multiple locations, bulky products, and cost and speed of delivery are of equal but moderate importance. _____

B. Which do you think would be the best choice of transportation mode for Music-stor? Why?

PRACTICE TEST

Multiple Choice – Circle the best answer

1. Which of the following is an activity that would not be considered a distribution function?

   a. storage
   b. transportation
   c. inventory
   d. production

2. Minimizing inventory and moving goods more quickly, using computers and other technology is called:

   a. supply chain management.
   b. channels of distribution.
   c. relationship marketing.
   d. quick response.

3. Which of the following statements is accurate regarding marketing intermediaries?

   a. Intermediaries add cost to products, but not value
   b. Intermediaries must adopt the latest technology to maintain their competitive position
   c. The functions performed by marketing intermediaries are easily eliminated
   d. Intermediaries have never performed their job efficiently, that's why they are being eliminated

4. In some areas of the country, Wal-Mart stays open 24 hours a day, most days of the year. This is an example of:

   a. service utility.
   b. place utility.
   c. time utility.
   d. possession utility.

5. McDonald's, Baskin-Robbins, and other franchisors are examples of a:

   a. corporate distribution system.
   b. contractual distribution system.
   c. retail cooperative.
   d. administered distribution system.

6. Mother Earth Pillows is a small retailer that offers a wide assortment of holistic and therapeutic remedies for stress and various types of illnesses, including pillows filed with herbal remedies, aromatherapy products, stress reduction products and more. Mother Earth is competing using

    a. Price.
    b. Location.
    c. Selection.
    d. Entertainment.

7. Because of improved, more customer-oriented logistics systems

    a. wholesalers have become obsolete.
    b. businesses carry less inventory, and costs have decreased significantly.
    c. certain transportation modes have been eliminated.
    d. final customers are now less likely to go direct to the manufacturer or to the wholesaler.

8. The largest percentage of goods are shipped by:

    a. air.
    b. ship.
    c. truck.
    d. rail.

9. When Hans Kaupfmann bought his car while on a trip to Germany, he wasn't sure how it would be shipped. The dealer assured him that many people buy cars and have them shipped, and it is a smooth transition from land to sea and back to land, by trucking the car to the port, loading the entire truck trailer on to the ship, then trucking again to the destination. This process is known as:

    a. piggyback.
    b. fishyback.
    c. bi-modal transportation.
    d. transatlantic transportation.

10. A _____ gathers, then redistributes, products

    a. distribution warehouse
    b. storage warehouse
    c. full-service wholesaler
    d. drop shipper wholesaler

11. The major difference between wholesalers and retailers is that:

   a. retailers sell only in certain parts of the country, while wholesalers are nationwide.
   b. wholesale organizations are generally more profitable than retail organizations.
   c. retailers sell only consumer goods, and wholesalers sell business to business goods.
   d. retailers sell to final consumers, while wholesalers sell to another member of the channel of distribution, not final consumers.

12. A(n) _____ is an independently owned wholesaler, that takes title to the goods they handle.

   a. broker
   b. agent
   c. merchant wholesaler
   d. manufacturer's agent

13. Sam's Club sells to retailers, but doesn't offer credit or transportation. Sam's will also allow a final consumer to shop, but charges an annual fee. They have begun to allow customers to use credit, but the store will not deliver. Sam's is an example of a:

   a. rack jobber.
   b. freight forwarder.
   c. drop shipper.
   d. cash and carry wholesaler.

14. Discount stores such as Wal-Mart, K-Mart and Target are hard to compete against, because these stores are the best at

   a. selection competition.
   b. price competition.
   c. location competition.
   d. service competition.

15. A_____ offers a very wide selection of a specific product category at prices that smaller retailers can't match.

   a. category killer
   b. department store
   c. discount store
   d. franchised store

16. Which of the following is not true regarding retailing over the Internet?

   a. most retailers can get away without going online
   b. the Internet has helped to boost sales for many small retailers
   c. e-tailers have had some problems with handling customer complaints
   d. online marketers are building brick and mortar stores so that customers can pick and choose which shopping technique suits them best.

17. After a few years of relying on the Internet to market their product, management at The Flying Noodle, a pasta company, has decided that it is time to get their product into the supermarket. This kind of basic pasta product will do best with

   a. selective distribution.
   b. intensive distribution.
   c. exclusive distribution.
   d. nonstore retailing distribution.

18. Nonstore retailing or out of store shopping is:

   a. declining as the Internet takes over.
   b. growing as the types of nonstore retailing grow.
   c. not a profitable method of retailing for most companies.
   d. consists primarily of vending machines and telemarketing.

19. Which of the following would not be an example of direct marketing?

   a. ordering a book from Amazon.com online
   b. buying Avon from your neighborhood Avon representative
   c. sending in an order form from an advertising supplement in the newspaper
   d. buying a soda from the vending machine at school

20. The biggest challenge for new online retailers with regard to supply chain management has been

   a. inbound logistics.
   b. materials handling.
   c. outbound logistics.
   d. transportation modes.

True-False

1. _____ A channel of distribution consists of marketing intermediaries who join together to store and transport goods in their path from producer to consumer.

2. _____ Companies are now able to carry lower levels of inventory because of supply chain management.

3. _____ Generally, it is much less expensive and much faster when we can avoid the use of a marketing intermediary and go straight to the producer.

4. _____ Providing service utility is becoming the most important utility for retailers, because without personal service they could lose business to other forms of retailing.

5. _____ In a corporate distribution system, a retailer signs a contract to cooperate with a manufacturer.

6. _____ The primary concern of supply chain managers is keeping costs down, regardless of anything else.

7. _____ Today, a majority of shipping is done by air.

8. _____ Merchant wholesalers do not buy what they sell, they primarily match buyers with sellers.

9. _____ The Internet has made wholesalers obsolete.

10. _____ Consumers will often pay a bit more for goods and services if a retailer will offer outstanding service.

11. _____ Smaller retailers can compete with category killer stores by offering lower prices .

12. _____ Multilevel marketing is not a good way to make money because it costs too much to get into.

You Can Find It on the Net

Compare shopping on the Internet to shopping in a store. Visit www.amazon.com or www.borders.com and check out the prices of three of your favorite c.d.s

How do the prices compare to the price you pay in the store?

How much does shipping add to the price of the c.d.'s?

How does the web site encourage you to buy the product?

What problems do you see with shopping for music over the Internet?

How does the web site overcome those problems?

Which type of shopping do you prefer, Internet or store? Why?

ANSWERS

LEARNING THE LANGUAGE.

1. Wholesale sale	12. Exclusive distribution	23. Cash & carry wholesaler
2. Utility	13. Service utility	24. Brokers
3. Wholesaler	14. Channel of distribution	25. Time utility
4. Administered distribution system	15. Retailer	26. Possession utility
5. Materials handling	16. Corporate distribution system	27. Retail sale
6. Form utility	17. Selective distribution	28. Contractual distribution system
7. Intensive distribution	18. Information utility	29. Merchant wholesalers
8. Telemarketing	19. Marketing intermediaries	30. Category killer stores
9. Place utility	20. Rack jobber	31. E-tailing
10. Intermodal shipping	21. Freight forwarder	32. Supply chain
11. Supply chain management	22. Drop shipper	

RETENTION CHECK

The Role of Distribution in Business

1. a. Wholesalers
    b. Retailers

2. Channels of distribution ensure communication flows and the flow of money and title to goods. They also help ensure that the right quantity and assortment of goods will be available when and where needed.

3. Marketing intermediaries perform marketing tasks like transporting, storing, selling, advertising, and relationship building more effectively and efficiently than most manufacturers could.

4. Brokers don't take title to, or own, the goods they deal with. They don't carry inventory, provide credit or assume risk. Some kinds of brokers are insurance brokers, real estate brokers, and stockbrokers.

5. Marketing intermediaries add efficiency to the distribution system by reducing the number of transactions necessary to get the product to the buyer. Marketing intermediaries are better at performing their functions than a manufacturer would be.

6. Technology has made it possible for manufacturers to reach consumers more efficiently. Some manufacturers, such as Dell Computer reach consumers directly on the Internet. Retailers, too, are so closely linked to manufacturers that they can get delivery as often as once or twice a day. All this means is that there is often no need for a wholesaler to perform functions such as storage and delivery. Wholesalers are not yet obsolete, but they need to change their functions to remain viable in today's rapidly changing distribution systems.

7. Some people believe that if they could get rid of the intermediary they could reduce the cost of what they buy. However, if we got rid of a retailer, for example, we may be able to buy a product for a little less, but we would still have to drive further and spend more time looking for the product. The value of intermediaries is that they make products available to us at times and places that are convenient for us. That often outweighs the cost they add to the product.

8. a. Marketing intermediaries can be eliminated, but their activities cannot

   b. Intermediaries have survived because they have performed functions more effectively and efficiently than others. They must adopt the latest technology to remain competitive.

   c. Intermediaries add cost, but the cost is usually offset by the value they create.

Utilities Created by Intermediaries

9. a. Time   d. Information
   b. Place   e. Service
   c. Possession   f. Form

10. Form utility is created mostly by producers. Form utility is created by taking raw materials and changing their form so that they become useful products.

11. Intermediaries add time utility to products by making them available when they're needed.

12. Place utility is added to products by having them where people want them.

13. Possession utility is added by doing whatever is necessary to transfer ownership from one party to another, including providing credit. Activities include delivery, installation, guarantees, and follow-up service.

14. Intermediaries add information utility by opening two-way flows of information between marketing participants.

15. Service utility is added by providing fast, friendly service during and after the sale and teaching customers how to best use products over time.

16. Service utility is becoming the most important utility for retailers, because without personal service they could lose business to electronic marketing or direct marketing. Personalized service is what distinguishes retailers from other types of nonstore marketing

Wholesale Intermediaries

17. A retail sale is a sale of goods and services to <u>consumers</u> for their own use. A wholesale sale is the sale of goods and services to <u>businesses and institutions</u> for use in the business or for resale.

18. Full-service wholesalers perform all distribution functions, such as transportation, storage, risk bearing, credit, market information, grading, buying, and selling. Limited function wholesalers perform only selected functions.

19.   a. Rack jobbers   c. Drop shippers
       b. Cash and carry   d. Freight forwarders

20. Rack jobbers furnish racks or shelves full of merchandise to retailers, display products and sell on consignment. They sell magazines, snack foods, etc.

21. A cash-and-carry wholesaler serves mostly smaller retailers with a limited assortment of products. Retailers go to them, pay cash, and carry the goods home.

22. A drop shipper solicits orders from retailers and other wholesalers and have the merchandise shipped directly from a producer to a buyer. They own the merchandise but don't handle, stock or deliver it.

23. Smaller manufacturers that don't make large shipments use freight forwarders. The freight forwarder puts many small shipments together to create a single large shipment that can be transported cost-effectively to a final destination. Some will offer additional services, such as warehousing and customs assistance, along with pick-up and delivery.

24. Much B2B wholesaling is being done over the Internet through sites like E-Bay's Business Exchange and Yahoo's Business-to-Business Marketplace.

Retail Intermediaries

25.   a. Price   d. Selection
       b. Service   e. Entertainment
       c. Location

26. Price competition is getting fiercer as Internet firms help consumers find the best prices on various items.

27. Retail service involves putting the customer first. This requires that all front-line people be courteous and accommodating to customers. It also means follow up service such as on-time delivery, guarantees, and fast installation. Customers are frequently willing to pay a little more for goods and services if the retailers offer outstanding service.

28. Services compete by having good locations. This explains why you will find automated teller machines in supermarkets and fast food places on college campuses. Some service establishments, like dry cleaners, will also pick up and deliver.

29. Category killer stores offer wide selection at competitive prices. They have been successful, but many are now being "killed" themselves, by discount department stores like Wal-Mart. Consumers are finding it more convenient to shop for multiple items at one store, rather than go out of their way to find stores selling only one category of product, like toys or sports equipment.

30. Smaller retailers compete with category killers by offering more selection within a smaller category of items. You may have successful smaller stores selling nothing but coffee or party products. Smaller retailers also compete with more personalized service.

31. Brick and mortar stores, in an effort to overcome the convenience of Internet shopping, have begun to make their stores more fun places to shop. The stores are becoming entertainment destinations with features like live music, giant aquariums, video games and skate parks.

32.   a. Intensive distribution
       b. Selective distribution
       c. Exclusive distribution

33. Intensive distribution puts products into as many outlets as possible and is used to sell products like cigarettes, gum and magazines.

Selective distribution is the use of only a selected group of retailers in a given area and is used to sell appliances, furniture, and clothing.

Exclusive distribution is the use of only one retail outlet in a given geographic area and is used by automobile manufacturers and for specialty goods.

Nonstore Retailing

34.   a. E-tailing   d. Direct selling

        b. Telemarketing   e. Multilevel marketing

        c. Vending machines, kiosks and carts   f. Direct marketing

35.   The major challenges, or battles, of e-tailing are getting customers and delivering the goods, providing helpful service, and keeping your customers.

36.   E-tailers have had problems with handling complaints, taking back goods that customers don't like and providing online personal help.

37.   The latest trend in e-tailing is for traditional retailers to go online. Further, online marketers are building "brick and mortar" stores, so that now customers can pick and choose which shopping form they prefer. Companies that want to compete in the future will probably need both a store presence and an online presence to provide consumers with all the options they want.

38.   The benefit of vending is their location in areas where people want convenience, such as airports, office buildings, schools and service stations. Kiosks and carts have lower costs than stores. Therefore they can offer lower prices on items such as T-shirts and umbrellas. Mall owners often like them because they are colorful and create a marketplace atmosphere. Customers enjoy interactive kiosks because they dispense coupons and provide information when buying products.

39.   Direct selling involves selling to consumers in their homes or where they work.

40.   Multilevel marketing sales people work as independent contractors. They earn commissions on their own sales and create commissions for the upliners who recruited them.

41.   In multilevel marketing, an "upliner" is an individual who has recruited others to sell for them. The "downliners" are the people who have been recruited to sell.

42.   The main attractions of multilevel marketing are

        a. great potential for making money

        b. low cost of entry

43.   Direct retail marketing includes:

        a. direct mail   c. telemarketing

        b. catalog sales   d. on-line shopping

Building Cooperation in Channel Systems

44.   a.   Corporate system

     b.   Contractual systems

     c.   Administered systems

     d.   Supply chains

45.   a.   Franchise systems

     b.   Wholesaler-sponsored chains

     c.   Retail cooperatives

46.   In a franchise system, the franchisee agrees to all of the rules, regulations, and procedures established by the franchisor. In a wholesaler-sponsored chains, each store signs an agreement to use the same name, participate in chain promotions and cooperate as a unified system of stores, even though each store is independently owned and managed. In retail cooperatives, the arrangement is much like a wholesaler-sponsored chain except it is initiated by the retailers.

47.   Retailers cooperate with producers in an administered distribution system because they get so much help for free.

48.   A supply chain is longer than a channel of distribution because it includes suppliers to manufacturers whereas the channel of distribution begins with manufacturers. Channels of distribution are part of the supply chain.

Supply Chain Management

49.   Inbound logistics brings raw materials, packaging, other goods and services and information from suppliers to producers.

50.   Factory processes change raw materials and parts and other inputs into outputs, such as finished goods.

51.   Outbound logistics manages the flow of finished products and information to business buyers and consumers.

52.   Materials handling is the management of goods within the company, for example, moving goods from the warehouse to the factory floor.

53.   The biggest problem for the new online retailers has been outbound logistics.

Choosing the Right Distribution Mode and Storage Units

54. A primary concern of supply-chain managers is selecting a transportation mode that will minimize costs and ensure a certain level of customer service.

55. A piggyback system means that a truck trailer is detached from the cab, loaded onto a railroad flatcar, and taken to a destination where is will be offloaded, attached to a truck, and driven to customers' plants. Fishyback systems work in the same way, except that truck trailers are placed on ships to travel, rather than railroads.

56.
   a. Railroad
   b. Motor vehicles
   c. Pipeline
   d. Water transportation
   e. Air

57.
   a. Cost
   b. Speed
   c. On-time dependability
   d. Flexibility in handling products
   e. Frequency of shipments
   f. Reach

58. Intermodal shipping uses multiple modes of transportation, including highway, air, water, and rail to complete a single long-distance movement of freight. Services that specialize in intermodal shipping are known as intermodal marketing companies.

59. About 25 to 30 percent of the total cost of physical distribution is for storage. This includes the cost of the warehouse and its operation plus movement of goods within the warehouse.

60.
   a. storage warehouses
   b. distribution warehouses

61. A storage warehouse stores products for a relatively long time, such as what is needed for seasonal goods. Distribution warehouses are facilities used to gather and redistribute products.

CRITICAL THINKING EXERCISES

1. The type of product will determine what kind of transportation and storage will be called for, and what kinds of stores (retailers) will carry the product. The type of transportation mode and the kind of storage will be a part of the final price of the product, as well as the kind of store - i.e. the image of the store and its pricing policies.

2. The channel of distribution for

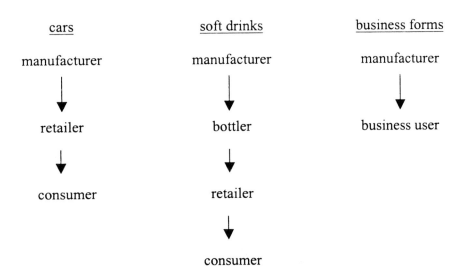

cars

manufacturer
↓
retailer
↓
consumer

soft drinks

manufacturer
↓
bottler
↓
retailer
↓
consumer

business forms

manufacturer
↓
business user

3. What Woody was trying to tell Joe is that, first, the outlet store is a type of middleman, called a retailer. Further, retailers and the other type of middlemen, wholesalers, add many things to a product that would be difficult to replace. In the first place, Joe would have to drive to wherever the suit he chose was manufactured, if he were to really avoid a middleman. That could be as far away as the Far East! The retailer is much closer. Secondly, if he decided to have the manufacturer ship the suit to him, he would have to pay for shipping the suit to his home, which could be expensive. He would have to contact the manufacturer during working hours, which for a manufacturer would probably be Monday - Friday, between 8a.m. and 5 p.m. Then he would have to try it on, figure out any alterations, and perhaps ship the suit back to be altered, or find someone to alter it for him. Further, Joe would not be able to see the suit before it was sent, or would have to spend hours looking through the manufacturer's warehouse looking through hundreds of suits (that is after having traveled to the Far East in the first place...) In short, middlemen provide value through adding convenience, such as transportation and storage, and enable us to shop for and find exactly what we want, at times convenient for us with far less effort.

Therefore, while middleman organizations can be eliminated, their functions cannot.

4.   a. Information
     b. Possession
     c. Time
     d. Place and possession
     e. Place

5.   Initially Music-stor may use some kind of wholesaler, who will then sell to a retailer. If we target primarily the auto industry, we will not necessarily need a wholesaler middleman, unless we use some kind of a broker in lieu of employing our own sales force. The channel of distribution will look like this:

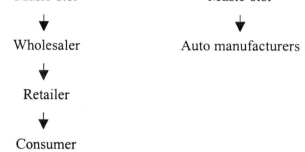

The most important utility for the end consumer may be information utility, as the consumer may need to know more about the product. Place utility is important, but is affected by our classification of Music-stor as either a shopping good or specialty good. This affects the kind of store we will choose, as shopping goods may be found in several kinds of stores and specialty goods will be found in fewer, different kinds of stores.

For the auto manufacturers, time and place utility will be important, as they will need the product delivered when they need it, where they need it.

6.   a. Cash and carry wholesaler   c. Drop shipper
     b. Rack jobber   d. Freight forwarder

7.   *Possible answer*: Eddy's gimmick of using sales associates on roller skates may actually be the key he is looking for! He apparently already knows that service is important to his customers; he may just need another way of approaching the idea! Retailers compete based on price, service, selection, location, or entertainment. Eddy needs to decide what is most important to his customers, what may draw new customers in, and what his strengths and weaknesses are. As a small retailer, he may be better able to specialize in a market, and compete with larger retailers by offering more selection within a smaller category of items. It is difficult for smaller retailers to compete with "category killers" based on price, but outstanding service may allow Eddy to charge a price that will help him stay in business and make a profit. Eddy's also has some entertainment value, with the sales associates on roller skates, and he may want to expand the entertainment value of his store to draw in new customers, and make the store a fun place to visit.

8.   a. Intensive
     b. Selective
     c. Intensive
     d. Exclusive
     e. Exclusive
     f. Selective

9.   a. Direct marketing
     b. Vending machines
     c. Direct selling
     d. Telemarketing
     e. Kiosks, carts
     f. Multilevel marketing
     g. E-tailing

10.   Music-stor will most likely be a part of an administered distribution system when we are using
      retailers. As a new company, we can't afford to own our own retail stores right away, which cuts
      out a corporate distribution system. Moreover, for this type of product, a corporate distribution
      system would not be practical. The same is true of a contractual distribution system. A
      franchise system is not appropriate without many more product lines, and wholesaler-sponsored
      chains and retail cooperatives don't fit either.

      As a new company, however, we will want to provide our retailers with as much service as we
      can until we become better known.

11.   A. 1. Air   4. Pipeline
          2. Truck   5. Railroad
          3. Water

      B. The best transportation mode for Music-stor would probably be by truck to both the auto
          manufacturers and the retailers. For auto manufacturers, which are located a considerable
          distance from Music-stor, a combination of rail and truck could be used for flexibility,
          number of deliveries and speed. The major problem with trucks is the cost, but it serves the
          other needs best.

PRACTICE TEST

MULTIPLE CHOICE

1.	d	11.	d
2.	a	12.	c
3.	b	13.	d
4.	c	14.	b
5.	b	15.	a
6.	c	16.	a
7.	b	17.	b
8.	d	18.	b
9.	b	19.	d
10.	a	20.	c

TRUE/FALSE

1.	T	7.	F
2.	T	8.	F
3.	F	9.	F
4.	T	10.	T
5.	F	11.	F
6.	F	12.	F

CHAPTER 16
PROMOTING PRODUCTS USING INTERACTIVE AND INTEGRATED MARKETING COMMUNICATION

LEARNING GOALS

After you have read and studied this chapter, you should be able to:

1. Define promotion, promotion mix, and integrated marketing communication.

2. Illustrate the seven steps of the selling process and discuss the role of a consultative salesperson.

3. Define advertising and describe the advantages and disadvantages of various advertising media, including the Internet.

4. Describe the role of the public relations department and how publicity fits in that role.

5. Explain the importance of sales promotion and word of mouth as promotional tools.

6. Describe integrated marketing communication and the role of interactive communications within it.

LEARNING THE LANGUAGE

Listed below are important terms found in the chapter. Choose the correct term for each definition and write it in the space provided.

Advertising	Personal selling	Pull strategy
Closing techniques	Promotion	Push strategy
Consultative salesperson	Promotion mix	Qualify
Infomercial	Prospect	Sales promotion
Integrated marketing communication	Prospecting	Sampling
Integrated marketing communication system (IMC)	Public Relations	Viral marketing
Interactive marketing program	Publicity	Word-of-mouth promotion
Interactive promotion		

1. Combining all the promotional tools into one comprehensive and unified promotional strategy is called _____.

2. The promotional tool known as _____ stimulates consumer purchasing and dealer interest by means of short-term activities.

3. Paid, nonpersonal communication, or _____, goes through various media by organizations and individuals who are in some way identified   in the message.

4. The management function of _____ evaluates public attitudes, changes policies and procedures in response to the public's requests, and executes a program of action and information to earn public understanding and acceptance.

5. A _____ is a promotional strategy in which heavy advertising and sales promotion efforts are directed toward consumers so that they will request products from retailers.

6. Ways of concluding a sale, or _____, include getting a series of small commitments and then asking for the order and showing the client where to sign.

7. The _____ is the combination of promotion tools that an organization uses.

8. A promotional tool that involves people talking about products they have purchased is called _____.

9. To _____ is to make sure that people have a need for the product, the authority to buy, and the willingness to listen to a sales message.

10. Researching potential buyers and choosing those most likely to buy is called _____.

11. A _____ begins by analyzing customer needs and then comes up with solutions to those needs.

12. The form of promotion known as _____ is any information about an individual, a product, or an organization that is distributed to the public through the media and that is not paid for, or controlled by, the seller.

13. A _____ is the strategy in which the producer uses advertising, personal selling, sales promotion and all other promotional tools to convince wholesalers and retailers to stock and sell merchandise.

14. A TV program exclusively to promoting goods and services are known as an _____.

15. The tool of _____ is the face-to-face presentation and promotion of products and services.

16. The process of _____is an attempt by marketers to inform people about products and to persuade them to participate in an exchange.

17. A tool known as _____ is a formal mechanism for uniting all the promotional efforts in an organization to make them more consistent and more responsive to that organization's customers and other stakeholders.

18. _____means changing the promotion process from a monologue, where sellers tried to persuade buyers to buy things, to a dialogue where buyers and sellers can work together to create mutually beneficial exchange relationships.

19. The term _____is used to describe everything from paying people to say positive things on the Internet to setting up multilevel selling schemes whereby consumers get commissions for directing friends to specific Web sites.

20. A system known as an _____ allows consumers to access company information on their own and supply information about themselves in an ongoing dialogue.

21. People with the means to buy a product, or _____also have the authority to buy, and the willingness to listen to a sales message.

22. Letting consumers have a small sample of the product for no charge is called _____.

RETENTION CHECK

Learning Goal 1   **Constant Change and the Promotion Mix**

1.   What are the tools of the promotion mix?

a._____   c._____

b._____   d._____

2.   According to the text, how is technology changing an organization's approach to working with customers?

Learning Goal 2   **Advertising: Persuasive Communication**

3.   How does the public benefit from advertising?

4.   List eight advertising media.

a._____   e._____

b._____   f._____

c._____   g._____

d._____   h._____

5.   List some of the advantages and disadvantages of each form of advertising media.

	Advantages	Disadvantages
a. Newspapers	_____	_____
	_____	_____
	_____	_____
	_____	_____
b. Television	_____	_____
	_____	_____
	_____	_____
	_____	_____
c. Radio	_____	_____
	_____	_____
	_____	_____
	_____	_____
d. Magazines	_____	_____
	_____	_____
	_____	_____
	_____	_____
e. Outdoor	_____	_____
	_____	_____
	_____	_____

f. Direct mail

＿＿＿＿＿＿＿＿ ＿＿＿＿＿＿＿＿

＿＿＿＿＿＿＿＿ ＿＿＿＿＿＿＿＿

＿＿＿＿＿＿＿＿ ＿＿＿＿＿＿＿＿

＿＿＿＿＿＿＿＿ ＿＿＿＿＿＿＿＿

g. Yellow pages

＿＿＿＿＿＿＿＿ ＿＿＿＿＿＿＿＿

＿＿＿＿＿＿＿＿ ＿＿＿＿＿＿＿＿

＿＿＿＿＿＿＿＿ ＿＿＿＿＿＿＿＿

＿＿＿＿＿＿＿＿ ＿＿＿＿＿＿＿＿

h. Internet

＿＿＿＿＿＿＿＿ ＿＿＿＿＿＿＿＿

＿＿＿＿＿＿＿＿ ＿＿＿＿＿＿＿＿

＿＿＿＿＿＿＿＿ ＿＿＿＿＿＿＿＿

＿＿＿＿＿＿＿＿ ＿＿＿＿＿＿＿＿

6. What are the top three media in terms of total expenditures?

7. What are the benefits of infomercials?

8. How do people react to ads on the Internet? What is the goal of advertising on the Internet?

9.   How does Customer Relationship Management software work?

10.   How will technology and the speed of the Internet affect Internet advertising and customer relationship management?

11.   What are the two approaches to advertising in the global market? Which does the evidence suggest often works the best?

12.   Distinguish between "globalism" and "regionalism" in advertising.

Learning Goal 3   **Personal Selling: Providing Personal Attention**

13.   How do we describe "effective selling?"

14.   How is technology aiding the salesperson of today?

15.   What are the seven steps in the personal selling process?

        a._____   e._____

        b._____   f._____

        c._____   g._____

        d._____

16.   In personal selling, what is the difference between prospecting and qualifying?

17.   What activities take place in the preapproach?

18.   What will be the objective of an initial sales call during the approach stage?

19.   What does the sales person do during the presentation?

20. What is the role of the salesperson in answering objections?

21. What activities are involved in closing a sale?

22. Identify the activities involved in the follow up.

23. According to the text, what are the two goals of a salesperson?

24. How is technology changing the role of the B2B salesperson?

25. According to the text, the role of both B2B sales persons as well as that of consumer sales person is to be a consultant. What does that mean, and why has that change occurred?

26.   Identify the three steps in creating a good public relations campaign.

   a. _____

   b. _____

   c. _____

27.   What is the responsibility of a public relations department? Why?

28.   What are three benefits that publicity has over other promotion mix variables, particularly advertising?

   a. _____

   b. _____

   c. _____

29.   What are three drawbacks of publicity?

   a. _____

   b. _____

   c. _____

30. List five types of B2B sales promotions.

a._____   d._____

b._____   e._____

c._____

31. List the kinds of consumer sales promotion

a._____   g._____

b._____   h._____

c._____   i._____

d._____   j._____

e._____   k._____

f._____   l._____

32. What are sales promotion programs designed to do?

33. Who are the targets of internal sales promotion and what is internal sales promotion designed to do?

34. What is a virtual trade show, and what is the benefit for customers?

35. Who are the targets after internal sales promotion is done?

36. What is the benefit of sampling as a sales promotion tool?

37. What is event marketing?

38. What is the idea behind word of mouth promotion?

39. What are some ways that companies are using word of mouth promotion?

40.   What is the trend regarding the use of the Internet in promotion, and how is that trend affecting traditional methods of promotion?

41.   How has promotion become interactive?

Learning Goal 6   **Managing the Promotion Mix: Putting It All Together**

42.   According to the text, what is the best way to reach:

a.   large homogenous groups

b.   large organizations

43.   What is the idea of a push strategy?

44.   What is the idea of a pull strategy?

45.   What is a total systems approach to marketing?

Integrated Marketing Communication (IMC)

46.   For a company, what is the result of an integrated marketing communication system?

47   What are the steps necessary to develop an interactive marketing program?

a. _____

b. _____

c. _____

CRITICAL THINKING EXERCISES

Learning Goal 1

1.   While we haven't yet decided on a promotion mix for Music-stor, (that will come shortly), the use of technology will no doubt play a part in the promotion mix. How would you incorporate the use of the Internet into our promotion mix?

Learning Goal 2

2.   There is a variety of media available to use for advertising. Using the chart in your text, determine what might be the most appropriate form of advertising media for: (there may be more than one answer for each)

a. A rock concert at an outdoor theater _____

b. Sales at the local mall _____

c. Products aimed specifically at women _____

d. A local news show _____

e. Long distance telephone service _____

f. Credit cards _____

g. Computer software _____

h. A storage case for CDs and tapes for the car _____

3. We're still working on a promotion mix for Music-stor, but we know it will most likely include some form of personal selling. Using the seven steps in your text, prepare an outline for a sales presentation to your automotive manufacturing customers.

Learning Goal 3

4. How will the presentation differ for selling Music-stor to a retailer?

5.   The Fox affiliate in large Midwestern city added a news broadcast to its lineup. In order to compete with the larger affiliates, the Fox affiliate (Channel 30) decided to air their program at 9:00 p.m. Before the news broadcast went on the air, the station surveyed viewers regarding their likes and dislikes about the current local news broadcasts. Shortly before the new show was to premiere, the station began promoting the show, the news anchors, and how this show was going to be different from current shows.

One of the changes the new show made was to avoid, as much as possible, the real "bad news" stories as leads to the broadcast, leaving them until later in the show. They made a point of finding "good news" stories about the city and the inhabitants. They did this because that's what viewers said they wanted. During the broadcast, just before a commercial break, a screen will show with the exact show times of each of the upcoming stories, in response to customer complaints that other stations will use upcoming stories as "hooks" but actually not air the story until much later in the broadcast. In promoting the show, and during the news broadcast, mention is made of the way the station is responding to viewer requests. Further, during the broadcast, the station's telephone number was flashed, and viewers were encouraged to call with complaints, requests, or suggestions.

How do these actions by the television station demonstrate a "good" public relations program?

6.   Identify three main groups that are the focus of sales promotion efforts, and a technique used to reach each group.

Group   Technique

a._____   _____

b._____   _____

c._____   _____

7. Consumers are frequently the targets of sales promotion techniques. Look through your mail, walk through a Sam's or a Wal-Mart, or shop at a grocery store. What kinds of sales promotion techniques do you notice? Do you notice the impact of technology on the promotion techniques vary? Have you seen the result of any "cookies" on your computer?

8. How do the other elements of the promotion mix affect word-of-mouth promotion?

    Product _____

    Sales promotion _____

    Advertising _____

    Publicity _____

    Personal selling _____

Learning Goal 1-6

9. Now that we have covered the promotion mix variables, you are an expert in designing an effective promotion campaign. What do you think would be the most effective promotion mix for Music-stor to use? Will it be more important to use a push or a pull strategy, a combination, or a "total systems" approach? Will you use the Internet? How?

10.   The Barucci family has run Barruci's Restaurant for 17 years. Most of the time it has only been marginally profitable, although the whole family worked diligently. After Papa Barucci died, the restaurant started to falter. No one seemed to be in charge, no one knew the suppliers, the inventory system, or much about managing the restaurant, as Papa had taken care of all that. Maria Barucci knew she had to do something fast. She began by finding out as much about the business as she could. She talked to the employees, looked at company records and other internal files. She asked the employees for their insights and recommendations. They gave her information about how the business was run, and many ideas for improvements. Maria kept all her information on the restaurant's computer, in a database and implemented the improvements her employees suggested.

Maria also talked to her competitors, other restaurant owners as well as suppliers and salespeople from several computer firms. From them, she learned the newest restaurant management techniques and technology. Maria and her employees learned how to implement many additional changes from some of the salespeople, which helped to make their job helping her, easier.

Maria spent a lot of time talking to customers, asking questions and asking for suggestions, and implemented many of those suggestions, too. Finally, Maria, along with her employees and others, began an advertising campaign, with the theme "You asked for it! You got it!" with advertisements in local newspapers and on the radio. She also included coupons with a bulk mailing company.

Lastly, Maria found a new company, just getting started, which agreed to develop a simple Internet-based advertisement for the restaurant, showing menus, specials, hours of operation, and so forth. She contacted several web servers and began negotiations for advertising on the Web, on her city's Web page and other appropriate formats. She began accepting take-out orders by e-mail. Maria also bought a fax machine, and started accepting take-out orders by fax.

The atmosphere at the restaurant became open, friendly, and helpful. A positive relationship between Maria, her employees, and her suppliers developed. The positive atmosphere carried over to the customers, who felt that the Barucci employees were among the most helpful and friendliest of any local restaurant. Barucci's became a bigger success than it had in the past.

a.   How did Maria Barucci implement an integrated marketing communication system?

b.   What advantages does a small business like Barucci's have in developing an integrated marketing communication system?

PRACTICE TEST

Multiple Choice – Circle the best answer

1.   Promotion is an attempt by marketers to

     a.   help retailers sell products.
     b.   inform and persuade people to buy.
     c.   segment markets to reach them more effectively.
     d.   search for new prospects.

2.   Technology has

     a.   had little impact on the area of advertising.
     b.   affected other areas of business more than advertising.
     c.   had a tremendous impact on promotion.
     d.   increased the need for personal selling.

3.   Which of the following would not be included in a discussion of the benefits of advertising, according to the text?

     a.   Advertising creates a lot of jobs
     b.   Advertisements are informative
     c.   Advertising pays for the production cost of television and radio
     d.   Some kinds of advertising, such as direct mail, allow a company to target very specific markets.

4.   Which media would be best if you are interested in targeting a specific audience, need flexibility, have a local market and don't have a lot of money to spend.

     a.   The Internet
     b.   Television
     c.   Outdoor
     d.   Radio

5.   Which of the following is an advantage of Internet advertising over other media?

     a.   Targets a specific audience
     b.   Local market focus
     c.   No competition from other material
     d.   Inexpensive global coverage

6. Which of the following would not be included in a discussion of the benefits of advertising using infomercials?

    a. They can show the product in great detail

    b. Infomercials are low in cost

    c. It is the equivalent of sending your best salesperson into the home

    d. Infomercials provide the opportunity to show the public how a product works

7. In personal selling, the relationship must continue for a long time, as the salesperson responds to new requests for information from current customers. This is an important part of the _____ step in personal selling.

    a. prospecting

    b. closing

    c. follow-up

    d. presentation

8. Which of the following is true regarding personal selling today?

    a. Automation has had a big impact on personal selling with the use of high-tech hardware and software.

    b. The objective of an initial sales call is to make a sale immediately.

    c. Big customers should always be treated with more care than small ones

    d. It is more difficult to find customers in the business to business market than in the consumer market.

9. Which of the following is not a part of developing a good public relations program?

    a. Listen to the public

    b. Inform people of the fact you're being responsive

    c. Develop policies and procedures in the public interest

    d. Advertise in a way that promotes positive word of mouth.

10. Which of the following is not considered to be a benefit of publicity?

    a. Publicity may reach people who wouldn't read an advertisement

    b. Publicity may be placed on the front page of a newspaper

    c. You can control when the publicity release will be used.

    d. Publicity is more believable than other forms of promotion

11. When Mary Lynn went to the grocery store last week, she took with her several coupons she had received in the mail that week. While at the store, Mary Lynn was offered samples of several food items, and she actually bought a few of those, using the in-store coupons. She also bought a particular brand of toothpaste because the tube came with a free toothbrush. Mary Lynn is taking advantage of:

   a. word of mouth.
   b. sales promotion.
   c. advertising.
   d. publicity.

12. Which of the following is not true regarding sales promotion efforts?

   a. Sales promotion efforts are aimed first at salespersons, then at the end consumer
   b. Sales promotion can be done both internally and externally
   c. Sales promotion programs are designed to supplement other promotion efforts
   d. Sales promotion efforts are designed to create long-term relationships

13. Mama Barucci's Restaurant has had a big increase in business since Mama implemented an integrated marketing communications system. Mama has learned that much of the new business is coming from customers who have recommended the restaurant to their friends and associates. People seem to be hearing about Mama Barucci's and want to try if for themselves. Mama's is benefiting from:

   a. publicity.
   b. advertising.
   c. word of mouth.
   d. sales promotion.

14. The city of San Antonio has made an effort to develop promotional materials for travel agents and bus tour companies that are within a 300-mile radius of the city. City officials are hopeful that these efforts will encourage tourism in the area when agents suggest the city to their clients. San Antonio is making use of a:

   a. push strategy.
   b. pull strategy.
   c. segmentation strategy.
   d. targeting strategy.

15. Microsystems advertises in several software publications, as well as the Internet. Their sales people call on computer stores, and often leave brochures and other materials describing their products and customer service programs. The company has a Web site where the customers can purchase products on-line. These efforts are part of the Company's

    a. marketing mix.
    b. promotion mix.
    c. push strategy.
    d. corporate platform.

16. Which of the following is not one of the basic steps of developing an interactive marketing communication system?

    a. Make it possible for customers to access information they need to make a purchase
    b. Respond quickly to customer information by designing wanted products
    c. Gather data about the groups affected by the organization
    d. Advertise in all media.

17. Which statement would not be included in a discussion of the advantages of interactive marketing on the Internet?

    a. Customers can access information any time they want
    b. Large companies can reach the markets more effectively than smaller companies
    c. Buyers and sellers can engage in a dialogue.
    d. Electronic ads and catalogs do not have to be printed, stored, or shipped

18. What is likely to be the impact of technology on television and other forms of mass advertising?

    a. The Internet has probably peaked as a form of advertising, and will not have a further impact on any other forms of advertising
    b. There is likely be a drop in TV and other mass advertising
    c. Technology will be a complementary effort, but will not increase in use as a tool for advertising
    d. Infomercials will probably replace the Internet as the primary form of promotion

19. _____allows customers to buy products by interacting with various advertising media without meeting a sales person face-to-face.

    a. Target marketing
    b. Market segmentation
    c. Direct marketing
    d. Promotion

20. Viral marketing is

    a. An Internet based form of notification of a potential computer virus.
    b. A term used to describe promotional efforts such as paying people to say positive things your product on the Internet.
    c. A system in which consumer can access company information on their own and supply information about themselves in an ongoing dialogue.
    d. A function that evaluates public attitudes and executes a program of action and information to earn public understanding.

True-False

1. _____ Most data indicate that personal selling is not a major force in our economy.

2. _____ In today's environment, B2B sales personnel will need to learn how to add value to the product they are selling.

3. _____ The idea of public relations is to establish a dialogue with stakeholders.

4. _____ One of the problems with publicity is that it is not believable.

5. _____ Sales promotion can be used as an attempt to keep salespeople enthusiastic about the company.

6. _____ Interactive promotion changes the promotion process from a monologue to a dialogue.

7. _____ One of the benefits of Internet advertising is that consumers tend to pay a lot of attention to the ads they see on the Internet.

8. _____ Evidence supports the theory that promotional efforts specifically designed for individual countries are not any more successful than more general advertising.

9. _____ When using a pull strategy, advertising and sales promotion efforts are directed at consumers.

10. _____ Companies are tending to use the traditional promotional tools less today because so much information about consumers is now available.

You Can Find It On the Net

You can visit virtually any web site to observe how companies implement the techniques we have discussed in this chapter. Here are a few suggestions.

Visit www.gap.com

Do they attempt to create a dialogue with the customer? How?

How do they attempt to use customer relationship management?

Visit www.cdnow.com

What sales promotion techniques does cd now use?

How does cd now make their website "user friendly?"

How does cd now promote to their buyers, or create a dialogue with their users?

Track the sites you visit over a few days. Can you remember the advertising you saw?

How effective do you think Internet advertising is?

LEARNING THE LANGUAGE

1. Integrated marketing communication	9. Qualify	16. Promotion
2. Sales promotion	10. Prospecting	17. Integrated marketing communication system
3. Advertising	11. Consultative sales person	18. Interactive promotion
4. Public relations	12. Publicity	19. Viral marketing
5. Pull strategy	13. Push strategy	20. Interactive marketing system
6. Closing techniques	14. Infomercial	21. Prospects
7. Promotion mix	15. Personal selling	22. Sampling
8. Word-of-mouth promotion		

ASSESSMENT CHECK

The Importance of Marketing Communication and Promotion

1. a. Personal selling
    b. Advertising
    c. Sales promotion
    d. Public relations

2. The Internet is changing the whole approach to working with customers. The latest trend is to build relationships with customers over time. That means carefully listening to what consumers want, tracking their purchases, providing them with better service, and giving them access to more information.

Advertising: Persuasive Communication

3. The public benefits from advertising because ads are informative. It provides us with free TV and radio because advertisers pay for the production costs. Advertising also covers the major costs of producing newspapers and magazines.

4. a. Newspapers   e. Outdoor
    b. Television   f. Direct mail
    c. Radio   g. Yellow pages
    d. Magazines   h. Internet

5. a. Newspapers   Good local coverage   Ads compete with other features;
                       ads place quickly   poor color; ads get thrown away
                       high acceptance;
                       ad can be clipped and saved

    b. Television   Sight, sound, motion   High cost; short exposure time
                       reaches all audiences;   takes time to prepare ads
                       high attention with no
                       competition

    c. Radio   Low cost; can target   People may not listen; short exposure
                       specific audiences;   time; audience can't keep ad
                       flexible; good for
                       local marketing

    d. Magazines   Target specific audiences; Inflexible; ads must be placed weeks
                       good use of color; long life; before publication; cost is relatively
                       ad can be clipped and   high
                       saved

    e. Outdoor   High visibility and   Limited message, low selectivity of
                       repeat exposures; low   audience
                       cost; local market focus

    f. Direct mail   Best for targeting specific High cost; consumer rejection as junk
                       markets; very flexible; ad mail; must conform to postal
                       can be saved   regulations

    g. Yellow pages   Great coverage of local   Competition with other ads;
                       markets; widely used by   cost may be too high
                       consumers; available at   for very small businesses
                       point of purchase

    h. Internet   Inexpensive global   Relatively low readership
                       coverage; available at
                       any time; interactive

6.   The three top media in terms of expenditures are television, newspapers, and direct mail.

7.   Infomercials allow the seller to show the product in detail, which helps the product to sell itself. They allow for testimonials and for showing the customer how the product actually works, and allow for the use of drama, demonstration, graphics, and other advertising tools.

8.   Most ads today on the Internet are ignored. Companies continue to use the Internet to advertise because ultimately the goal is to send customers and potential customers over to a web site where they can learn more about the company, and vice versa.

9.   Customer relationship software makes it possible to track customer's purchases and answer their questions online.

10.   New technology will greatly improve the speed and potential of Internet dialogues. Companies will be able to provide better online videos, online chat rooms, and other services that will take customers to a virtual store where they will be able to talk to other customers, talk to sales people, examine goods and services and buy products.

11.   The two approaches to advertising in the global market are to develop a promotional strategy that can be implemented worldwide, and to design promotions that are targeted at specific countries and or regions. Evidence supports the theory that promotional efforts specifically designed for individual countries often work best. The challenge is to conduct the research needed to determine the wants, needs and culture of each specific country and then designing appropriate ads and testing them.

12.   Globalism is the idea of producing one ad for everyone in the world, and regionalism is to develop specific ads for each country and /or for specific groups within a country.

Personal Selling: Providing Personal Attention

13.   Effective selling is a matter of persuading others to buy and helping others to satisfy their wants and needs.

14.   Sales people can use the Internet, portable computers, pagers, and other technology to help customers search the Net, design custom-made products, look over prices, and generally do everything it takes to complete the order.

15.   a. Prospect and qualify   e. Answer objections
      b. Preapproach   f. Close sale
      c. Approach   g. Follow-up
      d. Make presentation

16.   To qualify people means to make sure that they have a need for the product, the authority to buy, and the willingness to listen to a sales message. People who meet these criteria are called prospects.

17.   Before making a sales call, the sales representative must do further research, which is done during the preapproach. As much as possible should be learned about customer's wants and needs.

18.   The objective of an initial sales call is to give an impression of professionalism, create rapport and to build credibility.

19.   During the sales presentation, the sales representative matches the benefits of his or her value package to the client's needs. The presentation will be tailored to the customer's needs, and will be relatively easy to present because the sales representative has done the homework of getting to know the customer.

20.   A salesperson should anticipate a prospect's objections, and to resolve the doubts a prospect may have.

21.   Closing techniques include getting a series of small commitments and then asking for the order and showing the client where to sign.

22.   The follow-up includes handling customer complaints, making sure that the customer's questions are answered, and supplying what the customer wants.

23.   The goals of a salesperson are to help the buyer buy, and to make sure the buyer is satisfied after the sale.

24.   With current technology, a salesperson has data about the customer, competitors, where products are in the supply chain, pricing and more. B2B sales people will have new roles to play as more customers buy over the Internet. Sales personnel will have to add value to the product and become a consultative salesperson.

25.   A consultative sales person begins by analyzing customer needs and then comes up with solutions to those needs. Often customers have already searched the Internet for information and will already know what they want. So the role of the sales person is to be a consultant, to provide enough helpful assistance that it will be worth dealing with the sales person. The sales person will have to be computer proficient, and be able to walk the customer through the exchange process quickly and easily.

Public Relations : Building Relationships With All Publics

26. a. Listen to the public
    b. Change policies and procedures
    c. Inform people that you're being responsive to their needs

27. It is the responsibility of the public relations department to maintain close relationships with the media, community leaders, government officials, and other corporate stakeholders. The idea is to establish and maintain a dialogue with those stakeholders so that the company can respond to questions, complaints, and suggestions quickly.

28. a. Stories are published for free, if the material is interesting or newsworthy.
    b. It may reach people who would not read an advertisement.
    c. It's believable.

29. a. No control over how or when the media will use the story.
    b. The story may be altered, and could end up not as positive as the original.
    c. Once a story has run, it won't be repeated.

Sales Promotion : Getting a Good Deal

30. a. Trade shows   d. Catalogs
    b. Portfolios for salespeople   e. Conventions
    c. Deals (price reductions)

31. a. Coupons   g. Bonuses (Buy one, get one free)
    b. Cents-off promotions   h. Catalogs
    c. Sampling   i. Demonstrations
    d. Premiums   j. Special events
    e. Sweepstakes   k. Lotteries
    f. Contests   l. Exhibits

32. Sales promotion programs are designed to supplement the other promotion mix variables by creating enthusiasm for the overall promotional program.

33. Internal sales promotion efforts are directed at salespeople and other customer contact people. It is an attempt to keep salespeople enthusiastic about the company through sales training and the development of sales aids, and participation in trade shows where salespeople can get leads.

34. A virtual trade show is a trade show on the Internet. This allows customers to see many products without leaving the office, and the information is available 24 hours a day.

35. After the company's employees have been motivated, the next step is to promote to distributors and dealers involved so that they are enthusiastic about helping to promote a product. After the companies employees and intermediaries have been motivated, the next step is to promote to final consumers using samples, coupons, cents-off deals, displays, store demonstrations, premiums, and other incentives like contests, trading stamps and rebates.

36. Sampling is a quick effective way of demonstrating a product's superiority at the time when consumers are making a purchase decision.

37. Event marketing means sponsoring events such as rock concerts or going at various events to promote products.

38. The idea behind word of mouth promotion is to get people talking about your products and your brand name so they remember them when they go shopping.

39. Companies have begun to create word of mouth by paying people to go into Internet chat rooms and talk favorably about various products and services. The term for this and other forms of Internet word of mouth promotion is viral marketing. Companies are creating word of mouth thorough sending testimonials, and paying commissions for sending people to specific Web sites.

40. As people purchase goods and services on the Internet companies keep track of those purchases and gather other kinds of information about consumers. Over time the company learns who buys what, when and how often. Because of the availability of so much information, companies are tending to use traditional promotional tools less and are putting more money into direct mail and other forms of direct marketing, including catalogs and the Internet.

41. Promotion has become interactive because you can search the net on your own and find the information about products when you want it. If you can't find the information you want, you can request it and get it immediately.

Managing the Promotion Mix: Putting It All Together

42.   a. large homogeneous groups of consumers are usually most efficiently reached through advertising

       b. large organizations are best reached through personal selling

43. In a push strategy, the producer uses promotion tools to convince wholesalers and retailers to stock and sell merchandise. If it works, consumers will walk into the store, and see the product and buy it. The idea is to push the product through the distribution system to the stores.

44. In a pull strategy, heavy advertising and sales promotion efforts are directed toward consumers so they'll request the products from retailers. If it works, consumers will go to the store and order the products. Seeing demand, the storeowner will then order them from the wholesaler. The wholesaler in turn will order from the producer. The idea is to pull products down through the distribution system.

45. A total systems approach to marketing is when promotion is a part of supply chain management. In such cases retailers would work with producers and distributors to make the supply chain as efficient as possible. Then a promotional plan would be developed for the whole system. The idea would be to develop a value package that would appeal to everyone.

Integrated Marketing Communication (IMC)

46. The result of an integrated marketing communication system is a unified image of the company in the public's mind.

47.
   a. Gather data constantly about the groups affected by the organization and keep the information in a database. Make it available to everyone.
   b. Respond quickly to information by adjusting company policies and practices and by designing wanted products and services for target markets.
   c. Make it possible for customers and potential customers to access information that they may need to make a purchase.

CRITICAL THINKING EXERCISES

1. The Internet is changing organizations' approach to customers, creating an environment in which a company will work with, rather than promote to, their customers. At Music-stor we will need to create a relationship with our customers by listening to what they want in terms of product and service, and giving them access to information. This will require our web site to be interactive so our customers can talk to us, and even to each other, ask questions and get as much information as possible. We could even add links to popular music sites, and provide concert information "personalized" to each region of the country.

2.
   a. Radio, newspaper
   b. Newspaper, radio
   c. Magazines, Internet sites aimed at women
   d. Outdoor, local TV, radio
   e. TV, Direct mail
   f. Direct mail, TV
   g. Magazines
   h. Newspaper, direct mail, Web site

3.   A sales presentation for Music-stor will have to begin with prospecting. Which carmakers are you going to target? Are you going to go after just one carmaker, or several? Initially, you will probably be wise to begin with just one. The question then becomes which maker to go after. After research, you may be able to make that decision more easily. Then, the preapproach will call for learning as much as possible about the products your customer sells. Which models will be the best suited for Music-stor? Which of the models could be most easily adapted? What's the production volume on those models? What's the competition doing? How could Music-stor benefit your customer? Making the approach will involve making an appointment with the right person, the decision-maker. You will need to look professional, so have a prototype of the product with you. Come prepared with questions geared to help you find out what they may seeking for. During the presentation, you will have to show the car maker how Music-stor will make their cars better than the competition. You could discuss the benefits of convenience, luxury, having something the competition doesn't have. You could come prepared with visuals demonstrating how easily Music-stor would fit into the interior of the car (with the magic of computer graphics!). You will also want to know something about who your customer's customers are, in order to be able to demonstrate how Music-stor will appeal to them. Objections will have to be overcome by showing how easily Music-stor will fit into existing models, perhaps by driving a car (one of their models of course) with Music-stor installed, and taking the customer for a ride to show them Music-stor convenience. You could show them how easily the interior could be adapted for Music-stor by using your computer graphics presentation. Eventually you will have to close the sale, perhaps by asking to make Music-stor an available option, or asking your customer to put Music-stor in some of their cars. Finally, always be available for questions, "hand-holding," and problems that may arise. Keep in mind that this process will take a lot of time, and won't be accomplished in one sales call.

4.   In order to convince retailers to sell the product, you will need to convince them that the shelf-space you are asking for will pay off. You will still need to determine which type of retailer will be most appropriate (prospecting and qualifying), research retailers in terms of who their customers are, then learn about the needs of the retailer, and exactly what they want from the products they carry. During the presentation, you will need to convince the retailer that this is a product consumers will want, why they will want it (convenience and the ability to store more tapes and CDs) and how carrying the product will benefit the retailer. You will need to have a sample of Music-stor with you and show the retailer how it works easily with most interiors and how easily it can be detached to take out of the car if need be.

5.   It sounds like the station really wanted to know what people thought of their programming, and what people wanted in a news program. The first step of a good public relations program is to do research to evaluate public attitudes, which is exactly what the station did, by researching the market before the premiere, and by publishing the station's phone numbers and encouraging viewers to call. The station also seems to have responded by avoiding, as much as possible, the "bad news" stories as lead ins, which is in the public interest, especially as the broadcast is at 9:00 p.m. when it is possible that children could be watching. They also seem to have avoided the scandalous stories upon which many TV news programs seem to have thrived. This is also illustrated by the fact that they tell the viewers exactly when a news story will air, allowing viewers to change the channel if children are likely to be watching a story that parents don't want them to see, for example. Lastly, during the broadcast and in their advertising they are

mentioning the specific ways in which they have responded to viewer requests, which is the third step in a good public relations program.

6.   Suggested answers:

Group	Technique
a. Salespeople	Sales training, conventions, trade shows
b. Dealers	Catalogues, special events, "deals"
c. Customers	Coupons, sweepstakes, displays, samples

7.   You may have received free samples at the store or coupons in the mail, entered a contest, bought a glass at a fast food restaurant, sent in a rebate to a manufacturer, gone to a trade show or even received a free pen with a company name on it. You may have received a disk or a cd in the mail promoting an Internet provider. The kinds of ads you see on your computer, or in your mailbox, may be the result of various sites you have visited on the Internet.

8.   Product - A good product will generate positive word of mouth because customers will be happy with the product and pass the word along.

Sales promotion - Techniques such as special events and contests often create positive word of mouth promotion

Advertising - When an advertisement is easily remembered or funny it will often create positive word of mouth. A good technique is to advertise to people who already use your product.

Publicity - A news story can create word of mouth by stimulating the public's interest in the product.

Personal selling - A good sales person can help the customer to develop a positive image of the product, thus creating positive word of mouth.

9.   Your response to this question will really depend upon whom you have selected as you primary target market. If you have decided to go after the automotive manufacturers as your primary market, then most likely your promotion mix will include lots of personal selling, some advertising in the form of brochures, perhaps, aimed at the car dealerships who will be selling the cars with your product installed. It should also include a well designed web site, with interactive features. If your research has been done, and a need for this kind of product has been established, you could design a public relations campaign for the auto manufacturer, indicating that the company listened to your need for a product like Music-stor, then made the product in response.

If your primary market is the retail market, then you must design a campaign aimed at encouraging the retailers to carry the product, so some kind of sales promotion will be appropriate such as price deals, incentives for the retailers selling the most product, and so on. You could participate in trade shows, featuring the latest car models, which are held all over the United States and are attended by thousands of consumers. You could use some advertising, after the retailers have been convinced to carry Music-stor. Any form of publicity could be useful, as will the word of mouth generated by satisfied customers.

You may have your own web site, with attractive graphics, interactive sales techniques. You may be able to advertise on-line, on Web sites that appeal to a younger market, for example, which may be more likely to purchase your product for their car. You may also consider direct marketing, such as order forms in music magazines.

Most likely you will use a combination of a push and pull strategy for the product. You will be using primarily a push strategy if you are aiming primarily at the automotive manufacturers. A combination will be most effective if you are aiming at the consumer market. Probably the best approach, once you are an established company, will be to work with your customers, retailers and develop a value package that will appeal to everyone, the manufacturers, retailers and consumers.

10.   A. Maria Barucci implemented an integrated marketing communication system first by developing a list of all her "stakeholders," all those groups affected by her company. She started the process by talking with and listening to her employees, and responded by implementing their suggestions. This committed the employees to the rest of the changes she wanted to make. Maria communicated with customers and other stakeholders, and implemented the changes they suggested. She kept a database with this information, so that the information could be continually updated. Further, she let her customers know she was responding by developing an ad campaign with the theme "You asked for it! You got it!" which tells customers that Maria has responded to their suggestions. She is using new technology to make it easy for customers to know what changes they have made, what is on the menu and so forth.

The new, more relaxed atmosphere created by these changes carried over to the customers in the restaurant. Although there is no mention made, it is probable that the open, helpful atmosphere created positive word of mouth and that customers responded by patronizing the restaurant and by telling others.

B.   Small businesses have the advantage of being closer to the customer, and of being able to respond more quickly to suggested changes. Small businesses may also find it easier to develop relationships that are more personal with their suppliers and other stakeholders. Small businesses are more flexible than big businesses, and the decision-making process takes less time. Small firms tend to be better listeners and have fewer layers of management, which enables them to be more responsive to market changes.

PRACTICE TEST

MULTIPLE CHOICE

1. b
2. c
3. a
4. d
5. d
6. b
7. c
8. a
9. d
10. c

11. b
12. d
13. c
14. a
15. b
16. d
17. b
18. b
19. c
20. b

TRUE/FALSE

1. F
2. T
3. T
4. F
5. T

6. T
7. F
8. F
9. T
10. T

CHAPTER 17
USING TECHNOLOGY TO MANAGE INFORMATION

LEARNING GOALS

After you have read and studied this chapter, you should be able to:

1.   Outline the changing role of business technology.

2.   Compare the scope of the Internet, intranets, and extranets as tools in managing information.

3.   List the steps in managing information and identify the characteristics of useful information.

4.   Review the hardware most frequently used in business and outline the benefits of the move toward computer networks.

5.   Classify the computer software most frequently used in business.

6.   Evaluate the human resource, security, privacy and stability issues in management that are affected by information technology.

7.   Identify the careers that are gaining or losing workers due to the growth of information technology.

LEARNING THE LANGUAGE

Listed below are important terms found in the chapter. Choose the correct term for the definition and write it in the space provided

Broadband technology	Internet 2	Public domain software
Cookies	Intranet	Push technology
Data processing (DP)	Knowledge management	Shareware
Extranet	Knowledge technology	Virtual private network (VPN)
Information systems (IS)	Network computing system	Virtualization
Information technology (IT)	(client/server computing)	Virus

1.   Technology called _____ supported existing business, and was used primarily to improve the flow of financial information.

2.   A private data network called a _____ creates secure connections or "tunnels" over regular Internet lines.

3. The new Internet system known as the _____ links government supercomputer centers and a select group of universities; it runs many times faster than today's public infrastructure and supports heavy-duty applications.

4. Sharing, organizing and disseminating information in the simplest and most relevant way possible for the users of the information is called _____.

5. Web software called _____ delivers information tailored to a previously defined user profile; thus it pushes the information to users so that they don't have to pull it.

6. Accessibility through technology, or _____ allows business to be conducted independent of location.

7. A semiprivate network known as an _____ uses Internet technology and allows more than one company to access the same information or allows people on different servers to collaborate.

8. Software that is copyrighted but distributed to potential customers free of charge is called _____.

9. A piece of programming code known as a _____ is inserted into other programming to cause some unexpected and, for the victim, usually undesirable event.

10. Technology called _____ helps companies to <u>do</u> business; it includes such tools as automated teller machines (ATMs) and voice mail.

11. Technology known as _____ delivers voice, video and data through the Internet.

12. Technology called _____ adds a layer of intelligence to filter appropriate information and deliver it when it is needed.

13. Computer systems that allow personal computers (clients) to obtain needed information from huge databases in a central computer are called a _____.

14. Technology called _____ helps companies to <u>change</u> business by allowing them to use new methods.

15. Software that is free for the taking is _____.

16. Information such as registration information or user preferences, known as _____ are sent by a web server over the Internet to a web browser that the browser software is expected to save and to send back to the server whenever the user returns to that web site.

17. A company wide network called an _____ is closed to public access, and uses Internet-type technology.

ASSESSMENT CHECK

Learning Goal 1   **The Role of Information Technology**

1. What is the difference between data and information?

2. What was the primary role and use of data processing?

3. How did Information Systems differ from data processing?

4. What does Information Technology allow businesses to do?

5.	What two barriers to doing business are being broken by information technology? How does breaking these barriers change the way business is done?

6.	What is a virtual office?

7.	What is the difference between information technology and knowledge technology?

8.	How does knowledge technology change the flow of information?

9.	How does KT change a businessperson's job?

Learning Goal 2   **Road to Knowledge: The Internet, Intranets, Extranets and Virtual Private Networks**

10.   How can a company prevent competitors getting into their intranets?

11.   What are some applications of an intranet?

12.   How is an intranet different from an extranet?

13.   How can an extranet be used?

14.   What is the potential problem with an extranet?

15.   How does a virtual private network solve the problems involved with the use of an extranet?

16.   How does broadband technology solve the problem of a "traffic jam" on the Internet?

17.   What is the Internet 2 used for?

18.   What is vBNS?

Learning Goal 3   **Managing Information**

19.   What is "infoglut?"

20.   List four qualities of useful information.

        a._____

        b._____

        c._____

        d._____

21.   What is high quality information?

22.   When is information complete?

23.   What is meant by timeliness and relevance, regarding information?

24.   What does push technology do?

25.   What is important to remember about information overload?

26.   What is knowledge mail, and how does it work?

27.   What does Moore's Law predict? How did Moore revise his statement?

28.   What are some of the hardware components?

29.   What will a human computer interface do?

30.   What are Internet appliances designed to do?

31.   How is the way we access the Internet changing, and what effect does that have on information we get from the Internet?

32.   Identify the major benefits of a computer network system.

a. _____

b. _____

c. _____

33.   Describe the drawbacks of networks. What have some companies looked into to avoid the drawbacks?

34.   What is a thin client network? What is the benefit?

35.   What is another option for companies looking to avoid problems with networks, besides thin client networks? What is the benefit?

Learning Goal 5   **Software**

36.   What are six major business uses of software?

a. _____

b. _____

c. _____

d. _____

e. _____

f. _____

37.   Identify the major elements of each of the following types of software

Word Processing	Desktop Publishing	Spreadsheets	Database	PIMs	Graphics/ Presentation
Communications Programs	Message Center Software	Accounting / Finance	Integrated Programs	Groupware	

Learning Goal 6   **Effects of Information Technology on Management**

38.   What impact has technology had on the human resources area?

39. What is the challenge technology poses for human resource managers? How is the problem being addressed?

40. What is telecommuting and what are some benefits of telecommuting?

41. What are some drawbacks of telecommuting?

42. How are companies attempting to alleviate the problems of telecommuting?

43. What is a hacker?

44. How are computer viruses spread?

45.   Why are antivirus programs not always effective? What should you do to avoid the problem?

46.   What are some of the privacy issues that arise from the use of technology?

47.   What is a key issue being debated over Internet privacy?

48.   What does a cookie do?

49.   How expensive are computer glitches to American businesses?

50.   What is causing computer glitches?

Learning Goal 7   **Technology and You**

51.   What are some of the reasons why being computer illiterate could be "occupational suicide?"

52.   What has been the impact of a shortage of information technology workers?

CRITICAL THINKING EXERCISES

Learning Goal 1

1.   Describe how business technology changed from the 1970's to the 1980's to the present.

2.   We have read in several previous chapters of the need to meet increasing global competition, and of the movement toward customized products and marketing. How does information technology change business to make those jobs possible?

3.   Using Figure 17.1 in your text, identify as many ways as possible that information technology has changed your school.

Learning Goal 2

4.   Compare intranets and extranets. Do you know a company that has an intranet? How is it used? what are the applications in this company?

Learning Goal 3

5.   What is one of the biggest problems with the age of information technology in terms of managing the information?

6.   Help! You are swamped by the data, reports, facts, figures, and tons of paper and E-mail being sent to you! It's your job as a entry level sales employee to manage the dissemination of all this "stuff" and make sure it makes sense to everyone who gets it- in other words, your job is to manage all that information! What can you do to make this information useful? How does push technology help to solve information overload?

Learning Goal 4

7.   How could a network computing system help with information overload?

8.   Major uses for or types of software include:

Writing (word processing)   Communicating

Manipulating numbers (spreadsheets)   Integrated software

Filing and retrieving data (databases)   Groupware

Presenting information visually (Graphics)

Match the application being used to the following examples:

a.   Richard Bolt uses this software to record his students' grades, average the grades and total the grades at the end of the semester. It's easy to change scores if an error is made, because the computer will automatically recalculate averages and totals when the new score is recorded. _____

b.   Ray Smith uses Outlook Express to send and retrieve messages from work. _____

c.   Steve Nicholson is a marketing manager who uses this type of software to keep track of all his sales people. He has all the information regarding territories, sales quotas, expenses, sales calls and more right at his fingertips. _____

d.   Ryan Charles used this software to create a more interesting report for his science project. After he had finished writing the report, he created a pie chart and a bar chart to illustrate the findings of his research. _____

e.   Lin Brinkman works in a law office. Whenever there is a need for a certain kind of document for a specific case, all Lin has to do is pull the document up on her screen and insert the relevant information._____

f.   Julie Andersen uses this to complete her accounting worksheet, design a chart that graphically represents her information, and write a report summarizing all the information, all with one software package. _____

g.   The Ford Mustang re-design team used this type of software to work together on their project all at the same time. Every time someone had a good idea, they put it into the memory for retrieval by anyone on the team at any time. _____

Learning Goal 6

9.   What do you think has happened to organizational structures as a result of the increased use of technology?

10.   What are some of the security and privacy issues that are important to recognize with the increasing use of information technology?

11.   What careers will be growing in the next few years? How can computers be used for such jobs as a physical therapist or personal and home health care aide?

PRACTICE TEST

Multiple Choice – Circle the best answer

1. In the 1980's, business technology changed from supporting business, to *doing* business by using
    _____.

    a. data processing
    b. information technology
    c. information systems
    d. knowledge technology

2. Using _____ a new employee can sit at a workstation and let the system take over doing everything from laying out a checklist of each thing required on a shift to answering questions and offering insights that once would have taken up a supervisor's time.

    a. data processing
    b. information technology
    c. knowledge technology
    d. virtualization

3. At MEMC Electronics, employees can update their addresses, and submit requisitions, timesheets and payroll forms online. The company's system is closed to public access, but all employees have access. MEMC is using an _____.

    a. intranet
    b. extranet
    c. internet
    d. electronic data interchange system

4. A problem managers have with the rapid advance of information technology has been

    a. the skyrocketing cost of information.
    b. the hardware and software products available can't keep up with the expansion of information.
    c. the increased layers of management.
    d. information overload, with the deluge of information available.

5.   Which of the following is not included in a list of characteristics of useful information?

a.   Timeliness
b.   Quality
c.   Completeness
d.   Accessibility

6.   When facing information overload a manger should

a.   set goals and do the best he or she can.
b.   hire an intern to take care of information which is not needed.
c.   look for a system which will handle the information more readily.
d.   make use of a file management system.

7.   _____includes pagers, cellular phones, printers and scanners and personal digital assistants.

a.   Software
b.   Multimedia
c.   Extranets
d.   Hardware

8.   In recent years, businesses have moved from:

a.   network computing systems to mainframe systems.
b.   client/server computing to network computing systems.
c.   database systems to information processing.
d.   mainframe systems to network computing systems.

9.   Which of the following is not a benefit of networks:

a.   more information is available.
b.   saving time and money.
c.   networks provide easy links across boundaries.
d.   allows employees to see complete information.

10. Which of the following projects would be best suited to a spreadsheet program?

a. Personalizing a standardized letter to clients
b. Recording the sales figures from several different stores, and calculating profits
c. Updating lists and schedules, keeping track of inventory
d. Making a presentation more appealing with sound clips, video clips, and clip art

11. A major difference between groupware and other types of software is that groupware

a. is less expensive than other forms of software because it is distributed free.
b. can replace more management functions than others.
c. allows computers to talk to one another.
d. runs on a network and allows several users to work on the same project at the same time.

12. For workers, perhaps the most revolutionary effect of computers and increased use of the Internet is

a. the amount of information which has been made available to managers.
b. the ability to allow employees to work from home.
c. the spread of viruses.
d. the amount of personal information available and people who can access it.

13. Which of the following is not considered a benefit of telecommuting?

a. Saves money by retaining valuable employees during long leaves
b. Involves less travel time and cost
c. Can increase productivity
d. Avoids isolation of workers

14. In the movie The Matrix, a rebel group breaks into government computers, and accesses some very sensitive information. The term to describe this group would be:

a. hackers.
b. viruses.
c. cookies.
d. computer illiterates.

15. One of the problems with today's direct, real-time communication is

   a. existing laws do not address the legal issues.
   b. public information is more difficult to obtain.
   c. communication is not face to face.
   d. having to be careful to constantly update antivirus programs.

16. What is expected to happen to the demand for information technology workers?

   a. Thousands of technology jobs will go unfilled in the next few years
   b.   Demand is expected to level off within the next 10 years
   c. Supply of workers will probably meet demand for workers
   d. There will be more workers than jobs by the year 2005

17. Which of the following would not be included in a list of the causes of computer glitches?

   a. computer error
   b. malfunctioning software
   c. human error
   d. software and hardware that is not complex enough to handle the systems

18. A system that runs 22,000 times faster than a traditional modem and supports heavy-duty applications is known as:

   a. broadband technology
   b. the Internet
   c. an extranet
   d. Internet 2

True-False

1. _____ A virtual office would include cellular phones, pagers, laptop computers, and personal digital assistants.

2. _____ Information technology creates organizations and services that are independent of location.

3. _____ An extranet is a company-wide network which is closed to everyone outside the specific company using the intranet.

4. _____ Generally, only the largest companies use the Internet to do business.

5. _____ The Internet 2 will support heavy-duty applications, such as videoconferencing, research, distance education and other sophisticated applications.

6. _____ With the increased use of the Internet, information has become easier to manage.

7. _____ Push technology will allow for customized news delivery to your computer after sorting through thousands of new sources.

8. _____ Companies are moving toward mainframe computer systems for the next decade.

9. _____ A computer network will help a company file, store and access data more easily.

10. _____ Personal information managers are actually word processing programs.

11. _____ Message center software teams up with modems to provide a way of making certain that phone calls, e-mail and faxes are received, sorted and delivered on time.

12. _____ Antivirus programs need to be updated on a regular basis.

You Can Find It On the Net

As we have discussed in this chapter, there is a lot of information on the web for just about any topic you can imagine. Let's find out what some of the employment statistics are for computer-related occupations.

Visit the Bureau of Labor Statistics at www.bls.gov. Link to the National Wage data, on the classification of 700 occupations by the SOC system.

What is the employment total for Computer and Mathematical occupations?

What is the mean salary?

Go back to the main page and look at the State wage data.

What is the total employment in your home state for Computer and Mathematical occupations?

What is the mean salary?

Return to the main page, and look in the Occupational Outlook Handbook A-Z Index for computer related jobs.

Which are declining? Why?

Which are expected to grow? Why?

ANSWERS

LEARNING THE LANGUAGE

1. Data processing (DP)	7. Extranet	13. Network computing system (client/server computing)
2. Virtual private network	8. Shareware	14. Information technology
3. Internet 2	9. Virus	15. Public domain software
4. Knowledge management	10.Information systems	16. Cookies
5. Push technology	11. Broadband technology	17. Intranet
6. Virtualization	12. Knowledge technology	

ASSESSMENT CHECK

The Role of Information Technology

1.   Data are raw, unanalyzed, and unorganized facts and figures. Information is the processed and summarized data that can be used for managerial decision making.

2.   The primary role of data processing was to support existing business by improving the flow of financial information.

3.   Information Systems went from supporting business to actually doing business, through such means as ATMs and voice mail.

4.   Information technology allows businesses to deliver products and services where and when it is convenient for the customer.

5.   Information technology barriers break time and location barriers. Breaking these barriers creates organizations and services that are independent of location. Being independent of location brings work to people instead of people to work. With Information technology, businesses can conduct work around the world continuously.

6.   A virtual office includes cellular phones, pagers, laptop computers, and personal digital assistants. This technology allows you to access people and information as if you were in an actual office.

7. Knowledge technology is information charged with enough intelligence to make it relevant and useful. It adds a layer of intelligence to filter appropriate information and deliver it when it is needed. Information technology makes information available, as long as you know how to use it and where to find it.

8. Knowledge technology changes the traditional flow of information from an individual going to the database to the data coming to the individual. Using KT business training software a company can put a new employee at a workstation and then let the system take over.

9. It will "think" about individual needs and reduce the amount of time finding and getting information. Businesspeople can then focus on decision-making, rather than spending time on just finding the information they need to make decisions.

Road to Knowledge: The Internet, Intranets, Extranets and Virtual Private Networks

10. Companies can construct a firewall between themselves and the outside world to protect corporate information. A firewall can be software, hardware or both.

11. Intranet applications can include allowing employees to update their addresses or submit company forms such as requisitions, timesheets, or payroll forms online.

12. An intranet is only within the company. An extranet is a semiprivate network that uses Internet technology so that more than one company can access the same information or so people on different servers can collaborate.

13. One of the most common uses of extranets is to extend an intranet to outside customers. It can be used to share data and process orders, specifications, invoices and payments.

14. An extranet can be accessed by outsiders with enough knowledge to break into the system.

15. Most companies want a network that is as secure as possible. A dedicated line is a way to achieve that, but a dedicated line is costly and limits use to computers directly linked to that line. A virtual private network solves the problem by creating secure connections, or "tunnels" over regular Internet lines. The idea is to give the company the same capabilities as dedicated lines at a much lower cost.

16. Broadband technology solves the Internet traffic jam problem by offering users a continuous connection to the Internet, and allowing them to send and receive large files faster than before. The more bandwidth, the bigger the pipe for the data to flow through. The bigger the pipe, the faster the flow.

17.   The Internet 2 supports heavy-duty applications, such as videoconferencing, collaborative research, distance education, digital libraries, and full-body simulation environments known as tele-immersion.

18.   BNS, or very high speed Backbone Network Service links government supercomputer centers and a select group of universities.

Managing Information

19.   Infoglut refers to information overload resulting from a deluge of information from a variety of sources.

20.   a.   High Quality
       b.   Completeness
       c.   Timeliness
       d.   Relevance

21.   High quality information is accurate and reliable.

22.   Information is complete when there is enough information for you to make a decision but not so much information that the issue is lost or confused.

23.   Timeliness means that information must reach managers quickly. Relevance refers to the fact that different managers have different information needs. Because there is so much information available, manager must learn which questions to ask to get the answers they need.

24.   Push technology consists of software and services that filter information so that users can get the customized information they need. Push technology pushes the information to you so you don't have to pull it out. These services deliver customized news to your computer after sorting through thousands of news sources to find information that suits your identified needs.

25.   The important thing to remember when facing information overload is to relax. Set goals for yourself and do the best you can.

26.   Knowledge-mail sorts through the millions of e-mail messages going through a company's system and tracks users' work. It can then alert an individual when others in the company are doing similar work, so that people can share information to solve problems.

The Enabling Technology: Hardware

27. Moore's Law predicts that the capacity of computer chips will double approximately every year. That has been true, but recently the speed of evolution has slowed. Moore said in 1997 that his prediction cannot hold good for much longer because chipmakers will run into a fundamental law of nature: the finite size of atomic particles will prevent infinite miniaturization.

28. Hardware components include computers, pagers, cellular phones, printers, scanners, fax machines, personal digital assistants, and personal information managers.

29. A human computer interface combines a video camera and computer. When you approach the PC it recognizes you, and determines what tasks you want to complete that day.

30. Internet appliances are designed to connect people to the Internet and to e-mail.

31. Wireless handheld devices like the Palm Pilot, smart phones and two-way paging devices allows people to take the Internet with them wherever they go. Because these devices are meant for mobile Internet access, they must be small. This changes the format in which Internet information can be delivered. The traditional format designed for big, high resolution monitors must be changed to deliver small bits of information using brief lines of text and tiny images.

32. A computer network system:
    a. Saves time and money
    b. Provides easy links to other areas of the company
    c. Allows employees to see complete information

33. Maintaining a large number of desktop computers can be expensive. Studies show that maintaining one corporate Windows-based desktop computer costs between $5000 and $10,000 a year. This incurs a cost in lost productivity, when computers are down, or being updated with new software. Adding new software often causes problems with PC's, as it often conflicts, or even disables, existing software.

    Some companies have looked at a hybrid of mainframe and network computing systems. In this model, applications and data reside on a server, which handles the processing needs for all the client machines on the network. The PCs lack the processing power to handle applications on their own. This is called a thin-client network.

34. With a thin client network, software changes and upgrades only need to be made on the server, so the cost is lower.

35. Another option to maintaining a server onsite is to contract with a remote service provider, or you can lease specific software applications. When you lease software from an applications service provider, or ASP, the provider maintains and upgrades the software on its servers. You connect to their servers via the Internet. You are then using the most current software without the hassles of upgrading software yourself.

Software

36. a. Writing using word processing
   b. Manipulating numbers using spreadsheets
   c. Filing and retrieving data using databases
   d. Presenting information visually using graphics
   e. Communicating
   f. Accounting

37. **Word Processing**: can personalize letters, update documents, revise forms to exact customer needs

   Desktop Publishing: Combines word processing with graphics to produce designs

   Spreadsheets: allows for quick calculations, is the electronic equivalent of an accountants worksheet, combined with other features

   Database: allows users to work with information normally kept in lists. Can create customized reports

   PIMs: specialized database allowing users to track business contacts

   Graphics/Presentation programs: allows visual summary of spreadsheet data

   Communications programs: allows computers to exchange files with other computers, retrieve database information, and send and receive mail

   Message Center Software: more powerful than traditional communications packages. Allows for more efficient way of delivering messages from phone, fax, or e-mail

   Accounting/Finance: helps users record financial transactions and generate financial reports

   Integrated Programs: offer two or more applications in one package

   Groupware: allows people to collaborate and share ideas by working on the same project at the same time

Effects of Information Technology on Management

38. Technology has made the work process more efficient as it replaces many bureaucratic functions. Computers often eliminate middle management functions and flatten organizational structures.

39. One of the major challenges technology poses for human resources management is the need to recruit and/or train employees proficient in technology applications. Often managers hire consultants to address these concerns, and outsource the technology training.

40. Telecommuting may be, for workers, the most revolutionary effect of the new technology. Mobile employees using computers linked to the company's network can transmit their work to the office from anywhere, and employees can also work from home. This involves less travel time and fewer costs, and often increases productivity. Companies may also save on commercial property costs, as fewer employees in the office means smaller, less expensive office space.

   Companies can retain valuable employees while they are on leave and take advantage of the experience offered by retired employees. Workers with disabilities will be able to be gainfully employed, and men and women with small children will be able to stay home. Employees can work extra hours at home rather than at work, and this may help to improve morale and reduce stress.

41. Some telecommuters report that consistent long-distance work gives them a feeling of being left out of the office loop. Some feel a loss of the increased energy people can get through social interaction. In addition to isolation, the intrusion that work makes into the personal life is an issue. Often people who work from home don't know when to turn off the work.

42. Companies are using telecommuting as a part-time alternative to alleviate some of the problems and complaints of this kind of work schedule.

43. A hacker is a person who breaks into computer systems for illegal purposes.

44. Computer viruses are spread by downloading infected programming over the Internet or by sharing an infected disk.

45. New viruses are being developed constantly, and the antivirus programs may have difficulty detecting them. It is important to keep your antivirus protection program up-to-date and to not download files from an unknown source.

46. The increase of technology creates major concerns about privacy. E-mail can easily be "snooped," and companies routinely monitor their employees' use of e-mail. The Internet allows Web surfers to access all sorts of personal information about individuals, from license numbers to real estate property records.

47. One of the key issues in the debate over protecting our privacy is: Isn't this personal information already public anyway? The difference is that the Net makes getting public information too easy.

48. A cookie contains your name and password that the Web site recognizes the next time you visit the site so that you don't have to re-enter the same information every time you visit. Other cookies track your movements around the Web and then blend that information with their databases and tailor the ads you receive accordingly.

49. It has been estimated that computer glitches account for as much as $100 billion in lost productivity each year.

50. Experts say that computer glitches are combinations of human error, computer error, malfunctioning software, overly complex equipment, bugs in systems, and naïve executives who won't challenge consultants or in-house specialists.

Technology and You

51. Being computer illiterate could be occupational suicide because workers in every industry are exposed to computers somewhat. It is estimated that by 2006 half of all American workers will be employed in information technology positions or within industries that intensively use information technology products and services.

52. A shortage of information technology workers could have severe consequences for American competitiveness, economic growth and job creation. As the demand has increased and worsened the shortage, pay scales have gone up dramatically.

CRITICAL THINKING EXERCISES

1. In the 1970's, business technology was known as data processing. It was used primarily to support the existing business, to improve the flow of financial information. In the 1980's, the name changed to information systems, and the role changed from supporting business to doing business. Customers interacted with the technology in a variety of ways. In the 1990's, businesses have shifted to using new technology on new methods of doing business, and the role of information technology has become to change business.

2. "In the old days" customers had to go to a business during business hours to meet their needs for consumer products, and employees had to "go to the office" to work. We went to the bank for a loan. Businesses decided *when* and *where* we did business with them. Information technology has changed all that. Information technology allows businesses to deliver products and services whenever and wherever it is convenient for the customer. Even further, IT has enabled businesses to become better and faster at serving customer needs by reducing product development times, getting customer feedback quickly, allowing companies to make changes in products easily and quickly, allowing companies to solve customer problems instantly by using databases, reducing defects, cutting expensive product waste. This has allowed businesses to become more customer oriented and thus more competitive.

3.   These are just some examples of how information technology has changed many schools. You may have lots of other examples:

Organization: Students can get grades over the net, find out school schedules, find out who is teaching certain courses, e-mail assignments to teachers, get syllabi and other course information. Teachers can enter grades online.

Operations: Students can register online, and order books online.

Staffing: With online registration and payments, the need for office personnel may be reduced.

New products: Online courses are cropping up at many schools in many different academic areas.

Customer relations: Students can communicate with instructors, and vice versa via e-mail with questions and problems.

New markets: With online courses, schools can reach students who wouldn't ordinarily attend a particular school, or who may not attend at all, without the online access.

4.   An intranet is a company-wide network closed to public access, which uses internet-type technology. An extranet is a semiprivate network that uses Internet technology so more than one company can access the same information, or so people on different servers can collaborate. One of the most common uses of extranets is to extend an intranet to outside customers.

5.   One of the biggest problems of information technology and the information highway is the overwhelming amount of information available. Today business people are deluged with information from voice mail, the Internet, fax machines, and e-mail. Businesspeople refer to this information overload as "infoglut."

6.   The first thing you need to do is to improve the quality of the information by combining the facts and figures into something that is meaningful. Put sales reports together and summarize weekly or monthly figures. Note any trends in sales over a given period, and double check for accuracy in all the information you use. (Quality)

Secondly, you will need to make sure that you are using the latest sales reports, and double-check your figures. Since you will be sending this information to various sales managers, check to be sure that you have included all the data needed to give the managers an accurate picture of how sales are going and why. You don't need to include anything that may not be relevant, such as reports from committees or other areas that don't pertain to sales. (Completeness)

In addition, you need to work fast! If a sales person is not meeting quotas, a few weeks is too long to wait to find out why. With E-mail, your reports can be sent out almost as soon as they're finished. (Timeliness)

Lastly, be sure that the sales reports you are sending are appropriate to the management level at which they'll be received. Lower level managers will need inventory information perhaps, but

7. The network would allow you to communicate quickly with other areas of the company through E-mail, which we already mentioned. With knowledge mail, you may more easily find someone in the company who could either answer questions you may have, or who could tell you exactly what kind of information they need, and in what format. Using a network means that you could put all the information you have into a database and anyone who needs it could access it. The network could, in fact, eliminate the need for your job altogether!

8. a. Spread sheet - to store and manipulate numbers

    b. Communications - to send and retrieve messages

    c. Database - to store and organize information

    d. Graphics- to make a pictorial presentation

    e. Word processing for writing

    f. Integrated software - to use more than one type of software at one time

    g. Groupware - to allow a team to work on a project simultaneously

9. Computers have often enabled businesses to eliminate middle management functions, and thus flatten organization structures. Perhaps the most revolutionary effect of computers and the increased use of the Internet and intranets may be the ability to allow employees to stay home and do their work from there, or telecommute. Using computers linked to the company's network, workers can transmit their work to the office and back easily, either from home, or from their virtual office.

10. One problem today is hackers, who break into computer systems for illegal purposes. Today, computers no only make all areas of the company accessible, but other companies with which the firm does business1 Another security issue involves the spread of computer viruses over the Internet. Viruses are spread by downloading infected programming over the Internet or by sharing an infected disk. A major concern is a problem with privacy as more and more personal information is stored in computers and people are able to access all sorts of information about you. One of the key issues in the privacy debate is: isn't this personal information already public anyway?

11. Careers that will be growing include database administrators, computer-support specialists, computer scientists, computer engineers, systems analysts, personal and home-care aides, and physical therapists

    Physical therapists will use computer software to help with planning a program of therapy for people with specific injuries, thus "customizing" a therapy program. In the future, computers will also help with a diagnosis as well as with a plan of therapy. Home health care aids can use the computer in the same way, and also create databases for their clients, to keep track of patients, the kind of care they have received, the number of visits made and when the visits were made.

PRACTICE TEST

MULTIPLE CHOICE

1.	c	10.	b
2.	c	11.	d
3.	a	12.	b
4.	d	13.	d
5.	d	14.	a
6.	a	15.	a
7.	d	16.	a
8.	d	17.	d
9.	a	18.	d

TRUE/FALSE

1.	T	7.	T
2.	T	8.	F
3.	F	9.	T
4.	F	10.	F
5.	T	11.	T
6.	F	12.	T

LEARNING GOALS

After you have read and studied this chapter, you should be able to:

1. Understand the importance of financial information and accounting.

2. Define and explain the different areas of the accounting profession.

3. Distinguish between accounting and bookkeeping and list the steps in the accounting cycle.

4. Explain the difference between the major financial statements.

5. Describe the role of depreciation, and LIFO and FIFO in reporting financial information.

6. Detail how computers are used to record and apply accounting information in business.

7. Explain the importance of ratio analysis and the budgeting process in reporting financial information.

LEARNING THE LANGUAGE

Listed below are important terms found in the chapter. Choose the correct term for the definition and write it in the space provided.

Accounting	Depreciation	Liabilities
Accounting cycle	Double-entry bookkeeping	Last in, first out (LIFO)
Annual report	Expenses	Liquidity
Assets	First in, first out (FIFO)	Managerial accounting
Auditing	Financial accounting	Net income or net loss
Balance sheet	Financial statement	Owner's equity
Bookkeeping	Fixed assets	Private accountant
Budget	Fundamental accounting equation	Public accountant
Cash flow	Gross margin (gross profit)	Revenue
Certified Internal Auditor	Income statement	Statement of cash flows
Certified Management Accountant (CMA)	Independent audit	Tax accountant
Certified Public Accountant (CPA)	Intangible assets	Trial balance
Cost of goods sold	Journal	
Current assets	Ledger	

1.   A yearly statement called the _____ covers the financial condition and progress of an organization.

2.   A company's _____ is the difference between cash coming in and cash going out of a business.

3.   Items known as _____ can be converted to cash within one year.

4.   A(n) _____ is a financial plan that sets forth management's expectations for revenues and that allocates the use of resources based on those expectations.

5.   Assets that are relatively permanent, are called _____ and include items such as land, buildings and equipment.

6.   A_____ is the book where accounting data are first entered.

7.   An accounting method called _____ is used for calculating the cost of inventory, and assumes that the last goods to come in are the first to go out.

8.   Assets minus liabilities is the formula for _____.

9.   A(n) _____ is a summary of all the data in the account ledgers to show whether the figures are correct and balanced.

10.   A _____ is trained in tax law and are responsible for preparing tax returns and developing tax strategies.

11.   How fast an asset can be converted into cash is its _____.

12.   A(n) _____ is an evaluation and unbiased opinion about the accuracy of a company 's financial statements.

13.   Accounting used to provide information and analyses to managers within the organization to assist in decision-making is called _____.

14.   A concept called _____ is a system of writing every transaction in two places.

15. An accountant called a(n) _____ passes a series of examinations established by the American Institute of Certified Public Accountants

16. The economic resources owned by the firm are called _____.

17. The accounting technique called _____ is a method for calculating the cost of inventory that assumes the first goods to come in are the first to go out.

18. A firm's _____ is how much the firm earned by buying and selling or making and selling merchandise.

19. Accounting information and analyses prepared for people outside the firm is called _____.

20. Revenue minus expenses equals _____

21. A financial statement called a _____ reports the financial condition of a firm at a specific time.

22. Accountants who work for a single firm, government agency, or nonprofit organization are called _____,

23. The recording, classifying, summarizing, and interpreting of financial events and transactions, or _____, provides management and other interested parties the information they need to make good decisions.

24. A company's _____ is the value of what is received from goods sold, or services rendered.

25. The job of reviewing and evaluating the records used to prepare the company's financial statements is called _____.

26. A(n) _____ is the summary of all transactions that have occurred over a particular period.

27. The six-step process called the _____ results in the preparation and analysis of two major financial statements: balance sheets and income statements.

28. A type of expense called the _____ measures the cost of merchandise sold or cost of raw materials and supplies used for producing items for resale.

29. A _____ provides accounting services to individuals or businesses on a fee basis.

30. Accounts known as _____ indicate what the business owes to others.

31. A specialized accounting book known as a_____ is one in which information from accounting journals is accumulated into specific categories and posted so managers can find all the information about one account in the same place.

32. A _____ is a professional accountant who has met certain educational and experience requirements and been certified by the Institute of Certified Management Accountants.

33. The recording of business transactions is called _____

34. The _____ shows a firm's profit after costs, expenses and taxes; it summarizes all of the resources that have come into the firm, all the resources that have left the firm and the resulting net income or loss.

35. The systematic write-off of the cost of a tangible asset over its estimated useful life is called _____.

36. Items known as _____ include items of value such as patents, and copyrights that have no real physical form.

37. The financial statement called a _____ reports cash receipts and disbursement related to a firm's major activities: operations, investment, and financing.

38. A _____ is an accountant who has a bachelor's degree, 2 years of internal auditing experience, and has successfully passed an exam administered by the Institute of Internal Auditors.

39. Assets equal liabilities plus owner's equity is the _____ and is the basis for the balance sheet.

40. Costs involved in operating a business, such as rent, utilities, and salaries are called
_____

RETENTION CHECK

Learning Goal 1   **The Importance of Financial Information**

1. Why is accounting different from other business functions such as marketing, management, and human resources management?

2. What are the inputs to the accounting system?

3. What are the important elements of processing in the accounting system?

4. What are the outputs of the accounting system?

5. What are two purposes of accounting?

a._____

b._____

6.   Who are the users of accounting information?

Learning Goal 2   **Areas of Accounting**

7.   List the four key working areas of accounting.

a. _____

b. _____

c. _____

d. _____

8.   Identify the areas with which managerial accounting is concerned.

9.   How does financial accounting differ from managerial accounting? Who receives financial accounting information?

10.   Where can you find the information derived from financial accounting?

11.	What is the difference between a public accountant and a private accountant?

12.	What are some of the things a public accountant might do?

13.	What does it mean when financial reports are prepared in accordance with GAAP?

14.	Why are audits performed? Who performs audits?

Learning Goal 3	**Accounting versus Bookkeeping**

15.	What do accountants do with data provided by bookkeepers?

16.	What is the first task of a bookkeeper?

17. What information is recorded in a journal?

18. What is the difference between a journal and a ledger?

19. What are the six steps in the accounting cycle?

a. _____

b. _____

c. _____

d. _____

e. _____

f. _____

Learning Goal 4 **Understanding Key Financial Statements**

20. Identify two key financial statements

a. _____   b. _____

21. List the three major accounts on a balance sheet.

a. _____   c. _____

b. _____

22. What is the fundamental accounting equation?

23. What kinds of things are considered assets?

24. In what order are assets listed on a balance sheet?

25. List the three categories of assets on a balance sheet.

a. _____   c. _____

b. _____

26. What are liabilities? What is the difference between current liabilities and long-term liabilities?

27. What are:

    a. accounts payable:

    b. notes payable

    c. bonds payable

28. What is "equity?" What is stockholder's equity?

29. What is the formula for owner's equity?

30. How does owner's equity in sole proprietorships and partnerships differ from that in a corporation?

31.   What is the formula for developing an income statement?

32.   How does one arrange an income statement according to generally accepted accounting principles?

33.   What is the difference between revenue and sales?

34.   What is the difference in gross margin between a service firm and a manufacturing firm?

35.   What are some kinds of operating expenses? What are two categories of expenses?

36.   What is the "bottom line?"

37.   What is a poor, or negative, cash flow? How does poor cash flow cause problems?

38.   List the three major activities for which cash receipts and disbursements are reported on a statement of cash flows.

a. _____

b. _____

c. _____

Learning Goal 5   **Applying Accounting Knowledge**

39.   How can depreciation affect a firm's net income?

40.   What are two methods of inventory valuation for cost of goods sold?

a. _____

b. _____

41.   What impact do LIFO and FIFO have on net income?

Accountants and the Budgeting Process

42.   What financial statements form the basis for the budgeting process? Why?

43.   For what activities do companies use the budgeting process?

Learning Goal 6   **The Impact of Computer Technology in Accounting**

44.   What benefits do computers have for accounting in a business?

Using Financial Ratios

45.   What do liquidity ratios measure?

46.   What is the formula for the current ratio?

47.   To what is the current ratio compared?

48.   Identify the formula for the acid test ratio. What does this ratio measure?

49.   What is a leverage ratio?

50.   What is the formula for the debt to equity ratio?

51.   What does it mean if a firm has a debt to equity ratio above "1?"

52.   What are profitability ratios?

53.　What are three profitability ratios?

a. _____

b. _____

c. _____

54.　What is the difference between Basic EPS and diluted EPS?

55.　What is the formula for determining Basic Earnings Per Share?

56.　What is the formula for return on sales? What does it measure?

57.　What is the formula for return on equity? What does it measure?

58.　What do activity ratios measure?

59. What is the formula for inventory turnover? What does it measure?

60. What is meant by inventory turnover ratios which are lower than or higher than   average?

CRITICAL THINKING EXERCISES

Learning Goal 1, 2

1. Match the following terms with the definitions listed below.

Auditing   Managerial accounting

Certified management accountant (CMA)   Private accountant

Certified public accountant (CPA)   Public accountant

Financial accounting   Tax accountant

Independent audit

a. The preparation and analysis of financial information for people and organizations outside the firm._____

b. They provide business assistance by designing an accounting system for a firm, selecting the correct software and analyzing the financial strength of a firm, and will conduct independent audits. _____

c. The job of this professional will grow with growing emphasis on global competition, company rightsizing, and organizational accounting. _____

d. As the burden of taxes grows, these accountants will become increasingly important to companies. _____

e. This accountant works for a single firm on a full time basis to help the company keep accurate financial information. _____

f. This happens internally, and often continually, to ensure that proper accounting procedures and financial reporting are being carried on within the company.

_____

g. These accountants have passed a series of examinations and meet the state's requirement for education and experience, and can work as a private or public accountant.

_____

h. This is concerned with measuring and reporting costs of production, marketing and other functions, preparing budgets, checking to see that units are staying within budgets, and designing strategies to minimize taxes. _____

i. This is conducted by an public accountant to determine if a firm has prepared its financial statements according to accepted accounting principles. _____

Learning Goal 3

2. Music-stor is doing very well! They need a bookkeeper to help them with their paperwork, and an accountant. You have been given the task of writing a brief job description for each job. How would you write the job description for each?

Bookkeeper –

Accountant –

3.   The Accounting Cycle is as follows:
        1) analyze documents
        2) record transactions in journals
        3) post to ledgers
        4) prepare trial balance
        5) prepare financial statements
        6) analyze financial statements

Identify which of the following activities is being described in each statement.

a. Joan Perez has finished analyzing and categorizing original documents, and is getting ready for the next step in the accounting cycle, which will be _____

b. Joan is summarizing all the data, to check that all the information is correct _____

c. The accountant for Joan's company is getting ready to evaluate the financial condition of the firm. _____

d. Joan is just beginning the bookkeeping process, and is in the process of dividing the firms transactions onto categories such as sales documents, purchasing receipts, and shipping documents. _____

e. While Joan has prepared the journals, the next step is often done by computer. _____

f. Once the summary statements show that all the information is correct, then the accountant will _____, so that she can analyze them.

4.   a. Two key financial statements are the <u>balance sheet</u> and the <u>income statement.</u>

Indicate whether each of the following accounts would be found on a balance sheet or an income statement.

1. _____   Cash

2. _____   Retained earnings

3._____   Accounts payable

4._____   Interest expense

5._____   Rent expense

6._____   Property

7._____   Commission revenue

8._____   Gross sales

9._____   Common stock

10._____   Supplies expense

11._____   Notes payable

12._____   Accounts receivable

13._____   Equipment

14._____   Advertising expense

15._____   Wages expense

16._____   Retained earnings

17._____   Utilities expense

18._____   Cost of goods sold

19._____   Inventories

20._____   Gross Margin

b. List the liquid assets from questions 4-a in order of liquidity.

1._____   3._____

2._____

5.   The balance sheet reports the financial condition of a firm at a specific time. The basic formula for a balance sheet is:

Assets = Liabilities + Owner's Equity

Total assets consist of current, fixed and intangible assets

Total liabilities consist of current and long term liabilities

Owner's Equity consists of various types of stock and Retained earnings

Using the following list of accounts, construct an accurate balance sheet for Music-stor, Inc.

BE CAREFUL! Not all of the accounts listed will be used for the balance sheet.

MUSIC-STOR, INC.

List of accounts

Accounts payable	$25,000	Utilities expense	$12,000
Net sales	$600,000	Supplies expense	$3700
Accounts receivable	$110,000	Investments	$45,000
Depreciation expense	$4000	Rent expense	$35,000
Inventories	$62,000		
Advertising expense	$28,000		
Wages and salaries expense	$125,000		
Notes payable (current)	$15,000		
Rental revenue	$3000		
Cost of goods sold	$313,000		
Net Property, plant, equipment	$200,000		
Cash	$18,000		
Retained earnings	$165,000		
Accrued taxes	$40,000		
Long-term debt	$60,000		
Common stock	$130,000		

MUSIC-STOR, INC.

BALANCE SHEET

December 31, 2000

6. The income statement reports all the revenues and expenses of a firm for a specific period of time. The basic formula for an income statement is:

Revenue - Cost of goods sold = Gross profit (gross margin)

Gross profit - operating expenses = Net income (loss) before taxes

Net income before taxes - taxes = Net income (loss)

Using the previous list of accounts construct an accurate income statement for Music-stor. Again, look at each account carefully! For purposes of illustration, assume a 28% tax rate on income.

MUSIC-STOR, INC.

INCOME STATEMENT

Year ending December 31, 2000

7. Cash flow problems arise when a firm has debt obligations that must be met before cash from sales is received.

Prepare a personal cash flow statement for two weeks. Include all projected income and all projected cash disbursements (payments) Do you have a cash flow problem?

Cash flow forecast	Week one	Week two
Projected income	_____	_____
Projected "outgo"	_____	_____
Surplus (Deficit)	_____	_____

8. Two methods of determining the value of inventory, and therefore the cost of goods sold, are:
LIFO, last-in, first-out

FIFO, first-in, first out.

The method chosen will directly affect the "bottom line," or profits.

The basic formula for cost of goods sold is: (See Figure 18.6)

Beginning inventory + purchases = Cost of goods available

Cost of goods available - ending inventory = Cost of goods sold

a. Determine the cost of goods sold, using FIFO and LIFO with the following information:

FIFO

Beginning inventory	20,000 units @ $10	$200,000
+ Purchases	7,000 units @ $12	84,000
= Cost of goods available	27,000 units	$284,000
- Ending inventory	5,000 units	_____

LIFO

Beginning inventory	20,000 units @ $10	$200,000
+ Purchases	7,000 units @ $12	84,000
=Cost of goods available	27,000 units	$284,000
- Ending inventory	5,000 units	_____

Cost of goods sold   FIFO _____   LIFO _____

b. What is gross margin on revenues of $450,000 using FIFO? LIFO?

FIFO   LIFO

9. The use of computers in accounting has increased dramatically. Do you know an accountant? Do you know anyone majoring in accounting? Make an appointment and talk to someone who is in the accounting profession, or to one of your classmates majoring in accounting. What can they tell you about their reliance on computers in their profession?   What kind of software are they familiar with? Do they do any accounting over the Internet? What kind of software are you and your classmates using in your accounting classes?

Learning Goal 7

10. Liquidity ratios measure a firm's ability to pay short-term debt. Using the balance sheet and income statement you calculated earlier:

a. Calculate the current ratio for Music-stor

b. Calculate the acid-test ratio for Music-stor

c. In what shape does Music-stor appear to be?

11. Leverage ratios refer to the degree to which a firm relies on borrowed money for its operations.

a. Calculate the Debt to owner's equity ratio for Music-stor

b. If the industry average is .75, how does Music-stor compare?

12.   Profitability ratios measure how effectively the firm is using its resources.

   a.   If Music-stor has approximately 30,000 shares of common stock outstanding, what is their Basic Earnings per share?

   b.   Calculate their Return on sales.

   c.   What is Return on Equity?

13.   Activity ratios measure the effectiveness of the firm in using the available assets.

   a.   If the average inventory for Music-stor is $70,000, what is the inventory turnover rate?

   b.   If the industry average is 3.5, what does that indicate for Music-stor?

Multiple Choice

1.   One purpose of accounting is to:

    a. allow for government tracking of business activities.

    b. make sure a business is paying its taxes.

    c. help managers evaluate the financial condition of the firm.

    d. provide a method of spending money wisely.

2.   Which of the following is not one of the activities associated with accounting?

    a. recording

    b. summarizing

    c. classifying

    d. promoting

3.   The type of accounting that is concerned with providing information and analyses to managers within the organization is called:

    a. financial accounting.

    b. managerial accounting.

    c. auditing.

    d. tax accounting.

4.   Jim Hopson is an accountant who works for a number of businesses as a "consultant." He has helped to design an accounting system, provides accounting services, and has analyzed the financial strength of many of his clients. Jim is working as a:

    a. private accountant.

    b. certified management accountant.

    c. certified internal auditor.

    d. public accountant.

5.   If you were a bookkeeper, the first thing you would do is:

   a.   record transactions into a ledger.
   b.   develop a trial balance sheet.
   c.   prepare an income statement.
   d.   divide transactions into meaningful categories.

6.   A specialized accounting book in which information is accumulated into specific categories and posted so managers can find all information about one account in the same place is a:

   a.   ledger.
   b.   journal.
   c.   trial balance sheet.
   d.   double entry book.

7.   The _____reports the firm's financial condition on a specific day.

   a.   income statement
   b.   cash flow statement
   c.   statement of stockholder's equity
   d.   balance sheet

8.   Which of the following would be considered a current asset?

   a.   accounts payable
   b.   accounts receivable
   c.   copyrights
   d.   buildings

   Use the information below to answer questions 9 and 10:

Net sales	30,000
Total Assets	16,000
Taxes	2,300
Cost of goods sold	12,500
Total Liabilities	8,000
Operating expenses	3,200

9. Net income is:

   a. 14,000
   b. 17,500
   c. 14,300
   d. 12,000

10. Stockholder's equity is:

    a. 16,000
    b. 24,000
    c. 8,000
    d. can't determine from information given

11. Which of the following would not be shown on a statement of cash flows?

    a. cash from operations
    b. cash paid for long term debt obligations
    c. cash raised from new debt or equity
    d. cash paid in donations

12. With regard to depreciation, companies are allowed to:

    a. choose one method of depreciation, but must stay with that method.
    b. write off only a certain percentage of depreciation as an expense.
    c. use one of several techniques, resulting in different net incomes.
    d. change techniques, as long as net income is not affected.

13. The LIFO method of inventory valuation is a method that:

    a. assumes the newest merchandise is used first.
    b. can make the cost of goods sold appear lower than other forms of inventory valuation.
    c. assumes the oldest merchandise is used first.
    d. has the lease effect on cost of goods sold.

14. Financial ratios

    a. are used to calculate profits from one year to the next.

    b. are a poor indicator of a company's financial condition.

    c. are only used by independent auditors.

    d. are helpful to use in analyzing the actual performance of a company.

15. Which kind of ratio is used to determine the ability of a firm to pay its short-term debts?

    a. activity ratios

    b. profitability

    c. debt

    d. liquidity

16. A debt to equity ratio of over 1 would mean:

    a. the economy has more debt than equity.

    b. the company has more equity than debt.

    c. by comparison with other firms, the company is probably in good shape.

    d. the company is in too much debt, and should restructure.

17. Earnings per share, return on sales, and return on equity are all

    a. activity ratios.

    b. profitability ratios.

    c. liquidity ratios.

    d. debt ratios.

18. Which of the following is not considered a part of the basis for the budgeting process?

    a. ratio analysis statements

    b. income statements

    c. balance sheets

    d. statement of cash flows

19. Which of the following is not true of the use of computers in accounting?

    a. most big and small companies use computers to simplify the task of accounting
    b. computers can provide continuous financial information for the business
    c. computers can make accounting work less monotonous
    d. computers have been programmed to make financial decisions on their own

20. One of the benefits of continuous auditing is:

    a. it allows firms to hire fewer accountants.
    b. it can help prevent financial difficulties by spotting trouble earlier.
    c. it makes financial errors much harder to detect.
    d. it reduces the need for small businesses to hire or consult with accountants.

True-False

1. _____ You must know something about accounting if you want to understand business.

2. _____ A major purpose of accounting is to report financial information to people outside the firm.

3. _____ Financial accounting is used to provide information and analyses to managers within the firm to assist in decision making.

4. _____ A private accountant is an individual who works for a private firm that provides accounting services to individuals or businesses on a fee basis.

5. _____ Trial balances are derived from information contained in ledgers.

6. _____ The fundamental accounting equation is assets = liabilities + owner's equity

7. _____ The "bottom line" is shown in the balance sheet.

8. _____ Cash flow is generally not a problem for companies that are growing quickly.

9. _____ Depreciation will most often not have any affect on net income.

10. _____ The four types of financial ratios include liquidity, debt, profitability, and activity ratios.

11. _____ Often, the accounting needs of a small business are significantly different from the needs of larger companies.

12. _____ The higher the risk involved in an industry, the lower the return investors expect on their investment.

You Can Find It on the Net

Do you know what your personal balance sheet looks like? For a way to find out, visit the web site at www.betheboss.com. Use the Be The Boss worksheet to develop your own personal financial statements. Any surprises? What's your net worth? Would you be a good risk for a business loan, or to get involved in franchising, as the web site describes? Why or why not?

ANSWERS

LEARNING THE LANGUAGE

1. Annual report	15. Certified Public Accountant (CPA)	29. Public accountant
2. Cash flow	16. Assets	30. Liabilities
3. Current assets	17. FIFO First In First Out	31. Ledger
4. Budget	18. Gross margin	32. Certified Management Accountant
5. Fixed assets	19. Financial accounting	33. Bookkeeping
6. Journals	20. Net income	34. Income statement
7. LIFO Last In Last Out	21. Balance sheet	35. Depreciation
8. Owner's equity	22. Private accountants	36. Intangible assets
9. Trial balance	23. Accounting	37. Statement of cash flows
10. Tax accountant	24. Revenue	38. Certified Internal Auditor
11. Liquidity	25. Auditing	39. Fundamental accounting equation
12. Independent audit	26. Financial statement	40. Expenses
13. Managerial accounting	27. Accounting cycle	
14. Double entry bookkeeping	28. Cost of goods sold(manufactured)	

ASSESSMENT CHECK

The Importance of Financial Information

1. Accounting is different from other business functions because most of us have limited understanding of accounting principles. As consumers, we have had some experience with marketing, and as workers or students we probably have some understanding of management. But most of us have little experience with accounting.

2. Inputs to accounting include sales documents, purchasing documents, shipping documents, payroll records, bank records, travel records, and entertainment records.

3. In the processing function, recording is done when entries are made into journals, classifying consists of journal entries which are posted into ledgers, and then all accounts are summarized.

4. Outputs consist of financial statements – income statements, balance sheets, and other outside reports.

5.   a.   To help managers evaluate the financial condition and the operating performance of the firm so they make better decisions.

        b.   To report financial information to people outside the firm such as owners, creditors, suppliers, employees and the government.

6.   Users of accounting information include government agencies, such as the IRS and other regulatory agencies, stockholders, creditors, financial analysts, suppliers, and managers of the firm.

Areas of Accounting

7.   a.   Managerial accounting
        b.   Financial accounting
        c.   Auditing
        d.   Tax accounting

8.   Managerial accounting is concerned with measuring and reporting costs of production; marketing, and other functions; preparing budgets; checking whether or not units are staying within their budgets; and designing strategies to minimize taxes.

9.   Financial accounting differs from managerial accounting because the information and analyses are for people outside the organization. This information goes to owners and prospective owners, creditors, and lenders, employee unions, customers, suppliers, governmental units, and the general public. These external users are interested in the organization's profit, its ability to pay its bills, and other financial information.

10.   Much of the information derived from financial accounting is contained in the company's annual report.

11.   A private accountant works for a single firm, government agency or nonprofit organization as a full time accountant. A public accountant provides his or her services to individuals or businesses on a fee basis.

12.   One example of how a public accountant can provide business assistance is by designing an accounting system for a firm, help select the correct computer and software to run the system and analyze the financial strength of an organization .

13.   The independent Financial Accounting Standards Board defines what are *generally accepted accounting principles* that accountants must follow. If financial reports are prepared "in accordance with GAAP" , users know the information is reported according to standards agreed on by accounting professionals.

14. Internal audits are performed by private accountants to ensure that proper accounting procedures and financial reporting are being performed within the company. Public accountants will also conduct independent audits of accounting records. Financial auditors examine the financial health of an organization and additionally look into operational efficiencies and effectiveness.

Accounting versus Bookkeeping

15. Accountants classify and summarize the data provided by bookkeepers. They interpret the data and report them to management

16. The first task a bookkeeper performs is to divide all of the firm's transactions into meaningful categories such as sales documents, purchasing receipts, and shipping documents.

17. The bookkeeper records the data from the original transaction documents into record books called journals. These are the books where accounting data are first entered.

18. A *ledger* is a specialized accounting book in which information from accounting *journals* is accumulated into specific categories and posted so managers can find all the information about one account in the same place.

19. a. Analyzing and categorizing documents
    b. Recording into journals
    c. Posting into ledgers
    d. Prepare a trial balance
    e. Prepare an income statement and balance sheet
    f. Analyze financial statements.

Understanding Key Financial Statements

20. a. Balance sheets
    b. Income statements

21. a. Assets
    b. Liabilities
    c. Owner's equity

22. The fundamental accounting equation is: Assets = Liabilities + Owner's equity

23. Assets include productive, tangible items such as equipment, building, land, furniture, fixtures, and motor vehicles that help generate income, as well as intangibles of value such as patents or copyrights.

24. Assets on a balance sheet are listed in order of their liquidity, which refers to how fast an asset can be converted into cash.

25. a. Current assets   c. Intangible assets
    b. Fixed assets

26. Liabilities are what the business owes to others. Current liabilities are payments due in one year or less; long-term liabilities are payments not due for one year or longer.

27. a. Accounts payable is money owed to others for merchandise and/or services purchased on credit but yet not paid. If you have a bill you haven't paid, you have an account payable.
    b. Notes payable is short-term or long-term loans that have a promise for future payment.
    c. Bonds payable is money loaned to the firm that it must pay back.

28. The value of things you own, assets, minus the amount of money you owe others, liabilities, is called equity. The value of what stockholders own in a firm minus liabilities is called stockholders equity.

29. Owner's equity is assets minus liabilities.

30. For businesses that are not incorporated, like proprietorships and partnerships, owner's equity means the value of everything owned by the business minus any liabilities of the owners. For a corporation, owner's equity represents the owners' claims to funds they have invested in the firm, such as capital stock, plus earnings kept in the business, which are called retained earnings.

31. a. Revenue - Cost of goods sold = Gross profit
    b. Gross profit - Expenses = Net income (loss) before taxes
    c. Net income before taxes - taxes = Net income (loss)

32.   Revenue
        <u>- Cost of Goods Sold</u>
        Gross Margin
        <u>-Operating Expenses</u>
        Net Income before Taxes
        <u>-Taxes</u>
        Net income (or loss)

33.   Revenue is the value of what is received for goods sold, services rendered, and other financial sources. Most revenue comes from sales, but there could be other sources of revenue such as rents received, money paid to the firm for use of its patents, interest earned, and so forth.

34.   It's possible in a service firm that there may be no cost of goods sold; therefore, net revenue could equal gross margin. In a manufacturing firm, it is necessary to estimate the cost of goods manufactured.

35.   Obvious expenses include rent, salaries, supplies, utilities, insurance, even depreciation on equipment. Two categories of expenses are selling and general expenses.

36.   The "bottom line" is the net income the firm incurred from operations.

37.   A poor, or negative, cash flow, indicates that more money is going out of the business than is coming in from sales or other sources of revenue.

        In order to meet the demands of customers, more and more goods are bought on credit. Similarly, more and more goods are sold on credit. This can go on until the firm uses up all the credit it has with banks that lend it money. When the firm requests money from the bank to pay a crucial bill the bank refuses the loan because the credit limit has been reached. All other credit sources may refuse a loan as well. The company needs to pay its bills or else its creditors could force it into bankruptcy.

38.   a. Operations – cash transactions associated with running the business
        b. Investments – cash used in or provided by the firm's investment activities
        c. Financing – cash raised from new debt or new equity capital, or cash used to pay expenses, debts, or dividends

Applying Accounting Knowledge

39.   A firm may use one of several different methods to calculate depreciation. Each method will result in a different depreciation amount, and thus a different expense to be taken from gross profit. This will then result in a different bottom line.

40.   a. LIFO, last-in, first-out

  b. FIFO, first-in, first-out

41.   If the accountant uses FIFO, the cost of goods sold will be different, usually lower, than if the accountant uses LIFO. In FIFO, older perhaps less expensive merchandise is used to value the cost of goods sold. That means the net income will be higher. In LIFO, newer goods are assumed to be used, so the bottom line will be lower, because costs are higher.

Accountants and the Budgeting Process

42.   Financial statements including the balance sheet, income statement, and statement of cash flows form the basis for the budgeting process. This is because financial information from the past is what is used to project future financial needs and expenditures.

43.   Innovative companies use budgeting to determine the profitability of individual products, customers and channels of distribution. Most companies use the budgeting process as an opportunity to plan and to improve the management of the business.

The Impact of Computer Technology in Accounting

44.   Computers allow managers to obtain up-to-the-minute financial information for the business. Continuous auditing helps managers to prevent cash flow problems and other financial difficulties by allowing them to spot trouble early. Today's accounting packages are easy to use, can be customized and offer efficient Internet functioning. Computers can also help make accounting work less monotonous.

Using Financial Ratios

45.   Liquidity ratios measure the company's ability to pay its short-term debts. Short-term debts are expected to be repaid within one year and are of importance to the firm's creditors who expect to be paid on time.

46. $$\frac{\text{Current assets}}{\text{Current liabilities}} = \text{Current ratio}$$

47.   The current ratio is compared to competing firms within the industry to measure how the company sizes up to its main competitors. It is also important that the firm evaluate its ratio from the previous year to note any significant changes.

48. $$\frac{\text{Cash} + \text{marketable securities} + \text{receivables}}{\text{Current liabilities}} = \text{acid test ratio}$$

This ratio measures the cash, marketable securities and receivables of a firm. This ratio is important to firms with difficulty converting inventory into quick cash.

49. Leverage ratios refer to the degree to which a firm relies on borrowed funds in its operations.

50. $\dfrac{\text{Total liabilities}}{\text{Owner's equity}} = \text{debt equity ratio}$

51. A debt to equity ratio of above 1 would show that a firm actually has more debt than equity. It is possible that this firm could be perceived as a risk to both lenders and investors. It is always important to compare ratios to other firms in the same industry because debt financing is more acceptable in some industries.

52. Profitability ratios measure how effectively the firm is using its various resources to achieve profits.

53. a. Earnings per share
     b. Return on sales
     c. Return on equity

54. Diluted earnings per share measures the amount of profit earned by a company for each share of outstanding common stock, as does basic EPS. However, diluted EPS takes into consideration stock options, warrants, preferred stock and convertible debt securities that can be converted into common stock.

55. $\dfrac{\text{Net Income}}{\text{Number of Common shares outstanding}} = \text{basic earnings per share}$

56. $\dfrac{\text{Net Income}}{\text{Net Sales}} = \text{Return of sales}$

     Firms use this ratio to see if they are doing as well as the companies they compete against in generating income on sales they achieve.

57. $\dfrac{\text{Net Income}}{\text{Total Owner's Equity}} = \text{Return on equity}$

     Return on equity measures how much was earned for each dollar invested by owners.

58. Activity ratios measure the effectiveness of the firm's management in using assets that are available.

59.
$$\frac{\text{Cost of Goods Sold}}{\text{Average Inventory}} = \text{Inventory turnover}$$

The inventory turnover measures the speed of inventory moving through the firm and its conversion into sales. Inventory sitting by idly in a business costs money.

60. A lower than average inventory turnover ratio often indicates obsolete merchandise on hand or poor buying practices. A higher than average ratio may signal lost sales because of inadequate stock. An acceptable turnover ratio is generally determined on an industry-by-industry basis.

CRITICAL THINKING EXERCISES

1. a. Financial accounting
    b. Public accountant
    c. Certified management accountant (CMA)
    d. Tax accountant
    e. Private accountant

    f. Auditing
    g. Certified public accountant (CPA)
    h. Managerial accounting
    i. Independent audit

2. Suggested answers: BOOKKEEPING JOB DESCRIPTION - The bookkeeper for Music-stor will be responsible for collecting all original transaction documents, and dividing them into meaningful categories (sales, purchasing, shipping, and so on). The information will be recorded into journals on a daily basis, using the double-entry method. The bookkeeper will also be responsible for recording the information from the journals into ledgers. Must be familiar with computer accounting applications.

    ACCOUNTANT JOB DESCRIPTION - The accountant for Music-stor will be responsible for classifying and summarizing the data provided by the bookkeeper. He/she will interpret the data, report to management, and suggest strategies for improving the financial condition and progress of the firm. Must be able to suggest tax strategies and be skilled in financial analysis. Must be a Certified Management Accountant.

3. a. Record in journals
    b. Take a trial balance
    c. Analyze financial statements

    d. Analyze source documents
    e. Post to ledgers
    f. Prepare statements

4. a.
1.	Balance sheet	11.	Balance sheet
2.	Balance sheet	12.	Balance sheet
3.	Balance sheet	13.	Balance sheet
4.	Income statement	14.	Income statement
5.	Income statement	15.	Income statement
6.	Balance sheet	16.	Balance sheet
7.	Income statement	17.	Income statement
8.	Income statement	18.	Income statement
9.	Balance sheet	19.	Balance sheet
10.	Income statement	20.	Income statement

b.
1. Cash
2. Accounts receivable
3. Inventories

5.   MUSIC-STOR, INC.   BALANCE SHEET
                   December 31, 2000

Assets

Current assets

    Cash $ 18,000

    Investments   45,000

    Accounts receivable   110,000

    Inventory   62,000

  Total current assets   **$235,000**

Net Property, plant and equipment

                                                    200,000

Total Assets   **$435,000**

Liabilities and Stockholder's equity

Liabilities

    Current liabilities

    Accounts payable $25,000

    Notes payable (current)   15,000

    Accrued taxes   40,000

Total current liabilities   **$80,000**

Long-term Debt   60,000

Total liabilities   **$140,000**

Stockholder's equity

Common stock $130,000

Retained earnings   165,000

Total stockholders equity   **$295,000**

Total liabilities and stockholder's equity   **$435,000**

6.

MUSIC-STOR, INC.

INCOME STATEMENT

Year ending December 31, 2000

Revenues		
Net sales	$600,000	
Rental revenue	3,000	
Total revenues		$603,000
Cost of goods sold		313,000
Gross profit		$290,000
Operating Expenses		
Wages and salaries expense	$125,000	
Rent expense	35,000	
Advertising expense	28,000	
Depreciation expense	4,000	
Utilities expense	12,000	
Supplies expense	3,700	
Total Operating Expenses		$207,700
Net Income Before Taxes		$ 82,300
Less Income Taxes (28%)		23,044
Net Income After Taxes		$ 59,256

7.   Everyone's answer will vary, obviously. The things to look at include your wages for the next two weeks, and any other income you will be receiving within the next two weeks (not including that $10 your friend owes you unless you <u>know</u> they're going to pay you!), and any expenses that will be due within the next two weeks, such as car payments, insurance, rent, groceries, utility bills, tuition, books, and so on.....

8. a. **FIFO**

Beginning inventory	20,000 @ $10	$200,000
+ Purchases	7,000 @ $12	84,000
=Cost of goods available	27,000 units	$284,000
- Ending inventory	5,000 @ $12	60,000
Cost of goods sold		**$224,000**

LIFO

Beginning inventory	20,000 @ $10	$200,000
+ Purchases	7,000 @ $12	84,000
Cost of goods available	27,000 units	$284,000
- Ending inventory	5,000 @ $10	50,000
Cost of goods sold		**$234,000**

b. Gross margin for :

	FIFO	LIFO
Revenues	$450,000	$450,000
COGS	224,000	234,000
Gross margin	$226,000	$216,000

In going from FIFO to LIFO the effect is to reduce gross profit. This will have the effect of reducing operating income, and tax liabilities.

9. Your answers will vary, of course, depending upon whom you talk with, and the various kinds of software used. The level of dependence upon computers will probably vary, depending upon how large the firm is.

10. a. Current ratio: $\frac{\$235,000}{\$80,000}$ = 2.9

b. Acid-test ratio: $\frac{\$173,000}{\$80,000}$ = 2.16

c. It seems that Music-stor is financially sound from the liquidity perspective, as their ratios are above the benchmark of the 2:1 ratio.

11. a. Debt/Owner's equity ratio: $\frac{\$140,000}{\$295,000}$ = .47

b. Music-stor seems to be in very good shape, and could actually afford to take on slightly more debt, according to the industry average.

12. a. Earnings per share: $\dfrac{\$59,256}{30,000} = \$1.98$ share

b. Return on sales: $\dfrac{\$59,256}{\$600,000} = 10\%$ approximately

c. Return on equity: $\dfrac{\$59,256}{\$295,000} = 20.1\%$

13. a. Inventory turnover: $\dfrac{313,000}{70,000} = 4.47$ times

b. Music-stor's turnover exceeds the industry average. This indicates they are turning their inventory faster than the industry average.

PRACTICE TEST

MULTIPLE CHOICE

1.	c	11.	d
2.	d	12.	c
3.	b	13.	a
4.	d	14.	d
5.	d	15.	d
6.	a	16.	a
7.	d	17.	b
8.	b	18.	a
9.	d	19.	d
10.	c	20.	b

TRUE/FALSE

1.	T	7.	F
2.	T	8.	F
3.	F	9.	F
4.	F	10.	T
5.	T	11.	F
6.	T	12.	F

LEARNING GOALS

After you have read and studied this chapter, you should be able to:

1. Explain the importance of finance.

2. Describe the responsibilities of financial managers.

3. Tell what financial planning involves and define the three key budgets of finance.

4. Recognize the financial needs that must be met with available funds.

5. Distinguish between short-term and long-term financing and between debt capital and equity capital.

6. Identify and describe several sources of short-term financing.

7. Identify and describe several sources of long-term financing

LEARNING THE LANGUAGE

Listed below are important terms found in the chapter. Choose the correct term for the definition and write it in the space provided.

Capital budget	Financial managers	Risk/return tradeoff
Capital expenditures	Financial management	Secured bond
Cash budget	Indenture terms	Secured loan
Cash flow forecast	Inventory financing	Short-term financing
Commercial finance companies	Leverage	Short-term forecast
Commercial paper	Line of credit	Term-loan agreement
Debt capital	Long-term forecast	Trade credit
Equity capital	Operating (master) budget	Unsecured bond
Factoring	Pledging	Unsecured loan
Finance	Promissory note	Venture capital
Financial control	Revolving credit agreement	

1. Organizations called _____ make short-term loans to borrowers who offer tangible assets as collateral.

2. In a process known as _____ a firm periodically compares actual revenues, costs and expenses with projections.

3. Borrowed capital that will be repaid over a specific time period longer than one year is called _____

4. A line of credit called a _____ is guaranteed by the bank.

5. A _____ is a promissory note that requires the borrower to repay the loan in specified installments.

6. An _____ is a loan that is not backed by any specific assets.

7. Managers called _____ make recommendations to top executives regarding strategies for improving the financial strength of a firm.

8. Funds known as _____ are raised from within the firm or through the sale of ownership in the firm.

9. The process of using inventory such as raw materials as collateral for a loan is called _____.

10. A written contract, or _____ is a promise to pay.

11. A _____ is a prediction of revenues, costs, and expenses for a period of one year or less.

12. Funds raised through various forms of borrowing that must be repaid is called _____.

13. A(n) _____ is the budget that ties together all of a firm's other budgets; it is a projection of dollar allocations to various costs and expenses needed to run or operate the business given projected revenue.

14. A _____ is a loan backed by something valuable, such as property.

15. A prediction of revenues, costs and expenses for a period of longer than 1 year, and sometimes as far as 5 or 10 years in the future is a _____.

16. A given amount of unsecured short-term funds or a _____ is what a bank will lend to a business, provided funds are readily available.

17. A bond backed only by the reputation of the issuer is an _____.

18. Raising needed funds through borrowing to increase a firm's rate of return is called _____.

19. The process of _____ is selling accounts receivable for cash.

20. A(n) _____ highlights the firm's spending plans for major asset purchases that often require large sums of money.

21. The process of _____ is using accounts receivable or other assets as collateral for a loan.

22. A(n) _____ is a prediction of revenues, costs and expenses for a period longer than one year, sometimes extending 5 or 10 years into the future.

23. An unsecured promissory note of $25,000 and up is known as _____ and matures in 270 days or less.

24. The practice of _____ is buying goods today and paying for them later.

25. The type of financing known as _____ refers to borrowed capital that will be repaid within one year.

26. The function in a business called _____ is responsible for acquiring funds for the firm and managing funds within the firm.

27. The principle of _____ means the greater risk a lender takes in making a loan, the higher the interest rate required.

28. A bond issued with some form of collateral is a _____.

29. The terms of the agreement in a bond issue are known as _____.

30. The _____ estimates a firm's projected cash balance at the end of a given period.

31. The job of managing the firm's resources so it can meet its goals and objectives is _____.

32. Major investments, or _____, focus on long-term assets such as land, buildings, equipment, or research and development.

33. Money that is invested in new companies that have great profit potential is known as _____.

ASSESSMENT CHECK

Learning Goal 1   **The Role of Finance and Financial Managers**

1. What is the difference between an accountant and a financial manager?

2. Describe three of the most common ways for any firm to fail financially.

   a. _____

   b. _____

   c. _____

3. To whom is an understanding of finance important?

4.   What activities are involved in acquiring funds and managing funds?

5.   What is the difference between a chief financial officer and a comptroller?

6.   List eight functions of a financial manager.

a. _____

b. _____

c. _____

d. _____

e. _____

f. _____

g. _____

h. _____

7.   Why is the collection of payments and overdue accounts particularly critical to small businesses?

8.   Why does tax management fall under the area of finance?

9.   What is the role of the internal auditor?

Learning Goal 3   **Financial Planning**

10.   What is the objective of financial planning?

11.   What are the three steps involved in financial planning?

    a._____

    b._____

    c._____

12.   What is the difference between a short-term forecast and a long-term forecast?

13.   What is a cash flow forecast based on?

14.   What is used as a basis for forecasting company budgets?

15.   Identify three types of budgets

       a. _____

       b. _____

       c. _____

16.   What is the primary concern in a capital budget?

17.   What information does a cash budget provide? When is a cash budget prepared?

18.   What is the function of an operating (master) budget?

19.   Why do companies establish financial controls?

Learning Goal 4   **The Need for Operating Funds**

20.   What are four basic financial needs affecting both small and large businesses?

   a. _____

   b. _____

   c. _____

   d. _____

21.   What is the financial challenge of managing daily business operations?

22.   Describe the time value of money. What is the importance of the time value of money?

23.   What do financial managers try to do with cash expenditures?

24.   Why do financial managers want to make credit available?

25.   What is a problem with offering credit?

26.   What is one way to decrease the time and expense of collecting accounts?

27.   What does inventory control have to do with finance?

28.   What job does a financial manager have with regard to capital expenditures?

Learning Goal 5   **Alternative Sources of Funds**

29.   What is the difference between long-term and short-term financing?

30.   Describe the difference between debt capital and equity capital.

Learning Goal 6   **Obtaining Short-Term Financing**

31.   Why do firms need to borrow short-term funds?

32.   What are six sources of short-term financing?

a._____   d._____

b._____   e._____

c._____   f._____

33.   Describe the invoice terms of 2/10 net 30, when using trade credit.

34.   When would a supplier require a promissory note?

35.   What steps are recommended when borrowing from family or friends?

a. _____

b. _____

c. _____

36.   Why is it important for a businessperson to keep a close relationship with a banker?

37.   Identify five types of bank loans.

a. _____   d. _____

b. _____   e. _____

c. _____

38.   What is meant by the term "collateral"?

39.   What kind of bank customer is most likely to get an unsecured loan? Why?

40.   What is the primary purpose of a line of credit?

41.   How do the interest rates of commercial lending companies compare to those of a bank? Why?

42.   How does factoring work?

43.   Why do many small companies make use of factoring?

44.   How can small businesses make factoring less expensive?

45.   What kinds of companies sell commercial paper?

46.   What are the benefits of commercial paper?

Learning Goal 7   **Obtaining Long-Term Financing**

47.   What are three questions asked in setting long-term financing objectives?

a. _____

b. _____

c. _____

48.   What is long-term capital used for?

49.   What are the two major sources of initial long-term financing?

       a. _____   b. _____

50.   What legal obligation does a firm have when using debt financing?

51.   What is an advantage of debt financing?

52.   What are some drawbacks to a long-term loan?

53.   What is the risk/return trade-off?

54.   What is a simple explanation of a bond?

55.   What does a potential investor evaluate in the purchase of a bond?

56.   What is a debenture?

57.   What is equity financing?

58.   Who are the owners of a corporation?

59.   What is the most favored source of long-term capital? Why?

60.   What is venture capital?

61.   What are some considerations to remember when exploring venture capital?

62.   What are the key jobs of the finance manager, or CFO?

63.   How can a firm use leverage to get a higher rate of return, compared to equity funding?

CRITICAL THINKING EXERCISES

Learning Goal 1, 2

1.   Finance is the function in a business that is responsible for acquiring the funds for the firm and for managing funds within the firm.

Among the functions a finance manager performs are:

Planning   Collecting funds (credit management)

Budgeting   Auditing

Obtaining funds   Managing taxes

Controlling funds   Advising top management

Match the correct function to each statement below. Use each function only once.

a. Before Music-stor sends out quarterly financial statements, Debbie Breeze does her job, which is to ensure that no mistakes have been made, and that all transactions have been treated in accordance with established accounting rules and procedures. _____

b. Joe Saumby determined that his firm's accounts receivable were too high, and developed a more effective collection system. _____

c. Ann Bizer decided to include money for a new bank of computers in the operating budget. _____

d. In an effort to generate capital, Gerald McMillian decided that his company should "go public" and make a stock offering. _____

e. A major automotive company developed a long-range objective of automating its production facilities, which would cost millions of dollars. _____

f. In order to monitor expense account spending, many companies require employees to submit a receipt for any expenditure over $25. _____

g. During a period of high inflation, the Kroger Company changed from LIFO to FIFO to determine their cost of goods sold, ultimately reducing the company's net income for tax purposes. _____

h. In a report to management, Joe Kelley outlined the effect of newly proposed pollution control requirements on the company's long-range profit forecasts. _____

Learning Goal 3

2.   There are three kinds of budgets

Operating (master) budget   Cash budget

Capital budget

Determine which type of budget is being described in each of the following:

a. St. Louis Community College District projects that $350,000 will be spent for attendance and participation in conferences and seminars. _____

b. Kevin Nelson, the finance manager for TNG Enterprises, has just finished work on the budget that will enable him to determine how much money the firm will have to borrow for the next year. _____

c. At Whitfield School, a fund raising activity helped the school add money to the funds allocated to purchasing computer equipment for student and faculty use. _____

d. Phillip Knott is the comptroller for a major stock brokerage firm. At their annual finance meeting, he presented a summary of al the budgets for board approval.

_____

Learning Goal 1, 2, 3

3.　　Planning is a critical element in the management process. What is the relationship between strategic planning and long-term financial planning and forecasting?

Learning Goal 4

4.　　Eric is upset! He has just stormed into Music-stor's finance manager's office " What's going on? I just looked at our inventory levels, and they're lower than what I think we ought to see. Don't we have the money to buy inventory? How are we going to fill our orders? And what's the idea of all these credit sales? Visa? MasterCard? And another thing! Why are we always paying our bills at the last minute? Are we that short of cash? " "Hold on" said Bill Whittier, the new finance manager, " things look pretty good to me. We're actually in great shape!" " What? I don't understand!" replied Eric. "You know, I want to look into building a new plant within the next 2 years. Sales are going to continue to go way up. I need to know whether or not we're going to be able to afford it. Right now, it looks as if we are too short of cash. Explain!"

Learning Goal 5, 6

5.　　There are several sources of short-term funds:

Trade credit	Promissory notes
Family and friends	Factoring
Commercial bank loans	Commercial paper

Match the correct type of short-term financing to each of the following:

a.　A major Midwestern retailer often sells its accounts receivable for cash._____

b.　Lou Fusz auto network finances its inventories, using the vehicles themselves as collateral for the loans. _____

c. During a recent recession, Van Nuys Enterprises had some problems paying their bills on time. Afterwards, in order for them to buy with credit, Van Nuys' suppliers required them to sign a written contract. _____

d. Echo Enterprises recently raised some "quick cash" through selling promissory notes. Echo agreed to pay the principle plus interest within 90 days of the sale. Monterrey Bay Co. bought Echo's promissory notes as an investment for their extra cash. _____

e. Kellwood bills its retail customers on a 2/10 net 30 basis. _____

f. To pay an unexpectedly high liability insurance premium, the owner of a small chemical company borrowed money from his best friend. _____

6. There are several kinds of loans:

Unsecured loans   Line of credit

Secured loans (including pledging)   Revolving credit agreement

Inventory financing   Commercial finance company loans

Match each type to the following examples:

a. Ternier Steel company is using their most recent shipment of coal as collateral for a short-term loan. _____

b. In their commodities brokerage business, Bartholomew Enterprises needs guaranteed loans without having to apply for the loans each time it is needed. They are willing to pay a fee for the guarantee. _____

c. Rivertown Insurance is having some short-term cash problems. They have substantial accounts receivable which they intend to use as collateral for a loan. _____

d. Danny Noble Enterprises has been in business for a fairly long time and has a great financial record. When they needed money they went to their banker and applied for the loan without needing to put up collateral. _____

e. Because they often have a need for short term funds with short notice, Binny and Jones Manufacturing applied to their bank for a sort of "continual' unsecured loan. The bank lends Binny a given amount without Binny having to re-apply each time. While not a guaranteed loan, the funds will be available if Binny's credit limit is not exceeded.

_____

    f.   Because they were considered a credit risk, PPI, Inc. had to pay a higher rate of interest, and pledge their inventory as collateral for the loan. They went to General Electric Capital Services. _____

Learning Goal 7

7.   There are 2 general sources of long-term funds, and several choices within each source.

Debt capital

    loans

    bonds

Equity capital

    stock

    retained earnings

    venture capital

Match the correct type of financing to each of the following statements:

    a.   These are commonly referred to as "debentures." _____

    b.   This is the last alternative for long-term financing. _____

    c.   Generally the most favored source of long-term capital. _____

    d.   These can be either secured or unsecured. _____

    e.   For this, a business must sign a term-loan agreement because of the long repayment period.

_____

    f.   The key word here is "ownership." _____

    g.   The number one source of funds for young, fast-growing companies. _____

h. Using this source saves the company interest payments, dividends and any underwriting fees, and won't dilute ownership. _____

i. The terms of agreement are called indenture terms. _____

j. Good sources of start up capital for new companies, they often want a stake in the ownership of the business. _____

k. With this, a company has a legal obligation to pay. _____

8. Eric and his finance manager, Joel, are in disagreement over how to finance the future growth of Music-stor. "I just want to stay out of debt if I can" says Eric, "so I think the best idea is to sell stock, go public." "Well, I understand your perspective Eric, but I'm not sure you have thought of all the consequences of selling stock. Do you like being your own boss?" asks Joel. "Yeah, sure!" replies Eric, " but what the heck does that have to do with wanting to sell stock in the company?" What does Joel mean, and what are the other arguments for and against each type of funding?

9. If leverage means raising money through debt, what do you suppose is meant by a "leveraged buyout"?

PRACTICE TEST

Multiple Choice – Circle the best answer

1. Which of the following is not included in a list of reasons why businesses fail financially?

   a. Inadequate expense control
   b. Poor control over cash flow
   c. Undercapitalization
   d. Stock is undervalued

2.	Jackie Jones is a finance manager for Pokey Poseys, a wholesale florist. As finance manager, which of the following would not be one of Jackie's responsibilities?

a.	preparing financial statements

b.	preparing budgets

c.	doing cash flow analysis

d.	planning for spending funds on long-term assets, such as plant and equipment

3.	Regular internal audits are important because:

a.	the firm needs to keep a constant look out for employees who may be committing fraud.

b.	internal audits help to make accounting statements more reliable.

c.	they aid in the development of financial statements.

d.	the firm uses the audits to determine LIFO and FIFO procedures.

4.	The process of analyzing short-term and long-term money flows to and from the firm is known as _____.

a.	internal auditing

b.	forecasting

c.	financial planning

d.	financial controls

5.	Ima Midas is currently in the process of projecting how much his firm will have to spend on supplies, travel, rent, advertising, and salaries for the coming financial year. Ima is working on the _____.

a.	master (operating)budget

b.	capital budget

c.	cash budget

d.	master budget

6.	Which of the following is not one of the steps involved in financial planning?

a.	Forecasting short-term and long-term financial needs

b.	Developing budgets to meet those needs

c.	Establishing financial controls to keep the company focused on financial plans

d.	Developing financial statements for outside investors

7. What is the major problem with selling on credit?

   a. Too much of a firm's assets could be tied up in accounts receivable
   b. You can't control when customers will pay their bills
   c. It makes production scheduling more difficult
   d. Customers who aren't allowed to buy on credit become unhappy

8. Companies must maintain a sizable investment in inventories in order to:

   a. be able of accept credit cards.
   b. keep customers happy.
   c. increase demand for their products.
   d. reduce the need for long-term funds.

9. The time value of money means that

   a. the value of money will fall over time.
   b. it is better to make purchases now, rather than wait until later.
   c. a monetary system will devalue it's money over time.
   d. it is better to have money now, than later.

10. Which of the following is not a source of short-term funds?

   a. The sale of bonds
   b. The use of trade credit
   c. Promissory notes
   d. The use of inventory financing

11. The credit terms 2/10 net 30 means:

   a. The full amount of a bill is due within 2-10 days.
   b. Customers will receive a 10 percent discount if they pay in 30 days.
   c. A 2 percent discount will be given if customers pay within 30 days.
   d. Customers will receive a 2 percent discount if they pay within 10 days.

12. When accounts receivable or some other asset are used as collateral for a loan, the process is called

   a. a line of credit.
   b. a promissory note.
   c. trade credit.
   d. pledging.

13. Commercial finance companies accept more risk than banks, and the interest rates they charge are usually _____than commercial banks
   a. higher
   b. about the same as
   c. lower
   d. more variable

14. Dave Sinclair Ford usually obtains its short-term financing by offering the cars they are selling as collateral for a loan. This form of financing is called:

   a. factoring.
   b. inventory financing.
   c. a revolving credit agreement.
   d. a line of credit.

15. Raising debt capital includes using _____ as a source of funds.
   a. the sale of bonds
   b. the sale of stock
   c. the sale of inventory
   d. the sale of accounts receivable

16. One of the benefits of selling bonds over selling stock as a source of long-term funds is that

   a. bonds don't have to be paid back.
   b. the company isn't required to pay interest.
   c. bondholders do not have a say in running the business.
   d. interest is paid after taxes are paid.

17. The most favored source of meeting long-term capital needs is

    a. selling stock.
    b. venture capital.
    c. selling bonds.
    d. retained earnings.

18. When starting his new software business, Bob Campbell considered using venture capital as a source of initial funding. One of the drawbacks of venture capital is that

    a. venture capitalists generally want a stake in the ownership of the business.
    b. venture capitalists charge a very high rate of interest.
    c. venture capital is very difficult to find.
    d. venture capital firms generally don't provide additional financing later on.

True-False

1. _____ Financial understanding is important primarily for anyone wanting to major in accounting, but not necessary for others involved in business.

2. _____ Financial managers are responsible for collecting overdue payments and making sure the company doesn't lose too much money to bad debts.

3. _____ The cash budget is often the first budget that is prepared.

4. _____ Financial control means that the actual revenues, costs, and expenses are reviewed and compared with projections.

5. _____ One way to decrease the expense of collecting accounts receivable is to accept bank credit cards.

6. _____ Equity capital is money raised primarily through the sale of bonds.

7. _____ Firms often need to borrow short-term funds to be able to pay unexpected bills.

8. _____ One benefit of borrowing from friends or family is that you don't have to draw up formal papers like you do with a bank loan.

9. _____ It is important for a businessperson to keep close relations with a banker because the banker may be able to spot cash flow problems early and point out problems.

10. _____ A line of credit guarantees a business a given amount of unsecured short-term funds.

11. _____ Long-term capital is generally used to pay for supplies, rent, and travel.

12. _____ Potential investors in bonds measure the risk involved in purchasing a bond with the return the bond promises to pay.

You Can Find It On the Net

What are some of the financial considerations of starting and managing your own small business? Visit www.entreworld.org, and click on the Growing your Business link.

What is an angel investor?

What sources of venture capital are described?

Describe the forms of alternative funding identified in this section

How can a strategic alliance help a small business?

ANSWERS

LEARNING THE LANGUAGE

1. Commercial finance companies	13.Operating budget	24. Trade credit
2. Financial control	14.Secured loan	25. Short-term financing
3. Long-term financing	15.Cash flow forecast	26. Finance
4. Revolving credit agreement	16.Line of credit	27. Risk/return tradeoff
5. Term loan agreement	17. Unsecured bond	28. Secured bond
6. Unsecured loan	18. Leverage	29. Indenture terms
7. Financial managers	19. Factoring	30. Cash budget
8. Equity capital	20. Capital budget	31. Financial management
9. Inventory financing	21. Pledging	32. Capital expenditures
10.Promissory note	22. Long-term forecast	33. Venture capital
11.Short-term forecast	23. Commercial paper	
12.Debt capital		

ASSESSMENT CHECK

The Role of Finance

1.　Financial managers use the data prepared by accountants and make recommendations to top management regarding strategies for improving the health of the firm.

2.　a.　Undercaptitalization - not enough funds to start with

　　b.　Poor control over cash flow

　　c.　Inadequate expense control

3.　Financial understanding is important to anyone who wants to start a small business, invest in stocks and bond, or plan a retirement fund.

What is Financial Management?

4.　Activities in acquiring and managing funds within a firm include preparing budgets, doing cash flow analysis and planning for the expenditure of funds on assets such as plant, equipment and property.

5.　Most organizations will designate a manager in charge of financial operations, generally the chief financial officer, CFO. A comptroller is the chief accounting officer.

6. a. Planning   e. Collecting funds
    b. Budgeting   f. Auditing
    c. Obtaining funds   g. Managing taxes
    d. Controlling funds   h. Advising top management on financial matters

7. Collection of accounts receivable and overdue accounts is critical to all types of businesses. However, small businesses typically have smaller cash or credit cushions than large corporations.

8. Tax payments represent an outflow of cash from the business, and therefore fall under finance. As tax laws and tax liabilities have changed, finance specialists have become increasingly involved in tax management by analyzing the tax implications of various managerial decisions, in an attempt to minimize taxes paid by the business.

9. The internal auditor checks on the journals, ledgers, and financial statements prepared by the accounting department to make sure that all transactions have been treated in accordance with established accounting rules and procedures. Without such audits, accounting statements would be less reliable.

Financial Planning

10. Financial planning involves analyzing short-term and long-term money flows to and from the firm. The overall objective of financial planning is to optimize the firm's profitability and make the best use of its money.

11. a. Forecasting both short-term and long-term financial needs
    b. Developing budgets to meet those needs
    c. Establishing financial controls

12. A short-term forecast predicts revenues, costs, and expenses for a period of one year or less. A long-term forecast predicts revenues, costs, and expenses for a period of longer than one year, sometimes as far as 5 or 10 years into the future.

13. A cash flow forecast projects the expected cash inflows and outflows in future periods. This is based on expected sales revenues and on various costs and expenses incurred and when they'll come due.

14. The basis for forecasting company budgets is historical cost and revenue information derived from past financial statements.

15.   a.   Operating (master) budgets   c.   Cash budgets

               b.   Capital budgets

16.   The capital budget primarily concerns itself with the purchase of such assets as property, plant, and equipment

17.   Cash budgets are important guidelines that assist managers in anticipating borrowing, repaying debt, cash needed for operations and expenses, and short-term investment expectations. Cash budgets assist the firm in planning for cash shortages or surpluses. The cash budget is prepared after other budgets have been prepared.

18.   The operating, or master, budget ties together all the firm's other budgets and summarizes a company's proposed financial statements. It is in this budget that the firm determines how much it will spend on supplies, travel, rent, advertising, salaries and other operating expenses.

19   Many companies hold monthly financial reviews as a way to ensure financial control. This helps managers identify deviations and take corrective action if necessary. These controls provide feedback to help identify which accounts, departments and people are varying from the financial plan.

The Need for Operating Funds

20.   a.   Funds to manage daily business operations

               b.   Managing accounts receivable

               c.   Obtaining inventory

               d.   Major capital expenditures

21.   The challenge of sound financial management is to see that funds are available to meet daily cash needs without compromising the firm's investment potential.

22.   Money has a time value. If someone offered to give you money today or one year from today, you would benefit by taking the money today. You could start collecting interest or invest the money you receive today, and over time, your money would grow. For a firm, the interest earned on investments is important in maximizing the profit the company will gain.

23.   Financial managers often try to keep cash expenditures at a minimum, to free funds for investment in interest-bearing accounts. It is not unusual for finance managers to suggest the firm pay bills as late as possible and collect what is owed as fast as possible.

24. Financial managers know that making credit available helps to keep current customers happy and attracts new customers. In today's highly competitive environment, many businesses would have trouble surviving without making credit available to customers.

25. The major problem with selling on credit is that as much as 25 percent or more of the business's assets could be tied up in its accounts receivable. That means that the firm has to use some of its available cash to pay for the goods or services already given to customers who bought on credit.

26. One way to decrease the time, and therefore expense, of collecting accounts receivable is to accept bank credit cards.

27. To satisfy customers, businesses must maintain inventories that often involve a sizable expenditure of funds. A carefully constructed inventory policy assists in managing the use of the firm's available funds and maximizing profitability.

28. Financial managers and analysts evaluate the appropriateness of capital purchases. It is critical that companies weigh all the possible options before committing what may be a large portion of its available resources.

Alternative Sources of Funds

29. Short-term financing comes from funds used to finance current operations, which will be paid in less than one year. Long-term financing refers to capital needed for major purchases, which will be repaid over a period longer than one year.

30. Debt capital is raised through borrowing that must be repaid. Equity capital is raised from selling stock or from within the company.

Obtaining Short-Term Financing

31. Firms need to borrow short-term funds for purchasing additional inventory or for meeting bills that come due unexpectedly. A business sometimes needs to obtain short-term funds when the firm's money is low.

32.
    a. Trade credit
    b. Promissory note
    c. Family and friends
    d. Commercial banks
    e. Factoring
    f. Commercial paper

33. Terms of 2/10 net 30 means that the buyer can take a 2 percent discount for paying within 10 days. The total bill is due (net) in 30 days from the date of invoice if the purchaser does not take advantage of the discount.

34. Some suppliers hesitate to give trade credit to organizations with a poor credit rating, no credit history, or a history of slow payment. In such cases, the supplier may insist that the customer sign a promissory note as a condition for obtaining credit.

35. a. Agree on specific terms
    b. Write an agreement
    c. Pay them back the same way you would a bank loan

36. It is important for a businessperson to keep friendly and close relations with a banker, because the banker may spot cash flow problems early and point out danger areas. Additionally, the banker may be more willing to lend money in a crisis if the businessperson has established a strong, friendly relationship built on openness and trust.

37. a. Unsecured loans   d. Line of credit
    b. Secured loans   e. Revolving credit agreement
    c. Inventory financing

38. Collateral is something valuable, such as property that is used to back a secured loan.

39. An unsecured loan doesn't require a borrower to offer the lender any collateral to obtain the loan. Normally, only highly regarded customers, long-standing customers or customer considered financially stable, will receive an unsecured loan.

40. The primary purpose of a line of credit is to speed the borrowing process so that a firm does not have to go through the hassle of applying for a new loan every time it needs funds.

41. Commercial credit companies will charge higher interest rates than commercial banks, because they are willing to accept higher degrees of risk than commercial banks.

42. In the process of factoring, a firm sells many of its products on credit to consumers and businesses, creating an account receivable. Some of these buyers may be slow in paying their bills, causing the company to have a large amount of money due in accounts receivable. A factor is a market intermediary that agrees to buy the accounts receivable from the firm at a discount for cash.

43. Small companies often cannot qualify for a loan, so they make use of factoring, or the sale of their accounts receivable, to raise needed cash.

44.   Factoring can be less expensive if the small business selling its accounts receivables agrees to reimburse the factor for slow paying accounts. Factoring charges are even lower if the company assumes the risk of those people who don't pay at all.

45.   Commercial paper is unsecured and is sold at a public sale, so only financially stable firms, mainly large corporations are able to sell it.

46.   Commercial paper is a way to get short-term funds quickly and for less than interest bank rates. It is also an investment opportunity for buyers who can afford to put up cash for short periods to earn some interest.

Obtaining Long-Term Financing

47.   a. What are the long-term goals and objectives of the firm?
      b. What are the financial requirements needed to achieve these goals and objectives?
      c. What sources of long-term capital are available, and which will fit our needs?

48.   In business, long–term capital is used to buy fixed assets such as plant and equipment and to finance expansion of the organization.

49.   a. debt capital   b. equity capital

50.   If a company uses debt financing, it has a legal obligation to repay the amount it has borrowed.

51.   A major advantage of a business using debt financing is that the interest paid on the long-term debt is tax deductible.

52.   Long-term loans are often more expensive to the firm than short-term loans, because larger amounts of capital are borrowed. In addition, since the repayment period could be as long as twenty years, the lenders are not assured their capital will be repaid in full. Therefore, most long-term loans require some form of collateral.

53.   The risk/return trade-off is the idea that the greater the risk a lender takes in making a loan, the higher the rate of interest it requires.

54.   To put it simply, a bond is like a company IOU with a promise to repay on a certain date. It is a binding contract through which an organization agrees to specific terms with investors in return for investors lending money to the company.

55. Potential investors in bonds measure the risk involved in purchasing a bond with the return the bond promises to pay.

56. A debenture is an unsecured bond, backed only by the reputation of the issuer.

57. Equity financing involves selling ownership in the firm in the form of stock, or using retained earnings the firm has accumulated and kept to reinvest in the business.

58. The purchasers of stock become owners in a corporation.

59. Retained earnings are usually the most favored source of meeting long-term capital needs, since the company saves interest payments, dividends, and any possible underwriting fees. There is also no dilution of ownership in the firm, which occurs with selling stock.

60. Venture capital is money that is invested in new companies with great profit potential.

61. The venture capital firm generally wants a stake in the ownership of the business. Venture capitalists also expect a very high return on their investment. It is also important that the venture capital firm be able to come up with and be willing to provide more financing if the firm needs it.

62. A key job of the finance manager or CFO is to forecast the need for and to manage borrowed funds.

63. If a firm's earnings are larger than the interest payments on the borrowed funds, then the business owners are realizing a higher rate of return than if they used equity financing.

CRITICAL THINKING EXERCISES

1.
   a. Auditing
   b. Collecting funds
   c. Budgeting
   d. Obtaining funds
   e. Planning
   f. Controlling funds
   g. Managing taxes
   h. Advising top management

2.
   a. Operating(master) budget
   b. Cash budget
   c. Capital budget
   d. Operating (master) budget

3. Strategic planning helps the firm to determine what businesses it should be in within the next 5-10 years. Decisions about which direction a company should take could not be made without some knowledge of the expense of entering certain markets, as well as the profit potential of

those same markets. Long-term forecasts give top management some sense of the income or profit potential with different strategic plans.

4. Eric doesn't understand some basic ideas about financial management. Bill needs to explain the financial needs of all businesses: managing daily operations, managing accounts receivable, obtaining needed inventory (including inventory management) and major capital expenditures, and how a finance manager deals with each area.

One of the first things a finance manager will do is to see that funds are available to meet daily cash needs, without using too much cash and not being able to take advantage of other investments. So, bills are paid at the latest date possible to allow the firm to take advantage of interest-bearing accounts. Music-stor allows for credit purchases because it helps to keep their customers happy and helps to attract new customers. With effective collection procedures, selling on credit can be a benefit to the firm. It's important to keep inventories at a level necessary to fill orders, but too high an inventory level will tie up funds that could be used elsewhere for investment. Programs like just-in-time inventory help to reduce the amount of funds a firm must tie up in inventory.

There is no way to tell if the firm can afford to build a new plant in two years, but the finance manager will be able to evaluate the various alternatives, such as buying a facility, expanding on a current facility or building their own building.

5. a. Factoring
    b. Bank loan (inventory financing)
    c. Promissory note
    d. Commercial paper
    e. Trade credit
    f. Family and friends

6. a. Inventory financing
    b. Revolving credit agreement
    c. Secured loan
    d. Unsecured loan
    e. Line of Credit
    f. Commercial credit company loan

7.
a. Debt financing - bonds
b. Equity financing
c. Equity financing - retained earnings
d. Debt financing
e. Debt financing - loans
f. Equity financing - stock

g. Equity financing - venture capital
h. Equity financing - retained earnings
i. Debt financing - bonds
j. Equity financing – venture capital
k. Debt financing – loans, bonds

8. Joels' point to Eric is that when you sell stock to the public, the common stockholders get voting rights, and management must answer to the stockholders. Creditors, such as lending institutions or bondholders generally have no say in running the business. The plus side of the equity financing is that there is no repayment obligation, as there is with debt financing, and the firm is not legally liable to pay dividends to the stockholders. Interest on debt is a legal obligation. However, the interest is tax deductible, whereas dividends are paid out of after-tax profits, and so are not deductible.

9. Leveraged buyouts occur when one firm purchases the assets of another using funds that were borrowed, either through selling bonds, obtaining loans, or a combination of both.

PRACTICE TEST

MULTIPLE CHOICE

1.	d	10.	a
2.	a	11.	d
3.	b	12.	d
4.	c	13.	a
5.	a	14.	b
6.	d	15.	a
7.	a	16.	c
8.	b	17.	d
9.	d	18.	a

TRUE/FALSE

1.	F	7.	T
2.	T	8.	F
3.	F	9.	T
4.	T	10.	T
5.	T	11.	F
6.	F	12.	T

CHAPTER 20
SECURITIES MARKETS: FINANCING AND INVESTING OPPORTUNITIES

LEARNING GOALS:

After you have read and studied this chapter you should be able to:

1. Examine the functions of securities markets and investment bankers.

2. Compare the advantages and disadvantages of issuing bonds and identify the classes and features of bonds.

3. Compare the advantages and disadvantages of issuing stock and outline the differences between common and preferred stock.

4. Describe the various stock exchanges and describe how to invest in securities markets and explain various investment objectives such as long-term growth, income, cash, and protection from inflation.

5. Analyze the opportunities bonds offer as investments

6. Explain the opportunities stock and mutual funds offer as investments and the advantage of diversifying investments.

7. Discuss specific high-risk investments, including junk bonds, buying stock on margin, and commodity trading.

8. Explain securities quotations listed in the financial section of a newspaper and describe how stock market indicators like the Dow Jones Averages affect the market.

LEARNING THE LANGUAGE

Listed below are important terms found in the chapter. Choose the correct term for the definition and write it in the space provided.

Blue chip stocks	Growth stocks	Par value
Bond	Income stocks	Penny stocks
Buying on margin	Insider trading	Preemptive right
Callable bond	Intuitional investors	Preferred stock
Capital gains	Initial Public Offering (IPO)	Principal
Commodity exchange	Interest	Program trading
Common stock	Investment bankers	Prospectus
Convertible bond	Junk bonds	Round lots
Cumulative preferred Stock	Limit order	Securities and Exchange Commission (SEC)
Debenture bonds	Market order	Sinking fund
Denomination	Maturity date	Stockbroker
Diversification	Mutual fund	Stock certificate
Dividends	National Association of Securities Dealers Automated quotations (NASDAQ)	Stock Exchange Stock splits
Dow Jones Industrial Average	Odd lots	Stocks
Futures markets	Over-the-counter market (OTC)	

1.   Preferred stock that accumulates unpaid dividends is _____.

2.   The _____involves the purchase and sale of goods for delivery sometime in the future.

3.   Stocks called _____ offer investors a high dividend.

4.   Large investors known as _____are organizations such as pension funds, mutual funds, insurance companies, and banks that invest their own funds or the funds of others.

5.   The _____is an exchange that provides a means to trade stocks not listed on national exchanges.

6. Evidence of ownership called a _____ specifies the name of the company, the number of shares it represents, and the type of stock being issued.

7. Stocks of high quality firms that pay regular dividends and generate consistent growth in the company's stock price are called _____.

8. Trading known as _____ means giving instructions to computers to automatically sell if the price of stock dips to a certain price, to avoid potential losses.

9. A(n) _____ gives common stockholders the right to purchase any new shares of common stock the firm decides to issue.

10. The most basic form of ownership of firms is _____, which includes voting rights and the right to share in the firm's profits through dividends, if allowed by the firm's board of directors.

11. A(n) _____ is a special provision of a bond that requires the issuer to retire, on a periodic basis, some part of the bond principle prior to maturity.

12. The use of knowledge or information that individuals gain through their position that allows the person to benefit unfairly from fluctuations in security prices is _____.

13. The face value of a bond is the _____.

14. The purchase of 100 shares of stock at a time is a _____.

15. A(n) _____ is a bond that can be converted into shares of common stock in the issuing company.

16. Instructions called a(n) _____ tell the broker to buy or sell a stock immediately at the best price available.

17. A(n) _____ is a stock that sells for less than $2. It is considered a risky investment.

18. High-risk, high-interest bonds are called _____.

19. A registered representative, who works as a market intermediary known as a _____, buys and sells securities for clients.

20. A bond called a(n) _____ gives the issuer of the bond the right to pay off the bond before its maturity.

21. An organization that is known as a(n) _____ is one whose members can buy and sell securities for companies and investors.

22. The exact date the issuer of a bond must pay the principal to the bondholder is known as the _____.

23. Stock called _____ gives its owner's preference in the payment of dividends and an earlier claim on assets if the business is forced out of business and its assets sold.

24. A(n) _____ is a specialist assisting in the issue and sale of new securities.

25. The _____ is a dollar amount assigned to shares of stock by the corporation's charter.

26. The payment the issuer of a bond makes to the bondholders to pay for the use of borrowed money is called _____.

27. A _____ is a bond that is unsecured.

28. The process of _____ is the purchase of stocks by borrowing some of the purchase cost from the brokerage firm.

29. The part of a firm's profits that may be distributed to stockholders as either cash payments or additional shares of stock are called _____.

30. Stocks known as _____ are stocks of corporations whose earnings are expected to grow faster than other stocks or the overall economy.

31. A(n) _____ is an action by a company that gives stockholders two or more shares of stock for each share they own.

32. The technique of _____ means buying several different investment alternatives to spread the risk of investing.

33. A(n) _____ is an instruction to a broker to buy or to sell stock at a specific price, if and when that price becomes possible.

34. Shares of ownership in a company are called _____.

35. A(n) _____ is an organization that buys stocks and bonds and then sells shares in those securities to the public.

36. A corporate certificate called a(n) _____ indicates that a person has loaned money to a firm.

37. The average cost of 30 selected industrial stocks called the _____ is used to give an indication of direction of the stock market over time.

38. The security exchange called a(n) _____ specializes in the buying and selling of precious metals and minerals and agricultural goods.

39. The _____ is the federal government agency that has the responsibility for regulating the various exchanges.

40. A condensed version of economic and financial information called a(n)_____ must be filed with the SEC before issuing stock; it must be sent to potential purchasers of the firm's stock.

41. The _____ is a nationwide electronic system that communicates over the counter trades to brokers.

42. The amount of debt represented by one bond is the bond's _____.

43. A person's_____ are the positive difference between the purchase price of a stock and its sale price.

44. When you purchase _____, you have purchased less than 100 shares of stock at a time.

45. An _____is the first public offering of a corporation's stock.

ASSESSMENT CHECK

Learning Goal 1   **The Function of Securities Markets**

1.   What are two major functions of securities markets?

2.   Explain the difference between the primary and the secondary markets.

3.   How would companies prefer to meet their long-term financial needs?

4.   What does an investment banker do for companies?

5.   What are some examples of institutional investors?

Learning Goal 2   **Debt Financing Through Selling Bonds**

6.   What is the legal obligation of a company when selling bonds?

7.   What is meant by the term "coupon rate" with regard to bonds?

8.   What affects the interest rate of a bond?

9.   If a bond has an interest rate of 10% and a maturity date of 2020, what does that mean to a bondholder?

10.   List the advantages of raising long-term capital by selling bonds.

        a._____

        b._____

        c._____

11.   What are the disadvantages?

        a. _____

        b. _____

        c. _____

12.   Describe the two classes of corporate bonds.

13.   Why are sinking funds attractive to firms and investors?

        a. _____

        b. _____

        c. _____

14.   What is the benefit to a company of a callable bond?

15.   Why would an investor convert a bond to common stock?

16.   What information is contained in a stock certificate?

17.   What is the difference between the interest on a bond and a dividend paid on a share of stock?

18.   List the advantages of raising funds through the sale of stock.

a._____

b._____

c._____

19.   What are the disadvantages?

a._____

b._____

c._____

20.   What are two classes of stock?

a._____

b._____

21.   Describe how preferred stock dividends differ from common stock dividends.

22.   How is preferred stock like a bond?

23.   How do preferred stock and bonds differ?

24.   What are some special features of preferred stock?

25.   What are two rights that holders of common stock have?

Learning Goal 4   **Stock Exchanges**

26.   What are the two major national exchanges?

27. What are regional exchanges?

28. Which stock exchange lists the largest companies? Which exchange has the largest number of listings?

29. What is the purpose of the over the counter market? What kinds of firms are traded on the OTC market?

30. How are stocks traded in the over the counter market?

31. What did the Securities Act of 1933 require? Why?

32. Discuss the Securities and Exchange Act of 1934 and the responsibility of the Securities and Exchange Commission.

33.   How does the Securities and Exchange Commission define the term "insider" in reference to insider trading?

34.   How does a stockbroker trade securities?

35.   What is the benefit of trading on-line?

36.   What kind of customers use online trading?

37. Describe the five criteria to use when selecting an investment option.

a. _____

b. _____

c. _____

d. _____

e. _____

Learning Goal 5   **Investing in Bonds**

38. What is the best investment for those who desire low risk and guaranteed income? Why?

39. What are two questions first time bond investors may ask? What are the answers to the questions?

40. What does it mean to sell a bond at a discount? At a premium?

41.   Which form of investment has offered the highest return, historically?

42.   What does the market price of a stock depend upon?

43.   What are "bulls and bears" in the stock market?

44.   What are four different investment opportunities in stock? (in other words, four different "kinds" of stocks?)

    a. _____

    b._____

    c. _____

    d._____

45.   Which of the kinds of stock is considered to be very risky?

46. What is the difference between a limit order and a market order?

47. Why would a company declare a stock split? How does a stock split work?

48. What is the benefit of a mutual fund for an investor?

49. What are some varieties of mutual funds?

50. What is the difference between a "no-load" and a "load" fund?

51. What is the difference between an open-end fund and a closed-end fund?

52.   What is a portfolio strategy?

Learning Goal 7   **Investing in High Risk Investments**

53.   Why are junk bonds considered "junk"?

54.   What is a "margin"? What does a 50% margin rate mean?

55.   What is the downside of buying on margin?

56.   What is a margin call?

57.   What kinds of items are traded on a commodity exchange?

58.   When an investor buys commodities, what are they hoping for?

Learning Goal 8   **Understanding Information From Securities Markets**

59.   How is a bond price quoted?

60.   What information is included in a bond quote?

61.   What information is contained in a stock quote?

a. _____

b. _____

c. _____

d. _____

e. _____

f. _____

g. _____

h. _____

62.   What information is contained in a mutual fund quote?

63.   What is meant by net asset value, or NAV, when quoting a mutual fund?

64.   How has the Dow Jones Industrial Average changed in the last 20 years or so?

65.   What is a criticism of the Dow Jones Industrial Average?

66.   What happened to the stock market in October of 1987, October of 1997, and April of 2000?

67.   What is speculated to be the reason for the drop in 1987?

68. What are circuit breakers, and what will trigger the market to halt trading?

69. What are day traders?

70. What lessons can be learned from the stock market crashes in the past?

CRITICAL THINKING EXERCISES

Learning Goal 1

1. The financial manager of Music-stor has convinced management that a bond issue should be made to raise needed capital for future growth. He wants to avoid the difficulty of looking for and marketing to potential investors himself, and prefers to let "experts" perform those functions. How should he go about issuing this new bond issue?

Learning Goal 2

2.   In discussing bonds, there are several terms with which you need to be familiar:

Bond   Secured bonds

Interest   Sinking fund

Principal   Call provision

Maturity date   Convertible bond

Unsecured bonds (debentures)

Match the correct term to each of the following descriptions: Use each term only once.

a.   Gerry Hoffman will receive this on the date her bond becomes due in the year 2010.

b.   Beth Galganski will receive the principal value of her bond on this date.

c.   Tom Huff is in finance with Music-stor, Inc. Each quarter he checks the amount of money the company has in this account to be sure the company can pay off their bond issue on the maturity date

d.   Because it has declared bankruptcy in the past, and the future is uncertain, Bridge Financial Systems would probably not issue this type of bond.

e.   Bonnie Andersen receives $100 per year from her bond.

f.   Mobil Oil issued an unsecured one at 14.4 percent due in 2020.

g.   TNG Enterprises issued their debentures with this provision because they forecasted a decline in interest rates in a few years, and wanted the flexibility of being able to pay off the bond early.

h.   Bill Paterson bought this type of bond because he anticipated exchanging it for common stock in the firm later.

i.   Caldwell Industries used real estate holdings as collateral for their bonds.

3.   In discussing stocks, there are several terms with which you need to be familiar:

Stock	Preferred stock
Stock certificate	Cumulative preferred stock
Par value	Common stock
Dividends	Pre-emptive right

Match the correct term to each of the following: Use each term only once.

a.   Carmen Arauz was considering buying this type of stock, but was somewhat concerned about the risk when she learned that as a stockholder of this type, if the firm closed, she would be the last to share in the firm's assets.

b.   When her grandson was born, Judi Burton bought 100 shares of her favored stock, and gave his parents this, as evidence of his ownership.

c.   As her grandson Burke grew, he received these periodic payments from his stock, which his parents invested for college.

d.   On Burke's stock certificate, there is a dollar amount per share shown, which has no relationship to the market value, but which is used to assign the dividends that he is paid.

e.   When Judi was deciding which kind of stock to purchase, she decided upon this type, because the dividends are fixed and must be paid before other dividends are paid. Further, there are no voting rights with this type of stock.

f.   What Burke doesn't have is the right of the stockholder to purchase new shares when the firm makes a new issue, so that his proportionate ownership in the company is maintained.

g.   One of the advantages of Burke's stock is that if the company misses his dividend, the company must pay it before it pays any other, and the missed dividends accumulate.

h.   Either common or preferred, this represents ownership in a firm

4.   Why did Judi Burton decide buy her grandson Burke preferred stock instead of common stock?

Learning Goal 4

5.   What are the differences between the NYSE, the AMEX, and NASDAQ?

6.   How are the exchanges regulated?

7.   Five criteria to use when selecting a specific investment strategy are

Investment risk	Liquidity
Yield	Tax consequences
Duration	

Read the following situations and evaluate the criteria in terms of the needs of the potential investors. More than one criteria may relate to each situation.

a.   A young couple wants to invest money to begin a college tuition fund for their 5-year-old child. Since the child has no income, they are going to put the account in his name to avoid taxes

b.   A two-career couple; both anticipate retirement within the next five years.

c.   A single person, just graduated from college, starting a high paying job and wants to build capital. Not concerned about losing money at first.

20-22

8.   There are several terms used in securities trading with which you should be familiar:

Stockbroker	Buying on margin
Growth stocks	Stock splits
Income stocks	Round lots
Blue chip stocks	Margin calls
Penny stocks	Mutual funds
Market order	Diversification
Limit order	Bulls
Bears	Prospectus
Capital gains	

Match the correct term to each of the following:

a.   In 2001 Ford Motor Company gave its stockholders one additional share of stock for every share they owned. This reduced the price from $80 per share to around $40 per share.

b.   Evelyn Minervi likes to dabble in the stock market. Last year she bought a number of stocks of this type, which each sold for $1.45 per share, but which were considered fairly risky.

c.   Joe Contino works for a major brokerage firm, buying and selling stocks and bonds for his clients.

d.   Ron Stahl recently purchased exactly 100 shares of Navistar

e.   Dexter Inholt wanted to buy 500 shares of Ford at $40 each. He only had $12,000 to invest, so he borrowed the $8,000 he still needed from his brokerage firm

f.   The stock of Ford, which pays regular dividends and has had fairly consistent growth in its stock price, would be considered a _____stock

g. Marina Vasquez called her broker and asked him to buy Pepsico stock at the best price he could get.

h. Hong Le believed the stock market was going to take a big jump after the most recent national elections, and purchased the stocks she wanted in anticipation of that.

i. Lee Kornfield, a prosperous doctor, has a lot of money invested in the market. He recently called his broker and told her to buy the stock of several firms after the price went down to a certain level.

j. When Ford's stock took a slight dip in price, Dexter Inholt got worried that his broker would ask him to come up with some money to cover the losses the stock suffered.

k. LaTonya Adams is a first time investor, unfamiliar with the market. She wants to get into the market, but diversify her risk, and invest in lots of firms. Her brother advised her to get into one of these

l. Because he is investing money for his son's college education, Tim Martin decided to invest in several public utilities, because they offer a high dividend yield for the investment.

m. The Chesterfield Investment Club always sends for a document, which discloses the financial information of the firms in which the club is interested in investing.

n. Monte McHewie sold many of the stocks he was holding after he heard some economic news that led him to believe prices in the stock market were going to decline soon.

o. Lindsey Schopp has a portfolio that consists of 10 percent high-risk growth stocks, 40 percent mutual funds, 30 percent government bonds, and 20 percent commodities.

p. Casey Argetsinger bought several shares of a relatively new company, for $1.35 per share. The stock paid no dividend, but was in the biotechnology field, and was predicted to grow by 20 percent per year over the next 10 years.

q. When Ben and Casey Miller decided to buy a house, they sold a number of the stocks they had been holding. They found that there was a significant difference between what they paid for the stock, and the price at which they were able to sell it. So much so, that they were able to make a substantial down payment on their new house. This difference in selling prices was called their _____.

9. Whereas the stock exchanges trade securities, commodities exchanges specialize in buying and selling goods such as grains, livestock, metals, natural resources and foreign currency.

Jordan Reish has a large farm in the Midwest. His primary crop is corn. Jordan usually sells the crop he will plant in the spring, in the fall <u>before</u> the crop is even planted. General Mills is always happy to see Jordan and others like him selling their unplanted crops, and spends a good deal of time buying these futures contracts. What are Jordan and General Mills doing? Why?

10. The financial section of the Wall Street Journal contains stock and bond quotes, the Dow Jones Index and mutual fund quotes. Complete the following exercises, using the Wall Street Journal, or your local newspaper if the information is available. You can also find most of this information online, at a variety of sites, such as <u>www.excite.com</u> or, for mutual funds, at <u>www.morningstar.com</u>

a. Trace the stock quotes for General Motors (or for a company your instructor assigns you) for three days, using the chart given below:

52 weeks					Yld		Vol				Net
Hi	Low	Stock	Sym	Div	%	PE	100s	Hi	Low	Close	Chg

1. What was the actual price of the stock at the close of the third day? _____

2. What was the net change in dollars on the third day? _____

3. What was the highest price the stock traded for in the previous year? _____

4. How many shares were traded on the second day? _____

b. Choose a bond from the NYSE Bond section. Complete the following information:

    1. Name of company   _____

    2. Interest rate   _____

    3. Date of maturity   _____

    4. Current yield   _____

    5. Close   _____

    6. Change   _____

c. Choose a mutual fund and answer the following questions:*

    1. What is the net asset value?   _____

    2. Is this a "no load" fund?   _____

    3. What is the change in the net asset value?   _____

    4. What is the year to date return?   _____

* All this information was available in the Wall Street Journal as of April 2001. Occasionally, the WSJ changes the type of information it provides in the quotations they publish.

d. Look at the Dow Jones Industrial Average during the time your class is studying this chapter. Answer the following questions:

    1. Have stock prices trended up or down over the last 6 months?

2. What was the highest Dow Jones Industrial Average in the last 6 months?

3. What was the lowest?

PRACTICE TEST

Multiple Choice – Circle the best answer

1.   Which of the following statements is not true?

    a.   The only time a corporation receives the money from the sale of stock is after the IPO.
    b.   The IPO is handled in the secondary market.
    c.   The first public offering of a corporation's stock is called an IPO.
    d.   Investors buy and sell stocks in the secondary market.

2.   An investment-banking firm underwrites a new issue of stocks and bonds by:

    a.   buying the entire bond or stock issue a company wants to sell at an agreed discount.
    b.   guaranteeing a minimum price in the market for a stock or bond.
    c.   selling the entire bond issue for the issuing firm.
    d.   putting up collateral for long term loans, such as bonds.

3.   Which of the following is not considered an advantage of selling bonds?

    a.   The debt is eventually eliminated when the bonds are paid off
    b.   Interest on the bonds is not a legal obligation
    c.   Bondholders have no say in running the firm
    d.   Interest is tax deductible

4.   A _____ permits a bond issuer to pay off the bond's principal prior to its maturity date.
    a.   sinking fund bond
    b.   convertible bond
    c.   callable bond
    d.   collateral trust bond

5.   Daddy Warbucks bought his daughter Annie some stock for her birthday. The type of stock Daddy bought has a fixed dividend, and if the dividend isn't paid when it is due, the missed dividend will accumulate and be paid later. Daddy bought Annie

    a.   common stock.
    b.   cumulative preferred stock.
    c.   convertible stock.
    d.   preemptive right stock.

6. Which of the following would not be included in a list of the disadvantages of selling equity?

   a. Stockholders have the right to vote and so can alter the direction of the firm

   b. Dividends are not tax deductible

   c. Management's decisions can be affected by the need to keep stockholders happy

   d. There is a legal obligation to pay dividends

7. Which stock exchange is a network of several thousand brokers who maintain contact with one another and buy and sell securities though an electronic system of communication?

   a. NASDAQ

   b. NYSE

   c. AMEX

   d. Chicago exchange

8. When the International Ladies Investment Club is deciding on which stock to purchase, the Club will request a _____ before making that decision.

   a. insider report

   b. income statement

   c. prospectus

   d. disclosure statement

9. Linda Hutton is considering investing in the stock market. Linda wants to be sure to be able to get her money back whenever she wants. Linda is concerned with

   a. growth.

   b. yield.

   c. tax consequences.

   d. liquidity.

10. One of the benefits of trading on-line is that:

   a. investing on-line is more accurate.

   b. when you invest on-line you are more likely to make a good decision.

   c. on-line trading services are less expensive than regular stockbroker commissions.

   d. insider trading is less likely on-line.

11. The type of bond that has the least risk is

    a. a convertible bond.
    b. a U.S. government bond.
    c. a discount bond.
    d. a callable bond.

12. A bond that sells for more than face value is called a

    a. premium bond.
    b. U.S. government bond.
    c. discount bond.
    d. callable bond.

13. Maria Chadwick is interested in investing in the stock of a corporation that pays regular dividends and generates consistent growth in the price of a share. Maria is interested in purchasing

    a. growth stocks.
    b. income stocks.
    c. blue chip stocks.
    d. penny stocks.

14. When the price of a share of U.S. On Line went up to $150 per share, the company declared a 3 for 1 stock split. The price of a share of U.S. On Line stock is now approximately:

    a. $100 per share
    b. $75 per share
    c. $50 per share
    d. $25 per share

15. The benefit of a mutual fund for investors is that

    a. mutual funds help investors to diversify and invest in many different companies.
    b. an investor doesn't have to do as much research.
    c. mutual funds are less expensive than most individual shares of stock.
    d. mutual funds don't charge a commission or up-front fee.

16. Ed Marino wants to invest in the stock of U.S. On Line, and is considering buying 100 shares at $50 per share. The problem is, Ed only has about $3500 in his bank. Ed can still purchase the stock through

   a. selling short.
   b. buying convertible stock, which is less expensive.
   c. waiting for a stock split.
   d. buying on margin.

17. If the paper reports the bond price as 89 ½ the price an investor would have to pay is

   a. $890.50
   b. $8950
   c. $895
   d. $89.50

18. Which of the following is not included in a stock quote from the paper?

   a. The average price over the last 52 weeks
   b. The highest price in the last 52 weeks
   c. The price to earnings ratio
   d. The net change in price from the day before

19. The Dow Jones Industrial Average

   a. identifies recessions from the last 30 years.
   b. gives an indication of the ups and downs of the stock market over time.
   c. compiles average stock prices of all stocks on the NYSE.
   d. shows the average stock price of 20 stocks for the last year.

20. After the stock market crash of 1997, the stock exchanges have made an agreement to

   a. halt trading if the Dow Jones goes up too quickly.
   b. publish the average every day.
   c. halt trading if the Dow Jones Average drops by 20 percent.
   d. continue trading as long as the Dow Jones Average doesn't change by more than 15 percent.

True-False

1. _____ In the securities markets, the primary markets handle the sale of new securities.

2. _____ An institutional investor is a large investor who buys the entire bond or stock issues a company wants to sell.

3. _____ A company is legally bound to pay the interest on a bond, but not the principal amount.

4. _____ A sinking fund is a provision allowing for a company to pay off a bond prior to its maturity date.

5. _____ Dividends may be distributed as cash payments or additional shares of stock.

6. _____ One of the advantages of raising capital through selling stock is that the stockholder's investment never has to be repaid.

7. _____ Common stock normally does not include voting rights.

8. _____ The NASDAQ only deals with small firms that cannot qualify for listing on the New York or American exchanges.

9. _____ A stockbroker is a registered representative who acts as an intermediary to buy and sell stocks for clients.

10. _____ A young person saving for retirement can afford to invest in higher risk stocks than a person who is nearing retirement age.

11. _____ One of the disadvantages of a corporate bond is that if you buy it, you must hold it to the maturity date.

12. _____ "Bulls" are investors who believe that stock prices are going to rise, so they buy in anticipation of the increase.

13. _____ A market order tells a broker to buy or sell a particular stock at a specific price.

14. _____ Mutual funds are probably the best way for smaller investors to get started.

15. _____ Buying on margin allows an investor to borrow money from a brokerage firm.

You Can Find It On The Net

How much would you have made, or lost, if you had invested in the stock market a year ago?

Go to www.yahoo.com , and click on Finance/Quotes. Go down to historical quotes, and follow the instructions.

If you had purchased $1000 of a blue chip stock, such as Coca-Cola, or IBM exactly one year ago, what would your capital gain, or loss, be as of today?

Calculate the same information for a technology-related company, such as Cisco, Microsoft or Yahoo.com Would you have a capital gain? How much?

Now, visit an online broker such as www.etrade.com or www.ameritrade.com How do their fees compare to trading online with a discount broker such as Charles Schwab – www.charlesschwab.com, or a traditional broker such as A.G. Edwards www.agedwards.com?

ANSWERS

LEARNING THE LANGUAGE

1. Cumulative preferred stock	15. Convertible bond	30. Growth stock
2. Futures market	16. Market order	31. Stock split
3. Income stocks	17. Penny stock	32. Diversification
4. Institutional investors	18. Junk bonds	33. Limit order
5. Over the counter market (OTC)	19. Stockbroker	34. Stocks
6. Stock certificate	20. Callable bond	35. Mutual fund
7. Blue chip stocks	21. Stock exchange	36. Bond
8. Program trading	22. Maturity date	37. Dow Jones Industrial Average
9. Preemptive right	23. Preferred stock	38. Commodity exchange
10. Common stock	24. Investment banker	39. Securities and Exchange Commission
11. Sinking fund	25. Par value	40. Prospectus
12. Insider trading	26. Interest	41. National Association of Securities Dealers Automated Quotations(NASDAQ)
13. Principal	27. Debenture bond	42. Denomination
14. Round lot	28. Buying on margin	43. Capital gains
	29. Dividends	44. Odd lots
		45. Initial Public Offering

ASSESSMENT CHECK

1. Two major functions of securities markets are to help businesses find long-term funding they need to finance operations, expand their businesses, or buy goods and services. Secondly, securities markets give investors a place to buy and sell investments such as stocks and bonds to build their financial future

2. The primary market handles the sale of new securities. This is the only time corporations make money on the sale of securities. After the corporation has made its money, the secondary market handles the trading of securities between investors.

3. Companies normally prefer to meet long-term financial needs by using retained earnings, or by borrowing from a lending institution.

4.   Investment bankers are specialists who assist in the issue and sale of new securities. They underwrite new issues, or in other words, the investment banker will buy the entire bond or stock issue a company wants to sell at an agreed upon discount and then sells the issue to private or institutional investors at full price.

5.   Institutional investors are mutual funds, pension funds, insurance companies and banks. Because they have such large buying power, they are a powerful force in the securities markets.

Debt Financing Through Selling Bonds

6.   By issuing bonds a company has legal obligation to pay regular interest payments to investors and repay the entire bond principal amount at a prescribed time, called the maturity date.

7.   The interest rate paid on bonds is also called the bond's coupon rate.

8.   The interest rate paid on a bond varies according to factors such as the state of the economy, the reputation of the company issuing the bond, and the going interest rate for government bonds or bonds of similar companies.

9.   A 10% bond with a maturity date of 2020 means that the bondholder will receive $100 in interest (on a $1,000 bond) per year until the year 2020, when the full principal must be repaid.

10.   a. Bondholders have no vote on corporate affairs, so the management maintains control over the firm.
       b. The interest paid on bonds is tax deductible for the firm.
       c. Bonds are a temporary source of funding. They are eventually repaid, and the debt is eliminated.

11.   a. Bonds are an increase in debt and could adversely affect the firm.
       b. Interest on bonds is a legal obligation.
       c. The face value of bonds must be repaid at maturity, which could cause cash shortage.

12.   Unsecured bonds, called debentures, are not supported by any collateral.. Generally only firms with excellent credit ratings can issue debentures. The other classes of bonds, secured bonds, are backed by some tangible asset, or collateral, that is pledged to the bondholder if bond interest isn't paid.

13.   a. They provide for an orderly retirement of a bond issue.

       b. They reduce the risk of not being repaid, and so make the bond more attractive as an investment.

       c. They can support the market price of a bond because of reduced risk.

14.   Callable bonds give companies some direction in long-term forecasting. The callable bond permits the bond issuer to pay off the bond's principal before its maturity date. The company can benefit if they can call in a bond issue that pays a high rate of interest, and re-issue new bonds at a lower rate of interest.

15.   If the value of the firm's common stock grew in value over time, bondholders can compare the value of the bond's interest with the possibility of a sizable profit by converting to a specified number of common shares.

Equity Financing Through Selling Stock

16.   A stock certificate specifies the name of the company, the number of shares it represents, and the type of stock being issued. They will sometimes also indicate a par value.

17.   Interest on bonds is a legal obligation that the company must pay, and interest is tax deductible, so it is paid before taxes. Dividends are a part of a firm's profits that _may_ be distributed to shareholders. Unlike bond interest, companies are not required to pay dividends.

18.   a. Because stockholders are owners, they never have to be repaid.

       b. There is no legal obligation to pay dividends.

       c. Selling stock can improve the condition of the balance sheet

19.   a. As owners, stockholders can alter the direction of the firm, through voting for the board of directors.

       b. Dividends are paid out of after tax profits.

       c. Management decision-making can be hampered by the need to keep the stockholders happy.

20.   a. Preferred stock

       b. common stock

21.   Preferred stock dividends differ from common stock dividends in several ways. Preferred stock is generally issued with a par value that becomes the base for the dividend the firm is willing to pay. The owner is assured that the dividends on preferred stock must be paid in full before any common stock dividends can be distributed. Common stock dividends are declared by the board of directors, and may or may not be declared in any given quarter.

22. Both preferred stock and bonds have a face (or par) value, and both have a fixed rate of return. Preferred stocks are rated by Standard and Poor and Moody's Investment Service just like bonds.

23. As debt, companies are legally bound to pay bond interest and must repay the face value of the bond on its maturity date. Even though preferred stock dividends are generally fixed, they do not legally have to be paid, and stock never has to be repurchased. Though both bonds and stock can increase in market value, the price of stock generally increases at a higher percentage than a bond.

24. Like bonds, preferred stock can be callable. This means a company could require preferred stockholders to sell back their shares. Preferred stock can also be convertible to common stock. An important feature of preferred stock is that it is often cumulative. If one or more dividends are not paid when due, the missed dividends of cumulative preferred stock will accumulate and be paid later.

25. Common stockholders have the right to vote for the board of directors and important issues affecting the company, and to share in the firm's profits though dividends declared by the board of directors.

Stock Exchanges

26. The two major national exchanges are the New York Stock Exchange (NYSE) and the American Stock Exchange (AMEX)

27. Regional exchanges deal mostly with firms in their own areas and handle the stock of many large corporations listed on the New York exchange.

28. The New York Stock Exchange lists the largest companies, while the NASDAQ has the largest number of listings.

29. The over the counter market provides a means to trade stocks not listed on the national securities exchanges. Originally the over the counter market dealt primarily with small firms that couldn't qualify to trade on the national exchanges. Today, well-known firms such as Cisco, Microsoft, Dell and Intel are traded on the OTC market.

30. The OTC market is a network of several thousand brokers who maintain contact with each other and buy and sell securities through a nationwide electronic system that communicates trades through the NASDAQ.

31. The Securities Act of 1933 protects investors by requiring full disclosure of financial information by firms selling new stocks or bonds. Congress passed this act to deal with the "free-for-all" atmosphere that existed during the Roaring Twenties.

32.   The Securities and Exchange Act of 1934 created the Securities and Exchange Commission, which has the responsibility at the federal level for regulating activities in the various exchanges. Companies trading on the national exchange must register with the SEC and provide annual updates. The Securities and Exchange Act of 1934 also established guidelines companies must follow when issuing stock, and guidelines to prevent insiders from taking advantage of privileged information.

33.   Originally, the SEC defined the term insider as consisting of a company's directors, employees, and relatives. Today, the term has been broadened to include just about anyone with securities information that is not available to the general public.

34.   Stockbrokers place an order with a stock exchange member who goes to the place at the exchange where the bond or stock is traded and negotiates a price. When the transaction is completed, the trade is reported to your broker who notifies you to confirm your purchase. The same procedures are followed if you sell stocks.

35.   On-line trading services are less expensive than regular stockbroker commissions.

36.   The on-line services are targeted primarily at investors who are willing to do their own research and make their own investment decisions without the assistance of a broker. The leading online brokers do provide marketing information.

37.   a.   Investment risk – the chance that your investment could go down in value in the future.
       b.   Yield - the percentage return
       c.   Duration – the length of time for which you are committing your assets
       d.   Liquidity – how quickly you can get back your money if necessary
       e.   Tax consequences – how the investment affects your tax situation

Investing in Bonds

38.   U.S. Government bonds are a secure investment backed by the full faith and credit of the federal government. Municipal bonds are also secure, and are offered by local governments, and often have advantages such as tax free interest.

39.   Two questions first time bond investors have are
       a.   "If I purchase a bond, do I have to hold it to the maturity date?" The answer is no.
       b.   " How do I know how risky a particular bond issue is as an investment?" Standard and Poor's and Moody's Investor Service rate the level of risk of many corporate and government bonds.

40. If your bond does not have features that make it attractive to other investors, you may have to sell your bond at a discount, which is a price less than face value. If the bond is highly valued, you may be able to sell it at a price above face value, which is a premium.

Investing in Stocks and Mutual Funds

41. Since 1925, the average annual return on stocks has been about 12 percent, the highest return of any possible investment.

42. According to investment analysts, the market price of a common stock is dependent upon the overall performance of the corporation in meeting its business objectives. If a company reaches its stated objectives, there are opportunities for capital gains.

43. Stock investors are called bulls when they believe that stock prices are going to rise, so they buy stock in anticipation of the increase. When overall stock prices are rising, it is called a bull market. Bears are investors who expect stock prices to decline. Bears sell their stocks before they expect prices to fall. When the prices of stocks decline steadily, it is referred to as a bear market.

44. a. Growth stocks, whose earnings are expected to grow at a rate faster than other stocks
    b. Income stocks, which offer investors a high dividend yield on their investment
    c. Blue chip stocks that pay regular dividends and generate consistent growth in the company stock price
    d. Penny stock, which sells for less than $2 a share

45. Penny stocks are considered very risky investments.

46. A market order tells a broker to buy or to sell a stock immediately at the best price available. A limit order tells the broker to buy or to sell a particular stock at a specific price if that price becomes available.

47. When investors cannot afford to buy shares of stock in companies selling for a high price, the company may choose to declare a stock split; that is, they issue two or more shares for every share of stock currently outstanding. This has the effect of dropping the price of a share, proportionately. For example, if a stock was selling for $150 and you had one share, after a two for one stock split you would have two shares, and each share would be valued at about $75.

48. The benefit of a mutual fund to an investor is they can buy shares of the mutual fund and share in the ownership of many different companies they could not afford to invest in individually. Thus mutual funds help investors diversify and provide professional investment management.

49.   A variety of mutual funds are available, ranging from very conservative funds that invest only in government securities or secure corporate bonds to others that specialize in emerging high-tech firms, foreign companies, precious metals, and other investments with greater risk. Some mutual funds even invest only in socially responsible companies.

50.   A no-load fund is one that charges no commission to either buy or sell its shares. A load fund would charge a commission to investors.

51.   An open-end fund will accept the investment of any interested investors. Closed-end funds offer a specific number of shares for investment. Once the fund reaches its target number, no new investors are admitted into the fund.

52.   A portfolio strategy involves a strategy of buying several different investment alternatives to spread the risk of investing. By diversifying investments, the investor decreases the chance of losing everything.

Investing in High Risk Investments

53.   Standard & Poor's Investment Advisory Service and Moody's Investor Service consider junk bonds as non-investment grade bonds because of their high-risk and high default rates. Junk bonds rely on the firm's ability to pay investors interest, and strong cash flow. If the company can't pay off the bond, the investor is left with a bond that isn't worth more than the paper it is written on.

54.   The margin is the amount of money an investor must invest in a stock purchase. If a margin rate is 50 percent, an investor may borrow 50 percent of the stock's purchase price from a broker.

55.   The downside of buying on margin is that investors must repay the credit extended by the broker, plus interest.

56.   If an investor's account goes down in market value, the broker will issue a margin call, requiring the investor to come up with more money to cover the losses the stock has suffered. If the investor is unable to make the margin call, the broker can legally sell shares of the investor's stock to reduce the broker's chance of loss.

57.   Items such as coffee, wheat, pork bellies, petroleum, and other commodities that are scheduled for delivery at a given date in time are traded on the commodities market. A commodity exchange specializes in the buying and selling of precious metals and minerals, and agricultural goods. Other commodities include corn, plywood, silver, gold, U.S. Treasury bonds, potatoes, cattle, and various foreign currencies.

58.   Investors in the commodities market are hoping to profit from the rise and fall of prices of the commodities traded.

Understanding Information From Securities Markets

59.   A bond price is quoted as a percentage of the face value.

60.   A bond quote in the paper contains the name of the company issuing the bond, the interest rate, the maturity date, the price of the bond, the volume and the current yield.

61.   a. highest and lowest price over the past 52 weeks
        b. abbreviated company name and stock symbol
        c. last dividend per share
        d. the dividend yield
        e. the P/E ratio
        f. the number of shares traded that day
        g. the high, low and closing price for the day
        h. the net change of the stock price

62.   The fund's name, the net asset value, the sale price and the net change in the NAV.

63.   The Net Asset Value, NAV, is the market value of the mutual fund's portfolio divided by the number of shares it has outstanding.

64.   New stocks are substituted on the Dow when it is deemed appropriate. The Dow was broadened in 1982 to include 30 stocks, and again in 1991, adding Disney to reflect the increased importance of the service sector. In 1997 the list was changed by adding different companies, and in 1999 other companies were added while some companies were dropped.

65.   Critics of the Dow Jones Average argue that if the purpose of the Dow is to give an indication of the direction of the broader market over time, the 30-company sample is too small to get a good statistical representation. Many investors and market analysts prefer to follow stock indexes like the Standard and Poor's 500 that tracks the performance of many more companies.

66.   On October 19, 1987 the stock market suffered the largest one-day drop in its history, at that time. The Dow Jones Industrial Average fell 508 points. In October of 18, 1997, and April of 2000 the Dow fell again, by even larger amounts. The market continued to drop in 2000, and in the early part of 2001.

67.   Many analysts believe that program trading was a big cause of the stock market drop in 1987. In program trading, investors give computers instructions to automatically sell if the price of their stock dips to a certain price to avoid potential losses.

68.   Circuit breakers were instituted after the crash of 1987. Under market rules, if the market falls 350 points, the circuit breakers kick in and halt trading for a half-hour and give investors a chance to assess the situation. Since 1997, U.S. stock exchanges have agreed to halt trading for the day if the Dow Jones Industrial average drops 20 percent.

69.   Day traders are investors who trade online and move rapidly in and out of stocks.

70.   Lessons to be learned are the importance of diversifying your investments and understanding the risks of investing with borrowed money that may have to be repaid quickly when prices fall. It is also wise to take a long-term perspective.

CRITICAL THINKING EXERCISES

1.   The finance manager of Music-stor has the opportunity to avoid the difficulties of a new issue by making use of specialists in the securities markets such as investment bankers. These companies will underwrite the new issue, by purchasing the entire bond issue for a discount. The investment banker will then sell the issue on the open market to either private or institutional investors, such as pension funds, mutual funds, insurance companies, or banks.

2.   a. Principal   f. Bond
      b. Maturity date   g. Call provision
      c. Sinking fund   h. Convertible bond
      d. Unsecured bond (debenture)   i. Secured bond
      e. Interest

3.   a. Common stock   e. Preferred stock
      b. Stock certificate   f. Pre-emptive right
      c. Dividends   g. Cumulative preferred
      d. Par value   h. Stock

4.   While both forms of stock represent ownership, there are several differences between preferred and common stock. First, an owner of common stock has the right to vote, and so can influence corporate policy. Judi probably did not consider this to be important, as Burke was a baby, and wouldn't really be concerned about such things! Further, common stock is considered to be more risky than preferred, because if a company closes, common stockholders share in assets only <u>after</u> bondholders and preferred stockholders. Also, while preferred dividends are fixed, and sometimes accumulate, common stock dividends will only be paid after both bondholders and

preferred stockholders receive their interest and dividends. If Judi were interested in starting a "college fund" for Burke, then the preferred stock was a better match for her needs.

5. The largest exchange in the United States is the New York Stock Exchange, NYSE. The NYSE, and the American Exchange, (AMEX) are called national exchanges because they handle stocks of companies from throughout the United States. They are both located in New York City.

   NASDAQ, or the over-the-counter market, is a network of several thousand stockbrokers who maintain contact with each other and buy and sell securities through a nationwide electronic system. The stocks traded on NASDAQ are not "listed" on the national securities exchanges

   While the NYSE handles most of the largest companies, the NASDAQ handles more companies than the NYSE. Originally, the over-the-counter market dealt mostly with small firms that could not qualify for listing on a national exchange, or did not want to bother with the procedures for listing. Now, many large and well-known firms prefer their stock to be traded over-the-counter.

6. The Securities and Exchange Commission regulates the securities market. Companies listed on the national exchanges must register with the SEC and provide regular updates. All firms selling stocks or bonds must fully disclose financial information to investors.

   Before an IPO, a firm must file a registration with the SEC. A condensed version of that registration is called a prospectus. This prospectus must be sent to potential investors. The SEC has also established guidelines regulating insider trading.

7. a. This couple would probably want a low to moderate risk investment, which will increase their principle over time. Tax consequences will be minimal, at least at first, as the child will have little income in the early years.

   (If they opt for an interest or dividend bearing type of account, the child will be earning income, and tax consequences may become a more important consideration). They will choose an investment that will yield a high return over the long run, and liquidity isn't important for now.

   b. Since this investment may be for retirement, this couple will probably want a low risk investment, with as high an after-tax yield as they can earn. It will be of short duration, since they plan to retire in five years, and they may want to keep it fairly liquid in case they retire in less than five years. A big factor will be the tax consequences, as they are a two-income family, and are probably in a high tax bracket with few deductions.

   c. A young, single person will choose a higher risk investment than the others, because they probably are not concerned with long-term considerations as retirement. Since they want to build capital, the yield will be important for the short term. This individual may want to keep investments of short duration in order to make a large return. In a few years, when they may want the money as a down payment for a house, for example they may want their investments liquid. Tax consequences will be important, as there are few deductions, and they may be in a relatively high bracket

8.
a. Stock split	j. Margin call
b. Penny stocks	k. Mutual fund
c. Stockbroker	l. Income stock
d. Round lot	m. Prospectus
e. Buying on margin	n. Bear
f. Blue chip	o. Diversification
g. Market order	p. Growth stock
h. Bull	q. Capital gains
i. Limit order	

9. In the commodities market, buying or selling goods for delivery sometime in the future, is known as the futures market. This allows farmers, like Jordan, to fix a price for their crops, and aids in planning, and allows buyers, like General Mills, to fix a price so that they may also plan. It prevents the risk of being caught by a price increase, and gives businesses a form of price insurance that enables them to continue business without worrying about fluctuations in commodity prices.

10. Your answers for each section will vary according to which companies you choose to study, and when you are studying this chapter. As for the Dow Jones Industrial Averages, stock prices trended upward in the mid-1990s and the average broke 9000 for the first time in early 1998. Stock prices quickly recovered from the drop in October 1997. By late 1999, the Dow Jones Industrial Average hit over 11,000. During 2000 the Average varied, and in early 2001, the Dow Jones fell rapidly, plunging to below 10,000.

PRACTICE TEST

MULTIPLE CHOICE

1.	b	11.	b
2.	a	12.	a
3.	b	13.	c
4.	c	14.	c
5.	b	15.	a
6.	d	16.	d
7.	a	17.	c
8.	c	18.	a
9.	d	19.	b
10.	c	20.	c

TRUE/FALSE

1.	T	9.	T
2.	F	10.	T
3.	F	11.	F
4.	F	12.	T
5.	T	13.	F
6.	T	14.	T
7.	F	15.	T
8.	F		

CHAPTER 21
UNDERSTANDING MONEY AND FINANCIAL INSTITUTIONS

LEARNING GOALS

After you have read and studied this chapter, you should be able to:

1. Explain what money is and how its value is determined.

2. Describe how the Federal Reserve controls the money supply.

3. Trace the history of banking and the Federal Reserve System.

4. Classify the various institutions in the American banking system.

5. Explain the importance of the Federal Deposit Insurance Corporation and other organizations that guarantee funds.

6. Discuss the future of the banking system.

7. Evaluate the role and importance of international banking and the role of the World Bank and the International Monetary Fund.

LEARNING THE LANGUAGE

Listed below are important terms found in the chapter. Choose the correct term for the definition and write it in the space provided.

Banker's acceptance	Electronic funds transfer system (EFT)	Nonbanks
Barter	Federal Deposit Insurance Corporation (FDIC)	Open-market operations
Certificate of deposit	International Monetary Fund (IMF)	Pension funds
Commercial and consumer Finance companies	Letter of credit	Reserve requirement
Commercial bank	M-1	Savings and Loan Association
Credit unions	M-2	Savings Association Insurance Fund (SAIF)
Debit card	Money	Smart card
Demand deposit	Money supply	Time deposit
Discount rate		World Bank
Electronic check conversion		

1. Non-profit, member owned financial cooperatives called_____ offer the full variety of banking services to their members.

2. An electronic funds transfer tool called _____ converts a traditional paper check into an electronic transaction at the cash register and processes it through the Federal Reserve's Automated Clearing House.

3. The _____is a percentage of commercial banks' checking and savings accounts that must be physically kept in the bank.

4. Organizations called _____offer short-term loans to businesses or individuals who either can't meet the credit requirements or regular banks or else have exceeded their credit limit and need more funds.

5. The technical name for a savings account is a _____, for which the bank requires prior notice before the owner withdraws money.

6. A _____is a promise that the bank will pay some specified amount at a particular time.

7. _____is anything that people generally accept as payment for goods and services.

8. The interest rate the Fed charges for loans to member banks is the _____.

9. Financial organizations known as _____ accept no deposits, but offer many of the services provided by regular banks, include pension funds, insurance companies, commercial finance companies, consumer finance companies and brokerage houses.

10. A time deposit (savings) account called a _____earns interest to be delivered at the end of the certificate's maturity date.

11. A computerized system known as _____electronically performs financial transactions such as making purchases, paying bills, and receiving paychecks.

12. The part of the FDIC that insures holders of accounts in savings and loan associations is called the _____.

13. An electronic funds transfer tools known as a _____ serves the same function as checks, in that it withdraws funds from a checking account.

14. The activity of _____ is the trading of goods and services for other goods and services.

15. A financial institution called a _____ accepts both savings and checking deposits and provides home mortgage loans.

16. The _____ is how much money there is to buy available goods and services.

17. A _____ is a promise by a bank that a given amount will be paid if certain conditions are met.

18. _____ are amounts of money put aside by corporations, nonprofit organizations, or unions to cover part of the financial needs of members when they retire.

19. A profit-making organization that receives deposits from individuals and corporations in the form of checking and savings accounts and uses some of these funds to make loans is called a _____.

20. The _____ is an independent agency of the U.S. government that insures bank deposits.

21. The buying and selling of U.S. government securities by the Fed is called_____ and has the goal of regulating the money supply.

22. _____ includes everything in M-1 plus money that takes more time to raise (savings accounts, money in money market accounts, mutual funds and certificates of deposit.)

23. The technical name for a checking account is a _____, from which money can be withdrawn anytime on demand by the owner.

24. The _____ assists the smooth flow of money among nations.

25. The _____, also known as the International Bank for Reconstruction and Development, is primarily responsible for financing economic development.

26. Money that is quickly and easily raised, such as currency, checks, traveler's checks, is called the _____ money supply.

27. A _____is an electronic funds transfer tool that is a combination credit card, debit card, phone card, and more.

ASSESSMENT RETENTION CHECK

Learning Goal 1   **The Importance of Money**

1.   What is a problem with the barter system when compared to money?

2.   Describe five characteristics of "useful" money?

   a. _____

   b. _____

   c. _____

   d. _____

   e. _____

3.   What is e-cash? How can you use it?

4.   What is the euro?

5.   What was the impact when the euro fell against the dollar?

6.   What is the difference between M-1 and M-2?

7.   What is meant by "too much money chasing too few goods?"

8.   What would happen if too much money were taken out of the economy?

9.   Why does the money supply need to be controlled?

10.   What does a "falling dollar" mean? What does a rising dollar mean? What does this mean for the prices of European goods?

11.   What makes our dollar "weak" or "strong"?

Learning Goal 2   **Control of the Money Supply**

11.   What organization is in charge of monetary policy?

12.   What are the five major parts of the Federal Reserve System?

a. _____

b. _____

c. _____

d. _____

e. _____

13.   What does the Board of Governors do? What is the primary function of the board of governors?

14.   Describe the Federal Open Market Committee.

15. What are some activities of the Federal Reserve?

   a. _____

   b. _____

   c. _____

   d. _____

   e. _____

   f. _____

   g. _____

   h. _____

16. List three ways the Federal Reserve uses to control the money supply.

   a. _____

   b. _____

   c. _____

17. Which tool is the most powerful?

18. What is the result of an increase in the reserve requirement? What is the result of a decrease in the reserve requirement?

19. What is the Fed's most commonly used tool? Why are the open market operations commonly used than the reserve requirement, which is more powerful?

20. Regarding selling U.S. securities, what does the Fed do to increase or decrease the money supply?

21. Why is the Fed often called the banker's bank?

22. What is the impact of raising the discount rate? What is the impact of lowering the discount rate?

23. After you write a check to your local retailer, what happens to the check?

24. If you write a check to a retailer while on vacation in another state, what path does your check take to get to your home bank?

25.   What measures have banks taken to reduce the use of checks?

Learning Goal 3   **The History of Banking and the Need for the Fed**

26.   Why were colonists forced to use barter for goods?

27.   Why did Massachusetts begin issuing its own paper money? Why did this continental currency
        become worthless?

28.   Why were land banks established?

29.   What was the central bank?

30.   What was the state of banking by the time of the Civil War? Why?

31.   What happened in 1907 in the banking industry, and what was formed as a result?

32.   What did the Federal Reserve Act of 1913 require?

33.   What led to the bank failures of the 1930's?

34.   Why did the government start the federal deposit insurance program?

35. What actions did the Fed take during the 1990's?

36. Why would businesses become concerned about higher interest rates?

Learning Goal 4 **The American Banking System**

37. Identify four types of banking institutions.

a. _____

b. _____

c. _____

d. _____

38. What are two types of customers for commercial banks?

a. _____

b. _____

39. How does a commercial bank make a profit?

40.   What are NOW and Super NOW accounts?

41.   Describe a certificate of deposit.

42.   What is the benefit of an ATM?

43.   Identify the services offered by commercial banks

a._____   i. _____

b._____   j. _____

c._____   k._____

d._____   l. _____

e._____   m. _____

f. _____   n._____

g._____   o. _____

h._____   p._____

44. What is another name for savings and loans institutions, and why are they known as such?

45. What services were savings and loans permitted to offer after the difficult period between 1979 and 1983? Why?

46. What services do credit unions offer their members?

47. What are five nonbank institutions?

a. _____   d. _____

b. _____   e. _____

c. _____

48. What has been the result of competition between nonbanks and banks?

49.   Who are a finance company's primary customers?

Learning Goal 5   **How the Government Protects Your Funds**

50.   List the three major sources of financial protection

a. _____

b. _____

c. _____

51.   What does the FDIC do in the case of a bank failure?

52.   Why were the FDIC and the FSLIC created?

53.   Why was SAIF formed?

54.   What does the NCUA provide for?

Learning Goal 6   **The Future of Banking**

55.   What law does the Gramm-Leach –Bliley Act replace, and what does the new law provide for?
        What is likely to happen to the cost of banking, as a result?

56.   What banking services from home are available to customers?

57.   What benefits can Internet banks offer to customers?

58.   How have customer responded to Internet banks? Why?

59. How will ATMs and online banking combine?

60. What will we see in the future in terms of the exchange of money?

61. What are the electronic funds transfer (EFT) tools?

62. How does electronic check conversion reduce the paper-handling processes of using checks?

63. Explain how a debit card works, and why it is different from a credit card.

64. How are smart cards different from other cards?

65.   What is a direct deposit?

66.   What is direct payment?

Learning Goal 7   **International Banking and Banking Services**

67.   What three services are offered to banks to help businesses conduct business overseas?

68.   How do banks make things easier for travelers and businesspeople traveling overseas?

69.   What could be the international impact of the Federal Reserve System changing interest rates?

70.   What has been the net result of international banking and finance?

71.   What is the World Bank responsible for?

72.   What criticisms have been aimed at the World Bank lately?

73.   What does the International Monetary fund require?

74.   What does the IMF oversee?

75.   Why has the IMF been in the news frequently?

76.   Why do debt relief advocates want the World Bank and the IMF to forgive the debts of poor countries?

CRITICAL THINKING EXERCISES

Learning Goal 1, 2

1.   What is the importance of the stability of the value of money, and controlling the money supply in the international marketplace today?

2   Music-stor has made it big! Congratulations! The company has done so well here in the U.S. that management is seriously considering expanding into overseas markets. It is your job to research the idea, and you want to begin by helping other top managers understand some of the considerations of "going global." Within the context of the "value" of money, what are some of the issues you will want to bring up to your managers? What might be two "non-money" issues that would be important?

Learning Goal 2

3.   The Fed uses three major tools to control the money supply

Reserve requirement

Open market operations

Discount rate

Complete the following chart illustrating how each tool is used, and its effect on the money supply and the economy:

TOOL	ACTION	EFFECT ON MONEY SUPPLY	EFFECT ON ECONOMY
Reserve requirement	Increase reserve requirement	_____	_____
	Decrease reserve requirement	_____	_____
Open market Operations	Buy government securities	_____	_____
	Sell government securities	_____	_____
Discount rate	Increase discount rate	_____	_____
	Decrease discount rate	_____	_____

4. When the Fed regulates the money supply using one of the three tools just mentioned, what happens to interest rates overall? What is stagflation?

5.   The American banking system has a long history. List the major events that led up to the establishment of the Federal Reserve System, and subsequent events that have affected the American banking system.

a. _____

b. _____

c. _____

d. _____

e. _____

f. _____

g. _____

h. _____

i. _____

j. _____

k. _____

l. _____

6.   What happened during the 1990's and the early part of this century, in terms of the Fed and interest rates? (do some research for the more recent events – mid 2001 and beyond)

7.   The American banking system consists of three types of organizations:

Commercial banks

Savings and loans

Credit unions

Match each of the following descriptions to the correct type of institution:

a.   Offers interest-bearing checking accounts called share draft accounts at relatively high rates. _____

b.   Also known as thrift institutions. _____

c.   Offer a wide variety of services, to depositors and borrowers, including ATMs, credit cards, short and long term loans, financial counseling, automatic payment of telephone bills, safe deposit boxes, tax deferred individual retirement accounts, overdraft checking account privileges. _____

d.   Have been able to offer NOW and Super NOW accounts since 1981. _____

e.   Since they are member owned and non-profit, they are exempt from federal income taxes . _____

8   a.   What is the difference between demand deposit and a time deposit?

b.   What are three kinds of checking accounts, and what is the difference between them?

      1.

      2.

      3.

c. What are two kinds of savings accounts offered by commercial banks, and how are they different?

1.

2.

9. How are credit unions different from commercial banks and S&Ls?

10. Describe how nonbanks are becoming an important financial force, and how they compete with traditional banking institutions.

Learning Goal 5

11. A. What is the difference between FDIC, SAIF, and NCUA? Why were the FDIC, and the predecessor to SAIF, (known as the FSLIC) created?

Learning Goal 6

12. Compare what you have learned in earlier chapters about the trends in businesses to become more efficient and competitive to the trends in the U.S. banking industry.

13. What is the difference between a credit card, a debit card, and a smart card?

14.   In previous chapters, we have discussed the global nature of the marketplace, and the need for U.S. businesses to become and stay more competitive. How does what we have learned in those chapters about U.S. business, relate to international banking, and the U.S. banking industry?

PRACTICE TEST

Multiple Choice – Circle the best answer

1. When eggs are used to buy admission to a movie, and sausages used to pay for electric power, a
    _____ system is being used.

    a. barter
    b. direct marketing
    c. monetary policy
    d. inflation

2. Which of the following would not be included in a list of characteristics of money?

    a. Portability
    b. Divisibility
    c. Stability
    d. Usability

3. When the price of a European coffee maker becomes less expensive to buy here in the United
    States, you could say that we are experiencing a

    a. falling dollar.
    b. inflated dollar.
    c. rising dollar.
    d. stable dollar.

4. Which of the following is <u>not</u> one of the functions of the Federal Reserve?

    a. buying and selling foreign currency
    b. supervising banks
    c. lending money to member banks
    d. setting inflation rates

5. When the Fed increases the reserve requirement,

    a. interest rates will go down.
    b. banks will have more money to lend.
    c. inflation could go up.
    d. banks have less money to lend.

6. The discount rate is the rate

    a. banks charge their best customers.
    b. the Fed charges for loans to member banks .
    c. the Fed charges for selling bonds.
    d. the amount of money member banks must keep on hand at the Fed.

7. The bank failures of 1907 and the resulting cash shortage problems led to the creation of

    a. the Federal Reserve System.
    b. the gold standard.
    c. monetary policy.
    d. the money supply.

8. After the stock market crash of 1929, and the resulting bank failures of that time, Congress passed legislation creating

    a. laws which prevented banks from failing.
    b. the Federal Reserve System.
    c. federal deposit insurance.
    d. nonbanks.

9. The technical name for a checking account is a

    a. demand deposit.
    b. time deposit.
    c. certificate of deposit.
    d. deposit insurance.

10. The difference between a NOW account and a savings account is that

    a.   a NOW account doesn't pay interest, and a savings account does.
    b. a NOW account has a maturity date, but a savings account does not.
    c. you can't withdraw money from a NOW account until the maturity date, but you can withdraw from a savings account any time.
    d. you can write checks on a NOW account, but not on a savings account.

11. Competition between banks and nonbanks, such as insurance companies and pension funds, has

   a. decreased with the deregulation of the banking industry.
   b. not changed in 50 years, since the creation of the Federal Reserve System.
   c. increased significantly as nonbanks offer many of the services provided by regular banks.
   d. stabilized with the bull stock market of the late 1990s.

12. The Federal Deposit Insurance Corporation insures accounts up to

   a. $10,000.
   b. $50,000.
   c. $100,000.
   d. $500,000.

13. Funds in savings and loan institutions are protected by

   a. Federal Deposit Insurance Corporation (FDIC).
   b. National Credit Union Association (NCUA).
   c. Federal Savings and Loan Insurance Corporation (FSLIC).
   d. Savings Association Insurance Fund (SAIF).

14. Recent banking trends include all but which of the following?

   a. Closures and foreclosures
   b. Offering insurance
   c. Increased efficiency using new technology
   d. Offering the sale of stocks and bonds

15. Smart cards

   a. are a new credit card offered by nonbanks.
   b. combine the functions of credit cards, debit cards, phone cards and other types of cards.
   c. are a form of direct deposit.
   d. allow employers to make direct payments to your creditors.

16. Which of the following is not a way banks help businesses conduct business overseas?
   a. guarantee a certain exchange rate.
   b. offer letters of credit.
   c. provide bankers acceptance.
   d. currency exchange.

17. The organization which is responsible for financing economic development is the

   a. Federal Reserve Bank.
   b. International Monetary Fund.
   c. World Bank.
   d. Bank of the Americas.

18. The World Bank:

   a. Makes loans only to countries that can afford to make payments of the loans.
   b. Has come under criticism from environmentalists.
   c. Has been praised for its world in developing nations by AIDs activists.
   d. Works with countries to eliminate sweatshops.

True-False

1. _____ The banking system is becoming more complex as the flow of money from one country to another becomes freer.

2. _____ The definition of M-2 money supply includes only currency, money that is available for writing checks and money that is held in traveler's checks.

3. _____ If there is too much money in the economy, prices would go up because people would bid up the prices of goods and services, causing inflation.

4. _____ An increase in the discount rate would encourage businesses to borrow money and thus stimulate the economy.

5. _____ The most commonly used tool used by the Fed is open market operations.

6. _____ Continental currency, the first paper money printed in the United States, became very valuable over the years as the first form of money used in the U.S.

7. _____ Stagflation is a situation of slow economic growth combined with inflation.

8. _____ Commercial banks have two types of customers – borrowers and lenders.

9. _____ Unlike a NOW account, a certificate of deposit has a maturity date, and that is when interest is paid.

10. _____ Commercial banks are offering a wider variety of services, such as brokerage services, financial counseling, automatic payment of bills, and IRAs.

11. _____ The only type of institution in which funds are protected by the U.S. government is a commercial bank.

12. _____ Most online banks have been very successful.

13. _____ The result of international banking has been to link the economies of the world into one interrelated system with no regulatory control.

14. _____ The International Monetary Fund has the responsibility of assisting the smooth flow of money among nations.

You Can Find It On The Net

How many U.S. dollars will buy a British pound? We can find out at www.xe.com/ucc

Check out this site and find out!

How many U.S. dollars does it take to buy a French franc?

How many U.S. dollars will it take to buy a Japanese yen?

How much did your tuition cost in Canadian dollars?

If you are traveling in France, and your hotel costs 1000 French francs per night, are you staying at the French equivalent of the penthouse at the Ritz?

ANSWERS

LEARNING THE LANGUAGE

1. Credit unions	10. Certificates of deposit	19. Commercial bank
2. Electronic check conversion	11. Electronic Funds Transfer System (EFTS)	20. Federal Deposit Insurance Corporation (FDIC)
3. Reserve requirement	12. Savings Association Insurance Fund (SAIF)	21. Open-market operations
4. Commercial/Consumer Finance companies	13. Debit card	22. M-2
5. Time deposit	14. Barter	23. Demand deposit
6. Banker's acceptance	15. Savings and Loan Association	24. International Monetary Fund (IMF)
7. Money	16. Money supply	25. World Bank
8. Discount rate	17. Letter of credit	26. M-1
9. Nonbanks	18. Pension funds	27. Smart card

ASSESSMENT CHECK

The Importance of Money

1.   The problem with barter is that the goods used may be difficult to carry around. People need an object that's more portable, divisible, durable and stable so that they can trade goods and services without actually carrying the goods around with them.

2.   a.   Portability – money needs to be easy to carry around
       b.   Divisibility – different sized coins are made to represent different values
       c.   Stability – the value of money is more stable (unlike the value, or prices, of bartered goods)
       d.   Durability – Coins last for a long time
       e.   Difficult to counterfeit – money must be hard to copy, so it must be elaborately designed

3.   Electronic, or e-cash is the latest form of money. You can e-mail e-cash to anyone using websites, and are able to make online bill payments.

4.   The euro is the common currency recently created by 11 European countries.

5.   When the euro fell against the dollar, it meant that Europeans had to pay more for U.S. goods and European goods were cheaper for U.S. purchasers.

6. M1 includes coins and paper bills, money that is available by writing checks and money that is held in traveler's checks, or, money that is easily available to pay for goods and services. M-2 includes all of that, but adds in money held in savings accounts and other forms of savings that is not as readily available.

7. "Too much money chasing too few goods" means that more people try to buy goods and services with their money and bid up the price to get what they want. That is called inflation.

8. If too much money were taken out of the economy prices would go down because there would be an oversupply of goods and services compared to the money available to buy them. If too much money is taken out of the economy, a recession could occur.

9. The money supply needs to be controlled because this allows us to manage the prices of goods and services. Also, controlling the money supply affects employment and economic growth or decline.

10. A falling dollar means that the amount of goods and service you can buy with a dollar goes down. A rising dollar means that the amount of goods and services you can buy with a dollar goes up. Thus the price you pay for a European good today is lower than a few years ago because of the rising dollar relative to the European euro.

11. What makes a dollar weak or strong (falling or rising dollar) is the position of the U.S. economy relative to other economies. When the economy is strong, people want to buy dollars and the value of the dollar rises. When the economy is perceived as weakening, people no longer want dollars and the value of the dollar falls. The value of a dollar depends upon a strong economy.

Control of the Money Supply

11. The Federal Reserve System (the Fed) is in charge of monetary policy. The head of the Fed (Alan Greenspan in 2001) is one of the most influential people in the world because he or she controls the money that much of the world depends on for trade.

12. The Federal Reserve System consists of
   a. The board of governors
   b. The Federal Open Market Operations
   c. 12 Federal Reserve Banks
   d. Three advisory councils
   e. The member banks of the system

13. The board of governors administers and supervises the 12 Federal Reserve System banks. The primary function of the board of governors is to set monetary policy.

14. The Federal Open Market Committee (FOMC) has 12 voting members and is the policy-making body. The committee is made up of the seven board of governors plus the president of the New York Reserve Bank. Four others rotate in from the other Reserve Banks. The advisory councils offer suggestions to the board and the FOMC. The councils represent the various banking districts, consumers, and member institutions, including banks, savings and loans, and credit unions.

15. The Federal Reserve
    a. buys and sells foreign currencies
    b. regulates various types of credit
    c. supervises banks
    d. collects data on the money supply and other economic activity
    e. determines the level of reserves that must be held by financial institutions
    f. lends money to member banks
    g. sets the rate charged for loans to member banks
    h. buys and sells government securities

16. a. Reserve requirements
    b. Open-market operations
    c. The discount rate

17. The most powerful tool the Fed has to regulate the money supply is the reserve requirement.

18. When the Fed increases the reserve requirement banks have less money to loan, and money becomes scarce. In the long run, this tends to reduce inflation. It is so powerful because of the amount of money affected when the reserve is changed. A decrease in the reserve requirement increases the funds available to banks for loans, so banks make more loans, and money becomes more readily available. An increase in the money supply stimulates the economy to achieve higher growth rates but can also create inflationary pressures.

19. Open market operations are the Fed's most commonly used tool. Open market operations are more commonly used than the reserve requirement because the reserve requirement is so powerful that it is rarely used.

20. If the Fed wants to increase the money supply, it buys government securities from individuals, corporations, or organizations that are willing to sell. To decrease the money supply, the federal government sells U.S. government securities to the public. The money it gets as payment is taken out of circulation, decreasing the money supply.

21. One reason the Fed is called the banker's bank is that member banks can borrow money from the Fed and then pass it on to their customers as loans. The discount rate is the interest rate that the Fed charges for loans to member banks.

22. An increase in the discount rate by the Fed discourages banks from borrowing and consequently reduces the number of available loans, resulting in a decrease in the money supply. Lowering the discount rate encourages member bank borrowing and increases the funds available for loans, which increases the money supply.

23. When you write a check to a local retailer, the retailer takes the check to its bank. If your account is at the same bank, your account is simply reduced by the amount of the check. It is a simple process.

24. When you write a check out of state, the process become more complex. From the retailer, our check goes the retailer's bank, which then deposits your check for credit in the closest Federal Reserve bank. That bank will send the check to your local Federal Reserve bank for collection. The check is then sent to your bank and the amount of the check will be deducted from your account. Your bank will authorize the Federal Reserve bank in your area to deduct the amount of the check. That bank will pay the Federal Reserve bank that began the process in the first place. It will then credit the deposit account in the bank where the retailer has its account. This is a costly process.

25. Banks take several measures to reduce the use of checks, thus reducing the cost of processing. These efforts include encouraging the use of credit cards and electronic transfers of money.

The History of Banking and the Need for the Fed

26. Strict laws in Europe limited the number of coins that could be brought to the New World by colonists, and besides, there were no banks in the colonies. So, colonists were forced to barter for goods.

27. Massachusetts issued its own paper money in 1690 because the demand for money was so great. This money was called continental currency, and it became worthless after a few years because people didn't trust its value.

28. Land banks were established to lend money to farmers.

29. In 1781, Alexander Hamilton persuaded Congress to form a central bank, a bank where banks could keep their funds and borrow funds if needed. It was the first version of a federal bank, but closed in 1811. It was replaced in 1816 because state chartered banks couldn't support the War of 1812.

30.   By the time of the Civil War, banking was a mess. Different banks issued different currencies. During the war, coins were hoarded because they were worth more as gold and silver than as coins. The problems with the banking system continued after the Civil War, for over 40 years, until 1907.

31.   Many banks failed in 1907. People got nervous about their money and went to the bank to withdraw their funds, a "run on the banks". Shortly after, the cash ran out and some banks had to refuse money to depositors. The cash shortage problems of 1907 led to the formation of an organization that could lend money to banks – the Federal Reserve System. It was to be a" lender of last resort" during emergencies, such as the cash shortage

32.   Under the Federal Reserve Act of 1913, all federally chartered banks had to join the Federal Reserve. State banks could also join. The Federal Reserve became the bankers bank.

33.   The stock market crash of 1929 led to bank failures in the early 1930s. The stock market began tumbling, and people ran to the bank to get their money out. In spite of the Federal Reserve, banks ran out of money, and states were forced to close banks.

34.   In 1933 and 1935 Congress passed legislation to strengthen the banking system, to further protect us from bank failures. The most important move was to establish federal deposit insurance.

35.   During the 1990s the Fed tried to keep the economy growing at an even pace. In the early 1990s the fed lowered interest rates to get the economy growing. When inflation threatened in the mid 1990s, the Fed increased interest rates, which threatened the stock market. (By 2000, the Fed began to lower interest rates, in an effort to get the economy moving again, as growth had slowed, and prices in the stock market were beginning to fall).

36.   Businesses are concerned with higher interest rates because higher rates mean a higher cost of borrowing money. If businesses stop borrowing, then business growth slows, people are fired, and the whole economy stagnates. It is possible to have both slow growth and inflation. That situation is called stagflation.

The American Banking System

37.   a. Commercial banks
        b. Savings and loan associations
        c. Credit unions
        d. Mutual savings banks

38.   a. Depositors
        b. Borrowers

39. A commercial bank uses customer deposits as inputs, on which it pays interest, and invests that money in interest-bearing loans to other customers, mostly businesses. Commercial banks make a profit if the revenue generated by loans exceeds the interest paid to depositors plus all other operating expenses.

40. A NOW account typically pays an annual interest rate but usually requires depositors always to maintain a certain minimum balance in the account, and may restrict the number of checks that depositors can write each month. A Super NOW account pays a higher interest to attract larger deposits. However Super NOW accounts require a larger minimum balance. They sometimes offer free, unlimited check-writing privileges.

41. A certificate of deposit is a time deposit, or savings account that earns interest to be delivered at the end of the certificate's maturity date. The depositor agrees not to withdraw any of the funds in the account until the end of the specified period.

42. Automated teller machines, or ATMs, give customers the convenience of 24 hour banking at a variety of outlets, such as supermarkets, department stores and so on, in addition to the bank's regular branches. Depositors can do much of their banking at their own discretion using an ATM card.

43.
a. Checking accounts	i. Traveler's checks
b. Savings accounts	j. Credit cards
c. Loans	k. Certificates of deposit (CDs)
d. Financial counseling	l. NOW accounts
e. Safe deposit boxes	m. Super NOW accounts
f. Certified checks	n. Online banking
g. Overdraft protection	o. Automated teller machines (ATMs)
h. Insurance	p. Brokerage services

44. S&L's are often known as thrift institutions since their original purpose was to promote consumer thrift, or saving, and home ownership.

45. Between 1979 and 1983 many savings and loan institutions failed. Faced with this, the government permitted S&Ls to offer NOW and Super NOW accounts, to allocate up to 10 percent of their funds to commercial loans, and to offer mortgage loans with adjustable Interest rates. Further, savings and loans were allowed to offer several other types of banking services, such as financial counseling to small businesses, and credit cards.

46. Credit unions offer their members interest-bearing checking accounts at relatively high rates, short-term loans at relatively low rates, financial counseling, life insurance and a limited number of home mortgage loans.

47.   a. Life insurance companies   d. Commercial finance companies
        b. Pension funds   e. Corporate financial services
        c. Brokerage firms

48.   The diversity of financial services and investment alternatives offered by non-banks has led banks to expand the services that they offer. In fact, banks today are merging with brokerage firms to offer full-service financial assistance.

49.   The primary customers of commercial and consumer finance companies are new businesses and individuals with no credit history. College students often turn to finance companies for loans to pay for their education.

How the Government Protects Your Funds

50.   a. Federal Deposit Insurance Corporation (FDIC)
        b. Savings Association Insurance Fund (SAIF)
        c. National Credit Union Administration (NCUA)

51.   If a bank were to fail, the FDIC would arrange to have its accounts transferred to another bank or pay off depositors up to a certain amount. If one of the top ten banks in the United States would fail, the FDIC has a contingency plan to nationalize the bank so that it wouldn't fail.

52.   The FDIC and the FSLIC were started during the Great Depression. Many banks and thrifts failed during those years, and people were losing confidence in them. The FDIC and FSLIC were designed to create more confidence in banking institutions.

53.   The government placed the FSLIC under the FDIC, in order to get more control over the banking system. When they did that, they gave it a new name, the Savings Association Insurance Fund, or SAIF.

54.   The NCUA provides up to $100,000 coverage per individual depositor per institution. The coverage includes all accounts, and additional protection can be obtained by holding accounts jointly or in trust.

The Future of Banking

55.   The Bramm-Leach-Bliley Act of 1999 replaces the Glass Steagall Act of 1933 which prohibited banks from owning brokerages. The new act allows banks, insurers, and securities firms to combine and sell each other services. This allows banking consumers to have one-stop shopping for all their financial needs. As companies compete for business, the total cost of banking and other financial services is likely to go down. This may also make it easier to calculate taxes, and in fact, the financial firm may do it for you.

56. Bank from home services include transferring funds, paying your bills, and checking on account balances. You can apply for a car loan or mortgage online and get a response immediately. You can also buy and sell stocks online.

57. Online banks can offer better interest rates and lower fees because they do not have the cost of physical overhead that brick and mortar banks have.

58. While many consumers are pleased with the savings and convenience, not all consumers are happy with the service they receive from Intern et banks.. Many are nervous about the security of banking online. People fear putting their financial information into cyberspace where others may see it. Also, consumers often want to talk to a knowledgeable person when they have banking problems. Overall it seems that Internet banking customers miss the one-on-one help, and the security of local banks.

59. In the future ATMs will do much more for consumers than they do today. Online banking will be combined with ATMs to provide new services to customers, such as brokerage services, check cashing, wiring money and even picking up tickets to an event.

60. In the future we will see more electronic exchange of money because it is more efficient.

61. EFT tools include electronic check conversion, debit cards, smart cards, direct deposit and direct payments.

62. ECC saves both time and money in check clearing. When a customer makes a payment with a check, it is run through a check reader where the information is captured electronically. The check is verified against a database for acceptance. The transaction is electronically transferred, and funds are debited from the customer's account and deposited automatically into the merchant's account. With this kind of electronic check clearing there are no trips to the bank, and the risk of lost or stolen checks is reduced.

63. A debit card serves the same function as a check, in that it withdraws money directly from a checking account. While debit cards *look* like credit cards, they function differently. The difference is that you can spend no more than is in your checking account. When you use a debit card to make a purchase, you swipe the card in a point of sale terminal at the retailer. When the sale is recorded, an electronic signal is sent to the bank, and funds are automatically transferred from your account to the retailer's account.

64. Smart cards are a combination of credit cards, debit cards, phone cards, and more. The magnetic strip found on other cards is replaced on a smart card with a microprocessor. The card can then store information, including a bank balance. Each merchant can use the information to check the card's validity and spending limits, and the transaction can debit the amount on the card. Some

smart cards are used to allow entrance into buildings and secure areas, such as university dorms, to buy items, and serve as ATM cards.

65.   Direct deposit is a credit made directly to a checking or savings account.

66.   A direct payment is a preauthorized electronic payment. A customer signs a form when he or she wants automatic payment to a certain company, and the designated company is authorized to collect funds for the amount of the bill from the customer's account.

International Banking and Banking Services

67.   Banks help businesses conduct business overseas by providing letters of credit, banker's acceptances, and money exchange.

68.   Banks are making it easier for tourists to buy goods and services through automatic teller machines offering foreign currencies. You can often get a better exchange rate with an ATM than from your hotel.

69.   If the Federal Reserve decides to lower interest rates, foreign investors can withdraw their money from the United States in minutes and put it in countries with higher rates. The opposite is also true, so that when the Fed raises interest rates, money could come into the U.S. just as quickly.

70.   The net result of international banking and finance has been to link the economies of the world into one interrelated system with no regulatory control. American firms must compete for funds with firms all over the world.

71.   The World Bank is primarily responsible for financing economic development.

72.   Environmentalists charge that the World Bank finances projects that damage the ecosystem. Human rights activists argue that the bank supports countries that restrict religious freedoms and tolerate sweatshops. AIDS activists complain that the bank does not do enough to get low-cost drugs to developing nations.

73.   The International Monetary fund was established to assist the smooth flow of money among nations. It requires members to allow their currency to be exchanged for foreign currencies freely, to keep the IMF informed about changes in monetary policy, and to modify those policies on the advice of the IMF to accommodate the needs of the entire membership.

74.   The IMF is an overseer of member countries' monetary and exchange rate policies. The IMF's goal is to maintain a global monetary system that works best for all nations.

75. The IMF was frequently in the news because it was lending money to nations whose currencies had fallen dramatically and whose banks were failing, as was happening in Asia and Russia.

76. Debt relief advocates want the World Bank and the IMF to forgive the debts of poor countries because many of them cannot afford to feed their people, much less pay back huge loans.

CRITICAL THINKING EXERCISES

1. The stability of the value of money in the global marketplace is important because if the value is not stable, other countries will not accept that money in trade. In other words, if the marketplace believes your money will not be valuable to use, the market will not accept your money as payment for what you want to buy.

   The money supply needs to be controlled in order to control prices, and in part, the American economy. If there is too much money in the economy, prices of goods and services will increase, because demand will be greater than supply. If there is less money, people will not be spending at the same rate, demand correspondingly goes down, and prices will go down. That could result in an oversupply of goods and services, and possibly a recession. What makes a dollar weak or strong is the position of the U.S. economy relative to other economies. When the economy is strong, people want to buy dollars and the value of the dollar rises. The value of the dollar depends on a strong economy.

2. Some of the "money" issues Music-stor will need to research relate to how strong the American dollar is compared to the currency of the countries in which Music-stor is interested. For example, if our dollar is weak, or falling, in comparison to the British pound, the Japanese yen, or others, Music-stor could be very affordable for their target market. If our dollar is strong, or rising, the price of Music-stor could be too high for some. Further, we would want to know what the forecast might be for the future of the U.S. economy. Is our economy expected to be strong? What are the forecasts for recession, inflation, and income growth, both here, and in our target countries?

   Some of the "non-money" issues revolve around: the target market, whether or not it is common to listen to tapes and c.d.'s in the car in other countries, how many cars are equipped with tape and c.d. players, whether or not our product is adaptable to the interior design of other models, how big the car market is, growth projections for the car market.

3.

Tool	Action	Effect on Money supply	Effect on Economy
Reserve	Increase	Decrease	Slows down
Requirement	Decrease	Increase	Stimulated
Open market	Buy securities	Increase	Stimulated
operations	Sell securities	Decrease	Slows down
Discount rate	Increase	Decrease	Slows down
	Decrease	Increase	Stimulated

4. When the Fed takes action to increase the money supply, (either by decreasing the reserve rate, decreasing the discount rate or buying government bonds) interest rates will go down. Think of interest as the price of money. When the supply goes up, the price will generally go down. Correspondingly, if interest rates have declined, demand for goods and services could go up, the economy begins to grow, and inflation may begin to heat up. The opposite effect occurs when the Fed reduces the money supply. Interest rates will rise, which will slow demand for goods and services, which slows economic growth. Inflation will also then slow down, as supply begins to be equal to or exceed demand, and prices will stabilize.

Stagflation occurs when economic growth has slowed, but there is a high rate of inflation.

5.   a. Paper money established in 1690.
     b. Land banks established to lend money to farmers.
     c. Central bank established in 1781.
     d. Central bank closed in 1811.
     e. Second central bank established in 1816 to support War of 1812.
     f. Division between state banks and central bank.
     g. Central bank closed in 1836.
     h. Civil War - banks issuing their own currency.
     i. Cash shortage problems in 1907; banks began to fail.
     j. Federal Reserve System established in 1907 to lend money to banks.
     k. Stock market crash of 1929 and subsequent bank failures in 1930s.
     l. Legislation passed to strengthen banking system, establishing federal deposit insurance in 1933 and 1935.

6. In the early 1990s the Fed stimulated the economy by lowering interest rates. Inflation began to threaten as a result, and the Fed took action to fight it by raising rates. That caused a threat to the stock market. Your research will show that during 2000, the Fed saw the economy slowing down, and lowered interest rates 3 times. In early 2001, as the stock market began to nose dive,

and companies began to announce layoffs and lowered profit expectations, there was talk of a recession. The Fed again lowered interest rates to ward off a recession. However, the reductions didn't satisfy stock market investors, and the stock market plunged in March 2001.

7.   a. Credit unions
        b. Savings and loan
        c. Commercial banks
        d. Savings and loan
        e. Credit union

8.   a. Demand deposits are the technical name for checking accounts. They have this name because the money is available upon demand from the depositor. Time deposits are the technical name for savings accounts, so called because the bank can require a prior notice before withdrawal of funds from the account.

        b. 1. Non-interest bearing checking accounts

             2. NOW accounts, which pay an annual interest rate and require depositors to maintain a minimum balance at all times. The number of checks that can be written is restricted.

             3. A Super NOW account pays higher interest than a NOW account. They require a larger minimum balance that regular NOW accounts, and typically offer free and unlimited check-writing privileges.

        c. 1. Passbook savings accounts, with which the depositor has no checking privileges, and can withdraw money at any time.

             2. Certificates of deposit that earn an interest rate to be delivered at the end of the certificate's maturity date. Funds may not be withdrawn without penalties, and the maturity dates vary from three months to five years. Interest rates vary depending upon the time to maturity.

9.   Credit unions offer services similar to banks and S&Ls, but differ in their ownership structure. Credit unions are financial cooperatives, owned by members, while banks and savings and loans are often publicly-held corporations. Credit unions are also not for profit institutions, while banks and credit unions are profit-making organizations.

10.   Nonbanks are financial institutions that accept no deposits but offer many of the services offered by regular banks. Nonbanks include life insurance companies, pension funds, brokerage firms, commercial finance companies, and corporate financial services. The diversity of financial

services and investment alternatives offered by nonbanks has caused banks to expand the services they offer. For example, life insurance companies invest the funds they receive from policyholders in corporate and government bonds. In recent years, more insurance companies have begun to provide long-term financing for real estate development projects. In fact, banks today are merging with brokerage firms to offer full service financial assistance. Pension funds typically invest in corporate stocks and bonds, and government securities. Some large pension funds lend money directly to corporations. Brokerage houses have made serious inroads into regular banks' domain by offering high-yield combination savings and checking accounts. In addition, investors can get loans from their broker.

11. The FDIC is a government agency that protects bank deposits of up to $100,000. In the case of a bank failure, the FDIC would arrange to have your accounts at that bank transferred to another bank, or pay you off up to $100,000. The FDIC covers about 13,000 institutions, which are mostly commercial banks.

SAIF insures the accounts of depositors in thrift institutions, or savings and loans. It is part of the FDIC. SAIF was originally called the Federal Savings and Loan Insurance Corporation.

NCUA is the agency that protects depositors in credit unions.

Both the FDIC and the FSLIC were established to protect the deposits of customers, and to create more confidence in the banking industry at a time when many institutions were failing. This was during the Great Depression, and hundreds of banks were failing. To get more control over the banking system, the government placed the FSLIC under the FDIC and gave it the name of The Savings Association Insurance Fund, SAIF.

12. Trends in the banking industry have paralleled changes we have seen in other industries. We have studied how companies have begun putting the customer first, and have streamlined their operations to better satisfy customer's needs at lower costs. Banks have begun to look at customer needs, and have made "one-stop shopping" available for all a customer's financial needs. One company can provide you with credit cards, mortgages, all kinds of insurance, and brokerage services. As the competition increases, costs will go down, benefiting consumers. Further, the Internet has made online banking available, in the same way that the Internet has made the purchase of all kinds of products available from Internet stores. The online banking industry has suffered from customer service problems, just like online stores have done, and so, like other retail businesses, we will likely have a combination of online and brick and mortar financial institutions.

13. Credit cards were issued as a way for banks to make banking more efficient, and reduce the cost of the traditional check clearing process. But, although credit cards reduce the flow of checks there is still paper to process. Debit cards serve the same functions as checks but eliminate the proper handling processes, and so are even more efficient than credit cards. Your account is automatically reduced by the amount of the sale at the time of the sale. Smart cards are a combination of credit cards, debit cards phone cards, drivers licenses, and more. They are

embedded with a microprocessor that stores a variety of information. Merchants can use the information to check validity and spending limits, and the transaction can debit the amount on the card. Smart cards can also be used to allow access to buildings, buy gas, and serve as ATM cards.

14.   The U.S. banking system is directly tied to the success of banking and businesses throughout the world. American firms must compete for funds with firms all over the world. If a firm in another country is more efficient than one here in the United States, the more efficient firm will have better access to international funds. Therefore, U.S. businesses must compete not only in the marketplace, but in the financial arena as well.

    Further, today's money markets form a global system, and international bankers will not be nationalistic in their dealings. They will send money to those countries where they can get the best return on their money with an acceptable risk. When the Federal Reserve System makes a move to lower interest rates in the U.S., foreign investors may withdraw their money from the U.S. and put it in countries with higher rates. To be an effective player in the international marketplace and financial worlds, the U.S. must stay financially secure and businesses must stay competitive in world markets.

PRACTICE TEST

MULTIPLE CHOICE

1.	a	10.	d
2.	d	11.	c
3.	c	12.	c
4.	d	13.	d
5.	d	14.	a
6.	b	15.	b
7.	a	16.	a
8.	c	17.	c
9.	a	18.	d

TRUE/FALSE

1.	T	8.	F
2.	F	9.	T
3.	T	10.	T
4.	F	11.	F
5.	T	12.	F
6.	F	13.	T
7.	T	14.	T

CHAPTER 22
MANAGING PERSONAL FINANCES: WHO WANTS TO BE A MILLIONAIRE?

LEARNING GOALS

After you have read and studied this chapter, you should be able to:

1. Describe the six steps one can take to generate capital.

2. Identify the best way to preserve capital, begin investing, and buy insurance.

3. Outline a strategy for retiring with enough money to last a lifetime.

LEARNING THE LANGUAGE

Listed below are important terms found in this chapter. Choose the correct term for the definition and write it in the space provided.

Annuity	Term insurance
Individual Retirement Account (IRA)	Variable life insurance
Social Security	Whole life insurance

1. Pure insurance protection for a given number of years is _____.

2. A(n) _____ is a tax-deferred investment plan that enables you and your spouse to save part of your income for retirement.

3. A contract to make regular payments to a person for life or for a fixed period is an _____.

4. The term _____is used to describe the Old-Age, Survivors, and Disability Insurance Program established in 1935.

5. Whole life insurance, or _____, invests the cash value of the policy in stocks or other high yielding securities.

6. Life insurance that stays in effect until age 100 is known as _____.

ASSESSMENT CHECK

Learning Goal 1   **The Need for Personal Financial Planning**

1.   In the opening profile of this chapter, there are several tips on how to become a millionaire. What are some of those tips?

2.   What does the text say about what it takes to find and keep a good job in business?

3.   List the government incentives for getting an education.

a._____   f._____

b._____   g._____

c._____   h._____

d._____   i._____

e._____   j._____

4.   What are six steps you can take today to get control of your finances?

a._____

b._____

c._____

d. _____

e. _____

f. _____

5.   How do you take a personal inventory? How do you value your personal assets?

6.   What's the best way to keep track of expenses?

7.   What items are important to include in a household budget?

8.   How is running a household's finances like running a small business?

9.   Why should you pay off debts, such as credit cards, as soon as possible?

10.   What's a good way to plan for large purchases, such as a car?

11.   What is the best way to save money in general?

12.   How is it that you can save $6 a day, and have accumulated a million dollars after 35 years?

13.   When should you borrow money?

Learning Goal 2   **Building Your Capital Account**

14.   How can you accumulate capital?

15.   What are the investment benefits of buying a home?

16. What are the tax benefits of home ownership?

17. What is the key element to getting an optimum return on a home?

18. What is one of the worst places to keep long-term investments? Why?

19. What, over time, has been one of the best places to invest? Why?

20. If you finance a purchase using a credit card, what will it do to the total cost of your purchase, when compared to paying cash?

21. What are three reasons why credit cards are an important element in a personal financial investment?

a. _____

b. _____

c. _____

22. Should you carry a balance on a credit card? Why or why not?

23. Identify the "dangers" of a credit card.

a. _____

b. _____

24. Why should people or businesses buy life insurance?

25 What is the difference between term life insurance, whole life insurance and variable life insurance?

26. What is multiyear level-premium insurance?

27. What is universal life policy?

28. When are insurance needs the highest?

    a. _____

    b. _____

    c. _____

    d. _____

29. When do insurance needs decline?

    a. _____

    b. _____

    c. _____

    d. _____

30. What is the difference between a fixed and a variable annuity?

31.   What is the danger of not having health and disability insurance?

32.   What is meant by guaranteed replacement cost when referring to homeowners insurance?

Planning Your Retirement

33.   What are the issues surrounding the Social Security system?

34.   What does a traditional IRA allow? What is meant by "tax deferred"?

35.   What is the basic difference between a Roth IRA and a traditional IRA?

36.   In general, who is a Roth IRA best for?

37.   What is a key point to remember about taking money out of an IRA?

38.   What are some investment choices for IRAs?

39.   What is the maximum yearly investment in an IRA?

40.   What is a simple IRA?

41.   What are the benefits of 401(k) plans?

        a. _____

        b. _____

        c. _____

42.   Describe the characteristics of 401(k) plans.

43.   Who is a Keogh plan for?

44.   What is the advantage of a Keogh plan?

45.   What are three ways a Keogh plan is like an IRA?

46.   What is a financial planner? What is a CFP?

47.   What is a financial supermarket?

48.   What are the areas a financial planner will cover?

CRITICAL THINKING EXERCISES

Learning Goal 1

1.   What is the benefit of investing in an education?

2.   What is the only way to accumulate enough money to start your own business, or to make investments?

Learning Goal 1, 2

3.   The six steps to get control of your finances are:

Take an inventory of your financial assets

Keep track of all of your expenses

Prepare a budget

Pay off your debts

Start a savings plan

Only borrow money to buy assets that have the potential to increase in value

We only have a short period of time, but in at least a week, do as many of the of these steps as possible. Use a separate sheet of paper so you're not limited by the space provided in this book:

Inventory of assets: Do you own a car? house? appliances? stocks? savings account? checking account? collectibles?

Expenses: What do you spend in a day on food? newspapers? travel? supplies?

What do you spend in a month on food? housing? car payments? utilities?

Are you spending more than you are earning? Keep a small notebook handy to record all your spending for one day for a week.

Budget: Listing all your sources of revenue, determine how much you can spend in a month. Set up accounts for money you are going to pay to yourself, for savings, and for major purchases you will want to make sometime in the future as well as for items which may not be paid every month, but will come due eventually, like a car or life insurance. Can you spend less than you are making?

Pay off your debts: Can you pay off your credit cards, if you have them? Are there any other debts that can be paid off now?

Start a savings plan: In your budget, did you pay yourself first?

Identify those loans that were for articles which will *depreciate* in value (educational loans don't count! Your education will help you accumulate capital in the long run!)

It's not easy, is it?!

4.   "The principle is simple: To accumulate capital, you have to earn more than you spend."

    A. Take a few minutes to think about the way you spend money (beyond money for tuition, books and other school related items.) Using your text for suggestions, list some ways in which you could begin to accumulate capital for the future:

        1._____

        2._____

        3._____

        4._____

    B. Investigate the real estate market in your area. Determine the amount by which home prices in your area have appreciated (or depreciated) in the last 5 years. You can probably find a source for this information in your campus library or on the Internet.

    C. Let's assume you have found a house in your area for $110,000. If, over time, inflation averages 3 percent, how long will it take for the value of your house to double? (Hint: remember the rule of 72, in chapter 2)

D. Interest on mortgage payments is tax deductible. Assume that you are in the 28% tax bracket and that the payments on your house are $1200 per month. What is your real cost?

5.   "Plastic!" Credit cards are a helpful tool to the financially careful buyer. If you have credit cards, you are probably aware of the advantages:

Useful for identification

Helpful to keep track of purchases

Convenient, in place of cash

You may also be aware of the disadvantages, primarily high interest rates and the convenience of purchasing something you cannot afford.

A. If you have credit cards, figure the amount you spent last month using each card, and for what purchases. What is the interest rate on your cards? Did you make purchases you would not have made without the card?

B. Look at the budget you developed earlier. Do you have an account for credit card payments? Did you budget to pay the entire amount, or only a portion of the bill?

C. How much did you pay in interest on credit card accounts over the last six months? The last year? That is the amount by which you could have increased your capital account.

6.   A. Why should you invest in an IRA as a young person?

B. Again, using the rule of 72, if you invest $1000 in something that earns 10 percent interest, how long would it take to double the amount?

C. How much would your $1000 be worth in 15 years, if you are earning 10 percent?

7. Why should young couples invest in life insurance? What other kinds of insurance should people have?

8. Compare and contrast a Keogh, 401(k) and an IRA.

PRACTICE TEST

Multiple Choice – Circle the best answer

1. The first step in taking control of your finances should be:

    a. keep track of all your expenses.
    b. prepare a budget.
    c. pay off your debts.
    d. take an inventory of your assets.

2. Jerry and Jane are having a discussion about their finances. They are wondering what to do about the amount of money they are spending, how to control their financial situation as well and how to reach their financial goals. One technique to help them would be to:

    a. prepare a budget.
    b. do an asset inventory.
    c. develop an income statement.
    d. quit spending money on anything but the bare basics.

3. When planning for the future, in financial terms, an investment in a college education will

    a. provide you with a new ideas.
    b. give you a chance to learn about different ways of life.
    c. improve your earning potential.
    d. all of the above.

4. To accumulate capital you have to

    a. get the highest paying job you can find.
    b. earn more than you spend.
    c. borrow money and invest.
    d. buy assets which appreciate in value.

5. The <u>first</u> thing you should do when you have extra money is:

    a. Pay cash for a car.
    b. Start a savings plan.
    c. Pay off your debts, particularly credit cards.
    d. Put a down payment on a house.

6. Historically, one of the better investments a person can make is in

   a. a home.
   b. cars.
   c. credit cards.
   d an apartment.

7. From a financial standpoint it is best to buy

   a. the largest home you can find in an neighborhood where homes are less expensive.
   b. the smallest home in the best neighborhood.
   c. the smallest home in the least expensive neighborhood.
   d. the largest home in the most expensive neighborhood you can find.

8. One of the worst places for a young person to keep their investments is in:

   a. a bank or savings and loan.
   b. a stock market mutual fund.
   c. the stock market in general.
   d. home ownership.

9. One of the dangers of a credit card is that

   a. it is difficult to keep track of purchases.
   b. it can be an inconvenience carrying too many credit cards around.
   c. merchants won't accept credit cards as a form of identification.
   d. consumers may buy goods they wouldn't normally buy if they had to pay cash.

10. _____ life insurance gives protection for a given number of years.

    a. A fixed annuity
    b. Whole
    c. Variable
    d. Term

11. Guaranteed replacement cost in homeowners' insurance means that

    a. the insurance company guarantees they will replace the lost items for you.
    b. the insurance company guarantees they will pay the current value of a lost item.
    c. the insurance company will pay you what it costs to replace the items.
    d. the insurance company will pay you something for lost items, but the amount can't be determined, so they guarantee an average of market value.

12. Which of the following is not likely to happen with the social security system in the future?

    a. serious cuts in benefits
    b. reduced cost of living adjustments
    c. later retirement age to collect
    d. lower social security taxes

13. A tax-deferred retirement plan that can be used as a supplement to a company sponsored plan is

    a. a Roth IRA.
    b. 401(k) plan.
    c. a Keogh plan.
    d. a traditional savings account.

14. The earnings in a traditional IRA account

    a. are taxed as you go along.
    b. are not taxed.
    c. subject to double taxation.
    d. are not taxed until they are withdrawn.

15. One of the benefits of a Roth IRA is that

    a. contributions aren't taxed.
    b. earnings grow tax free.
    c. you can take the money out before the age of 59 ½ without penalty.
    d. you can invest up to 12,000 a year.

16. A tax sheltered retirement program designed to encourage small-business owners and self-employed people to invest for retirement is called a(n):

a. Keogh Plan.

b. 401(k) plan.

c. Roth IRA.

d. Simple IRA.

True-False

1. _____ In developing an income statement for yourself, your pay check would be considered as revenue.

2. _____ One of the best ways to keep track of your expenses is to carry a notepad with you everywhere you go and record what you spend as you go through the day.

3. _____ It could be said that running a household is similar to running a small business.

4. _____ The statistics indicate that a majority of the population in the U.S. has accumulated enough money by retirement to live comfortably.

5. _____ The first steps to accumulating capital are finding employment and living frugally.

6. _____ One of the investment benefits of owning a home is that it is a way of forced savings.

7. _____ Home ownership generally provides few tax advantages.

8. _____ Credit card limits prevent people from spending too much with a credit card.

9. _____ Other than life insurance, you should also carry health, disability, and auto insurance policies.

10. _____ One of the benefits of a 401(k) plan is that employers often match part of your deposit.

You Can Find It On The Net

There are two things a college student would like to have more of: Time and Money! Well, we all have the same amount of time, but we vary in how much money we have. But, all of us can find ways to use and spend our money more effectively!

Visit www.thebudgetbook.com and find out what this book can do to help you keep your finances in line and start you on the road to becoming a millionaire!

Also visit www.savvystudent.com Click on the budget worksheet, and develop your personalized monthly budget.

What are 10 ways this site suggests to save money?

What is the tip of the week to save money?

ANSWERS

LEARNING THE LANGUAGE

1 Term insurance	4. Social Security
2. Individual Retirement Account (IRA)	5. Variable life insurance
3. Annuity	6. Whole life insurance

ASSESSMENT CHECK

The Need for Personal Financial Planning

1. The opening profile indicates that, in order to be a millionaire, you need to:get an education, work hard, save your money, and make purchases carefully.

2. In order to find and keep a good job it usually means learning how to communicate well, how to use a computer, and how to apply some of the skills you have learned in classes and in life. It also means staying out of financial trouble.

3.
    a. Scholarships
    b. Lifetime Learning Credit
    c. Hope Credit
    d. Traditional and Roth IRAs
    e. Education IRA
    f. Employer's Educational Assistance
    g. Interest paid on student loans
    h. Qualified State Tuition Programs
    i. Education as a deduction
    j. U.S. Savings bonds

4.
    a. Take an inventory of your financial assets
    b. Keep track of all your expenses
    c. Prepare a budget
    d. Pay off your debts
    e. Start a savings plan
    f. If you have to borrow money, only borrow it to buy assets that have the potential to increase in value.

5. To take a personal inventory, you need to develop a balance sheet for yourself. You can develop your own balance sheet by listing your assets, such things as a TV, DVD, computer and so on, as assets on one side, and your liabilities, like mortgages and car loans, on the other side. Your assets are evaluated on their current value, not the purchase price.

6. The best way to keep track of expenses is to carry a notepad with you wherever you go and record what you spend as you go through the day. At the end of the week, record your journal entries into a record book. Develop certain categories to make the task easier and more informative.

7. Items that are important to include in a household budget are mortgage or rent, utilities, food life insurance, car insurance and medical care.

8. It takes the same careful record keeping, the same budgeting process and forecasting, the same control procedures and the same need to periodically borrow funds to run a household's finances as it does to run a small business.

9. Debts often carry high interest rates. Credit card debt may be costing you 16 percent or more a year. It's better to pay off the debt at 16 percent than to put the money in the bank earning only 3 percent or so.

10. A good way to plan for large purchases such as a car is to save some money each month in a separate account. Then when it comes time to make the purchase, you'll be able to pay cash, and avoid finance charges.

11. The best way to save money is to pay yourself first. That is, take your paycheck, take out money for savings, and then plan what to do with the rest.

12. If you save $6 a day, for 35 years, you will have saved $76,440. If you invest that money at 12 percent, compound interest, it will be worth $ 1 million.

13. You should only borrow money to buy assets that have the potential to increase in value, or to cover the most unexpected expenses.

Building Your Capital Account

14. To accumulate capital, you have to live frugally and earn more than you spend.

15. A home is an investment you can live in, payments are relatively fixed, and as your income rises, the payments get easier to make, and it is a good way to force yourself to save. Also, interest on home mortgages is tax deductible.

16. Interest on mortgage payments and real estate taxes are tax deductible. During the first few years, almost all the mortgage payments go for interest on the loan so almost all the early payments are tax deductible.

17. The key element to getting the optimum return on a home is a good location. A home in the "best part of town", near schools, shopping and work is usually a sound financial investment.

18. One of the worst places for young people to keep long-term investments is in a bank or savings and loan. The reason for this is that interest paid on savings accounts is relatively low compared to other investment choices, such as the stock market.

19. One of the best places to invest over time has been the stock market. The stock market has historically paid a higher rate of return than other investment choices.

20. If you finance a large purchase with a credit card, you may end up spending more than if you pay with cash, because of the finance charges on a credit card.

21. a. Credit cards are needed as a form of identification
    b. They are a way to keep track of purchases
    c. Credit cards are convenient

22. If you use a credit card, you should pay the balance in full during the period when no interest is charged. Not having to pay 16 percent interest is as good as earning 16 percent tax-free.

23. a. Consumers are tempted to make purchases they would not make if they had to pay cash or write a check, and pile up debt as a result
    b. High rates of interest

24. Today, with so many two-career couples, the loss of a spouse means a sudden drop in income. To provide protection from such risks, a couple or business should buy life insurance.

25. Term life insurance is pure insurance protection for a given number of years, that costs less the younger you buy it. The premium could increase as you grow older. Whole life insurance stays in effect until age 100. Some part of the money you pay goes toward pure insurance and another part goes toward savings. Variable life insurance is a form of whole life insurance that invests the cash value of a policy in stocks or higher-yielding securities.

26. Multiyear level-premium insurance is a term insurance policy that guarantees you'll pay the same premium for the life of the policy.

27. A universal life policy is a form of whole life insurance that lets you choose how much of your payment should go to insurance and how much to investments.

28. Insurance needs are highest when:
    a. Children are young and need money for education
    b. Mortgage is high relative to income
    c. There are auto payments and other bills to pay
    d. Loss of income would be disastrous

29. Insurance needs decline when:
    a. Children are grown
    b. Mortgage is low or completely paid off
    c. Insurance needs are few
    d. Retirement income is needed

30. An annuity is a contract to make payments to a person for life or for a fixed period. A fixed annuity is an investment that pays the policy holder a specified interest rate. A variable annuity provides investment choices identical to mutual funds.

31. Hospital costs are too high to risk financial ruin by going uninsured. It is a good idea to supplement health insurance policies with disability insurance that pays part of the cost of a long-term sickness or an accident. Your chances of becoming disabled at an early age are much higher than your chances of dying from an accident.

32. Guaranteed replacement cost means that the insurance company will give you whatever it costs to buy all of the items you have insured, rather than the depreciated cost of the items.

Planning Your Retirement

33. The issues surrounding the Social Security system stem from the fact that the number of workers paying into social security is declining, but the number of people retiring and living longer is increasing dramatically. The result is likely to be serious cuts in benefits, a much later retirement age, reduced cost of living adjustments and/or much higher social security taxes.

34. A traditional IRA allows people who qualify to deduct the money they put into an IRA account from their reported income. These deductions are tax deferred, which means you pay no current taxes. The earnings gained in the IRA are taxed as income when they are withdrawn from your IRA account.

35.   A Roth IRA is the newest kind of IRA. People who invest in this kind of IRA don't get up-front deductions on their taxes like they would with a traditional IRA, but earnings grow tax free and are tax free when they are withdrawn.

36.   In general a Roth IRA is probably best for younger workers because their savings can compound year after year with no further taxes being paid.

37.   A key point to remember with IRAs is that you can't take the money out of either type of IRA until you are 59 ½ years old without paying a 10 percent penalty and paying taxes on the income.

38.   Some choices for IRAs included a local bank, savings and loan or credit union. Insurance companies also offer IRAs. You can also put funds into stocks, bonds, mutual funds, or precious metals.

39.   The yearly investment limit in an IRA is $2000 per year, but at the time of this writing Congress is considering an increase to $5000 a year.

40.   A simple IRA can be offered by companies with fewer than 100 employees. Employees of these companies can contribute up to $6000 of their income annually compared with the $2000 limit of regular IRAs. This makes for a good employee benefit for smaller companies.

41.   The benefits of 401(k) plans are
        a.   The money you put in reduces your present taxable income
        b.   Tax is deferred on the earnings
        c.   Employers often match part of your deposit

42.   Normally you can't withdraw funds from a 401(k) account until you are 59, but often you can borrow from the account. You can usually select how the money in the plan is invested: stocks, bonds, and in some cases real estate. If the policy is held until you die, no income taxes will be due on the investment gains that have built up in the policy.

43.   A Keogh plan is for small business people who don't have the benefit of a corporate retirement system. This can be an alternative for doctors, lawyers, real estate agents, artists, writers and other self-employed people.

44.   The advantage of Keogh plans is that the maximum that can be invested is more than $30,000 per year.

45.   A Keogh plan is like an IRA because funds aren't taxed until they are withdrawn, nor are the returns they earn. As with an IRA account, there is a 10 percent penalty for early withdrawal. Also, funds may be withdrawn in a lump sum or spread out over the years like an IRA.

46.   A financial planner assists in developing a comprehensive program that covers investments, taxes, insurance, and other financial matters. A CFP is a certified financial planner. This person will have completed a curriculum on 106 financial topics and a 10-hour exam.

47.   A financial supermarket provides a wide variety of financial services ranging from banking services to mutual funds, insurance, tax assistance, stocks, bonds, and real estate.

48.   Most financial planners begin with life insurance, and explore health and disability insurance. Financial planning covers all aspects of investing all the way to retirement and death. A financial planner can steer you into the proper mix of IRA investments, stocks, bonds, precious metals, real estate and so on.

CRITICAL THINKING EXERCISES

1.   History has shown that an investment in education has paid off regardless of the state of the economy. We have studied in previous chapters about the need for constant updating. This includes education! Statistics show that a person with an undergraduate degree earns about twice as much as someone with only a high school diploma.

2.   The only way to accumulate enough money to start your own business or to make investments is to live frugally and make more than you spend. There are six steps to get control of your finances and build a capital account, including: taking an inventory of your assets, keeping track of all your expenses, preparing a budget, paying off your debts, starting a savings plan, and only borrowing money to buy assets which will increase in value.

3.   Obviously, everyone will have different answers. This is primarily to get you started on the road to good personal financial planning!

4.   A. This is another section where each individual will have varied answers. Some suggestions may include: living at home while going to school, buying used books, keep clothing allowances to a minimum, walking or riding a bike when you can, eating at home, or if you are in a house or apartment, making meals at home. For students returning to school after being out for a while, the methods of accumulating capital will be different - and you may already have discovered ways of your own!

        B. Prices in different parts of the country vary widely. Some areas that have been hit by unemployment may have seen a decline in the price of homes. Other areas may have seen above average increases.

C. Using the rule of 72 you can calculate how long it will take for the value of any asset to double. In this case, the rate of inflation is 3 percent. 72 divided by 3 = 24. So the value of a $110,000 house will double to $220,000 in 24 years. If you have a 30 year mortgage, your house will be almost paid off, and you will have a $220,000 asset! (If you put money in a savings account in a bank and earn 3% interest, it will take 24 years for the savings to double, if you don't make any additional deposits. That's how the rule of 72 works.)

D. In this example, with a house payment of 1200, and a 28% tax bracket, you can calculate your real cost by multiplying 1200 x .28 which equals $336. Subtract $336 from $1200 and your real cost will be $864 with an interest deduction.

5. Your answers will vary. If you have no credit cards yet, use this information to make good decisions about whether to apply for a credit card, and how to use it.

6. A. An IRA is a good deal for a young investor, because the invested money is not taxed. When you put money into an IRA you save taxes. If you continue to invest in an IRA, you will have a significant amount of money by the time you retire. The earlier you start, the better. For example if you start putting $2000 a year in an IRA between the ages of 23-28 at 12% interest, you would have *invested* only $13,000, but even if you never add another penny by the time you are 65 you will have almost $900,000, because of compounded interest. If you continued nonstop from age 23 until age 65, you would have almost $2 million.

B. 72 divided by 10 = 7.2 years. Your $1000 would double to $2000 in 7.2 years.

C. If your money doubles every 7.2 years, in approximately 15 years your money will have doubled twice, to $4000.

7. Because so many couples today are two career families, the loss of the income of one spouse can have a devastating financial affect. It is for that reason that young couples need to invest in some kind of life insurance plan. Health insurance is necessary because of the high cost of medical care. Disability insurance is needed to make up for lost income in the event one spouse is injured and can 't work for an extended period, or at all.

8. The money invested in an IRA is not taxed. Earnings are not taxed until you take them out when you retire, presumably when you are at a lower tax rate. The money cannot be taken out until the age of 59 without paying a penalty. An IRA is for workers to use as a supplement to a company-sponsored retirement plan and Social Security. It is not connected with your employer. A 401(K) plan is offered by employers, who will often match your contribution. Further, you can borrow the funds from a 401(K), whereas that isn't an option in an IRA.

The Keogh plan is for small business people who do not have the benefit of a corporate retirement system, whereas the 401(K) is a company sponsored program. The benefit over an IRA is that the maximum amount that can be invested is much greater.

A Keogh is like an IRA and the 401(K) in that the funds are not taxed, nor are the earnings, and there is a penalty for early withdrawal. All these plans are designed to protect people from the decline in the value of the Social Security system.

PRACTICE TEST

MULTIPLE CHOICE

1.	d	9.	d
2.	a	10.	d
3.	c	11.	c
4.	b	12.	d
5.	c	13.	b
6.	a	14.	d
7.	b	15.	b
8.	a	16.	a

TRUE/FALSE

1.	T	6.	T
2.	T	7.	F
3.	T	8.	F
4.	F	9.	T
5.	T	10.	T

Listed here are important terms found in this appendix. Choose the correct term for each definition below and write it in the space provided.

Health maintenance organizations (HMOs)

Insurable interest

Insurable risk

Insurance policy

Law of large numbers

Mutual insurance company

Preferred provider organization (PPOs)

Premium

Pure risk

Risk

Rule of indemnity

Self-insurance

Speculative risk

Stock insurance company

Uninsurable risk

1. A _____ is a type of insurance company owned by stockholders.

2. A written contract known as a(n) _____ is between the insured and an insurance company that promises to pay for all or part of a loss.

3. The _____ says that an insured person or organization cannot collect more than the actual loss from an insurable risk.

4. The threat of loss with no chance of profit is called _____.

5. The _____ is a principle that if a large number of people are exposed to the same risk, a predictable number of losses will occur during a given period.

6. A chance of either profit or loss is called _____.

7. The chance of loss, the degree of probability of loss, and the amount of possible loss is called _____.

8. A _____ is a type of insurance company owned by its policyholders.

9. Health care organizations known as _____ require members to choose from a restricted list of doctors.

10. The feel charged by an insurance company for an insurance policy is a _____.

11. An _____ is one that no insurance company will cover.

12. The practice of setting aside money to cover routine claims and buying only "catastrophe" policies to cover big losses is called _____.

13. An _____ is a risk that the typical insurance company will cover.

14. Health care organization, which allow members to choose their own physicians for a fee are called _____.

15. The possibility of the policyholder to suffer a loss is called _____.

ASSESSMENT CHECK

Managing Risk

1. What are two kinds of risk?

    a._____   b. _____

2. What is the difference between the two?

3. Which kind of risk is of most concern to business people?

4. List four methods businesses use to manage pure risk.

    a. _____

    b. _____

    c. _____

    d. _____

5.   How can a firm reduce risk?

6.   How do some companies avoid risk?

7.   Why are some firms turning to self-insurance?

8.   When is self-insurance most appropriate?

Buying Insurance to Cover Risk

9.   What are four kinds of uninsurable risk?

    a. _____

    b. _____

    c. _____

    d. _____

10.   Identify the guidelines used to evaluate whether or not a risk is insurable.

    a. _____

    b. _____

    c. _____

    d. _____

    e. _____

11.   How are the premiums for an insurance policy determined?

12.   What is the difference between a stock insurance company and a mutual insurance company?

Types of Insurance

13. What are six types of insurance to cover losses?

    a. _____

    b. _____

    c. _____

    d. _____

    e. _____

    f. _____

14. What are three major options for health insurance?

15. What are some features of an HMO?

16. What are some complaints about HMOs?

17. What are some characteristics of a PPO?

18. Why do most businesses and individuals choose to join an HMO or a PPO?

19. Describe disability insurance.

20. Who provides worker's compensation and what does it guarantee?

21. Who does professional liability insurance cover?

22. What is product liability insurance?

23. What should you do about insurance coverage if you have a home-based business?

The Risk of Damaging the Environment

24. What are some environmental risks we are facing?

CRITICAL THINKING EXERCISES

1. Businesses have four options to avoid losses stemming from pure risk situations.

    Reduce the risk   Buy insurance to cover the risk

    Avoid the risk   Self-insure against the risk

Read the following situations, and determine which option the firm is choosing in each case.

Use each option only once.

a. The president of an asbestos removal firm in Merriam, Kansas closed his firm for four months.

b. A group of 27 accounting firms formed its own insurance company to insure themselves.

c. Workers and visitors on construction sites are required to wear hard hats.

d. Senoret Chemical Company experienced a 1600% increase in its liability coverage premium.

2. Many variables determine which risks are insurable. Using your text, determine which

   of the following situations would constitute an insurable risk.

    a. TNG Enterprises would like to buy insurance to cover loss of computer equipment

       from power surges and possible spills.

    b. Gilmores, Inc. a retail store in Kalamazoo, would like to insure against losses occurring

       when a competitor, Steketees, implements an aggressive marketing campaign.

    c. Chrysler wants to buy insurance to cover losses created by a breakdown with their

       robotic and computer driven manufacturing systems.

    d. PPI, a small manufacturing firm, wants to insure themselves against losses created

       by damage from a fire set accidentally.

e.   Residents in Morgan City, Louisiana, East Lansing, Michigan and Valley Park, Missouri want to buy flood insurance.

f.   Residents of Morgan City, Louisiana, however, face a high risk of flooding, because the Mississippi River is cutting a new tributary through that city, and floods regularly.

g.   Boeing has extensive contracts with the government to build fighter planes. The company wants insurance to cover losses that may occur if Congress cuts the defense budget by over 20%.

3.   What are some forms of public insurance?

4.   Distinguish between HMOs and PPOs.

PRACTICE TEST

Multiple Choice – Circle the best answer

1.   When Macy's orders inventory for the Christmas season, the company has to predict what their customers will want to buy that season. The kind of risk being described is

   a.   speculative risk.   c.   insurable risk.

   b.   pure risk.   d.   self-insurance.

2.   Which of the following is not one of the options a firm has available to manage risk?

   a.   reduce the risk

   b.   avoid the risk

   c.   buy insurance against the risk

   d.   find another company to take the risk

3.   It is when a company has several widely distributed facilities that _____ is the most appropriate.

   a.   reducing the risk   c.   self-insurance

b.   avoiding the risk   d.   finding another company to take the risk

4.   An insurable risk is one in which

   a.   the loss is measurable.

   b.   the loss is not accidental.

   c.   the risk is dispersed.

   d.   the policyholder has no insurable interest.

5.   The idea that an insured person or organization cannot collect more than the actual loss from an

   insurable risk is called the

   a.   law of large numbers.   c.   disability insurance.

   b.   rule of indemnity.   d.   insurable interest.

6.   A type of insurance that requires members to choose from a restricted list of doctors is called a

   a.   health maintenance organization.

   b.   preferred provider organization.

   c.   disability insurance.

   d.   professional liability insurance.

7.   Disability insurance

   a.   replaces all your income if you become disabled.

   b.   starts immediately after your disability.

   c.   is required from employers.

   d.   replaces a portion of your income.

8.   Which of the following is not a type of property and liability insurance?

   a.   Professional liability

   b.   Credit life insurance

c. Business interruption insurance

d. Computer coverage

9. If a person is injured when using product and sues the manufacturer, the company is covered by

a. workers compensation.

b. disability insurance.

c. product liability insurance.

d. business interruption insurance.

10. Which of the following is not an environmental risk faced by businesses?

a. tornadoes

b. global warming

c. nuclear issues

d. damage to the ozone

True-False

1. _____ A firm can reduce risk by establishing loss prevention programs such as fire drills, health education and accident prevention programs.

2. _____ One type of risk that cannot be covered is loss from accidental injury.

3. _____ The rule of indemnity is the principle that if a large number of people are exposed to the same risk, a predictable number of losses will occur during a given period.

4. _____ One of the complaints about an HMO is that members can't choose their own doctors.

5. _____ To save money, HMOs generally must approve treatment before it is given.

6. _____ PPOs are less expensive than HMOs because you can choose your own doctor.

7. _____ Employers are required to provide worker's compensation insurance.

8. _____ Many professionals other than doctors and lawyers are buying malpractice insurance.

ANSWERS

LEARNING THE LANGUAGE

1.   Stock insurance company

2.   Insurance policy

3.   Rule of indemnity

4.   Pure risk

5.   Law of large numbers

6.   Speculative risk

7.   Risk

   8. Mutual insurance company

9.   Health Maintenance Organization (HMO)

10.   Premium

11.   Uninsurable risk

12   Self insurance

13.   Insurable risk

14.   Preferred Provider Organization (PPO)

15.   Insurable interest

ASSESSMENT CHECK

Managing Risk

1.   a.   speculative risk   b.   pure risk

2.   Speculative risk involves a chance of either profit or loss. It includes the chance the firm takes to make extra money by buying new machinery, acquiring more inventory and making other decisions in which the probability of loss may be relatively low and the amount of loss is known. An entrepreneur takes speculative risk on the chance of making a profit.

Pure risk is the threat of loss with no chance for profit. It involves the threat of fire, accident or loss. If such events occur, a company loses money, but if the events do not occur, the company gains nothing.

3. The risk that is of most concern to business-people is pure risk.

4. Firms can manage risk by

   a. Reducing the risk

   b. Avoiding the risk

   c. Self-insure against the risk

   d. Buy insurance against the risk

5. A firm can reduce risk by establishing loss-prevention programs such as fire drills, health education, safety

   inspections, equipment maintenance, and accident prevention programs.

   Retail stores use mirrors, video cameras, and other devices to prevent shoplifting for example.

6. Companies avoid risk by not accepting hazardous jobs and by outsourcing shipping and other functions. For

   example, the threat of lawsuits has driven away some drug companies from manufacturing vaccines, and some

   consulting engineers refuse to work on hazardous sites.

7. Many companies and municipalities have turned to self-insurance because they either can't find or can't afford

   conventional policies. Such firms set aside money to cover routine claims and buy only "catastrophe" policies to

   cover big losses. Self-insurance lowers the cost of insurance by allowing companies to take out insurance only

   for large losses.

8. Self insurance is most appropriate when a firm has several widely distributed facilities.

Buying Insurance to Cover Risk

9. a. Market risks (from price changes, style changes, new products)

   b. Political risks (from war or government restrictions)

   c. Personal risks (from loss of job)

   d. Risks of operation (strikes or inefficient machinery)

10. An insurable risk is evaluated using the following criteria

    a. The policyholder must have an insurable interest.

    b. The loss should be measurable.

    c. The chance of loss should be measurable.

d.   The loss should be accidental.

e.   The risk should be dispersed

f.   The insurance company can set standards for accepting risk.

11.   Premiums for insurance policies are determined by using the law of large numbers. This states that if a large number of people or organizations are exposed to the same risk, a predictable number of losses will occur. The higher the risk the higher the potential cost to the company, and the higher the premium. Today, however, higher premiums are being charged to cover higher anticipated court costs and damage awards.

12.   Stock insurance companies are owned by stockholders, like any other investor-owned company. Mutual insurance companies are owned by their policyholders. A mutual insurance company does not earn profits for its owners. It is a nonprofit organization and any excess funds go to the policyholders/investors in the form of dividends or premium reductions.

Types of Insurance

13.   a. health insurance   e. life insurance for businesses

             b. liability insurance   f. "other"

             c. disability insurance   g. insurance for home based businesses

             d. workers compensation

14.   Three major options for health insurance are health care providers, such as Blue Cross/Blue Shield, health maintenance organizations (HMOs) and preferred provider organizations (PPOs).

15.   HMOs offer a full range of health care benefits. Emphasis is on helping members stay healthy instead of on treating illnesses. Members do not receive bills and do not have to fill out claim forms for routine service. HMOs employ or contract with doctors, hospitals and other systems of health care and members must use those providers. HMOs are less expensive than comprehensive health insurance providers.

16. Members complain about not being able to choose doctors or to get the care they want or need. Some physicians complain that they lose some freedom to do what is needed to make people well and that they often receive less compensation than they feel is appropriate for the services they provide.

17. Preferred provider organizations contract with hospitals and doctors, but do not require members to choose only from those physicians. Members have to pay more if they don't use a doctor on the preferred list. Also members have to pay a deductible before the PPO will pay any bills. When the plan does pay, members usually have to pay part of the bill. This payment is called co-insurance.

18. Most individuals and businesses choose to join a PPO or an HMO because they can cost as much as 80 percent less than comprehensive individual health insurance policies.

19. Disability insurance replaces part of your income if you become disabled and unable to work. Usually, before you can begin collecting there is a period of time you must be disabled. Many employers provide this type of insurance, but some do not.

20. Workers compensation insurance guarantees payment of wages, medical care, and rehabilitation services for employees who are injured on the job. Employers in all 50 states are required to provide this type of insurance. This insurance also provides benefits to the survivors of workers who die as a result of work-related injuries.

21. Professional liability insurance covers people who are found liable for professional negligence, such as lawyers, doctors, dentists, mortgage brokers, and real estate appraisers.

22. Product liability insurance provides coverage against liability arising out of products sold.

23. Homeowner's policies usually don't have adequate protection for a home-based business, so you may need to add an endorsement to increase the coverage. If you have clients visit your office and receive deliveries regularly, you may need home-office insurance, which protects you from slip and fall lawsuits and other risks associated with visitors. More elaborate businesses may need other kinds of insurance.

The Risk of Damaging the Environment

24.   Some environmental threats included global warming and resulting damage to ozone level,

chemical gas leaks, and nuclear issues.

CRITICAL THINKING EXERCISES

1. a.   Avoid risk

    b.   Self-insure against the risk

    c.   Reduce the risk

    d.   Buy insurance to cover the risk.

2. a.   Yes, companies can buy insurance against the loss of computer equipment.

    b.   No, this would be an uninsurable risk.

    c.   No, a company cannot insure against inefficient machinery or machinery that breaks down or doesn't work

    d.   Yes fire damage can be insured against

    e.   Yes, probably, unless the occurrence of loss has been too high

    f.   No, most likely because the probability of flooding in Morgan City is too high.

    g.   No this would be a "political risk" and is uninsurable.

3. Some state and federal agencies provide insurance protection, which is known as public insurance. Some forms of public insurance are unemployment compensation, for unemployed workers, social security which provides retirement, health and disability insurance, the FHA, Federal Housing Administration, which provides mortgage insurance, and National Flood Insurance. Other types of insurance are provided to property owners in high-crime areas, compensation for damaged crops and insurance against pension loss if a company declares bankruptcy.

4. Health car Maintenance Organizations and PPOs have a number of similarities. Both contract with hospitals and doctors. However, while HMOs require members to use the doctors in the plan, preferred provider organizations allow members to choose from other doctors, at a cost. HMOs are less expensive than PPOs for that reason, and because they generally do not require a co-insurance payment, as PPOs require.

PRACTICE TEST

Multiple Choice

1.	a	6.	a
2.	d	7.	d
3.	c	8.	c
4.	c	9.	c
5.	b	10.	a

True-False

1.	T	5.	T
2.	F	6.	F
3.	F	7.	T
4.	T	8.	T